Anne Carson

Anne Carson

The Glass Essayist

ELIZABETH SARAH COLES

OXFORD
UNIVERSITY PRESS

Oxford University Press is a department of the University of Oxford. It furthers
the University's objective of excellence in research, scholarship, and education
by publishing worldwide. Oxford is a registered trade mark of Oxford University
Press in the UK and certain other countries.

Published in the United States of America by Oxford University Press
198 Madison Avenue, New York, NY 10016, United States of America.

© Oxford University Press 2023

All rights reserved. No part of this publication may be reproduced, stored in
a retrieval system, or transmitted, in any form or by any means, without the
prior permission in writing of Oxford University Press, or as expressly permitted
by law, by license, or under terms agreed with the appropriate reproduction
rights organization. Inquiries concerning reproduction outside the scope of the
above should be sent to the Rights Department, Oxford University Press, at the
address above.

You must not circulate this work in any other form
and you must impose this same condition on any acquirer.

Library of Congress Cataloging-in-Publication Data
Names: Coles, Elizabeth Sarah, 1983– author.
Title: Anne Carson : the glass essayist / Elizabeth Sarah Coles.
Description: New York : Oxford University Press, 2023. |
Includes bibliographical references and index.
Identifiers: LCCN 2023014225 (print) | LCCN 2023014226 (ebook) |
ISBN 9780197680919 (hardback) | ISBN 9780197680926 (epub)
Subjects: LCSH: Carson, Anne, 1950—Criticism and interpretation.
Classification: LCC PS3553.A7667 Z66 2023 (print) | LCC PS3553.A7667 (ebook) |
DDC 811/.54—dc23/eng/20230417
LC record available at https://lccn.loc.gov/2023014225
LC ebook record available at https://lccn.loc.gov/2023014226

DOI: 10.1093/oso/9780197680919.001.0001

Printed by Integrated Books International, United States of America

For Amador & Amador Lucian

Contents

Acknowledgments ix
A Note on the Text xi

Introduction 1

PART I. VARIATIONS IN CRITICISM

1. The Eros Variations 31
2. Criticism and the Gift: (Carson with Celan) 61

PART II. GLASS ESSAYS

3. On Not Being Emily Brontë 85
4. Lyric Transparency and the "Fictional Essay" 100

PART III. SPECULATIVE FORM

5. *Decreation*, or the Art of Disappearance 125
6. Fake Women 146

PART IV. OPEN TRANSLATION

7. Grief Lessons: (Two Stories of Translation) 175
8. Sappho in the Open 202

Postscript: Short-Talking 224

Notes 235
Bibliography 299
Index 319

Acknowledgments

The story of this book condenses in my mind to a sequence of four or five frames. I would like to name and thank the people whose presence, warmth, wisdom, or example endures in and between them; those whose encouragement has kept them moving; and those without whom there would be no book, and my own story would tell quite differently.

I started writing about Carson more than a decade ago, and wouldn't have produced anything like this book without the support of Jacqueline Rose, to whom I owe a pressing debt of gratitude. Jacqueline remains a model of intellectual courage and charisma I never hoped to equal, but the influence of her thinking leaves its mark throughout these pages. Her belief that I could write the book has made its writing possible.

Others at Queen Mary, University of London, and at the Psychoanalysis, History, and Political Life Forum, which Jacqueline co-founded and which I later co-ran at the School of Advanced Study in Russell Square, I have been lucky enough to call my colleagues and friends. The generosity and kindness of Shaul Bar-Haim, Shahidha Bari, Katie Fleming, Peter Howarth, Cora Kaplan, Daniel Pick, Bill Schwarz, and Helen Tyson gave me ground to stand on. Peter in particular has supported this book's evolution in very tangible ways, reading early draft material and encouraging me to keep going when I was almost ready to bow out. He put me in touch with two individuals to whom I'd also like to express my gratitude: David James, who pointed out the project's virtues and shortcomings, and suggested Oxford University Press as a potential home; and Reena Sastri, whose friendship and correspondence with me on all things Carson has been a source of insight and companionship. My thanks to two women, Beverley Clack and Lisa Ruddick, for words of encouragement not forgotten.

Earlier still, before I'd ever read Carson or knew who she was; reading Virginia Woolf's spring-loaded prose and sublimely defensive "happening" words: I owe a debt of gratitude to my teachers, mentors, and friends at St. Catharine's College, Newnham College, and the Faculty of English at Cambridge. To Elizabeth Andrew, Colin Burrow, Alexander Dougherty, Caroline Gonda, Christos Hadjiyiannis, Paul Hartle, Alison Hennegan, Mary Jacobus, David Nowell-Smith, and Dan Wakelin. To Marina Voikhanskaya, for her humor and intelligence. To Yulia Yamineva, whose friendship is one of my greatest treasures. It's my pleasure to thank Loveday Why for sending me a copy of *Decreation* to review back in 2006, and Simon Jarvis for introducing his MPhil students to *Economy of the Unlost* the same year.

Several fellowships and prizes have made it possible for me to read and write for a living, and, almost two years ago, to return to full-time academic work. I would like to acknowledge the Isaac Newton Trust, University of Cambridge; the Wood-Whistler Medal and Scholarship, Newnham College, Cambridge; the Arts and Humanities Research Council; la Coordinación de Humanidades, UNAM; the Haas Library at the Universitat Pompeu Fabra and a Javier and Marta Villavecchia Fellowship; and, last but not least, the European Commission Horizon 2020 research and innovation program, whose Marie Skłodoswka-Curie Actions fellowship has enabled me to write a significant portion of this book. Especial thanks to Sonia Arribas for her support and encouragement during a time of seismic change in my life, and to Miquel Bassols, Neus Carbonell, Antoni Esquerra, Rosa Sellarès, and Mariona de Torres *per la seva complicitat*.

I would like to thank my generous and gifted editors at OUP, Hannah Doyle and Brent Matheny, and the two anonymous readers who reviewed this manuscript and gave me the courage to revise it. My wholehearted thanks also go to the individuals and publishers who gave their permission to reproduce poems, prose excerpts, and images without which this book would be much the poorer: to Anne Carson, her agent, Nicole Aragi, and Brenda Leifso at Brick Books for permission to reproduce three of the glorious "Short Talks"; to Little Brown Book Group LLC and Penguin Random House for the use of two fragments of Sappho in Carson's translation, and to Penguin Random House for permission to reproduce a selection of material from *Float*; to Routledge and Rosemarie Waldrop for an excerpt from her translation of Paul Celan's correspondence, and to Suzanna Tamminen at Wesleyan University Press for permission to reproduce a prose poem from John Cage's late "Composition in Retrospect." To the Estate of Betty Goodwin and to Gaétan Charbonneau for his kindness in providing me with a digital reproduction of *Seated Figure with Red Angle* (1988), and to Terence Byrnes, for generously allowing me to use his portrait of Carson on the cover of this book.

My last and dearest thanks are to my son, Amador Lucian, whose arrival in late 2020 lit the last stages of an early draft; and to his father, Amador, for living with me, thinking with me, and for his courage. Love is untrammeled freedom. This book is dedicated to them.

A Note on the Text

I use no abbreviations or acronyms for the short titles of Carson's published works, so *Eros the Bittersweet*, not *Eros* or *EB*. The spellings I use for Greek words in Latin script are Carson's, so Kreon, not Creon. All translations from the Greek and Latin are Carson's unless otherwise stated. Greek words appear in Latin script throughout, except where Carson does not transliterate, so "If not, winter" / δ]ὲ μή, χείμων[.

Introduction

Anne Carson studies a canvas by the American-born painter, Cy Twombly, on which the name "CATULLUS" is scrawled with a trained insouciance. Twombly's all-caps Latin is "gauche," Carson recalls from Roland Barthes's famous reading.[1] His "graffiti"—"VIRGIL," "LEDA," "CASSANDRA"—claims the canvas surface, not in the name of these paramours, but of the here-and-now of their coming to mind.[2] What Twombly's declarations perform, and what captures Carson's attention, is a "visible action" of line that "scratches out from idleness," in Barthes's words, "as if it were a matter of making time itself visible."[3] The time that shows up in Twombly is a present tense exposed, almost embarrassed, by the strength of its claim: that nothing—no Catullus—exists beyond its impressions. "Everything lives in the present," Carson quotes Twombly: "it's the only time it can live."[4]

A similar claim might be made in the name of Carson (b. 1950), the poet, classicist, translator, and performer known, in the very simplest terms, for making the ancient "live in the present." In more intrepid terms—those of the British painter and video artist, Tacita Dean—for "ripping" the classics "out of the past, shocking them back to life as if with electrical voltage, bringing the monsters of Greek myth to walk among us, slouch, punch, kiss, go back to bed, kill."[5] Twombly's claim goes further—but then so does Carson, whose work has made a discipline of foiling expectations, categories, and constraints. The ancients share their now-time in Carson with whatever happens to be lying beside them on her desk: with "whatever I bump into" in a library or etymological dictionary, in Hegel, in Woolf, in Brecht's FBI file, or the annals of her own intimate history.[6] This is Carson's "everything" and it matches Twombly's in its performance of philia and affinities, and its exposure of an active working present. "All time is now," says Carson in conversation with Dean. Anachronism? "There's no such thing."[7]

In the prismatic present tense that Anne Carson's readers now take for granted, Paul Celan's lines sharpen those of Simonides of Keos (and vice versa), with each poet "placed like a surface on which the other may come into focus."[8] Immanuel Kant and Monica Vitti, or Euripides's Helen and Hollywood's Marilyn, speak to—or speak for—one another, "and yet no conversation takes place."[9] Augustine, from whom Carson and Twombly draw their philosophy of time, "wanders across the back" of Edward Hopper's sultry interiors and the result is "Hopper: *Confessions*," ten short verse mise-en-scènes shot, as it were, at Carson's worktable. These wild-card comparative readings, whose studied errancy is almost unanimously acclaimed, are where her project turns out to be easiest to come to grips with.[10] How exactly that project is performed (*per formam*) is another matter. For just as there's "no such thing" as anachronism, so for Carson there's "no such thing" as form and genre beyond the needs and conditions thrown up by her source texts and collaborators. These makeshift constraints are made-to-measure, and recognizable forms are broken or repurposed to meet their demands. (Harold Bloom, a known admirer of Carson, described "the breaking of form" as the condition for its revelation as "a place of invention".)[11] When Carson does invoke formal categories, which is often, it is as a set of terms—"talk," "lecture," "essay," "fictional essay"—that stage their greater or lesser misalignment with the forms on the page, a greater or lesser indistinction between source text and commentary, commentary and adaptation, literature and criticism. Descriptors that seem to hold for one work evaporate like a mirage facing another. Terms and categories, in or out of her outré nomenclature, question as much as they affirm. This irrepressible staging of invention is a problem for some readers. The formal and thematic cabaret of *Men in the Off Hours* (2000) for one reviewer "begs the question: what now? What lands left to conquer?"[12] There is surely "a limit," sighs a more skeptical reader of *Float* (2016), "to pretending there's no limit."[13]

We would be right to wonder what a writer who "takes risks, subverts literary conventions, and plays havoc with our expectations" or who "takes risks, gambles with exposure" can hope to expose once her risk-taking has become de rigueur; or how a programmatic irreverence can sustain its own promise of danger.[14] Yet to understand Carson's project as experiment for experiment's sake, its rationale the shock of the new, is, I suggest, to miss the point. In the poet-critic Charles Bernstein's much-cited declaration that "*poetry is aversion of conformity* in the pursuit of new forms," it is a pun that tells us how aversion is itself *a version* of conformity: that to be averse—or to "subvert literary convention"—is a form of passionate attachment to the refused antecedent, where "new forms" are bound to sound out the old.[15] Anne Carson is a writer who not only has no problem with such attachment to literary history, but who actively cultivates and seeks it out. A classicist by training, many of her best-known works derive explicitly from the literatures of antiquity: her versions of the *Antigone* (2012, 2015), her triple-author *Oresteia* (2009), and her single-author devotion to Euripides, the essay-elegy *Nox* (2010), and verse-novel *Autobiography of Red* (1998), or the spare lyricism of *If Not, Winter: Fragments of Sappho* (2002). Beyond her translations and adaptations, go in search of novelty in Carson and you will almost always find highly original ways of being derivative: reproducing, riffing on, or otherwise preserving what she calls the "facts" of "the texts I deal with."[16] Carson's handling of her source texts rarely coincides with what we have come to expect from scholars. Yet this book makes the case for Carson's writing as an extraordinary experimental mode of scholarship, a project that rehearses scholarly methods while slipping their strictures of form and emotion. What transcends formal categories in her work, and what frees us from their bind as we read her, is Carson's unresting attention to the work of others, set to form in a decades-long reckoning with the tasks, modes, and moods of the scholar and close reader. And Carson, it is argued here, is one of the most creative and exacting *readers* writing now.

Understanding her work as primarily responsive, her experiments in composition as lessons in interpretive attention and textuality, invites us to read Carson more or less as she reads herself. Which is to say—though taking Carson at her word is a complex business—that it allows us to see her many modes of written creation and, more recently, live performance, as part of a single continuous inquiry sustaining no working distinction between the academic and the non-academic. So Carson tells Kevin McNeilly, who puts it to her in an interview that "some would say the academy is not the place for poetry, that it thrives outside its interpretation": "I practically don't separate them," says Carson; "I put scholarly projects and so-called creative projects side-by-side in my workspace and I cross back and forth between them or move sentences back and forth between them, and so cause them to permeate one another."[17] Her mode of exchange between these inseparables has clearly paid off. *The Beauty of the Husband: A Fictional Essay in 29 Tangos* (2001), an essay in verse whose inquiry into truth begins with its own unblushing formal anomaly, won Carson the T. S. Eliot Prize in the year of its publication.[18] The imperatively titled "Possessive Used as Drink (Me): A Lecture on Pronouns in the Form of 15 Sonnets," staged in collaboration with the Merce Cunningham Dance Company, joins a long list of experimental lectures and opera libretti performed across and beyond North America, where the bestselling *Autobiography of Red* earned Carson an early cult following.[19] Arguing for a project or vision behind what can seem a scattershot relationship to form and genre is something existing scholarship on Carson, which now includes two multi-author collections of essays, has neither sought nor been able to do.[20] Yet to affirm Carson the reader, indivisible from Carson the writer, is only the beginning of the story.

Beyond her sheer breadth of range, something that complicates any critical approach to Carson—and this book is no exception—is how much and how shrewdly Carson reads herself. From mock-scholarly prefaces and "Notes on Method," to lectures that compare their "perilous" composition to involuntary discomposures of the mind, Carson builds self-reading into her writing, telling us what she's doing and performing it in one or several iterations, anticipating qualms, and theorizing her (and our) emotions as she goes. So exposed is this apparatus of commentary that in several works the performance of method and working emotion becomes the focus and foreground, not just the backstory, of her reading of a source text. Even where these exposures of thought saturate or subsume their sources, producing a an autofictional approach to John Keats in *The Beauty of the Husband*, a tendentious, citation-rich glossary of Catullus 101 in *Nox*, or the translation-commentary of Euripides's *Herakles* titled *H of H Playbook* (2021)—recently dubbed a "performance of thought"—, they do not compel our assent or agreement. What they do is splay out a reading in which the facts of a source text move among and exchange valency with other facts, textual or (auto)biographical: from the life of Carson's late, long-estranged brother, or her "story of a marriage" and the wider philosophical inquiry to which its breakdown gives rise in *The Beauty of the Husband*. The zoom-in on Carson in these texts, the fact that it is so clearly Carson who is speaking, puts in shot an errant reflective throughline—a *person*—whose effect as a reader addressing herself to readers is (to tilt Neil Hertz's phrase) the pathos of certain agency.[21] Carson's readings move us, in part, because they address us in situ, as though the thinking is still happening, caught up at the scene of composition. Whatever her prefatory notes, drafts, and interpolated commentary represent—too much self, too much scholarship, or "sleight of hand," the choice is ours—a reader, agile, spontaneous, and self-examining, is exposed to view.[22]

The trace of Carson the scholar and teacher is unmistakable across her experiments in form, including—and perhaps especially—in readings that square even less with what we might expect from, say, an essay or a translation. In another much-quoted interview, Carson describes poems as "an action of the mind captured on a page, and the reader, when he engages it, has to enter into that action . . . [you] feel when you're in it that you're moving with somebody else's mind through [the] action."[23] It is an idea of mimesis as a "captured," capturing performance that recurs across her work, from early scholarly essays that read for and begin to reprise the "sensible forms" of prosody, to the recent "interactive lectures" that revive the micro-essays of *Short Talks* (1992) as thirteen-second vocal happenings.[24] Carson takes this deceptively simple idea to great lengths. A performative, iconic quality observed in the syntax of Simonides ("mimesis in its most radical mechanism") or in Sappho ("lyric mimesis," in an early essay on Aristotle's *Poetics*) is made available in Carson's own compositions as a strong mode of response to other writing, recruiting structure, citational poetics, meter, and mise-en-page in the performance of a style of thought or argument, sometimes—as in *The Albertine Workout* (2014), the *Denkbild*-styled *Short Talks*, or her lecture in sonnet form—in lieu of an argument explicitly being made. In an early conversation with John D'Agata, Carson called this mimetic shorthand a "painting notion," "painting with thoughts and facts," designed to preserve "just the facts" with no story to put them into order.[25] She speaks often of her scholarly training and invokes its moods, methods, and apparatus across much of her work. Yet Carson pushes against the descriptive and expository métier of scholarship in pursuit of documentation, formal immediacy, variation, unexpectedness, and emotive effect—and the *effect* is often captivating.

The recruitment of "non-academic" form for scholarship and scholarly paratext for narrative or verse work—Carson, we have seen, has no truck with these distinctions—has strong consequences for us as readers, and this book is interested in how, even perhaps why, these consequences are afforded. From the book's opening chapter, which reads her dazzling essay *Eros the Bittersweet* (1986) alongside several later works reprising its questions, we will see form take a decisive role in the way argument happens and the way source texts are presented. Though some of these works appear to have been composed to free the play of Carson's material, opening thought to unforeseen destinies, the structure or syntactic pattern of others is not only compelling, ostentatious as form, but *compels*: reprising an action of mind or an action of text in her source, these performative forms would have us go through the motions again ourselves, perhaps without even realizing it (the reader, Carson says, "*has to* enter into that action").[26] Performative form, a "strong form" in Bloom's terms, works against what Carson calls "the boredom of a story" and against the ennui and expository force of academic essays; but the breaking of scholarly form doesn't always mean greater freedom—our freedom—to think and feel. Form carries the weight of expectation at the crossing of critical scholarship, literature, and translation. The variety of arrangements produced in their exchange—from structural imitations of sources to variable structures of reading—matters for each of these disciplines, whose undisciplining by Carson is also an inquiry into how she (and how her reader) reads.

Just as Carson's form is complex in its relation to the conventions of scholarly writing, so her commentary and exposures of method, I have begun to suggest, offer something trickier and more provocative than a set of instructions for readers. For all her deliberateness and self-explanation, Carson is not Susan Sontag's "overcooperative" author, whose inbuilt critical presentations (in Sontag's example of Thomas Mann) pander to the reader, or, in Eve Kosofsky Sedgwick's words, "demand the least" from him.[27] Instead, Carson's critical presentations are uncertain in status: they can hover between reflection and reckoning; autofiction, send-up, and sabotage; a way of blindsiding scholars or beating critics at their own game. We are granted an arresting degree of access to how Carson works, thinks, and feels around her sources, but the same transparency—not the usual transparency and accountability of scholars—can disorient. Her cleverness, and her constant courting of ours, can be "overpowering."[28] If anything, this book argues, Carson's apparatus of reflection invites a complicity that her tic for addressing us directly merely makes explicit. Christopher Ricks has described "a contractual model in literary understanding" that invites us to accept fictions, incongruities, and factual inaccuracies as part of the work of literature.[29] Carson offers us another version of the contract. Her reckoning with scholarship not only happens in our midst—talks to us of its troubles, plays openly with its forms—but recruits us as an accomplice. There is an "understanding," and it is that we will suspend our disbelief when Carson interviews Stesichoros, speaks as Euripides, has fiction slip her reading of Keats, or theorizes her writing for us: not at the expense of doubt, but on the understanding that there is nothing like doubt, error, staged fiction, and incongruity, nothing so inviting as direct address and assumed complicity, to throw our own thinking into relief. Whether or not we enter into this understanding—as Carson herself would say—depends on us.

Anne Carson: The Glass Essayist is a portrait of a singularly polyphonic reader of literature, whose polyphony or "hybridity" is no restive postmodern symptom.[30] Nor does the book understand Carson's complex mediating transparency—"I am writing this to be as wrong as possible to you"; "There is too much self in my writing"; "I am to imitate a mirror like that of water"—as a post-authorial performance, swapping the "I" of authorship for designed exposures of its fabrication or failure.[31] Across its eight chapters and postscript, in close readings and wider-angle commentary, this book suggests we understand Carson's performance of scholarship as uniquely personal and dexterous in its handling of personality, as well as significant beyond her own much-vaunted singularity of style. Carson has found a way to exercise an essentially speculative distinction between critical scholarship and literature, and by doing so, to turn what it is we need both of these to be into an object of thought. It is this speculation, high on erudition, that has made Carson not only a writer of extraordinarily widespread appeal and acclaim, but a particular penchant of academic critics, owing, perhaps, to her status as a striking limit-case in the contemporary academy.

In the more than forty years since her doctorate, Carson has combined teaching posts at Princeton, McGill, Michigan, and Cornell with residencies at New York's 92nd Street Y, Bard College, and the "Library of Water" at Stykkishólmur in Iceland; single-author essays, translations, verse and performance works with high-profile commissions and intermedia collaborations. Pipped to the Oxford Professor of Poetry Chair by (scholar and non-poet) Ricks in 2004, Carson's 2018 Clark Lectures at Trinity College, Cambridge, put a licensed exchange of action between literary creation and criticism, as between cultural and occupational performance, center stage. Such exchanges have long been par for the course in her writing, where the demands of academic scholarship are set to "literary" compositional rigors, and offset by reactions and moods unsanctioned, if not effectively outlawed, by the profession. Rather than erased in the exchange, these demands—together with the "I" who parses them and bears their weight—come under the most sustained and expansive scrutiny.

Carson's exercise of this "I," an "I" who has already processed our most sophisticated postmodern objections, is one of the boldest throughlines of her writing career. Examining her project, its speculations with form and bold exchanges of action, this book makes a broader case for the importance of reading Carson—and reading her as a reader of literature—now.

*

This book was written at a moment of some creative dissent in the Anglophone academy around the moods and methods of literary scholarship, and the distinctions these enable or disable between critical attention and literary creation, between criticism and other interpretive forms and media, and between the academic and non-academic (the "lyric" or even belletrist) essay. A mainstay of the discussion concerns the methodologies and emotions associated with "critique," the dominant oppositional reading style that is the subject of acclaimed work by Rita Felski, Eve Kosofsky Sedgwick in her remarkable essay on "paranoid reading," and other scholars in their wake.[32] Critical writing suffers from a "frame lock" as well as a "tone jam," observes Charles Bernstein.[33] It culls rather than cultivates surprise, says Sedgwick.[34] (Carson suggests that a similar conviction about academic lectures spurred her to write *Short Talks* while teaching at Princeton.)[35] The glaring exception from most of these conversations is form. Bar a handful of high-profile outliers—scholar-poets whose work is marked experimental and returned undercover to "literature"—the scholarly or critical-interpretive essay suffers from a *form lock*.

Anne Carson's "Every Exit Is an Entrance: A Praise of Sleep," a short essay from the multiform concept volume *Decreation: Poetry, Essays Opera* (2005), was anthologized in a collection that sought to ask the form question in the field of the critical essay. *Creative Criticism: An Anthology and Guide* (2014) places Carson alongside Barthes, John Cage, and Jacques Derrida—all of whom she cites in her writing—and alongside other authors (Geoff Dyer, Kevin Kopelson, Sedgwick) with whom her "creative-critical" approaches share little more in common than a knack for creative resignification.[36] An introduction to the anthology traces a lineage for "creative criticism" back to the freeform modernist essays of H. D., Wyndham Lewis, Ezra Pound, and Laura Riding, for which the editors owe a significant debt to Lisa Samuels's 2001 genealogy of "the Other Criticism": defiant, formally driven interpretive writing from Pound and Riding through Georges Bataille, Charles Olson, Angela Carter, and the American scholar-poets, Bernstein and Susan Howe.[37] A range of recent alt-critical examples might also be cited here, from "slow burn" collective readings of Elena Ferrante in epistolary form, to the theoretical and ekphrastic poem-essays of Ann Lauterbach.[38] Bernstein, whose "thought opera" on Walter Benjamin premiered in 2005, and Howe, whose "anarcho-scholasticism" and form-sensile critical testimonies presage the author of *Nox*, *Men in the Off Hours*, and "The Glass Essay," are perhaps Carson's truest peers in the unlocking of form for scholarship.[39] Comparison might be drawn, too, with the "lyric philosophy" of Canadian scholar-poet Jan Zwicky, whose compositions amplify the formal arrangements and philosophical complexities of her principal source and emotive event, Ludwig Wittgenstein.[40] Like Howe, like Bernstein, and like Carson, there is something non-negotiable in Zwicky's citational poetics, as though the end of paraphrase—the start of an art of copying down—is where close reading comes into its own.

Arguments for "the essay as form" and a "search for style" have a stronger, less timid, and better known history in European philosophy, where what Sontag calls "the specter of banished 'content'" has been kept more successfully at bay.[41] The years of Carson's doctoral research ("Odi et Amo Ergo Sum," University of Toronto, 1981) are the Anglo-American advent of French post-structuralism and *écriture*, of Jacques Derrida's seminal, mimetic reading of Plato's *Phaedrus*—the dialogue at the heart of Carson's thesis and, later, *Eros the Bittersweet*—and Barthes's famous formal "simulation" of a lover's discourse, perhaps the closest kin to Carson's essay on desire.[42] (Carson praises Barthes's "golden persuasions" in her essay on Twombly and quotes him in numerous other works.)[43] These are also the late summit years of Language poetry, Howe, Bernstein, and Bruce Andrews's materialist arts of sound. In 1994, the period of *Short Talks* and "The Glass Essay," after *Eros the Bittersweet* and before *Men in the Off Hours*, a conference in Miami titled "Reinventing the Poet-Critic" set out to address "experiments in criticism that explode conventional genres and categories," defining its aims against the complaint that "even as we redefine the objects and goals of scholarship, our essays and books, considered as writing, are often as boring and predictable as ever."[44] Bernstein, one of the conference keynotes, would later speak of "criticism's blindness to the meaning of its forms."[45] The poet and essayist Rachel Blau DuPlessis, another of the keynotes, would go on to scour the recent history of experimental essays on the trail of a certain recklessness of form, where the "essay" is easily misrecognized but where its brief of "writing-as-reading" comes into the sharpest focus.[46]

We will recognize this brief, and these misrecognitions of the essay, throughout the pages of this book. "Essay," less a strict purview than a soft pretext for my inquiry, is a term Carson herself handles breezily. Under its loose-drawn aegis are *Eros the Bittersweet: An Essay* (a subtitle removed from later editions); a roughly lineated "Essay on What I Think About Most," paired in *Men in the Off Hours* with an elliptical redraft, "Essay on Error," alongside "Irony Is Not Enough: Essay on my Life as Catherine Deneuve" and "Dirt and Desire: Essay on the Phenomenology of Female Pollution in Antiquity." There is the extended scholarly essay, *Economy of the Unlost: (Reading Simonides of Keos with Paul*

Celan) (1999); "Decreation: How Sappho, Marguerite Porete and Simone Weil Tell God," reprised as "Decreation: An Opera in Three Parts," and other "essays" glossed in the subtitle of *Decreation: Poetry, Essays, Opera*, including "Foam (Essay with Rhapsody): On the Sublime in Longinus and Antonioni." There is *Short Talks*, whose prose poems Carson has called both "essays" and "lectures"; *The Beauty of the Husband: A Fictional Essay in 29 Tangos*; scripts for performance pieces, including "Variations on the Right to Remain Silent," "Cassandra Float Can," and "Uncle Falling: A Pair of Lyric Lectures"; and a handful of more conventional lectures, referred to in their published versions in the journal *Critical Inquiry* as "essays."[47] Several of these titles do strong performative work, which is to say they make the essay an "essay" simply by calling it one, where otherwise it might be taken for erudite narrative fiction, say, or a philosophical poem with footnotes. A lecture in sonnet form, similarly, pulls the expectational weight of a lecture—as Cage's intermedia masterpiece, "Lecture on the Weather," did several decades earlier—because the title awakens such expectations even as it obliges us to revise them.[48] Many works that do not announce themselves as essays or lectures exercise a similarly imperative appeal. The imperative voice that Elaine Scarry suggests is "the voice under which we compose" when we describe ("Imagine this. Now. Do it. Fast") is given an edge in Carson by her tic for deixis and direction ("Let's look at this," or "drop the sound. Listen to the difference / Shatter").[49] Yet the imperative gets softened, even sabotaged, by Carson's repertoire of scholarly paratexts and paraphernalia, whose mimicry of critical apparatus exposes its fantasies, processes, and contingencies, and is usually on the verge of sending itself up.

An early example of this is Carson's Introduction to the poem sequence, "The Life of Towns," which tells us, with ironic self-regard, what a scholar is and how this particular scholar has already managed to wrongfoot "you," the reader:

> A scholar is someone who takes a position. From which position, certain lines become visible. You will at first think I am painting the lines myself; it's not so. I merely know where to stand to see the lines that are there. And the mysterious thing, it is a very mysterious thing, is how these lines do paint themselves. Before there were any edges or angles or virtue—who was there to ask the questions? Well, let's not get carried away with exegesis. A scholar is someone who knows how to limit himself to the matter at hand.[50]

What category of statement is this, whose address assumes an intimacy its irony bleaches out? Are we being taught a lesson, or asked to go along with our own duping? What is our position on this scholar—a "painter of writing," to borrow Barthes's term for Twombly—who both theorizes her work and curtails its exegesis, and whose confident exposure of operations tells us these operations happen all by themselves?⁵¹ Carson's work is full of scenic events like this one: performances of intent that invite us to cede to their artifice "just for the thrill"; prefaces, appendices, glossaries, botched quotations, lesson plans, and fake testimony that take the expectation they rouse of security and, more or less explicitly, dash it.⁵² The Carson paratext is a romp through scholarly form that builds misadventure into the work of commentary, but which understands our awareness of erring, like our awareness of mistakes or of being duped, as an unrivaled source of insight and invention.

Invention here is our prerogative as well as Carson's. For we, it turns out, are one of her main motives in the unlocking of scholarly form: "If I'm totally professional and locked in to my credentials as a professional, I can't let you have a thought about what I am telling you," remarks Carson; "It's not teaching, it's closing off teaching."⁵³ In the same set of remarks, it also turns out that "being an amateur"—(from the Latin *amare*, *amator*), for whom to love your objects is to play rough with them—might actually make you a better teacher. In any case, the separation of "amateur" or "belletrist" from professional reading has, in Eric Hayot's words, "made the literary academy increasingly self-absorbed and thus increasingly irrelevant."⁵⁴

Interviewing Carson back in 1997, D'Agata asked her what she thought of the essay form. Carson, at this point in their conversation, has already declared form to be "a rough approximation of what the facts are doing," a remark that delegates to form the tasks of proximity—as in likeness, mimesis—and interpretation. When D'Agata speaks about form in Carson's "very formal" oeuvre, he confesses he's "not sure"—not ever sure, the suggestion is—"what the form is" or "where it comes from." Carson affirms: "that's because it arises out of the thing itself."⁵⁵ By this account, then, we have form that is not just approximate to facts but wholly contingent on them: form whose entire raison d'être is response. Essays, it seems, are a way of formalizing the arrangement; but the arrangement doesn't exactly stop there:

> When you write an essay, you're giving a gift, it seems to me. You're giving this grace, as the ancients would say. A gift shouldn't turn back into the self and stop there. That's why facts are so important, because a fact is something already given. It's a gift from the world or from wherever you found it. And then you take that gift and you do something with it, and you give it again to the world or to some person, and that keeps it going.⁵⁶

More than asking what a form is in Carson, we might do better to ask where it comes from, how it responds to a given set of "facts," how and whom it addresses, what or where are its destinies. To borrow Susan Howe's words for her own, in some ways comparable mode of response to other authors, the question for

Carson is "what form for the form"—in what shape, measure, or metric the echo of an original is sustained in her work, as tempo, unsettled structure, rhyme, symbol, or copy, potentially (though not necessarily) including verbatim citation.[57] This idea of form also sends us back to Oscar Wilde, an idol of Carson's youth and an inspiration behind her decision to study Greek, who wrote in "The Critic as Artist" that the critic "exhibits to us a work of art in a form different from that of the work itself," his formal task indivisible from his interpretive one.[58] Carson's remarks about grace, gifts, and the essay, from which Chapter 2 of this book takes its cue, imagine a form that keeps on forming—a *forma efformans*, in Coleridge's term—in the continued production of points of arrival: a form that wants to be "found," that lets us "have a thought" of our own about it, and that, to do so, must expose its dependencies and its incompletion.[59] Yet Howe's protocol, and Carson's, I propose, is where the essay as such starts to disappear. In the tautological fit between "form" and "form," where the essay only exists as a counter-gift to given facts, there is no "essay form" to speak of (though there might be an essay "*as form*"). Not just because it changes shape—as Carson has said, her work is continually altered "in performance or medium, making a book a dance, or a dance a sculpture"[60]—but because its definition, its defining condition of possibility, is always elsewhere.

We can start to speak, then, of the Carson "essay"—in scare quotes for the moment—as transparent, prismatic, contourless, speculative, imitative, or mirroring. An "open work" in the modernist sense (as the artist Kim Anno calls "open reading" the effect she sought to create in collaboration with Carson): performing its dependency on other works and its intent to go on meaning and producing in the future; a form that foregrounds the interpretation—hers as well as ours—without which, it is supposed, it would not exist.[61] It is on these grounds that Carson's works that bear the term "essay" in their titles blend into works that don't, and into her translations, adaptations, fiction, ekphrases, and verse compositions. Beyond the task of approximation, staging form as a findable measure of other finds, there is no rubric for Carson's essaying with form save the requirement to reflect on it: a doubling expressed as commentary, academic paratext, rehearsal (drafts, iterations, "cuts," "workouts"), and exposures of the kinds I have tried to sketch out here. A reading that begins as a prose essay, thinking of the essays of *Decreation*, gets redrafted as an ode, rhapsody, or libretto to perform its dependency on the facts and to "keep [attention] from settling."[62] Close readings and critical reflections pass their prerogatives to autobiography, fiction, verse, or the protagonists of Greek tragic drama ("The Glass Essay," *The Beauty of the Husband, Autobiography of Red, Antigonick, H of H Playbook*). The "Note on Method" heading *Economy of the Unlost* begins with a line from Hölderlin's river poem, "The Rhine," that reflects on the essay in its wake: *Nur hat ein jeder sein Maas*—"Yet each of us has his measure."[63] Carson's measure, unmeasured and unmeasurable by most standards, is set by the texts and collaborators she works with. Measuring facts is what her essaying does best, as well as what defines it, perhaps, as essay (from *exagiare*, to weigh): the "weighing," in Brian Dillon's words, "of something outside of itself."[64]

There is, of course, the essay whose title this book explicitly calls upon. "The Glass Essay," the long opening verse composition of *Glass, Irony and God* (1995) and the focus of Chapter 3, is a reading of the life and work of Emily Brontë in situ—embedded, that is, in site-specific, real-time reflections on the story of a broken love affair.[65] Ian Rae has described "The Glass Essay" as an attempt "to create a broader interpretative context, one capable of mirroring the speaker's mental and emotional states, out of fragments of biography, theology, and literary analysis."[66] In this seamless, edgeless essay, *everything* comes to bear on Brontë, and vice versa. Every fact, every conversation, every moment's reflective underside, is fair game. "Fishing up facts of the landscape from notes or memory," a working method claimed for *Economy of the Unlost*, is given a rich narrative mise-en-scène in "The Glass Essay," as textual finds and inquiries occur while the narrator is out "stumping over the mud flats" or "strid[ing] over the moor," bruised and brooding on her reclusive source and alter ego.[67] With the reading wide open to recollection and landscape, it *is* its situation in place and time, the facts of its source text just some among the other facts that surround them. The reading as such is almost completely transparent. The essay as essay, a tautology of the kind Carson is so good at exposing, almost isn't there at all.

I began this Introduction with Twombly's scribbled shout-out to Catullus that, in Carson's words (in which Barthes's words show through), "mingle[s] together exposure and erasure" of the author's hand.[68] Exposure and erasure—both gestures toward transparency and both with their quotient of threat—are methods and moods to be found in greater or lesser degrees of tension throughout Carson's writing. Like Twombly's self-effacing line, Carson's exposure/erasure of the essay on Brontë is "a matter of making time itself visible": the time of thinking and walking and talking in which the reading errs and evolves. ("I want to make you see time" is an admission of *The Beauty of the Husband,* another kind of "glass essay" on another nineteenth-century poet, and the subject of Chapter 4 of this book.) Carson's Emily Brontë—like Howe's *My Emily Dickinson* (1989)—is also the object of a recovery, a commitment to the suppressed errancies of handwritten textuality and to what Howe, in her errant scholarly monograph, imagines as the mirroring of her source: "A poet is a mirror, a transcriber" (a premise unsettled in Carson's express commitment "to imitate a mirror like that of water" at the start of *Short Talks*).[69] Brontë is Carson's looking glass, as Carson is offered as hers, and it is in this putatively uncritical exchange that the speculative activity in all reading appears on the scene. It is here in "The Glass Essay" that reader and source, Carson and Brontë, start—though they will not continue—to tell the same story. Carson's early confession in the work, "I feel I am turning into Emily Brontë," exposes an erasure of boundary—one of the first taboos of academic criticism—that the essay's formal equivocations perform from the first.

Anne Carson's insertion of herself in the dilemmas, lives, and literatures of her objects, from Brontë to Catherine Deneuve, Euripides to Simone Weil, is an admission of the unsanctioned emotional life of scholarship, where boredom can be potent ("I will do anything to avoid boredom") and identifications delirious ("Essay on My Life as Catherine Deneuve").[70] Mirroring, pastiche, even impersonation, far from lapses in critical attention, are, more often than not, rehearsals of a critical difference. For all their baffling ironies and the riot they run with scholarly procedure, these maneuvers, and the kinds of experience they express, are not perhaps the outliers they might seem in the study of literature. At the end of an early essay, Barthes sketches a short vignette about criticism and literary interpretation. "In adding his language to that of the author and his symbols to those of the work," he says, "[the critical reader] reproduces yet again, like a sign which is lifted out and varied, the sign of the works themselves."[71] This may not be an action we either recognize or aspire to if we write academic prose or teach literature for a living; then again, it might be just what we long to do with literature's singularities, after hours in the company of the texts we deal with. The lifting and variation of signs is the soft power that criticism shares with literature, and Carson, this book hopes to show, has fixed this soft power, its allure, and its negotiations with form, at the center of her work.

Carson, it bears restating, is in good company in these negotiations—alongside Bernstein on Benjamin, Howe on Dickinson, Zwicky on Wittgenstein. We find variation and identification, too, as the operative modes of authors known primarily for their critical or theoretical writing: Barthes, of course, but also Hélène Cixous in her readings of Clarice Lispector, Julia Kristeva in her extraordinary autofictional novel-essay on Teresa of Ávila, and Carol Mavor in the luxurious mimetic prose of *Reading Boyishly*.[72] "The Glass Essay" itself has given rise to at least one mimetic variation: "A Glass Essay," a recent piece by American scholar Sarah Chihaya, varies Carson's verse essay by reflecting on what it means to feel she is "turning into" Anne Carson.[73] D'Agata reminds Carson that "people still call 'The Glass Essay,' for example, brilliant literary criticism and a brilliant poem, together in one form, in one consistent voice."[74] Where Carson's scholar-narrator says "I am turning into Emily Brontë," Barthes's hypothetical reader-critic, whose first-person voice fuses with the source text, declares in her own "combined voice": "*I am literature*" (*je suis littérature*), a protest against our taboos and perhaps a cry of vindication, too.[75] For "I," the self-effacing "I" of literary interpretation, is the sum of its encounters.

Some quick lifting and variation of Carson's symbol, finally, lets us call upon *glass* not just as the medium of mimesis and illusion, but as the medium that problematizes medium per se.[76] Glass is the reluctant matter that, depending on where we're standing, either effaces or exposes its mediation—another way of saying that it keeps the idea of mediation open. As it moves in and out of perceptibility, between exposure and erasure, it *is* and *is not* the same as the forms it reveals, though expert at concealing its non-identity. In fact, its easy exchange of identity with the world of its surroundings has made glass the medium of choice for the modern assault on art from within, from Marcel Duchamp's *The Large Glass*—which makes a cameo in *The Beauty of the Husband*—to the invisible proscenium of performance art.[77] Metaphors of glass plumb the paradoxes of writing whose author seeks to pass unnoticed, or which stages its own lapses of presence. For the Scottish poet W. S. Graham, the "white / Crystal of Art" in which the poet "could not speak" stifles this presence, like the "atmosphere of glass" into which Carson and her mother fall in "The Glass Essay."[78] (For Carson, on the contrary, exercising transparency, speaking in the decommissioned words of others, sometimes makes it possible to speak.) For Howe, the poet's words "like the sun against glass, may recoil false meaning back on herself": to write is to be dazzled by misrecognitions.[79] In another poet, Joan Brossa, on the Catalan avant-garde, the poem can do performative contradiction just as well as its analogue: "These lines were written / to go as unnoticed as / glass."[80]

*

The strong emotional claims that share reading's present tense, put so disarmingly to scrutiny in "The Glass Essay," are first broached in the text that inaugurates Anne Carson as a scholar of classics. "Odi et Amo Ergo Sum," the doctoral thesis whose title riffs on the opening of Catullus 85, is a theory of desire and the lyric poem in the advent of writing. For the Carson of "Odi et Amo," written script changes minds. The lyric poems of Sappho, Alkman, Anakreon, and Archilochos, dramas of desire under straits, were composed to be sung and recited before audiences. The desire they stage is public insofar as it is proclaimed audibly and circulates openly at the scene of their performance. Yet for Carson, the arrival of semi-literate and literate culture brings to these poems a new performative dimension from which public desire is exempt. The transcribed poems enclose the desire they mimic and the desire they awaken in new and compact borders. The quiet concentration of reading sharpens sensory edges, heightens the stakes of their breaching, and in this parsing of edges is the early rubric of a "science of self."[81] For the celebrated classicist, Bruno Snell, "the discovery of the mind" (and the "theory" of other minds) begins as a confrontation with bittersweet *erōs*, "the love which has its course barred."[82] So writing begins as an index of ethical value—but it is first, and perhaps foremost, an inducement to eros, a scene of self-regard and self-possession on which the arrival of "a sudden, strong emotion from without cannot be an unalarming event."[83] At the erotic "crisis of contact" between lovers, transcription is the lyric poet's accomplice, as reading nurtures the very conditions of possibility for the love to which he pays tribute: the love that assaults the senses and shakes the mind.

Carson's thesis gets reworked five years later as *Eros the Bittersweet*, an essay whose compositional and citational arrangements mark a shift from the thesis and portfolio of academic articles she had already begun to compile. Its formal rehearsals and central account of the complicities of writing and desire will return in various iterations across her work, the "Eros variations" of this book's opening chapter.

This is the scene Carson sets for eros:

> As Sokrates tells it, your story begins the moment Eros enters you. That incursion is the biggest risk of your life. How you handle it is an index of the quality, wisdom, and decorum of the things inside you. As you handle it you come into contact with what is inside you, in a sudden and startling way. You perceive what you are, what you lack, what you could be.[84]

Carson's story as a scholar begins with this uplit cautionary tale. The stakes of the "incursion" are so high, she says, not just because of the contact they augur with someone else, but because of the contact they compel with "you" yourself. The rulebook of Carson's "decorum" is written in real time, as relation and self-relation, then and now, suddenly and startlingly coincide. Elsewhere in *Eros the Bittersweet*, as in the doctoral thesis, she describes a "voltage of decorum" shocking between lovers and halting incursive eros in its tracks. Against the desire to possess is a contrast sensation, *aidōs*, defined by Carson as "an instinctive and mutual sensitivity to the boundary between them."[85] This bittersweet compromise, for Carson (on the trail of Snell), is what transforms erotic desire into a crisis of personal sovereignty. Channeled in the erotic tableaux of Greek lyric, amped up by the reading and speaking of written words in solitude, Carson's "voltage of decorum" carries down its currents a shiver of anxiety around the phenomenon of literary mimesis. The *mimēsis* that proved so troubling to Plato, moving mind and body undetected, finds concentrated expression in the tight textual spaces of early love lyric, whose written marks electrify the edges of readers. They transport us, but they also put us in our place.

Carson talks to McNeilly about her work in terms that bring *aidōs* to mind, describing a "scholarly hesitation" in her contact with the classical canon.[86] Awareness of incursive or possessive designs on the fragments of Sappho, for instance, which have been filled out, bowdlerized, and versioned since Catullus, leads her quite literally to stop at their edges—to preserve those edges, as she does in *If Not, Winter*—as though a crisis of contact or drama of non-identity were the prized object of classical translation (and perhaps, in a way, all translation).

Yet halting restraint is not how most readers would describe Carson's handling of the texts she deals with. Not least Tacita Dean, whose evocation of Carson's Ancient Greek archive and cast—"shocking them back to life as if with electrical voltage"—ramps up Carson's "voltage of decorum," the boundary-sensitivity of *aidōs*, almost beyond recognition. Though the glossing of Catullus 101 in *Nox* opens a thoroughgoing "hesitation" to scrutiny, poring over facts of the poem and facts from her brother's life, other works can look like reading on a rampage. *Antigonick*, *Autobiography of Red*, *H of H Playbook*, *Norma Jeane Baker of Troy* (2019), a "Twelve-Minute Prometheus (After Aiskhylos)" (2008), and "Oh What a Night (Alkibiades)" (2020)—an "unusual" version of Plato's *Symposium*—are headlong incursions into source texts that shake up or shirk their philological details; that redesign these texts as immanent commentaries, caricatured, shorthand versions, or dramatizations of lives and scenarios millennia apart. Where the materially compromised and textually conjectured classics might seem to ask for more *aidōs* than, say, Proust's *À la recherche* or Weil's notebooks, Carson submits her classical sources to form-driven readings and imaginative revisions no less intrepid than her responses to Proust or Weil, Marguerite Porete or Emily Brontë. In each of these cases, there is no doubt that what we're reading is a version of the facts, and that this version is Anne Carson's.

This book pays close attention to moments in Carson's writing where she confronts the sheer personality of her scholarship directly; where its consequences are processed, as it were, so that we don't have to. In the introductory notes to *If Not, Winter*, where Carson sets out the case for hesitation, she describes her working method and its subtending "fantasy":

> In translating I tried to put down all that can be read of each poem in the plainest language I could find, using where possible the same order of words and thoughts as Sappho did. I like to think that, the more I stand out of the way, the more Sappho shows through. This is an amiable fantasy (transparency of self) within which most translators labor.[87]

Carson is certainly not "most translators." Yet the fantasy she professes to share with them is one she will revisit across the contexts of translation, critical prose, and freeform interpretive composition. *Economy of the Unlost*, the comparative study derived from her Martin Classical Lectures, begins its "Note on Method" with the declaration, "There is too much self in my writing," but the "Note" proceeds almost immediately to a taut lyrical paean to thought's "best moments," where introverted or "windowless" aesthetic work is set against scholarship's "landscape of science and fact where other people converse logically and exchange judgements."[88] Fast-forward several years and the problem of self—now the "brilliant assertiveness of the writerly project" with its "big, loud, shiny center of self"—is the reflexive center of "Decreation: How Sappho, Marguerite Porete and Simone Weil Tell God" (discussed here in Chapter 6), where the dilemma of "too much self" is pursued through three—or four—very different repertoires for self-undoing.

This inquiry into subjectivity, its exposure, and its derailing, continues to shape her work. Speaking to Eleanor Wachtel in 2012, Carson describes an ongoing struggle to "get every Me out of the way" (the expression is John Cage's).[89] The most recent incarnation of this struggle is "The EgoCircus Collective," an experimental art and performance lab founded in 2020 by Carson and her husband, the performance artist Robert Currie.[90] The project bears the hallmarks of the Cage/Merce Cunningham creative duo, both of whom cultivated non-intentional and chance composition, and whom Carson has said "represent the ideal form" of collaboration.[91] The same struggle is, perhaps, the backstory to Carson works whose composition hinders the assimilation of material: from essays in verse, draft, or notational form, to fake paratexts, incomplete syntaxes, randomized lineation, variable structures, and other constrained writing techniques popular in the mid-century literary avant-garde.[92] Her play for alternatives to argumentative synthesis and the rerouting of interpretive attention might be called phenomenological in its pursuit of immediacy, the suspension of ego, and the exposure of experiential or compositional time. (Carson's affinities with phenomenology, implicit and explicit, crop up at several points in this book.) We might simply call it experimental, taking up Cage's definition of experiment as "an action the outcome of which is not foreseen," where the unforeseen shows up the mind and exposes its judgments.[93] In any case, a strong push-pull between the ideal of transparency—the condition of medium or optic for another work—and the sheer textual conspicuousness of so many of Carson's readings and versions, tautens her writing voice against its own means, sending a vibration of hesitancy across her full range of forms. Cage's "every Me out of the way" couldn't be more apt in this regard as it recognizes, as Carson does, that authors obstruct their work by overdetermining and overidentifying with its possibilities, seeing themselves ("*every* Me") everywhere they look.

We can understand the transparency/exposure, fidelity/errancy, or even *aidōs*/eros push-pull as the site of a struggle of competing virtues in Carson and declare the matter more or less closed (arguments for verisimilitude, as for and against authorial virtue, can often have that effect). Instead, I propose we approach Carson's claims, and the "big, loud, shiny" non-identity of many of her responses to source texts, as a late polemical event in the history of literary imitation, in particular, the imitation of other authors (*imitatio*). For the little her most vociferous critics have understood about Carson's work, their objections at least affirm that something—if something scandalous—is going on with regard to imitation. An early critique attacks her "negative biomimicry" and her "lines *conceptually* downloaded" from other authors, objections that, in the era of "uncreative writing," "unoriginal genius," and "the iterative turn," look decidedly dated.[94] Another reader is concerned by Carson's "sleight of hand" and an "artless grafting-on of academic materials" that blurs the difference between real literary scholarship and a literary simulacrum, critical writing and poems in critical drag.[95] Derrida uses the expression "*trompe-l'oeil*" (translated by Barbara Johnson as "sleight-of-hand") to gloss Plato's theorization of *mimēsis*, not in relation to the tragic poets, as in *The Republic*, but in relation to philosophy, in the late dialogue *The Sophist*.[96] Contra the bona fide philosopher, the sophist is "the imitator of him who knows" or "mimic of the wise man" (*mimētēs tou sophou*), a simulator and creator of effects, whose impostor knowledge threatens the real thing with contamination.[97] It also exposes the fact, for Derrida, that the contamination has already taken place: that there is no non-mimetic philosophy, no truth content free of the shifting forms of the *logos*. The essay form, for Adorno, likewise "salvages a moment of sophistry."[98] No wonder, then, that Carson's uses of literature, like her uses of scholarship, cause a certain unrest among readers who would prefer to keep scholarship and literature apart.

Without realizing it, the author of the "biomimicry" attack alights on one of the central complexities of imitation, a complexity whose history goes back almost as far as the concept itself. In his superb *Imitating Authors* (2019), Colin Burrow argues that the elasticity and unruliness of *imitatio*—how it blurs into paraphrase, translation, adaptation, etc.—is central to both the anxiety it arouses and its historic appeal. (When Daphne Merkin called Carson "one of the great pasticheurs," she surely had this appeal in mind.)[99] Not only has *imitatio* always confounded categories; its blurring action also makes literary and literary-critical history: "Imitating authors are also readers, who are observing features of the texts they read, which are passed on through their texts to their own readers. So *imitatio* can blend outwards into the history of reading."[100] The notion is so obvious it almost passes unnoticed: that to imitate, parody, or reproduce the form or idea of a source text, you first have to interpret it. The history of *imitatio* is an alternative history of critical reading.

Reena Sastri, Robert Stanton, and Gillian Sze have produced bold and interesting work on the ideas and iterations of "errancy" or "wild constancy" at work in Carson.[101] Sastri recognizes the simple but extraordinary fact that, in Carson, fidelity to a source text is often indivisible from its creative estrangement. Yet how can we speak of her errant readings as close or as mimetic—reading Euripides's *Helen* through Marilyn Monroe, for example—without capsizing the very idea of imitation? How to vindicate imitation as an interpretive strategy, capable, that is, of performing a critical difference? Burrow calls attention to a passage in *The Sophist* that explains how even the most divergent adaptations, versions, readings, or creative misreadings, in which a source's lexical or contextual particularities are trashed, can still be mimetically invested in their originals.[102] Describing what he calls "formal imitation," Burrow explains how the "idea" of a work ("akin to a Platonic Form"), a pattern of symbolism, or an argumentative structure, can be reproduced without necessarily imitating any of its verbal details.[103] He cites the claim made by Gérard Genette that "*it is impossible to imitate a text . . . one can imitate only a style: that is to say, a genre*," a proposition that resonates strongly with Carson's claim to derivative form: form that approximates without exactly reproducing a set of facts.[104] Plato makes a distinction in *The Sophist* between *eidōla* (simulacra, copies, illusions; the popular sense of imitation drawn from *The Republic*) and likeness produced "by following the proportions of the original in length, breadth, and depth, and giving, besides, the appropriate colours to each part," which Plato includes in this late, revised definition of *mimēsis*.[105] Plato's "proportions of the original"—*tou paradeigmatos summetrias*, "the proportions of the paradigm" is Burrow's suggested gloss— permit a kind of likeness that retains the structural geometry of its source without reproducing any of its details.[106] What Guy Davenport called Carson's "mathematics of the emotions" in his preface to "The Glass Essay" brings this way of likening to mind, a structural mimetic sensibility applied equally and interchangeably to the facts of emotional life and the facts of texts.

All this talk of measure and proportion—like Carson's talk of "hesitation"— falls dissonant if we expect it to mean an orderly, transparent correspondence between original and likeness. If anything, approximating its geometry gives license to Carson to catastrophize her source, not only "ripping" it "out of the past," in Dean's words, but subjecting it to exorbitant demands: making Monica Vitti speak for Kant, or ventriloquizing Simone Weil, who sings alongside her mother on the emotional life of nonagons in *Decreation*. Formal imitation can be a form of "strong reading"—"strong *misreading*" is Bloom's more famous term—, which is to say that there is something necessarily "transgressive" and "aggressive" in parsing Euripides's *Helen* through a replacement cast and scenario from the life of Monroe, camping up Simone Weil's final struggles, or reading Brontë by assimilation to Carson's biography.[107] Mimetic desire—for René Girard "the source of all disorder"[108]—is what we saw Barthes ascribe to all critical attention, whose disorderly energies are an important part of living and working with texts. This is not Woolf's involuntary "shadow-shape" that endures like an afterimage of the books we have read, but the crafted and deliberate form ("something hard and lasting") she insists must be made from it.[109] Even Adorno's "exact fantasy," a mimetic critical attention that takes its proportions (its exactitude) from the facts under scrutiny, prizes the element of fantasy and misrule at the same time as it prizes a form of imitation.[110]

Whatever her interest in approximation, in proportionality in the sense introduced in *The Sophist*, this is to say, all Carson's readers know about *disproportion* in her writing. If you have read *Autobiography of Red* alongside the fragments Carson reproduces from its source, the *Geryoneis* of Stesichoros, you will know Carson's verse novel is extravagant in its rendition, throwing Stesichoros off course and off kilter; exorbitant (*ex orbita*) in the sense she theorizes in another recent essay.[111] Readers of *The Beauty of the Husband* will recall its outrageous autofictional confessions ("I broke the glass and jumped") and its account of a love that slips the equations set for it, first among which is Keats's "Beauty is truth." (Reading against Keats, Carson's narrator declares her intent *not* "to produce / a golden rule.")[112] Following on the trail of the far-fetched, the disproportionate, the camp, and the exorbitant takes us from adaptations such as the "Decreation" libretto and mise-en-scènes such as the "TV Men" sequence or "Hopper: *Confessions*," to all manner of essays and lectures, cropped and verse-lineated or simply sprawling in their associative range. Our expectations are the first line of assault in Carson's readings. For her, "you don't think when you're comfortable. You just doze off."[113]

Staying with this willed discomfort for a moment. I suggested at the start of this Introduction that there is something in the way Carson's "mimesis" works, in its most concentrated expressions, that might be called imperative; whose strong performative effect, seeking to decompress thought and expose its workings, might in fact compel us to think in particular ways. In the McNeilly interview, Carson describes the mimetic action I introduced in the opening pages, calling it first "imitation" and then "performance":

KEVIN MCNEILLY: Is it fair to say some of [your] poems are gestures at process or at attempt?

ANNE CARSON: Well that's what imitation is for the ancients. It's simply a mirroring of the activity of the thought that you had at the time that you had it, and at attempt *to make that activity happen again* in the mind of the listener of [*sic*] the reader. Probably that's always what I'm trying to do.

KM: Is this why you say things like "irony is a verb" or "desire is a verb," as opposed to the nominal. You point often towards process or to action or to performance.

AC: Yes, performance, I think so. The ancient poets thought of the publication of a poem as the time of saying it, and the time of saying it is also the time of it being heard, and that's the time when there's an exchange of that action, that verb, whatever the verb is that's being described. The verb happens.[114]

"Desire is a verb"—"Desire moves. Eros is a verb" are Carson's actual words— because desire compels, moving transitively between individuals, but also because it does to us the way a performative utterance *does*. A verb that "happens" is the kind of performance we take for granted in poems, yet it can be thrilling, if perplexing, as an action of lectures, critical essays, or bespoke forms that share their purpose. An instinct for the performative, traceable across so much of Carson's writing—and to which the above remarks allude—, is driven by pursuit of the kind of "imitation" we have already seen her describe: an approximation of what a given set of facts is "doing." An interest in shorthand, the synthetic and synchronic, the "economy" of gesture of *Economy of the Unlost*, drives Carson's "imitation" to what she has since described as "an art of pure shape": an abstract, suggestively visual mimesis charged with leaving an impression in the mind "no matter what the words mean." Whether, that is, these words are station names of the London Underground, words from Donne's "Woman's Constancy," or from Bertolt Brecht's FBI file, as they are in her consecutive translations of Ibykos fragment 286 in *Nay Rather* (2013).[115]

Nonverbal or post-verbal impressions in the mind are effects we more readily ascribe to visual art, arts of sound, and the "visual performativity" of concrete poems, which Johanna Drucker has so powerfully described.[116] Carson's "art of pure shape," though, discussed in the final chapter of this book, is the aspiration behind a hypothetical "Essay on Translation," which Carson claims to have spent her life rewriting. This potential text, a version of which is performed in the lecture that describes it, is an essay in pursuit of its own disappearance; it moves, or wants to move, she says, through a reduction of continuous prose to broken paragraphs, ending up a smattering of clipped lines and single words. Carson's claims for the compelling synchronic effect of "performance" recall her remarks on the painter Francis Bacon's relation to what he also calls "the facts." "By 'facts,'" Carson explains, "[Bacon] doesn't mean to make a copy of the subject as a photograph would, but rather to create a sensible form that will translate directly to your nervous system the same sensation as the subject."[117] This is the nervous jolt that, for Carson, makes thinking happen. With Bacon as her exemplum, though, we know we are on potentially uncomfortable terrain. "Mak[ing] activity happen again in the mind of the reader" is no reasoned, or necessarily reasonable, transaction. It ups the voltage, so to speak, on an imperative latent to all description.[118]

Carson first theorizes this performative force in an early essay on Aristotle, whose arguments subtend her reply to McNeilly more than a decade later. " 'Just for the Thrill': Sycophantizing Aristotle's *Poetics*" (1990) talks about "the thrill of lyric mimesis," where the emotions inspiring lyric song "happen again" for the reader or listener in micro-dramas of form, grammar, and meter.[119] The reader of lyric and the willing dupe of its metaphors, explains Carson, experiences the movements of her own "emotive reasoning" (*dianoia*) in an exchange of action with the subject of lyric song.[120] It is interesting, as an aside, that the catch-all category of the "lyric" is now characterized by some of its principal theorists as a reading effect, as though twentieth-century literary criticism had need of such an object—a "lyric" voice "in solitary speech," nonimperative and unperformed—and invented it.[121] Jonathan Culler's theory of the lyric strikes on a quality of performativity—"the iterative and iterable performance of an event in the lyric present"—that is closer to Carson's ideas and is especially suggestive in relation to the iterative here-and-now of her scholarship, whose lyric "event" is addressed to readers.[122] Carson's essay on "lyric mimesis" offers arguments that will later appear revamped in "Essay on What I Think About Most" and "Essay on Error" (both in *Men in the Off Hours*) on metaphor as the careful production of a felicitous mistake.[123] The wrongness or disproportion of a metaphor throws our fresh-cut reasoning into relief, "translating to [our] nervous system" the very sensation of thinking.

It is in this essay, too, that Carson's identification of her work with visual art acquires a makeshift philosophical history. For it is visual spectacle (*opsis*), for Aristotle, that "captures the mind," or, in the translation provided in Carson's essay, "kidnaps your soul" (*psychagōgikon*: root of the modern "psychagogy," the therapeutic influencing of behavior).[124] Some of the strongest recent writing on Carson goes on the trail of the visual and para-literary in her work, pursuing the Carson of collaborations (with Currie, and with visual artists such as Bianca Stone and Roni Horn), as well as Carson the collage artist and ekphrasist, who painted and drew before she wrote, and who declares in an early interview, "I mostly think of my work as a painting."[125] *Opsis* is the lyric mode Northrop Frye ascribes to the riddle, and it is easy to spot the occult logic and spectacular appeal of riddles in works that avoid marking explicit argumentative lines; whose lines of inquiry—in Carson's words—seem to "paint themselves."[126] There is something sublimely *unreasonable* about this mode of emotional reasoning, especially when we have been led by a text's apparatus, descriptors, or sources to expect a different approach, one more closely aligned to scholarship's conventions of transparency and exposition. Listening to Carson lecture or "short-talk" on Sylvia Plath or on Rembrandt van Rijn's *The Three Crosses*, it is interesting to ask ourselves if we are willing or unwilling hostages, accomplices in our own capture of mind. For scholarship is no safe space in Carson. The self-sensing and suspension of disbelief she courts in us invite us to wonder whether these are not always our endgames when we read; not just poetry, drama, and narrative fiction, but critical and philosophical essays, too.

It comes as little surprise, finally, to find Anne Carson at ease with this particular soft power of writing, whether that writing is filed under scholarship, criticism, or literature. She names as much as a special prerogative of the essay: "an essay is a broaching, an interference, a disruption, a breaking in of me upon you—your mind a quiet lake, me jumping into it."[127] There is nothing ambiguous about this record of activity, which has the essay commit the incursions and crises of eros with impunity. Such effects are, of course, speculations by Carson about what she would like her essays to do to us. Their actual effects—compelling, disrupting, thrilling, or nonplussing—depend on our disposition and on the disposition of our categories (poem, essay, talk, etc.). Her activity in the essay that ventures the above reflection is, we will see, precisely that: speculation. The "mirroring" and "performance" of speculative activity, an exposure of thought almost, it seems, as it happens.

"Criticism *is* speculative," writes Simon Jarvis—in whose seminars I first read Carson—"where speculation is opposed to certain knowledge."[128] Cross back to DuPlessis and we find her affirming that "an essay, like a theory, can be described as a speculative performance" and "[e]ssay is the play of speculation."[129] If Carson's performance of her scholarship asks us to go along with its ventures or suspend our disbelief—and if in the end we do so—, it is because, in place of other guarantees, other forms of transparency and accountability, she offers a subject on whom we can rely to process the work's complexities; even where—and perhaps because—that subject has put herself in doubt, as the fictional essayist of *The Beauty of the Husband* does, or as the translator-mourner in *Nox* does. This belief-effect (which Raoul Eshelman has called "performatism") is a rebuff to certain trends in postmodern authorship, for which staged failures of presence are obligatory.[130] Carson's newness consists, in part, in the story she tells of her work, a story of what a scholar, a poet, and a translator is, and of what this particular scholar feels about and wants from the texts and images she handles. Form, for this extraordinary writer and performer, is not only a measure of what happens, but a measure of what matters. If the "crisis of contact" with literature is a means of sudden and startling self-perception, it is also a means of presenting us with its sharpest limits. The sensible, thinkable "edges" of self are where speculation and literature begin.

*

This book approaches Carson through variations and overlaps of the following four modes: academic criticism, the poem-essay, the multiform concept volume, and translation, ending with a postscript on Carson's lectures and the interactive, live-performative turn of her recent work. Throughout the book, attention is paid to individual compositions—poems, essays, lectures—as well as to whole collections and other multi-work publications, with the aim of showing, in the latter case, how Carson's readings of a single set of source texts or a single unifying idea produce variable structures or a range of different formal rigors. Consistent with Carson's "very formal" oeuvre (D'Agata), the book seeks to pay her writing the very closest formal attention: to read Carson with and against her own inset commentary and, in some cases, through the optics of her scholarly essays, approaching her, as far as possible, on her own terms. These opening pages have placed Carson's writing in a specific moment in time, in the company of other experimental and post-critical scholars working new kinds of relation between their scholarship and its source texts and readers. The chapters to follow focus principally on the affiliations Carson performs herself, and on the terms she sets—terms we can take or leave, but which either way bear scrutiny—for understanding her work.

Part I explores variations on the function and forms of academic literary criticism in Carson's work, focusing on the two major examples of her published scholarly writing: *Eros the Bittersweet* (1986) and *Economy of the Unlost* (1999). These opening chapters address Carson's engagement with the concepts of *erōs* and *xenia* or gift exchange, arguing for her respective readings of Plato, Simonides of Keos, and Paul Celan as grounding and anticipating the interpretive modes of later compositions. These early works show Carson's scholarship taking a crucial turn toward performance in the imitation of an original action or paradigm, which is reproduced in the form, structure, or stylistics of the reading. Chapter 1 examines a series of variations on Carson's early reading of desire in *Eros the Bittersweet*, tracing its most striking formal and theoretical legacies in the light-footed literary-critical sketch, *The Albertine Workout* (2014), and in "Possessive Used as Drink (Me): A Lecture on Pronouns in the Form of 15 Sonnets" from the performance-oriented pamphlet series, *Float* (2016). This short history of the theory of eros in Carson—and of a distinctive approach to interpretive form—shows how the relationship between writing and desire in her early work becomes the framework for a longer-term inquiry into the emotions of reading literature.

Following this opening chapter is a study of the interpretive "conversation" or "exchange" at the center of Carson's acclaimed (though not uncontroversial) comparative critical essay, *Economy of the Unlost: (Reading Simonides of Keos with Paul Celan)*. Out of the Simonides/Celan constellation comes an inquiry into what is at risk for the poet writing poetry, but also, in Carson's strong confessional identification with Celan, for the poet *reading* poetry and writing criticism. The chapter close-reads Carson's richly imitative prosody in an essay whose interpretations are voiced, the chapter argues, in a parallel exchange of poetic "gifts" between Carson and Celan. An adapted version of her Martin Classical Lectures, Carson's extended essay is a complex case of performed reading, fusing personal aesthetic declaration, direct reader address, a reciprocal critical style, and one of the most striking confessions of what is at stake for Carson herself in the psychic economies of poetry.

The chapters of Part II examine the lyric voice in Carson's readings more closely. These chapters approach two less formally conventional examples of her self-described "essays"—"The Glass Essay" and *The Beauty of the Husband*—with an eye for how the two works use autobiography, autofiction, and the lives and writing of Emily Brontë and John Keats to stage the compelling power games of interpretation and romantic love. Reading her use of two very different literary oeuvres, these chapters explore the formal, citational, and affective bonds these hybrid "essays" form with their source texts. In its first-person narration of a strong identification with Brontë, Chapter 3 argues, "The Glass Essay" introduces a form of transparency that surfaces in later works such as *The Beauty of the Husband*, *Decreation*, and *Nox* that reproduce the processes, sites, and emotions of their composition. Parsing Brontë's biography and close-reading her oeuvre, the narrator's strong critique of Brontë's reception and editorial regularization doubles as a story of the narrator's own, personal vindication. Bronte's story of subjection and liberty serves as her confessional double, the reading and its emotional valence are seamless; but close-reading Brontë is also where the narrator finds her resistant to assimilation. This inquiry into equivalences of literature and personal need is a study, too, of their refusal to coincide.

Chapter 4 reads *The Beauty of the Husband*, the subtitled "fictional essay" whose blurb describes it as "an essay on Keats's idea that beauty is truth, and the story of a marriage": a philosophically minded verse narrative studded with fragments of Keats marginalia, yet not in any direct sense "about" Keats. Like "The Glass Essay," in this "essay," the reading of Keats collapses into its autofictional backstory; fragments from Keats, and a host of inconsistently attributed quotations from other authors, exchange valence with the "facts" of Carson's story in a continuous, "horizontal" lyric texture.[131] Like "The Glass Essay," too, the reading is transparently personal. Yet the question of fiction (mimesis, sophistry, infidelity, lie), unsteadying the personal story, performs a critical response to "Keats's idea that beauty is truth" aslant. The chapter makes the case for an extreme form of lyric transparency, in which the reading of Keats is boundaryless, both nowhere and everywhere to be found, and in which "story" and "essay" displace and expose one another's purposes. The interweaving of textual fact, critical discourse, and autobiography/autofiction in both "The Glass Essay" and *The Beauty of the Husband* produces a distinctive lyric style that skews, as it speaks directly to, our expectations of what an essay and a reading should be. Both force (in us) the question of their limits: the limits of "essays" and, at the heart of that lesser concern, where receptiveness to other writing becomes its absorption.

Part III explores Carson's engagement with the problem of "self" in the essays and iterative forms of *Decreation: Poetry, Essays, Opera*. Reading close to the work of the philosopher Simone Weil—theorist of "decreation" or self-undoing—, alongside Carson's other interlocutors in the book, these two chapters consider why the high-stakes dilemmas of Christian mysticism interest Carson as problems of knowledge, writing, and desire.[132] Chapter 5 approaches a range of individual poem sequences and prose narratives from *Decreation*, exploring how Carson's set of intimate scripts for essaying and embodying Weil's concept also places a limit on the idea that self-undoing can be voluntary or performed. The chapter shows, on the one hand, how the variorum or concept volume is a performative form, a format that stages the displacement of its central event and that studies the self-shattering métier by miming its ideals and points of tension. On the other, it is argued, *Decreation* structures in a crucial constraint on the possibility of performative artifice: the possibility of a voluntarily "decreative" writing.

Chapter 6 is an inquiry into the idea of the "fake" that emerges in the title essay, "Decreation: How Women Like Sappho, Marguerite Porete and Simone Weil Tell God," and its companion piece, the libretto "Decreation: An Opera in Three Parts." The chapter explores Carson's striking gloss of the term "fake woman" (*pseudo-mulier*), which reorients it from a term of indictment—in the inquisitorial case against fourteenth-century mystic, Marguerite Porete—to a descriptor of radical psychological insight. The chapter compares the two interpretive forms—essay and opera—directly. Where the essay presents Carson's source material verbatim, arguing for the contradictions of decreative writing, the libretto reprises the same material aslant, in a riotous critical remix. Weil's aspiration to "undoing the creature" is performed alongside the creatureliness and contradiction that hamstrings it: the praise, masochism, and desire that make Sappho, Porete, and Weil both so complex and so compelling as theorists of contradiction. The chapter closes with a discussion of "fake women" from across the Carson oeuvre. Splaying out the category of the "fake," the chapter also confronts one of the most well-known critiques of Carson herself to date: the charge of imitator, phony, fraud.

The fourth part of the book addresses one of the most complex and rich modes in Carson's work, where classical philology meets experimental dramaturgy and poetic form. Although the essays and verse discussed at earlier points in the book draw heavily on Carson's academic classicism, it is in her translations and adaptations of classical source texts that the quality of her scholarship and her creative originality have garnered the highest praise. These adaptations and versions of myth, drama, lyric, and epic poetry are numerous and, bar a small number of tonally orthodox translations of Greek tragic drama, most bear Carson's signature misalignments of tone, purpose, form, and of the classical unities (unity of action, time, and place). From the early poem sequence "Mimnermos: The Brainsex Paintings" (1995) to "Twelve-Minute Prometheus (After Aiskhylos)" (2008), "Pinplay: A version of Euripides's *Bacchae*" (2016), *Norma Jeane Baker of Troy*, a "version" of Euripides's *Helen*, and her recent translation of his *Herakles*, *H of H Playbook*,[133] perhaps the best-known of Carson's "versions" is the verse novel *Autobiography of Red*, and its jauntier sequel, *Red Doc>* (2013), which adapt the myth of Herakles's tenth labor as preserved in the fragments of Stesichoros's *Geryoneis*.[134] The full catalogue of Carson's classical adaptations, unbinding myth from the textual and historical particularities of its literary sources, unquestionably merits a study apart—and one such study, Laura Jansen's impressive multi-author volume *Anne Carson/Antiquity* (2022), arrived in the final stages of preparation of this book.[135] The chapters in this last section approach a selection of these works, whose tonal, formal, and contextual anomaly not only "rip[s]" Carson's sources "out of the past" but performs her working present. Carson's scholarship, self-involved, self-parodic, saturated in a lifetime of reading, is at the forefront of this performance.

Chapter 7 approaches two of Carson's most striking translation projects: *Nox*, an elegy, multimodal prose commentary, and translation of Catullus 101; and *Antigonick*, an illustrated, frenetic adaptation of Sophokles's *Antigone*, of which a more tonally orthodox Carson translation was staged to acclaim in 2015.[136] The subject matter of both source texts is grief and its afterlife following the loss of a brother, yet in Carson's versions, the texts become strikingly different expressions of the dilemma of how to comprehend the lives and languages of others. Both works tell stories—apocryphal stories, critical histories, personal associations— to which the source text has been bound. Both open the translator's artifice to scrutiny by way of commentary, asides, interpolations, and the hand-produced documents of which both texts are facsimiles. Where *Nox* stages Carson's work of translation, its component parts and accrued reflections, *Antigonick* is a version of the Greek drama radically capable of reading and scrutinizing itself. The chapter considers the ways these works remain "open": open to collaboration, permeable to personal and critical histories, and refusing closure of both the project of translation and the wounds of grief and tragic violence. The chapter situates the confessional transparency of Carson's translations in relation to her scholarship's wider self-exposure.

The final chapter approaches Carson's minimalist, textually driven, and materially committed translation of the fragments of Sappho, an oeuvre whose textual history combines rigorous scholarship with fictional interpolation, misquotation, and a good deal of erotic fantasy. The chapter asks what kind of intervention—and underlying it, what kind of reading—Carson's uncluttered, hands-free edition is exactly, in view of her stated intent to reproduce the "drama" of the papyrus fragment and to translate under the fantasy she calls "transparency of self."[137] The chapter reads *If Not, Winter: Fragments of Sappho* as the unlikely work that perhaps best illustrates what form—and especially performative form—is for Carson, as well as what is at stake in its effects. This particular drama of form is not Sappho's, yet nor exactly is it Carson's. Carson's text reproduces Sappho's extant material, but the textual imitation of materiality produces an extreme, high-voltage lyric form whose drastic spaces, stray words, and hedged brackets still-frame the solitary speech of reading them. The role of negative form, of unmarked pages, is to capture what it is we want and need from Sappho, amplifying our logic at the edge.

The book ends with a reflection on the performance-orientation of Carson's most recent work and a brief history of her approach to the lecture form: from *Short Talks* to the performance scripts of *Float* (2016) and more recent collaborations such as "Lecture on the History of Skywriting" (2019). "Lecturing is not easy for me," Carson admitted in 2001: "A lecture is not a conversation, you don't get to ask the other people in the room what they think until the end, you have to expose yourself first."[138] The performance aesthetics of these late works herald a decisive move away from literature (and its study) as the private lyric experience Carson theorizes in *Eros the Bittersweet*—and which so many of her works chronicle and expose—toward a public, collaborative, and intermedia scene for the products of scholarship. At the same time, I offer, the move toward multi-sensory, site-specific performance is anticipated in Carson from the very beginning.

PART I
VARIATIONS IN CRITICISM

1

The Eros Variations

To watch them fall fills you with an inexpressible odd longing.
Perhaps it is the longing for what Streb calls "a real move."[1]

"Elizabeth Streb is a Brooklyn choreographer who teaches her dancers to fall straight down from a height of thirty-two feet, flat on their faces or flat on their backs or sideways through the air as if flying," explains Lecturer II in Carson's "Uncle Falling: A Pair of Lyric Lectures with Shared Chorus," staged in 2010 in collaboration with Streb and others.[2] The dancers, Lecturer II tells us, "fall as fast as stars and look like gods for an instant. They redeem the shame of falling, an act we usually associate with being very young or very old or very lost or not the master of oneself."[3] The art of falling—"a motion lexicon that all humans recognize," says Streb—is a performance of contradiction.[4] For the onlooker who can't quite believe his eyes (who is obliged to make his own leap of faith), this controlled fall from a height is ever the analog to an accident: to that "real move" we would postpone indefinitely and yet, Carson says, we also unspeakably long for. Falling between accident and intent, control and release, the Streb dancer embodies their split-second convergence in a mistake that, finally, and to our audible relief, turns out not to be one. The fall can be reprised an infinite number of times—fall again, fall better—and each time, in a collective intake of breath, the "real move" buzzes into earshot. Streb's performative contradiction is so shocking, so sharply honed, that no sooner have accident and intent converged than we would force them apart midair, or cover our eyes until the dancer stands again to her feet. An artful fall never quite escapes a brush with the real thing.

The scene with which I begin this chapter is the kind of scene that interests Carson. In the words of her "Essay on What I Think About Most" (1999), a disquisition on mistake in stanzas of unrhyming verse, the "wilful creation of error" is the action of the "master contriver"—the poet: "what Aristotle would call an 'imitator' of reality."[5] Like the "true mistakes of poetry," the matter Carson confesses to "think about most," Streb's choreographed falls perform the conversion of human error into an art form. Under the dancer's regime, and by an extraordinary coup of artifice, the emotions of mistake—shame, exposure, thrill—are handed to us, putting our own contradictions and "odd longings" center stage.

In this regard, the controlled fall of the Streb dancer crystallizes certain things germane to Carson's project. Insofar as "Streb and her dancers imitate real falling by falling according to plan," the episode replicates a sense in Carson's work that imitation—*mimēsis, imitatio*, but also parody, unattributed quotation, pastiche, even the outrageously fictive or fake—can be a strong form of reading, a performance that reveals something raw and essential about an original set of facts or experiences. It evokes, too, an equally pervasive sense in her work of something ostensibly haphazard going very precisely to plan. While *Float*, the collection of unnumbered pamphlets in which "Uncle Falling" appears, can be read in any order—"Reading can be freefall"—Carson's commentaries on this and other serendipitous "accidents" lend her work a deliberate, self-theorizing quality, a redoubling of artifice that has become one of her signature modes.[6] In "Uncle Falling," a two-voice "lyric lecture" on vulnerability complete with its own tragic Chorus, a double first-person fulfills the functions of autobiographical narrative and real-time analysis: as the lecture moves through these modes, we can feel we have been saved by such commentaries from precisely the kinds of disorientation it describes. While Streb holds her audience in a ruthless present tense, as much desired as desired to be over, the real-time, performative aspects of Carson's writing can get weighed down by a sense that we are being micromanaged in our readings. Facing so self-studying a work, one that names its resonances and schedules its mischief, the critical reader of Carson can be left chasing after something that has already occurred, something all but over before it has really begun.[7]

This said, what the Streb scene far more vividly brings to life is an experience Carson doesn't talk about in her lecture: another kind of falling and another scenario of risk whose exploration begins in the very earliest Carson texts. The "fall" of falling in love is an untidy agon of contradictory and inexpressible longings, channeled, for Carson, in the lover's confrontation with time. The lover seeks out the "present moment of desire" (*Eros the Bittersweet*, 126) and wants to stay there, yet also wants the same moment over and done with. The longed-for "real move" of an erotic "crisis of contact" means high risk and mutual exposure, where desire's very expression threatens to drink it dry. What happens in this amplified present tense must be brought to an end, in order, put simply, for it to happen again. It is only to be expected, Carson says, that "Eros traditionally puts the lover in the position of genuinely desiring both points at once" (126)—the "now" and the "then," risk and its mitigation, the present indicative and the perfect tense.

This chapter follows Carson's working of the contradictions of eros through a series of examples ranging from 1986 to 2016. Each of these works, beginning with *Eros the Bittersweet: An Essay* (1986), places high demands on itself as literature because each, in its way, asks how writing can sustain these contradictions and how it might in fact be complicit in their power. Each deals with a difference already compromised between "real moves" and their imitation. Through *Eros the Bittersweet*, her first full-length book and a sharpened lyrical reworking of her 1981 doctoral thesis, "Odi et Amo Ergo Sum," Carson draws an inquiry into what is at stake in the emotions of falling in love and the experiences of writing about it.[8] While her title plays on Sappho's contradiction of "bittersweet" or sweet-bitter desire (*glukupikron*), it is Plato's late dialogue, the *Phaedrus*, that runs the full length of Carson's disquisition on the paradoxes—the now and then, the *odi et amo*—of erotic love. It is with Plato that Carson thinks through the charged and complex relations between desire and writing, imitation and the real, atemporality and sensible time, whose charge can be felt, and whose relation traced, in Carson's own approaches to writing.

Carson's reading of Plato runs more or less as follows. Phaedrus, Socrates's dreamy young interlocutor, has fallen "in love with a written text" (122). What charms Phaedrus about this *erotikos logos*, the transcript of a treatise on love by the sophist Lysias, is the protection it promises against erotic risk. Lysias extols the virtues of the lover not-in-love, a "nonlover" for whom, "having no special commitment to pleasure in the present," time affords no emotions of crisis. His "particular vantage point on time" is what separates "all that a nonlover feels and thinks and does from what a lover feels, thinks or does" (124). It is the nonlover who, Carson says, "looks at a love affair from the point of view of the end"— the "then" at the expense of the "now" (124). Phaedrus, it turns out, is not only in love with the idea of nonloving but with the writing that, in contrast to the spoken word, sets it, too, outside time. (Phaedrus, says Socrates, asked for the speech to be repeated over and over, until "in the end he secured the script.")[9] The "nonlover" trope is deliberately perverse: "Lysias' speech is designed to alarm standard sentiment and displace preconceptions about love" (124), says Carson. His godlike mastery of the erotic scenario "redeems the shame of falling," but redeems it that bit too much. For at the zero degree of shame is zero tension, zero emotional strife, and no convergence of tenses, a timeless fait accompli that is all but over before it has really begun. The "conventional lover," on the other hand, confronts his own sensitized time at every turn. His "Ice-pleasure"— Carson on Sophokles's metaphor, the "ice crystal in the hands"—compels him one way and the other, to hold on to the present and throw it over fast: "an affair of the moment, transparently" (112, 113). His desire is braced by a "voltage of decorum," the *aidōs* or "shamefastness" that marks "the fact that two are not one" (20, 21). "A Lysian theory of love" plants the lover outside love's contradictions, "violates these natural currents of physical and spiritual change that constitute our human situation in time" (137). This against the risk-prone lover of the lyric poets: "Candidly, he wants to keep on desiring" (136).

In an interview in 2000, Carson made the following observation: "our subjects call us. *Eros the Bittersweet* was a book based on my PhD dissertation (*Ode* [sic] *et Amo Ergo Sum*: Toronto, 1981) and I notice that PhD students frequently choose a doctoral subject that isolates a main issue of their being."[10] Carson has drawn the issue of her thesis—the complicities of writing and erotic emotion—through works as diverse as *Eros the Bittersweet*, the philosophical verse essay *The Beauty of the Husband* (2001), the concept volume *Decreation* (2005), her essay in blueprint form, *The Albertine Workout* (2014), and the performance-oriented pamphlets of *Float* (2016). In Carson's reading, artful writing can't quite be kept apart from the emotional cache of eros. Both Carson's doctoral thesis and its reworking as *Eros the Bittersweet* offer that the advent of literacy and its proliferation in early classical lyric culture, when poetry began to be written down and read in private, has a marked set of consequences for the felt experience of desire.[11] Drawing on the work of classicists Bruno Snell and Denys Page, Carson has it that the written word not only records erotic experience, as a glance at the lyric poets might suggest, but is also its active accomplice. Unlike her oral and semi-literate counterparts, the solitary reader must close off her nonvisual senses at the expense of the social world; the crisis of desire, when this reader puts down her Alkman or her Sappho, then assaults those newly sensitized edges with increased force. Under these conditions, the text of eros—*erotikos logos*—is a contract with her own intimate life and an object of desire in its own right.[12] Carson asks, after Plato, how close writing can get to the "real moves" of desire. Her answer, caught up in the taut mimetic structures of poems, is that writing is not quite the safe space Phaedrus would wish it to be.

What I will be calling Carson's eros variations are an inquiry that joins her early essay to later compositions that rehearse its concerns. An inquiry into desire and its structure of paradox, the texts that form these variations on a theme also test one of its most compelling commitments—to the written text as a player in desire, and the idea consequent upon it that *form* matters for how desire moves in the minds of readers.[13] This is an inquiry that not only thinks in strong ways about written form, that draws our attention to form and its lures, but whose thinking on desire itself also *happens* through form. The chapter follows three formally very different iterations of Carson's early theory of desire, beginning with *Eros the Bittersweet*, where the idea that writing channels the reasoning of eros first appears. Then to *The Albertine Workout* (2014), Carson's sketch for an essay on Albertine Simonet, muse and captive of Marcel in Marcel Proust's *À la recherche du temps perdu*, and to conclude with a reading of "Possessive Used as Drink (Me): A Lecture on Pronouns in the Form of 15 Sonnets" (2016), a performance work published in *Float* alongside Carson's lyric lecture on falling. Each of these works is a variation on the essay or lecture forms. The first two are structured around readings of other works, while the third is a series of reflections on spoken and written grammar, and the workings of the possessive pronoun. All three talk about and respond formally to the notion that one of the principal desires activated by language is the desire to possess or master. "Mastery of this relation is part of the study of letters," Carson has said of the enduring perversity of our relation to the written word (121), and these three works each find ways to capture, circumvent, or sabotage this default.

Carson's approach to desire here, then, is also an approach to form. In these three studies in the complexity of erotic relation, self-relation, and possession, Carson's arguments are rehearsed in the formal organization of the work, with a view to performing and eliciting a particular mode of thought in the real time of reading or, in the case of the sonnet-form lecture, in the time-bound experience of its staging. The shifts that occur between *Eros the Bittersweet*, *The Albertine Workout*, and "Possessive Used as Drink (Me)" take us through various degrees of performative form, pulling further by degrees from full-bodied, referenced, and indexed critical prose toward more haphazard forms of argument that happen as an effect of form and/or live performance. Carson has said, we saw, that form "arises out of the thing itself"; that, faced with a set of facts, "form is a rough approximation of what the facts are doing." When asked to explain what she means by this, she adds: "when we say that form imitates reality or something like that it sounds like an image. I'm saying it's more like a tempo being covered, like a movement within an event or a thing."[14] Each of these eros variations makes an argument by tempo, the approximation of a movement, as well as, or instead of, an exposition. In their pursuit of such effects, all three works express something essential about the emotional life of desire, and they infer something, in turn, about the emotional life of their readers or audience. While their concerns derive from the "main issue" of Carson's thesis, all three works err from established modes of scholarly writing, modeling new acts of exchange between the critical gesture and its objects of study.

Eros the Bittersweet

Five years after completing her doctoral thesis, Carson published *Eros the Bittersweet* with Princeton University Press.[15] In his praise for the book, the poet and essayist Guy Davenport wrote that it showcases to readers a scholar "with a mind as fresh as a spring meadow."[16] In the "Essay on What I think About Most," first published in *Raritan* in 1999, Carson reflects on the quality of "freshness." She begins her close-reading inquiry into what she calls "true mistakes" with a quotation from Aristotle on the three categories of words—strange, ordinary, and metaphorical: "Strange words simply puzzle us; / ordinary words convey what we know already; / it is from metaphor that we can get hold of something new & fresh."[17] "In what," she asks, "does the freshness of metaphor consist?"

> Aristotle says that metaphor causes the mind to experience itself
> in the act of making a mistake.
> He pictures the mind moving along a plane surface
> of ordinary language
> when suddenly
> that surface breaks or complicates.
> Unexpectedness emerges.[18]

The kind of language Carson "thinks about most," and the kind of language she argues is sought by the first lyric poets to express the innermost paradoxes of desire, is a language that moves minds to feats of self-awareness like this one. Carson continues, paraphrasing the arguments of her early scholarly essay, " 'Just for the Thrill': Sycophantizing Aristotle's *Poetics*": "Metaphors teach the mind // to enjoy error / and to learn / from the juxtaposition of *what is* and *what is not* the case."[19] "Error. / And its emotions" (the poem's first lines) continue to be a central concern of Carson's, reappearing as recently as her 2021 essay on "Stillness," which reproduces verbatim lines from the "Essay on What I Think About Most" and ponders "mistakes" that perform irreverent revelations, from John Cage's silences to Meister Eckhart's syntactic inversions.[20] It is here that Carson describes the essay form as a performance of unexpectedness, in which surfaces break and complicate: "an essay is a broaching, an interference, a disruption, a breaking in of me upon you—your mind as a quiet lake, me jumping into it."[21] If *Eros the Bittersweet* is a stage for Carson's incipient freshness of mind, it is perhaps because the disruptive function of metaphor is not only the object of a scholarly exposition, but is structured into the form and argumentative texture of the essay.

The early tonal crescendo of *Eros the Bittersweet* is a short, quotable buzz-phrase on the effects of desire: "Desire moves. Eros is a verb" (17). Eros is a force of momentum that compels individuals, but the movement of its "volts," for Carson, discloses something else about eros: that erotic voltage runs its charge through words, "replacing erotic action with a ruse of heart and language," as Carson argues Sappho does, and as Carson begins to do here in her elegant deductive ruse.[22] The appearance of the phrase is the first time we come across the idea in the book that there is something about eros that requires its thinking and description to move into the terrain of the counterfactual. Flaunting a category mistake, Carson's theatrical turn of phrase performs the kind of unexpectedness she ascribes to metaphor, but which, by this point in the essay, she has also attributed to the "subterfuge" of desire. The verbality of eros is a "true mistake," in the terms of Carson's "Essay on What I Think About Most," to express *what is* and *what is not* the case—that eros is, and is not, a verb. Since the earliest surviving Greek lyric, the principal source texts of *Eros the Bittersweet*, language has been stretched and compressed under the demand to inspire and perform desire; into neologism and coinages like Sappho's *glukupikron* and through all available densities of metaphor. One of the most memorable and outrageously kinetic of the Ancient lyric similes quoted by Carson is this from Anakreon: "With his huge hammer again Eros knocked me like a / blacksmith / and doused me in a wintry ditch."[23] Hot and cold, Carson says, converge in a delighted masochistic blow.

It is a striking beginning for Carson's theory of eros: that a study of the logical scandals and grammatical acrobatics of lyric should follow suit with a counterfactual move of its own. What interests Carson in the grammatical and syntactic moves of lyric is a quality of performativity structured into them. She will call this quality "lyric mimesis" in the essay " 'Just for the Thrill,' " where she argues that the smallest shifts in declension or tense, all the way to the boldest arrangements of metaphor, are designed to mime (and to replicate in the reader) the high-line reasoning of erotic love.[24] Her own slightly dazzling instance—"eros is a verb"— is no exception. Where the doctoral thesis shares much in common with its sharper, snazzier rewrite at the level of argument and philological detail, what makes Carson's scholarship in *Eros the Bittersweet* "fresh," in Davenport's words, is its reliance on metaphor as a structural principle, a mimetic "form for the form" of desire.[25] Metaphor in Carson's book—*metaphora*, transferral or movement from one place to another, a movement of reach—is the epistemological structure that not only best allows us to understand desire, but that most closely mimics it.[26]

In his introductory remarks to *Glass, Irony and God* almost a decade later, Davenport spoke of a "mathematics of the emotions" in Carson. Her writing, he wrote, is structured around "daring equations and recurring sets and subsets of images."[27] Carson's early theory of eros takes the form of a *Bilderreihen* or image sequence, a constellation of vivid tableaux, metaphors, and analogies, among them the triangle, the ruse, the apple of Daphnis and Chloe, the Greek alphabet, the ice-crystal of Sophokles, gardens, wings, cicadas, and so on. The triangle, a figure with iterations all over Carson's writing, first appears in her reading of Sappho's fragment 31, one of the few near-complete poems in the extant *fragmenta*.[28] In fragment 31, which reappears in the title essay of *Decreation* twenty years later, desire circulates through the angles of three pronouns—"He," "you," and "me." The poem stages two parallel acts of attention: a listener ("He") who "listens close," and an onlooker ("me") who observes the listener and his attentions to her beloved ("you") at a distance at once grievous and delicious.

> He seems to me equal to gods that man
> who opposite you
> sits and listens close
> to your sweet speaking . . .

Carson uses these first lines of the fragment to consider what it might mean to be a lover "equal to gods," who seems—perhaps as the Streb dancers look "like gods for an instant"—to be almost impervious to risk. Sappho's lyric subject knows this kind of risk only too well. In thrall to what she witnesses, erotic delirium threatens her with annihilation: "for when I look at you, a moment, then no speaking / is left in me . . . / . . . greener than grass / I am and dead—or almost / I seem to me."[29]

The fragment traces out the familiar geometry of mimetic desire: "He" is the kind of lover the poem's "I" would like to be but isn't; interceding between the lover and her beloved, *his* desire (as René Girard would have it) is part of what makes the beloved so desirable in the first place. For Girard, mimetic desire is "the source of all disorder"—not least the kind of sensory disorder experienced in abundance by Sappho's lover-in-waiting.[30] "It is not a poem about the three of them as individuals," in Carson's words, "but about the geometrical figure formed by their perception of one another, and the gaps in that perception" (13). This geometrical figure, the triangle, arcs and pulls into order the "lines of force" that circulate in the disorderly forms of human eros.

The triangle, with its bold psychosexual trigonometry, is the first explicit instance in the book of Carson's "mathematics of the emotions." Following on from it is a series of single, clear-cut, still-frame metaphors that picture the complex grammars of erotic desire in a sequence of interconnected, interchangeable shapes. *Eros the Bittersweet* comprises thirty-four short chapters—the shortest just a paragraph in length—, each of which boasts an alluringly cryptic title ("Ruse," "Edge," "Ice-pleasure," "Realist," "Read Me the Bit Again"). The book moves from one still-frame to the other with little pause for recollection, summary, or what in academic parlance is sometimes called "signposting" for the reader. Structured as an unbroken syntax of figures, none of which claims argumentative predominance, Carson's inquiry performs the circulation of eros, its variable "lines of force" and its dance in which "desire moves," in the real time of reading. We are passed, as desire is parsed, through one figure after another, as though what Carson wants is for desire to be simply "a mood of knowledge" (66). A recent review of her writing claims, "you read her work with the prevailing sense that you're getting something and getting it fast."[31] Here, the prerogatives of lyric exchange action with critical scholarship. Their shared métier: to make desire "happen," make it dance, in the tempo of thinking about it.[32]

In her conversation with Kevin McNeilly, the term Carson uses to cover these effects is "imitation," and she defines it as "simply a mirroring of the activity of the thought you had at the time you had it, and an attempt to make that activity happen again in the mind of the listener [or] the reader . . . the verb, whatever the verb is that's being described. The verb happens."[33] While Carson's comment couldn't be a more lucid justification for "eros is a verb," it also indicates an intention in her writing to exchange what we might call an author-centered argumentative form with a reader-driven, performative one. John D'Agata has described the essay form as the seat of "lyric" action: as "an art form that tracks the evolution of consciousness as it rolls over the folds of a new idea, memory, or emotion . . . capturing that activity of human thought in real time."[34] Yet Carson's essay seems to go one step further. Her figure sequence captures the activity of thought, but it also scripts a kind of choreography for ours, compelling us to "think" desire as we read. As another recent reader writes, "when we read Carson, we do the thinking."[35]

So far, so consistent with Carson's claim to derive form from "what the facts are doing." An early reviewer described *Eros the Bittersweet* as "a literary embodiment" of the structural metaphors of desire, recalling, the same reviewer remarks, "the critical approaches introduced by Derrida's seminal interpretation of the *Phaedrus* in *La Dissémination*," published in the English translation the year Carson's doctoral thesis was submitted.[36] There are certainly affinities with Derrida, for whom writing—the *pharmakon*, poison-remedy of philosophy—is the true, disavowed object of desire in the *Phaedrus*. For philosophy, he says, writing represents the "inexhaustible adversity of what funds it and the infinite absence of what founds it."[37] (Unlike lyric poetry, philosophy seldom acknowledges the lack that is its generative condition.) Derrida's polemical account, his translator Barbara Johnson observed, "mimes the movement of desire rather than its fulfillment."[38] Yet the kind of "paraliterature" that results, Gregory Ulmer has written, "enacts or performs (mimes) the compositional structuration of the referent"—the semiological unconscious of Plato's text—with a view to exposing as unviable its founding opposition between philosophy and sophistry, or metaphysics and writing.[39] Derrida's mimetic account mimes, or performs, to critique. Carson's account mimes—"My Page makes love," she quotes Montaigne—just for the thrill.[40]

In this, Carson's paraliterary reading of eros is far closer to Roland Barthes, whose *Fragments d'un discours amoureux* (1977; *A Lover's Discourse: Fragments*, 1978) makes an appearance in the chapter epigraph to "Now Then" (117), and whose writing surfaces, cited or otherwise, across her work. Barthes's famous account of desire is summoned by the structure and conceits of *Eros the Bittersweet*. In its opening pages, Barthes lays claim to what he calls a "structural" portrait composed of "figures" ("the body's gesture caught in action and not contemplated in repose"), "non-syntagmatic, non-narrative," to perform the "amorous subject" as an effect of writing: "the description of the lover's discourse has been replaced by its simulation," he announces.[41] Like Carson's—thinking of her breezy citations of Woolf, Sartre, Kierkegaard, rather than her readings of Plato or the lyric poets—, Barthes's performative account is capricious in its citational style, "not invoking guarantees, merely recalling, by a kind of salute given in passing, what has seduced, convinced, or has momentarily given the delight of understanding (of being understood?)."[42] As well as the performance of a speech act, miming how desire "sounds" as it leaves through other people's words ("So it is a lover who speaks and who says: . . . "), Barthes's text is a performance of his thinking, full of "reminders of reading, of listening"; the kind of remembrances scattered all across Carson's writing—in her translations, *Nox*, *Antigonick*, *H of H Playbook*, and *Norma Jeane Baker of Troy*, as across her essays in prose and verse.[43] The genre of these paraliterary readings was never an issue for their authors. The writing, under the same laws as its object of study, was quite simply that—*écriture*; and *écriture*, as Anastasia-Erasmia Peponi has suggested, is in the air when Carson revises her thesis as the essay, *Eros the Bittersweet*.[44]

If *Eros the Bittersweet* is a "literary embodiment" of its object, it is one that not only hopes to perform the duress of desire at the level of form, in the here and now of its readings. Carson's performative here-and-now participates in a logic of desire that pitches it directly opposite the "then" of Plato's "nonlover," who is happier to engage in describing—defining, mastering—desire than performing and ceding to its strictures; which would mean, finally, being unable to pin it down. What happens to the essay under the pressures of this formal imitation, and in the case of so erratic and compelling an object, is perhaps the same that happens to the *subject* of desire, whose story, Carson tells us at the end of *Eros the Bittersweet*, only truly begins with the incursion of eros: "the biggest risk of your life"—forcing you "to come into contact with what is inside you, in a sudden and startling way" (152–153). Earlier in the book, Carson states directly that "[t]here would seem to be some resemblance between the way Eros acts in the mind of a lover and the way knowing acts in the mind of a thinker" (70), a nod to Plato's argument for philosophy in the *Phaedrus*, but also a reading of interpretation and the interpretive impulse, one in which her own thinking emphatically includes itself. As eros moves the mind to self-awareness, Carson pursues the same movement in writing.

Just what was *Eros the Bittersweet* for Carson? We have seen her suggest that the thesis from which the book derives isolated a "main issue of [her] being." In the same interview with D'Agata, however, Carson also claims that, in terms of what it achieved, *Eros the Bittersweet* was a one-off. The 1986 essay on desire was, she says, "possibly the last time I got those two impulses to move in the same stream—the academic and the other [the 'poetic']. After that, I think I realized I couldn't do that again."[45] She goes on to say that "I can't come back together to replicate *Eros [the Bittersweet].*"[46] For Carson, it seems, there is no reliable return "again and again" to this particular text of desire, in which scholarship and *poiesis* moved to the same rhythm, converged "in the same stream." There was, she says, a "clean" quality to the work that she feels is now irretrievable.

The second part of this chapter returns to the strategy of real-time or performative form that arises out of *Eros the Bittersweet*, and which Carson has continued to rehearse in later works engaging questions of desire, difference, and mastery. Before moving on to these, I want to stay for a moment with the particular fate of *Eros the Bittersweet*, which for Carson remains a shining instance of something—the moving of scholarship and *poiesis* "in the same stream"—to which she still aspires in her writing.

One effect of the discourse of desire seems to be precisely the kind of irretrievability Carson spoke of in reference to *Eros the Bittersweet*: an acute sense (shared with one-to-one expressions of desire) that no sooner is such a discourse expressed than it has—or *we* have—shifted shape. In the *Phaedrus*, Socrates talks about the presence of paradox and ambivalence in his characterization of erotic love. Love, he suggests, is a naturally dialectical state, with knock-on effects for its description and definition: so it is, Phaedrus notes, that Socrates ends up having to "describe [love] as a curse to lover and loved alike, and then to turn round and assert that it is the greatest of blessings."[47] Socrates gets so caught up in the description that an earlier theorization of love, which he outlined to Phaedrus with the full force of conviction, slips into oblivion: "But tell me," he says, addressing his young interlocutor: "—I've been so carried out of myself that I've quite forgotten—did I define love at the beginning of my speech?" Phaedrus's answer is yes: "in the most emphatic manner conceivable."[48] Socrates's moment of oblivion, in which he is "carried out of myself" like Aristotle's "kidnapped" subject of *opsis*, or even like the ecstatic, self-observing narrator of Sappho's fragment 31, recalls a similar moment in Longinus's "On the Sublime." Longinus, too, finds himself possessed "by a spirit not [his] own" as he reverts to rhetorical strategies—among them the imitation of other writers—in order to describe the sublime. Carson will allude to something like this capture in "Foam (Essay with Rhapsody): On the Sublime in Longinus and Antonioni" (2005), where she describes the sublime as not just a sensation but a "documentary technique" that mimics it, replicating the sensation as a feature of the text.[49]

The possession of an author by her object—moving as desire moves, as Barthes sought to do in the delirious "dramatic method" of *A Lover's Discourse*—is one explanation of what happens to Carson in her essay on desire; an effect that, depending on how we feel toward it, is either to its credit or its detriment as an essay.[50] Carson's thesis has it, in D'Agata's words, that "the real lover and recipient of . . . desire is language itself," a romance that seems to give permission for Carson's own text to get carried away.[51] (It echoes Barthes's sentiments, too, that "intellectual effort should be directed toward a secondary sexuality, in particular toward the sexuality of language").[52] In an emphatic critique of *Eros the Bittersweet* a year after the book's publication, and picking up on the image of Kafka's "spinning top" from Carson's preface to the book, T .J Sienkewicz remarked that "in her sheer joy of the spinning top she creates, [Carson] falls into an illusion of fragmentary wholeness, a temporary delusion that the fragmentary state of Greek lyric is structurally intentional."[53] Carson's readings of Sappho in *Eros the Bittersweet* center on an aesthetics of fragmentation that is, this book's final chapter suggests, the silver lining of the Sappho canon's extreme material impoverishment; an aesthetics, Carson has admitted, that has influenced her entire approach to writing.[54] It is an aesthetics that results (she acknowledges) from historical accident, misquotation, and faulty preservation: material loss, here, as for the Hellenophile poets of Imagism, equals poetic gain.[55] A remark on Sappho fragment 105a all but admits the contradictions of such a position: "the poem is incomplete, perfectly"; imperfection as perfect serendipity, or even perfect form (27). Sienkewicz is right to imply that Carson is more interested in the shimmer of "fragmentary wholeness" than the extreme historical contingency of these texts, perhaps allowing herself even to labor under a "temporary delusion." The thrill of the fragment's accidental perfection is an emotion—a "drama," in *If Not, Winter*—that we almost expect in lyric poetry, but that, in Sienkewicz's reading, puts the integrity of scholarship at risk.

Carson is clear that some degree of rhetorical possession goes with the territory of eros. She devotes several chapters to the ways in which punning, doubling language enters into the discourse of eros ("It seems impossible to talk about or reason about erotic lack without falling into this punning language," 33). Her own "sheer joy" of reading and composition picks up harmonies with the Platonic lover, for whom all signs, however arbitrary and contingent, point to the beloved object. For this lover, there is no accident—no fragment or parataxis—that is not somehow predestined in its address, a kind of perfect, poetic incompletion. In a sense at which Derrida might have smiled, Carson's theory of eros works under the sway ("under the influence") of its object, which is never quite divisible—Carson's own essay seeks to show—from the logic of writing. If Sienkewicz's suggestion is that it is writing that carries Carson away, writing that has made her delirious, we might respond that this delirium—the lucid performance of desire—is what makes her account so compelling. We might add, with Derrida, that getting caught up in the *logos*—Carson and us—is what makes it seductive; that an un-deferred *logos* "would not seduce anyone."[56] Carson's "temporary" delusion lasts as long as it takes us, her readers, to do the thinking she wants us to with regard to a fragment of verse. The synthetic effects she theorizes in relation to lyric poetry, which I talk about in Chapter 8 in her readings of Sappho, appeal to just this kind of captive, here-and-now emotional reasoning, in which we see ourselves thinking and hear ourselves parsing words.

If there is a risk to mimicking the analogical movements, repeated iterations, and emotional reasoning of eros, it is perhaps because this reasoning cannot be reconciled with the logic and rationale of historicist and materialist academic scholarship, for which "now" and "then" are never simultaneous, and "perfect" textual incompletion is inconceivable. As Carson says in *Economy of the Unlost* of the "landscape of science and fact where other people converse logically and exchange judgments": "I go blind out there." Yet what threatens the argumentative integrity of Carson's essay is to its advantage as a performance. The concerns of Carson's essay continue to crop up across her writing, and each time they do, they produce consequent, performative forms to carry off, or carry away, her thinking. *The Albertine Workout*, Carson's blueprint for an essay on Albertine Simonet, muse of Marcel Proust's *À la recherche du temps perdu*, matches its arguments about possession, desire, and the desire to know, with a "form for the form" for reading Proust.

The Albertine Workout

If *Eros the Bittersweet* teaches us one thing about eros—eros the "verb"—, it is that it compels and requires continual movement, a requirement that jars with the wish to hold time and the beloved in suspense. Formally committed to this lesson, Carson's book shows how desire gets libidinally tangled up in the substance of its expression (a fact Barthes's "lover's discourse" made the center of its own mimetic confession). The suggestion is, in *Eros the Bittersweet*, that what we cannot defy in time, we can somehow get to grips with in writing that rehearses the erratic tempo of eros; a performative script in which "the verb happens."

Eros the Bittersweet is a case of such writing entering and unsettling the domain of critical scholarship. Carson's first book-length essay is, we saw, the result of a confluence of two impulses conventionally kept apart: "the academic" and "the poetic"; the stylistics and formal shape of their complicity constitutes an imitative enactment of Carson's theory of eros and a playful engagement with the central concern of Plato's *Phaedrus*. Yet a number of later works return to the book's arguments in new and more obviously experimental essay forms. These iterations of the original theory plumb the principle Carson calls "exchange of action"—an exchange of the action of thinking from author to reader, from exposition to performance—to produce new and less familiar "essay" forms.

In 2013, at a staged reading from "59 Paragraphs About Albertine," a work unpublished at the time, Carson described her experience of reading Marcel Proust, in French, for thirty minutes at breakfast, every day for seven years—"one of the best seven years of my life," she quips. She explains what happened next:

> The interval of reading Proust is immediately followed by something else, that I call the desert of After Proust. And it's a space of life where all you want is for Proust to go on. But there is no more. And so for a while you kind of make do with other sorts of reading material—biographies and literary studies of Proust, and word indexes and books by other people who write similarly to Proust, and it's all futile, there is no more Proust and that's that, and eventually you accept this and settle back into the grey tedium of a life without Proust.[57]

Out of this scholarly ennui came a series of fifty-nine sequentially numbered paragraphs of varying length, published under the title "The Albertine Workout" in 2014 in the *London Review of Books* with an extended pamphlet edition published by New Directions less than a month later.[58] In the extended version of the work, the fifty-nine numbered paragraphs are followed by a series of sixteen allusively titled appendices numbered non-sequentially: "appendix 4 on Samuel Beckett" is immediately followed by "appendix 8 on capture myopathy," finishing with "appendix 59 on a bad photograph," an arrangement that suggests the remaining, hypothetical appendices (and the prose to which they refer?) are missing in action. The paragraphs themselves, sometimes discontinuous, sometimes in an unbroken flow, turn on the subject of Proust's Albertine Simonet, the elusive and difficult love object of Marcel in *À la recherche du temps perdu*. The entries making up the main body of the work consist of stray concordance data (e.g., "2. Albertine's name occurs 2,363 times in Proust's novel, more than any other character") interwoven with a fragmented account of Marcel's singular fixation on Albertine, allusions to possible avenues of critical inquiry, and a series of drily lyrical observations that quote or mimic Proust's descriptions of Albertine.[59] In the appendices, by contrast, Carson's associations to the data and vignettes are allowed to bloom. Like the "bonsai-shaped appendices" to her doctoral thesis, into which, she says, "all of the imaginative sections [of her research] had to be forced," the rhizomatic appendices of *The Albertine Workout* point down discontinuous lines of inquiry, offering associations and commentary on the details and scattered images that piqued Carson in the course of her reading.[60]

Carson's notes form a cumulative picture: a kind of painting-by-numbers of the central dilemma in which Albertine finds herself caught in *La Prisonnière* (*The Captive*), volume five of *À la recherche*. Imprisoned by Marcel in his home and at the mercy of his overactive erotic suspicions, Albertine's story is both a story of victimhood and the chronicle of a strange form of resistance to Marcel's banal possessiveness. Despite her imprisonment, Carson suggests in her numbered notes, Albertine is an object that continues to evade capture, her mind and her desires ultimately impossible to pin down. Marcel's is a "usual boundless uncertainty" around what Albertine might be doing or thinking, "an uncertainty too indeterminate to be painless" (*relativement à ce que faisait Albertine . . . mon infini doute habituel, trop indéterminé pour ne pas rester indolore . . .*).[61] In his attempted total possession of Albertine, Marcel uncovers the tedium not only of having what he wants, but of robbing himself—by robbing Albertine—of new objects of scintillation, new material to master.[62] In *The Albertine Workout*, Marcel's iconic ennui, along with the totalizing desire that produces it, is staged as a commentary on another, parallel set of desires and their consequences. For Carson's broken narration of what happens in *La Prisonnière* is a designed exposure of how and why she reads it in the form she does—in a deliberately incomplete, draft- or blueprint-form essay, whose structure performs the process, rather than the finished article, of a critical reading.

Hermeneutic possessiveness is precisely what *The Albertine Workout* works against in its sparse and erratic exercise. It is a reading that, while listing them in an inconclusive collage arrangement, refuses to be drawn on the facts collected in and around Proust's novel. Rather, as Carson hints in her remarks on the piece at its first public outing, *The Albertine Workout* takes its cue and its raison d'être from the limits of its object: from the bare, incontrovertible fact that "there is no more." "The desert of After Proust" (a phrase that also makes an appearance in "appendix 15 (a) on adjectives") is a state to which Carson's exercise both acquiesces, by listing the bare residual facts of the work, and resists, by performing their unfinished interpretation. In the relation of the appendices to this list, the desire for "more" is staged in the exposed movements of a mind unmooring itself from the facts. As one reviewer of the *Workout* notes, in Carson's text, "an appendix pointing toward a text cannot match the text precisely, but can think around it, imprecisely."[63]

The sometimes downright bizarre associations to Proust in the appendices recall the kind of discontinuous desire-led inquiry undertaken and theorized by Barthes, and which often, in his case, came to rest on the figure of Proust, too. Indeed, Barthes—whom Carson refers to in *The Albertine Workout* as "that late-born pre-Socratic philosopher" and whose theory of the photographic image she cites in the final appendix[64]—said of his own encounters with Proust: "Proust is what comes to me, not what I summon up; not an authority, simply a circular memory."[65] Carson's list-plus-appendix format allows her to formalize a fresh, untheorized relation between the facts of Proust's novel and the circulation of memory and association around it; to set down anecdotally what she calls the "sparks"—what Barthes, in *Le Neutre*, calls *scintillations*—lit in the course of her research.[66] Barthes's course delivered at the Collège de France includes notes for sessions on Proust, whose own blueprint form—a form anticipating a future performance, as was explicit in his final course, *The Preparation of the Novel*, whose "novel" was never written—makes us think of Carson's "workout" as awaiting a similar realization: that its endgame, where the work "happens," is somewhere other than the text itself.[67] To write up her notes in conventional essay form would be, as it were, to end the affair, extinguishing its spark and inducing an ennui worthy of Marcel himself.

A sketch for an essay suspended in time, then, whose completion remains pending and possible, *The Albertine Workout* stages its own "mathematics of the emotions" in response to an object that, for Carson, is always more than the sum of its parts. Its spare list of facts and associations recalls the *Bilderreihen* or image sequences that give *Eros the Bittersweet* its fragmented structure and that make desire "happen" in the process of reading. The workout pulls on the aesthetics of the fragment, whose allure derives from what is omitted from its clipped forms. These forms are, as such, always provisional and always an invitation to the reader: Kim Anno, who collaborated with Carson in the artist book edition of *The Albertine Workout*, spoke of their desire to create "an open reading that readers and viewers can make on their own."[68] The fragment "designates a presentation," as Philippe Lacoue-Labarthe and Jean-Luc Nancy have written, "that does not pretend to be exhaustive" ("the empty place that a garland of fragments surrounds is a precise drawing of the contours of the work").[69] It is in this committed design not to exhaust—not to exhaust Proust, in this case—that Carson's work sets itself up as a reading of Albertine that has learned the lesson that Marcel's reading of her within the novel has not. Carson's elliptical statements perform her reading as "process" as they gesture toward a possible whole that is at once desired and actively delayed. Carson's workout is, in this sense, less an effort to "*work out* who Albertine is" (as one reader has argued[70]) than the contrary impulse: to hold her decipherment and capture at bay, so to keep desire in circulation. Where it documents the profound pleasure of *la recherche*—the pursuit of something whose dimensions are yet to be determined (the "empty place" the collection of notes "surrounds"), and of course, the pleasures of scholarly *research*—its inconclusive form passes that pleasure on to the reader, so that it "happens again" in the action of reading.

In addition to its performative form, the workout's comment on its own strategy is explicit at several key points. Early on in the work, Carson explores a possible interpretation of Albertine's sexual enigma in the form of the so-called transposition theory—the theory that the Albertine character is in fact a female version of Proust's chauffer, Alfred Agostinelli, which, as Carson explains, exhibits parallels between the circumstances of their deaths and the gifts given to Agostinelli and Albertine by the two Marcels, author and protagonist.[71] In entry 57, following a climactic exposition of the theory, Carson bluntly disqualifies it by bringing its totalizing biographical scoop into symmetry with Marcel's paranoid reading of Albertine: "57. Granted the transposition theory is a graceless, intrusive and saddening hermeneutic mechanism," she says, though she admits, continuing, that "in the case of Proust it is also irresistible" (p. 20). The analogical relation between Albertine and Agostinelli is worked and unworked, tossed and turned, all the way through the workout, as part of a wider to-and-fro in the work between the consequences of a desire to comprehend Albertine: capture and liberation, facts and the allure of possibility beyond them. The workout, finally, works in pursuit of the "something that facts lack"—words Carson uses in *Nox* under the influence of a very different impulse. "Overtakelessness," she writes there, "is a word told to me by a philosopher once: *das Unumgängliche*—that which cannot be got round."[72] Rather than overtaking or closing down the question of Albertine, Carson's inquiry approaches what it is in her that fascinates Marcel and eludes his own theories—that which cannot be got round, which remains indecipherable—by performing its painstaking non-decipherment.

While the transposition theory episode functions as a manifesto against overpossessive theorization, there is a playful ambivalence throughout the piece toward interpretation and its double allure: the allure of possibility and of its calculated constraint. Reflecting on the transposition theory, Carson tells her readers that what interests her are the "spark[s] to be struck from rubbing Alfred [Agostinelli] against Albertine, as it were" (57, p. 20). The last of these sparks to be struck in the workout comes from the stanza by Mallarmé that Proust had inscribed "on the fuselage of Alfred's plane—the same verse Marcel promises to engrave on the prow of Albertine's yacht," Carson writes. The stanza consists of four verses from the second poem of the tetrad "Plusieurs sonnets," "Le vierge, le vivace et le bel aujourd'hui." Carson explains in the entry preceding her reproduction of the fragment that the four verses are "about a swan that finds itself frozen into the ice of a lake in winter." "Magnificent," Carson's translation reads, "but / without hope of setting himself free / for he sailed to sing / of a region for living / when barren winter / burned all around him with *ennui*."

58.

> *Un cygne d'autrefois se souvient que c'est lui*
> *Magnifique mais qui sans espoir se délivre*
> *Pour n'avoir pas chanté la région où vivre*
> *Quand du stérile hiver a resplendi l'ennui.*
> (Mallarmé, "Le vierge, le vivace and [*sic*] le bel aujourd'hui")

Mallarmé's swan moves in these lines from an affirmation (*c'est lui*, "it is he"— *Magnifique*, Magnificent) to its near destitution (*mais qui sans espoir*, "but / without hope"). The change of condition staged here, from natural possibility to its immobilization, evokes the captive Albertine, but also a form of paralysis closer to home for Carson the poet. For the swan's capture pictures a resistance to possibility within the poem, or even a warning of poetry's failure—*Pour n'avoir pas chanté*, "for he failed to sing"—while the poem continues to sound. This freezing mid-movement pictures the detention of meaning and a mind that has ceased to move, unhappy result of a reading that seeks to hold the poem still in time (a rush to the "then," at the expense of the "now"). The detention of meaning is a state the poem names *stérile hiver*, a barren winter and an *ennui* to match not just Marcel's—stricken with boredom by the success of his capture—but the tedium of completion that Carson's exercise wards off.

Carson's remarks on the Mallarmé fragment in the preceding entry present it to us in an undeniably sad light: "What a weird and lonely shadow to cast on these two love affairs [Marcel-Albertine, Proust-Agostinelli], the fictional and the real; what a desperate analogy to offer of the lover's final wintry paranoia of possession" (57, p. 20). A wan shadow it casts, too, over the possibility of paranoid reading, interpretation that seeks to possess its object by suspecting (and proving) what it "really means." "Paranoid reading," Eve Kosofsky Sedgwick's term for reading under the injunction of suspicion—whose signature affects are, in Lisa Ruddick's words, "deadness and meanness"—is the kind of criticism whose verve for what the text "really means" leads it to immobilize a poem's action, along with the surprise and vertigo it can inspire (Sontag even speaks of the work's "freedom to 'mean' nothing").[73] Its affair with the text is always risk-averse because it seeks in the text that which is finally reducible to the reader's suspicions. Marcel, paranoid reader par excellence, refuses to recognize that his version of the beloved object is one of many possible fictions. His capture of Albertine, like the swan that becomes her motif, marks the hopeless sterility of possession. And yet, the following and final entry in the workout, quoting Marcel's uncertain epiphany in *La Prisonnière*, acknowledges such possession is always in any case a fantasy: "59. 'Everything, indeed, is at least double,' *La Prisonnière*, p. 362," a phrase echoed in Samuel Beckett's remarks on the "double sign" of Proustian action—that which is always at least double what it seems.[74]

The double impulse of interpretive fascination—toward possession on the one hand and possibility on the other; captivation by theory and by what slips its moorings—is set up, then, to mirror the paradox of possessive desire at the heart of *À la recherche*. One of the more significant achievements of *The Albertine Workout* is the communication of such a reading without explicitly making the case for it: the form of Carson's essay, I have been suggesting, is a powerful interpretive act, sustaining her argument by producing the coincidence of a dilemma with a form for reading it. In no single sentence or entry does Carson tell us her precise reading of the Albertine question; rather, she follows lines of inquiry that replicate the outline of its central dilemma. Within Proust's novel, for example,

Marcel discovers that what he finds so troubling and, at the same time, so alluring in Albertine is the non-reducibility of her actions to one or other possible reading of them, never more so than when she is asleep. Sleep is where Albertine slips her bonds. Carson reports the following in some of the workout's most clipped and elliptical entries: "24. The state of Albertine that most pleases Marcel is Albertine asleep." "27. a) Sometimes in her sleep Albertine throws off her kimono and lies naked. b) Sometimes then Marcel possesses her. c) Albertine appears not to wake up." The question Carson draws out of the conundrum of Albertine's sleep is what kind of control is being exercised here and by whom. For in her sleep, Albertine is alluring for the same reason as she is, or seems to be, non-consenting: remaining asleep while "Marcel possesses her," Albertine begins to represent for Marcel the creeping presence of fiction, the slippery realm of the "double sign"—what Carson, in her entries, calls "the bluff." Marcel, Carson remarks, "appears to think he is the master of such moments," and yet "he gets himself tangled up in the wiles of the woman. On the other hand, who is bluffing whom is hard to say." The bluff is so difficult, to intractable, because it refuses all efforts to trace out its edges (the same way Carson's notational form in *The Albertine Workout* avoids staking lines of argument, lapsing or 'sleeping' between its numbered entries). Where its contours cannot be traced, the bluff becomes the sign of impossible possession, the unmasterable because incomplete.

In his readings of *À la recherche*, René Girard remarked on the refusal of Marcel's mother to kiss him goodnight that such a refusal "is both the instigator of desire and a relentless guardian forbidding its fulfillment."[75] Girard points to the double role of what he calls "internal mediation," by which Albertine, too, both instigates and prohibits desire.[76] Just as the "bluff" of Albertine's sleep both instigates and prohibits Marcel's "hermeneutic" desire, it is also the fiction that cantilevers Proust's novel off balance, undercutting the sovereignty of a single narrative perspective. Mediator of another's desire, the bluff—whoever it is, finally—is at the heart of *La Prisonnière*. Several versions of Proust's Albertine in contemporary works of fiction, featuring more or less explicit iterations of the sleep scenes, have sought to tease out the complexity of this "bluff." In Jacqueline Rose's novel *Albertine* (2001), a psychoanalytic reading of Proust that puts the fantasy life of the erotic object at its center, Albertine is awake during the episodes of possession; it is Marcel who is the object of a sustained manipulation.[77] In Angela Carter's so-called theoretical fiction, *The Infernal Desire Machines of Doctor Hoffman* (1972), the "glass woman" Albertina, daughter of the novel's internal weaver of fictions, the eponymous Doctor Hoffman, is a mirror for Carter's protagonist in ways that both excite and repel him—much as Proust's Marcel is constituted, to his considerable frustration, by his own difficult object of desire. Albertina is killed by Carter's protagonist in an ironic victory of fact over psychic fiction, a fiction that, after the event, he continues to long for. Whether intentionally or otherwise—and like other metafictional "versions" such as Jean Rhys's *Wide Sargasso Sea* (1966), Marina Warner's *Indigo* (1992), and Jeanette Winterson's *Frankissstein* (2019)—these novels have a mind for the theoretical cultures of their time, composing their iterations of Albertine as works of feminist literary revisionism and, in a roundabout way, as works of criticism.[78] Yet while these novels anticipate their own critical reception—what Martin Paul Eve calls a "literature against criticism"—*The Albertine Workout* has an altogether different relationship to critical culture: namely, Carson's essay wants criticism out of the way. It features an interpolated letter that Carson has Proust address to Heraklitos—"*Dear Heraklitos*, he wrote, *theory is good but it doesn't prevent things from existing*" (theory, this fiction suggests, is no antidote to the real).[79] The work's rebuff to possessive or paranoid interpretive theories such as the transposition theory occurs most powerfully by way of its form. An essay in the making, the work comments on how the critical essay can, as it were, go wrong, falling into the trap of suspicion and possessive desire. In what it performs, it is a cautionary tale of how not to read literature.

A wider question that emerges in this fascinating case of performative form might be said to concern form itself. What does it mean to "give form" to a critical inquiry? How do formal constraints (sequential numbering, blooming appendices, or the organized paragraphs of academic prose) translate, and translate into, a set of emotional experiences derived from reading? Certainly, the minimalism of Carson's interpretive routine does its best to conceal her; yet the essay-in-waiting is also one of her most theatrical forms, staging an appeal to the very expectations that judge it incomplete. Carson asks us to do the thinking work her reading of Proust tells us is best left unfixed. We have seen how *Eros the Bittersweet* might "capture the mind" with its kaleidoscopic image repertoire and pointillistic structure, in which the circulation and displacement of key images translate, and translate into, the circulation of desire. In the final text studied in this chapter, we will see the emotional intensities transacted by formal constraint rise in temperature.[80] We will also see the onus of *theorizing* possession passed even more decisively to us, as we read (or listen to) the lecture in sonnet form.

The Albertine Workout draws most clearly on *Eros the Bittersweet*, finally, when Carson names as "Marcel's theory of desire" a theory that matches Carson's own almost exactly. Marcel's theory, Carson says, "equates possession of another person with erasure of the otherness of her mind, while at the same time positing otherness as what makes another person desirable" (entry 18). Later, we read Marcel's own words to this effect: " 'One only loves that which one does not entirely possess,' says Marcel" (entry 52). Another way the workout reprises *Eros the Bittersweet* is in the reappearance of the trope of the "verb" and its place in grammars of desire. At first glance, the verb trope makes its first appearance by omission, as part of Carson's reflections on grammar and its relationship to the different forms and degrees of possession. In "appendix 15 (a) on adjectives," Carson surmises that "Adjectives are the handles of Being. Nouns name the world, adjectives let you get hold of the name and keep it from flying all over your mind like a pre-Socratic explanation of the cosmos"—or like a swan, or a poem, or like a beloved whose being won't be fixed either. She continues these reflections in "appendix 15 (b) on adjectives" by bringing our attention to Barthes's suggestion "viz. to craft a language with no adjectives at all, thereby to outwit 'the fascism of language' and maintain 'the utopia of suppressed meaning,' as he [Barthes] deliriously put it."[81]

Language with the capacity to free a captive, to dominate or abandon dominion over another language, to establish or cede sovereignty over another way of speaking, has obvious resonances with Albertine and with Carson's exercise in keeping Proust going. Her reading is interested in "the utopia of suppressed meaning" precisely because it is its suppression, its unavailability as representation, that goes on releasing ever more meaning into circulation—a vital source in "the desert of After Proust." The adjective is also opposed implicitly to the action of the verb, which makes an appearance in one of the final appendices—"appendix 34 on getting rid of your slave," where the verb, it turns out, is precisely the grammar to undercut possessive desire. In the logic of *Eros the Bittersweet* ("eros is a verb"), desire moves because its object claims his or her own volition. In *The Albertine Workout*, the presence of the verb is a recognition of the other as such. Withholding it means a refusal to recognize the other as agent of her own desire, a refusal of erotic risk, and worse, it turns out. "Marcel's ultimate reference to Albertine on the last page of the novel [*The Captive*]," Carson explains, "is a sentence without a main verb: Profound Albertine, whom I saw sleeping and who was dead."

Carson's inquiry into the grammars of desire and possession can be traced throughout her writing: whether in the form of circulating, interchangeable pronouns, where desire refuses to settle in any one configuration ("pronouns do the dance called washing" in *The Beauty of the Husband*); in the love triangles of Carson's autobiographical verse essays; or in the ecstatic delivery from self-relation explored in *Decreation*. In the work I turn to in the final part of this chapter, Carson continues her long-standing inquiry through a return to the spoken word—the orality privileged by Plato over writing as the "real" move in the discourse of eros. It is a work in which the sonnet form, conventional seat of the lyric voice and one of the most common forms of love poem, hosts an unconventional inquiry into the limits between beings, the contingencies and rules—physical, emotive, grammatical—governing their difference.

"Possessive Used as Drink (Me)"

In "Uncle Falling," the lyric lecture with which I began this chapter, Lecturer II offers some remarks on the lecture form:

> The best connections are the ones that draw attention to their own frailty so that at first you think: *what a poor lecture this is—the ideas go all over the place* and then later you think: *but still, what a terrifically perilous activity it is... how unprepared and unpreparable is the web of connections between any thought and any thought.*[82]

Those "unprepared" connections that "draw attention to their own frailty" might be just what we find in the loose, non-sequitur connections of *The Albertine Workout*, the risk or "peril" being that we might just lose our thread. The single remark—"reading can be freefall"—printed on the back cover of *Float* suggests that, in the case of the lyric lecture, taking its place at random among Carson's unnumbered pamphlets, losing our thread is precisely the idea.

In 2006, following a commission from Harvard University, Carson performed a lecture on the subject of pronouns.[83] "Possessive Used as Drink (Me): A Lecture on Pronouns in the Form of 15 Sonnets" is, as its title suggests, a lecture written in sonnet form, first performed with the on-stage support of sound artist Stephanie Rowden, video artist Sadie Wilcox, and three dancers from the Merce Cunningham Dance Company, whose improvised choreography accompanied Carson's reading.[84] The text of her "Lecture on Pronouns" is reproduced in *Float* alongside "Uncle Falling" and other performance-oriented prose and verse works with similarly associative lines of inquiry, such as "Cassandra Float Can" and "Variations on the Right to Remain Silent." "Possessive Used as Drink (Me)" is a series of sonnets and slight variations on the traditional fourteen-line verse form. The etymology of the word "sonnet" (*sonetto*, a diminutive deriving from *suono*, a sound), rather than perhaps the stricter sense of orthodox sonnet lineation, might be what inspired this particular lecture form, which appeals to sound and cadence to draw out differences, as well as sliding elisions, between pronouns and the possession they ascribe. As Carson's offbeat title hints, the "Possessive Used as Drink (Me)" proposes and performs the use of grammar as inebriant—or, in parentheses, as a muffled erotic imperative—by which boundaries between persons, possession and self-possession, might be put to the test. "Washing the pronouns in the water to remove the mud," in the terms of one of the sonnets (the "Sonnet of the Pronoun Event"), the sonnet sequence harnesses the aesthetics of live vocal performance to play with muddying and clarifying identities, sovereignties, and ownership, in an inquiry that performs feats and failures of the grammatical "possessive."

The tenth sonnet in the sequence, "Merce Sonnet," a three-column "blended text" of the kind we also find in *Decreation*, offers an indication of where Carson is going, not just with her pronouns but with the performance aesthetics of the lecture. An inquiry "of pronoun / the etymology," the poem splays its meanings out horizontally, across the three-column lines: from "instead of" and "earlier, prior, before," to another, more haphazard history:

Perhaps in this way	came to us	dancing—
very early,	starry, stumbling,	chancing,
that first into hour	of air blueblack	and bold
before of our names	the terrible gusto	took hold.[85]

The pronoun, we hear across these horizontally plotted stanzas, both precedes and replaces the name. It is a form of naming too early for the ("terrible") specificity of the noun, and strongly affiliated to the contingent moves of "dancing"—"very early, starry, stumbling, chancing"—as though the rhyme itself were fumbled or happened upon by accident, a chance affinity between columns of text as between bodies in motion. The sonnet alludes both in the title and text to "Merce"—the dancer and choreographer, Merce Cunningham, from whom the dance company that first performed Carson's lecture takes its name. Cunningham envisaged modern dance as an art that deals in contradiction, whose forms of physical freedom embrace the possibility of total internal unfamiliarity, including acts of self-sabotage and what Roger Copeland, in his study of Cunningham, and remembering John Cage's "chance operations," calls "chance procedures."[86] (Copeland quotes a remark from Marcel Duchamp, a strong influence on Cunningham, that appears as the epigraph to Carson's "Sonnet Isolate": "I force myself to contradict myself in order to avoid conforming to my own taste"—an argument for the pursuit of non-self-possession through deliberate self-contradiction).[87]

The debut performance of Carson's lecture featured unchoreographed contact dance, accompanied by a live video recording of the dancers and live sound—both reading and song—that weave in and around one another, undermining and magnifying cadence and rhythm in the sonnets. This interdisciplinary operatic event, in the sense theorized by Linda Hutcheon, brings scored sound and movement to bear on a spoken libretto, much in the way Carson's "Decreation" libretto did several years earlier.[88] If the lecture is, as Carson says in the lecture-essay on "Stillness," "a broaching. An interference. A disruption. A breaking in of me upon you," then the intermedia lecture makes space for the breaking-in of chance and accident on the lecture form—a move against the intensified privacy of the written interpretive event. In this inquiry into how relations move in and among their grammatical names, Carson returns to the ruses of dance of *Eros the Bittersweet*. From the permutatory partnerships of the "dance called Jealousy," the *bassa danza* she cites in that essay, to the improvisatory contact of the dance "before our names": desire moves one toward and against another.[89] Dance literalizes this movement and exposes our agendas for desire: to script its moves or let them unspool.

While the vocal accompaniment to Carson's recital is scored and choreographed, the lecture is also open to the contingencies of performance, including moments of improvisation and accident, risks that become points of fruition in the course of the argument. Carson's husband and collaborator Robert Currie explains:

> Just prior to the performance [of the sonnets] Merce Cunningham passed away and of course all three dancers were from the Cunningham Company. There's this great moment during the Merce sonnet when Marcie [Munnerlyn] goes back to the edge—way upstage—and she dances one of his solos completely out of the score. It was simply beautiful.[90]

If dance expresses a contingent and versatile grammar of relations between distinct, visible bodies ("starry, stumbling, / chancing"), the voice in its onstage address opens the play of relations in ways that the "Merce Sonnet" anticipates. The sonnet, read in private or addressed to a live audience, speaks to an "us" both particular and universal. Particular universality is a mode the poem locates before the name ("before our names / the terrible gusto / took hold"); a pro-nominal, primordial chaos in which we stumble upon and fumble for our edges, moving in an "air blueblack / and bold."

In contrast with naming, here, the pronoun is an open, non-accusative form of address, an embracing form with the potential to signify beyond particularity. (As the recent practice of listing preferred pronouns has shown, pronoun identity can trump the particularities of biology.)[91] When sounded and echoed, as it is in Carson's performance of other sonnets in the sequence, the pronoun is set adrift from all singularity of reference. Where the speaking "I" is fixed to the speaker onstage, "you" and "she/he" or "thou" roam freely across multiple simultaneous possibilities of relation. Pronouns, Carson says at another point in the lecture, are "a system that argues with its shadow / like Venetian blinds," so dialectical; a Platonic space for the contrary and counterfactual.[92] In this crucial sense, Carson makes the pronoun the defining moniker of theater: a compact play of shadows in which identity flickers between beings, and in which no one on stage is in full possession of themselves. It is a transitive address from fiction to fiction, assumed identity to assumed identity. An address that assumes it does not know to whom it is speaking.

As we saw in *Eros the Bittersweet*, the love triangle is the form in which the circulation of desire and its relational possibilities is most clearly visible. If the pronoun is a grammar of difference, measuring off one being from another, it is also a grammar for their exchangeability: "I" will be "you" to my interlocutor, "I" will be "she" in the third point of a love triangle; one gives necessary contour to the others, but their exchanges of valency allow for potent confusions. We see this confusion staged in the subheadings of "The Glass Essay," where "SHE" is Carson's mother and/or Emily Brontë, one or other of "three silent women at the kitchen table." We see the pronoun as event in the love triangle of *The Beauty of the Husband*, where "PRONOUNS DO THE DANCE CALLED WASHING" and "her" is a word that bursts into flames.[93]

Carson's long, languid "Drop't Sonnet," with a parenthetical annex that falls diagonally across the page, describes what happens when a pronoun goes missing—when "language drops a distinction." The "thinning" of grammatical and vocal possibility thins conditions of possibility for relation. With the loss of a grammatical distinction, a form of life and a vital expression of tension is lost: "a lowering of arms, / a thinning of air inside the whole system, / a sadness in the sparrows, a slipping away of prefixes and wisdom." The sonnet then plunges diagonally into a parenthesis, a precipitance of synonyms and analogies running at 45 degrees across the page. The narrator talks about an emotional event for which she struggles to find the words. By the end of this headlong verbal/visual slide, the poem arrives at the understanding that what was needed was a pronoun—a category of the possessive fallen into disuse. Something about the event—

this

mineshaft,
    cataract,
        toboggan slide (waterslide, landslide), . . .

this

          streaming
          downspout
          of voodoo pine—
           cried out to be addressed
                      as
                          thine).

The mise-en-page of Carson's sonnet is a sensible form in its own right, miming the synonymic rush and slide, and its abeyance once the pronoun is arrived at, in the concrete visual image of the poem. In live recital, this fragment of "lecture" is "published" (to borrow Carson's term from the McNeilly interview) as the lecturer's voice mimics the plunge through associations to their arrival at earth ("*thine*"). That "lyric mimesis"—the performativity of poems—is a function of this lecture is pretty much beyond doubt.

Carson's "Lecture on Pronouns" begins with a sequence of three sonnets titled "Triple Sonnet of the Plush Pony," the text of which was first published in the *London Review of Books* in 2007.[94] In the live performance of these poems, the phenomenon of voice becomes the principal object of a question posed in Part I of the "Triple Sonnet" regarding the classification of bodily effects as "alienable" and "inalienable"—as "a personal possession or as something you can sell." The question of what is "me" and "not me," a distinction around which Part I assumes a basic troublesomeness, finds its articulation in a lecture form premised on sounds and images that perform the kinds of straying and convergence described in the poem: whose nonlinear argument moves between incongruous scenarios and never quite returns to itself. Most strikingly of all, the "Triple Sonnet" leads its inquiry through the analogy of a toy pony, whose ontological status as "plush" (imitation) and/or "meat" (sentient, real) is tried and tested through the possessive pronouns of "yours" and "his." The first sonnet sets out the case for the fragile intelligibility—and often dramatic consequences—of such distinctions: "Such thinking," Carson says, "will affect how a word like rape is defined" or "how you feel in your mind / when you address animals." Some of these animals, the sonnet ends, "depend on their owner to keep or dispose. But your pony you cannot sensibly classify with those."

In Parts II and III, by way of performance of the hypothesis of Part I, an argument is made through the release of sound in euphonic internal rhyme, harmonics and dissonance, forms of meaning that, in their live recital, perform without need of description, and almost, at moments in Part III, without need for the words to mean. Instead, sound performs Carson's argument as the rhythmic circulation of metered breath and voice, turning on the variable difference between the "alienable" and "inalienable"—in this case, between body and breath. The "Triple Sonnet" is a live theory of possession that performs its question without resolution. Its inquiry vacillates, instead, through rhythmic song.

Triple Sonnet of the Plush Pony Part II[95]

Another thee.
A summer's day.
Double vantage me.
Never to repay.
and Will in overplus.
Making addition thus—
your pony is all these to you—and more:
he can detect the smell of danger

and will not take you through a door
if there is doom or pain there.
So at the end of his life if you want to sell him for meat
you'll have to change the pronoun with which you greet
at dawn his shaggy head,
at dawn his shaggy head.

Triple Sonnet of the Plush Pony Part III

A body in the dawn.
A body in the cold.
A body its breath.
Its breath a plume.
A dance a plume.
A dance not thou.
A thou, a thee.
Thou, breath.

There stands.
Breath, plume.
How cold is.
A dawn is.
How still stands.
Thy breath.

The "Triple Sonnet" casts its inquiry out wide, such that the question around bodily parts and effects, and the "thinking that will affect how a word like rape is defined"—surely the sharpest way to ask about possession and self-possession—shares its dilemma with the commodification of the animal and, in the final part, the sublime duet of body and breath. "Your pony" is, in the first two sonnets, an abstract figure for a relational other who is—depending on the pronoun we grant him—either sovereign and autonomous, or a dispensable extension of the "you" to whom Carson addresses her inquiry. Part II then establishes that if the pony belongs to the possessive pronoun category "thee" ("thou")—"Another thee," linked by the arch rhyme to "Double vantage me" and given a reverb echo, a double vision to match his shaky ontology, in the sung performance of the sonnet—then his commodification and sale will require a change in category: "you'll have to change the pronoun with which you greet / at dawn his shaggy head."

Part III is where this piece of verse thinking comes into its own. Even without the winding, echoing vocals of Carson's collaborative debut recital, as we read it on the page, the poem manages to approximate the circulation of breathing: "Its breath a plume. A dance a plume," making two full iambic breaths (inhale, exhale; inhale, exhale). Body and breath begin in this poem as an equivalence, whose statement of fact follows the same formula as the descriptions that precede it: "A body in the dawn. / A body in the cold. / A body its breath." The two then begin to separate out as the statements of fact continue ("Its breath a plume. / A dance a plume") until their difference is confirmed. The lines "A dance not thou. A thou, a thee" mark the breath's constitution as an entity in its own right in a dance of distinctions and equivalences ("Thou, breath," "Breath, plume"). This pronominal dance was mirrored in the aesthetics of Carson's debut performance of the work, where the bodies moving onstage are echoed by a video projection that stalks, shadows, and recapitulates their moves.

One of the most striking things about this last of the three sonnets is the absence of verbs, with one exception. All of the poem's motility, the flux it performs as rhythmic action, is tied to the verb "stands," a verb whose subject, in both instances in which it appears, is the breath: "There stands. / Breath, plume" and "How still stands / Thy breath." That the breath is the agent of this poem is clear, both in the organization of meter in the sonnet and the "alienable/inalienable" inquiry it shares with the preceding two poems (when does the breath cease to belong to the body?). It also shares affinities with *The Albertine Workout*, where Carson ponders how a writer can "disenfranchise, disempower or delete his slave *grammatically* by taking away the part of speech in which she acts as a subject connected to a predicate" ("appendix 34 on getting rid of your slave"). Yet the breath is agent of another exchange of action, too. The poem as a work of breath, as *pneuma*, passes from the poet into circulation—into language and into the world, as Paul Celan imagined it—, bringing with it its own natural quotient of alienation. In the performance cited above, the circling vocal accompaniment to Carson's recital transforms her still, cropped syntax into truncated questions or statements awaiting completion, iterated and changed as they pass from one breath to another ("How cold is. A dawn is": suspended affirmations awaiting a verbal agent to bring them to life). Here, the verb "happens" only when the poem is performed, the breath imitated in the tonalities of speaking voices.

By the final line of the "Triple Sonnet," the breath returns and rests at its source: the "plush pony" is once again in possession of his ("thy") breath. The agency of the breath, which moves between equivalence with physical being and an analogy for it, becomes the third point of a triangle: the lines of this triangle run from "you" to "your pony" to "its breath." It is a movement we rehearse when we read the poem aloud, as the meter reaches outward (exhales) and inward (inhales) in an iambic flow. Where the first two parts of the "Triple Sonnet" approach the relation between the possessive pronoun and ontology—what kind of object the pony is, or our bodily effects are—the third sonnet reduces

Carson's inquiry to what she calls elsewhere in *Float* "an art of pure shape."[96] The third sonnet's compact pneumatic dance performs the throes at the heart of Carson's inquiry, but it performs them in ways that the argumentative exposition of a conventional lecture cannot. The sonnet in recital is an exquisite case of what Jean-Luc Nancy calls *partage des voix*: the sharing or splitting of voices, where meaning is offered and abandoned (*Le sens se donne, il s'abandonne*) in an exchange between description and sound, whose "dialogical rhapsody" takes place in the dividing and joining of voices.[97] In the sensible immediacy of this rhapsody is the longed-for "real move" of poems. Its descriptive imitation of the breath is also, in recital, the real-time lyric performance of the breath in motion, where artful imitation and a "real move" become inseparable.

We have seen Carson say that oral and literate cultures think, express themselves, and fall in love differently. In Carson's words in *Eros the Bittersweet*, "[in] oral poetics, . . . Eros and the Muses clearly share an apparatus of sensual assault" (50). She goes on to explain how the audience of an oral recitation is "as Herman Fränkel puts it, "an open force field" into whom sounds are being breathed in a continuous stream from the poet's mouth" (50). Yet the written word is no such "all-pervasive sensual phenomenon." Literacy, Carson says, "de-sensorializes words and reader" (50). If *Eros* and the Muses share an apparatus of sensual assault, then this assault matters not just for poetry, but for philosophy too. In his mythic hymn to Love, following his performance and recantation of a speech in favor of the "nonlover," Socrates (in Catherine Pickstock's words) harnesses for "the philosophic life" the madness (*mania*) of eros against what Pickstock calls "purely 'mortal' and parsimonious modes of self-control": an *erotikos logos* contra the "*pharmako-logos*" of Derrida's Plato.[98] This *mania* is expressed—happens— as the "sensual assault" of oral, as opposed to written, poetics; what Pickstock calls the liturgical origins and "consummation" of philosophy. As Pickstock sees it in her groundbreaking reading of the *Phaedrus*, Socrates's critique of sophistry does not—as Derrida claimed—lead him to disavow the written word in favor of the "metaphysical presence" of the spoken ("a supra-linguistic philosophical logos, independent of time and place").[99] He disavows it because this philosophical logos, suspended in time—where "a piece of ice melts forever"—is fundamentally not to be trusted. The spoken word is where breath and voice, body and word, are staked in real time, time-bound to a unique moment of exchange. Carson's lecture in sonnet form harnesses this sensual apparatus to make an argument that risks its own self-control in favor of a live, formally and vocally involved exchange of action, where whether and how argument "happens" is contingent on the bodies of speaker, dancer, and audience.

The poet Jorie Graham has spoken of the "arguments" of poems as arguments "that don't want to make the reader 'agree.' They don't want to move through the head in that way. They want to go from body to body."[100] In its performative rendering of breath in movement, or of a dance of pronouns that displaces the lyric "I" from its putative center, it is easy to see how Carson's lecture on pronouns moves "from body to body" in a mode of argument that abandons linear exposition and the production of agreement. It is a mode of argument that, like Carson's reading of Albertine, puts its own argumentative self-possession at risk; a form of reasoning that, like *Eros the Bittersweet*, hands itself over to the movements and scintillations of desire, and, in doing so, hands the prerogatives of desiring and thinking desire over to the reader. This sensual, non-argumentative form of argument sets the authority of the lecture and the essay off kilter, yet it remains a powerful form of suggestion and persuasion. The intermedia performances in which Carson is increasingly involved are where variations on her own earlier writing—iterations, remixes, and verbatim use of older material—look and sound like attempts to break out from the authority and imperativity of written interpretive form. These performance pieces herald a move further away from description and toward the kind of "sensible form" Carson attributes to the paintings of Francis Bacon: form "that will translate directly to your nervous system the same sensation as the subject"—form in which an original sensation "happens" again and in which this reprised sensation persuades.[101] What is risked in the performative arguments is the sovereignty of criticism, ceded in exchange for other soft powers.[102] Reaching toward reader and audience in an exchange of action, the performative argument is strong as form and weak as exposition, a play for more radically uncertain forms of thought.

2
Criticism and the Gift
(Carson with Celan)

> *Poems are also gifts—gifts to the attentive. Gifts bearing destinies.*
> —Paul Celan[*1]

There is a kind of gift, says the Romanian-born poet Paul Celan, that, once given, is never the same again. The "poem" is, for Celan, a "unique instance of language": though it can be reproduced—its gift offered—any number of times, in print or in recital, no moment of reading or sounding is equal to another. This gift, the poem, is the sum of its iterative destinies, infinitesimal possibilities addressing recipients beyond number, whose point of continuous arrival and departure is the embodied human voice. It was in his public address on receipt of the Georg Büchner Prize for literature ("The Meridian," 1960), reflecting on some of language's darkest fates, that Celan declared this gift from voice to voice to be nothing short of salvific. He spoke of poems as "detours from you to you" and as "paths on which language becomes voice. They are encounters, paths from a voice to a listening you."[2] It is a strange kind of conversation to which Celan alludes, one whose interlocutors do not share the same place and time but who meet, as it were, on the unlit paths of sound. For Celan, this "encounter" was not enough to redeem a language pushed to obscure, violent, and unrecognizable ends. Yet something vital was salvaged, for him, in the simple act of poetic address: voices given, voices received, and voices returned, knit together in a double-blind exchange of gifts. An anonymous exchange of grace, and a form of life difficult to extinguish.

In *Economy of the Unlost: (Reading Simonides of Keos with Paul Celan)* (1999), Carson examines "what exactly is lost to us when words are wasted" and what is preserved when words and breath are "saved" (3). The language of "losses," "waste," and "saving," ubiquitous in the book, accounts for the twists and turns of what Carson calls *poetic economy—economy* in the sense of a system of organization, a grammar of exchange between verbal facts and their consequences as thought and sound, but also *economy* as a driven compactness of form. What Carson shows as she reads Simonides of Keos—Greek poet of the fifth century

BC and the first to commerce with the poem in exchange for money—with twentieth-century German-speaking poet Celan is that the two share a commitment, in response to wildly different demands, to sustaining multiple, sometimes contradictory meanings in the most economical of written forms. Both poets, she argues, use negation to express possibility and its curtailment in the same move. In Carson's bold feat of comparative reading, "riddled with flaws and insights" according to one critic, this commitment to poetic constraint links together the origins of poetry as a written and commercial culture with the extreme demands placed on the form by the atrocities of the twentieth century.[3] In both scenarios—the poem in the Hellenic gift economy and the poem after Auschwitz—the formal and imaginative economy of poetry gives us "two realities for the price of one," making it both eminently marketable (value for money) and the guarantor of an invaluable, unexchangeable singularity: a currency for guest-friendship and encounter, and, at the same time, a vindication of incommunicable inwardness.

It is surely because she is a poet—and a poet who, regardless of formal or disciplinary affiliation, seeks to "approximate what the facts are doing"—that Carson is not content to account for the poetic "gifts" of Simonides and Celan without responding in kind. This chapter examines how Carson reads Simonides and Celan, paying special attention to how her essay functions, not just as a medium for what she calls their "conversation" and exchange, but as a return of such "gifts." In Carson's book, the critical essay—one of the many destinies of poems—is a form of reciprocal gift to the poems' lexical and metrical facts. Prosody is the principal currency for this exchange, as well, we will see, as the essay's structure of address, and the stakes of writing that Carson, in one of the more grandiose moments of her reading, professes to share with Celan.[4] The kinds of approximation and reciprocity we find in *Economy of the Unlost* are less formally decisive than those of the verse essay/long poem "The Glass Essay," published four years earlier, in which Carson's exchange of emotive claims and registers with Emily Brontë exposes the fantasy life of critical attention to her source. Yet Carson's response to Simonides and Celan not only participates in the same mimetic compositional strategies—"arising from the thing itself" or approximating "the facts"—pursued throughout this book. What she tells us she is doing in *Economy of the Unlost*, alongside her declared affinities as a poet with some of Celan's keenest hopes for language, gives us crucial insight into how and why her essay responds in the ways it does to the "gifts" of poetry. The book's added value (to re-angle one of Carson's terms) is its modeling of how poetry can enrich the traditional close reading forms of the essay and the lecture.

Like *Short Talks* or "The Life of Towns" poem sequences before it, and like so much of Carson's writing in its wake, *Economy of the Unlost* begins with an intervention of the kind that, in the early poem "Now What?" she calls *scholia*: prefatory or appendix material whose traditional function is to tell us what is going on in the work it adjoins.⁵ With its paratactic jumps between Simonides and Celan and a constellatory structure of sub-headings, not unlike the chapters of *Eros the Bittersweet* a decade earlier, *Economy of the Unlost* is an academic prose essay and an unorthodox one for several reasons—not least among them, the pairing of two authors writing more than two millennia apart. This chapter will begin, then, with the *scholia* Carson adds to her essay: the "Note on Method" in which she introduces her singular work of reading, and the "Prologue: False Sail."

The first words of *Economy of the Unlost* take the form of an epigraph from Friedrich Hölderlin's river poem, "The Rhine": *Nur hat ein jeder sein Maas*—"Yet each of us has his measure."⁶ The line looks forward to the contracted "measure" of verse economy in both Simonides and Celan, but the measure alluded to in the "Note on Method" also refers unequivocally to Carson's own writing. In classicist Steven Willett's remarks on the essay, the "Note on Method" tells us "that Carson must go her own way according to her own individual standards."⁷ What she describes is a deliberate measuring off of her experience of and attention to "facts," whose names and activity are "noted down," she tells us, and the complementary act of excision she calls the "clearing" of "everything I do not know." This act of measuring is figured using an image from the Hungarian philosopher and critic, György Lukács—*Eine fensterlose Monade* ("a windowless monad").⁸ Carson's disquisition on the image begins with the strong, self-exposing declaration, "There is too much self in my writing," and is followed by a halting stream of caveats. She describes a long struggle to push her thought into "the landscape of science and fact where other people converse logically"; for her, Carson says, writing is a constant "dashing back and forth" between "that darkening landscape where facticity is strewn and a windowless room cleared of everything I do not know." She speaks of her task as copying the names and noting the activity of all that remains in the "windowless room," then she wonders how the "clearing" actually happens:

> Lukács says it begins with my intent to excise everything that is not accessible to the immediate experience (*Erlebbarkeit*) of the self as self. Were this possible, it would seal the room on its own boundaries like a cosmos. Lukács is prescribing a room for aesthetic work; it would be a gesture of false consciousness to say academic writing can take place there. And yet, you know as well as I, thought finds itself in this room in its best moments—
>
> locked inside its own pressures, fishing up facts of the landscape from notes or memory as well as it may—vibrating (as Mallarme would say) with their disappearance. (vii)

Perhaps the most important takeaway from this extraordinary manifesto is the distinction it entertains, and, in the end, bypasses, between academic and aesthetic work. It is one of the most striking achievements of Carson's writing that such a distinction—between the academic and aesthetic as métiers with distinct sets of consequences for form—is shown to be a false choice. Our implicit agreement with Carson is taken for granted ("you know as well as I") that, were such a distinction meaningful to begin with, thought's "best moments" occur when it is disbanded. Carson's wide-open caesura, the line break left ajar after "best moments—," seems almost to measure out in the mise-en-page the fleeting contours of a "room" of our own, vibrating with possibility alongside Carson's. These "best moments" are what we find compressed in the lapidary microlectures of *Short Talks*, whose associative readings are cut loose from constraints of historical fact; in the absence of facts, the edges of these moments—whose affiliation to "aesthetic work" is clearer and sharper than *Economy of the Unlost*— "shine," in the words of one reviewer.[9] Directly addressed to her readers, Carson's brief performative vignette not only makes us Carson's accomplices in reading. The "Note on Method," locked in stylistic "pressures" of its own, introduces *Economy of the Unlost* as a work cognizant from the start of the origins and potential destinies of its own aesthetic gestures.

Striking, too, is the relationship Carson claims to "facts," "activity," and "names." For one, Carson reduces her entire critical agency to the actions of "copy[ing] down the names of everything left in [the room] and not[ing] their activity" or "fishing up facts of the landscape from notes or memory"; "once cleared," she tells us, the room for aesthetic work simply "writes itself."[10] The act of copying down also has an important antecedent in *Short Talks*, a book that begins with its own statement of intent and an admission that its work is to "copy out everything that was said . . . things vast distances apart."[11] Second, of equal importance to these "names and activity" is their arising out of what Carson calls the "vibration" of their aftermath, trailing the "disappearance" of thought's "best moments." Setting the scene for the essay that follows it, the "Note on Method" declares absence, negativity, the invisible, and the immaterial as the conditions of all poetic affirmation. The economical poems of Simonides and Celan, Carson will argue, plumb the dialectical capacity of language to pull on precisely this kind of felt vibration of absence, much in the way "unlost"—Celan's *unverloren*—marshals a vibration of "lost" (*verloren*). (Whether you call this form of saying "a waste of words or an act of grace," Carson says, "depends on you," 121.) Carson's introduction to the work recalls Hans Georg Gadamer's own lyrical admission that in his readings of Celan, he took to the facts of the poems "without any scholarly aid": "I lay in a sand pit in the Dutch dunes and mulled the verses over, 'listening earnestly in the damp wind,' until I thought I understood them. Of course," Gadamer continues, "it is an entirely different question to what extent exegetical words can represent such an encounter without diminishing it."[12] Carson's "Note"—and indeed, the entire essay—could almost be seen to respond to Gadamer's "different question" head-on. For what she suggests she will do in the essay is represent the "encounter," not by exegetical words alone, but by the same material and immaterial conditions of affirmation she ascribes to the poetry—naming activity and "vibrating" with the disappearance of thoughts and verbal facts. Carson declares her essay to be conditioned by more or less the same intuitive aesthetic "work" as her object of study, drawing on the generative capacities of absence and memory.

The "Note on Method," then, offers an argument for why we can read *Economy of the Unlost* alongside less formally conventional Carson "essays" like *The Albertine Workout*, whose form—a drastic hermeneutic minimalism, we saw—is explicitly conditioned by the copying down of facts in list form and the noting of their activity, afterimages, and lacunae in the appendices.[13] Charting the disappearance of facts and the intuition of "what goes beyond them" is the work of *Nox*, Carson's glossary-translation and essay on Catullus poem 101, which stages an "encounter" between two very different languages for loss in the work of two very different elegies ("the last gift owed to death").[14] Carson's reasoning around the negative poetics of Simonides and Celan, along with the "copying" and "noting" work of her readings in *Economy of the Unlost*, makes this an essay that speaks amply to her wider concerns and compositional modes, as well as one that dissuades us in no uncertain terms from drawing any meaningful division between Carson's academic and aesthetic work. The close reading that follows this manifesto, we will see, is an object lesson in literary-critical "attention" unlocked from the tonal constraints of academic prose, a form of attention mimicking the kinds of affirmation it finds in poetry.

The "Note" is also, finally, where Carson sets out the rationale behind the "conversation" she stages between Celan and Simonides:

> Attention is a task we share, you and I. To keep attention strong means to keep it from settling. Partly for this reason I have chosen to talk about two men at once.... Moving and not settling, they are side by side in a conversation and yet no conversation takes place. (viii)

It may or may not be a coincidence that Carson couches her approach in the essay in such similar terms to those Celan uses to describe the "encounter" (*Begegnung*) staged by poetry: a mysterious form of proximity, movement "from a voice to a listening you," but also movement from "soliloquy" to "conversation." (Celan's preparatory notes for his speech sketch out the following scheme: "Direction (wherefrom, whereto), language → soliloquy → conversation.").[15] "Celan's lyrics," says John Felstiner, "seek 'an addressable thou'": sometimes addressable because "thou" or "you" is a known individual, as in the indelibly poignant "Epitaph for François," or the "you" and "your God" in "Zurich, at the Stork," dedicated to Nelly Sachs; at other times, because of an urgent, unshakeable faith that someone—"something indeterminable, present only because the speaker calls it *du*"—is there to receive it.[16] In the poetic encounter Celan describes in "The Meridian," as in the critical encounter Carson stages in *Economy of the Unlost*, voice approaches voice, but through no direct address; there is no audible conversation, no face to face meeting, but an askance proximity or oblique intimacy. The gifts transferred in Celan's conversation-that-is-not-one are, we saw, "gifts to the attentive." If for Celan, the conversation only happens because we are attentive to it, for Carson, the inverse is true; attention, strong attention, is a result of the conversation being staged. It is a strategy Carson will rehearse time and again, in verse and prose alike: in reading Sappho with Marguerite Porete and Simone Weil in *Decreation*, or Plato with Defoe in an early essay, with the same aim of staging unexpected lines of convergence and auguring errant, unforeseen destinies.[17]

Yet Carson, as well as hosting one conversation, also invites another, addressing her writing at several key moments in the book—"you know as well as I" is the first of these—to a "you" of her own. In the example above, the same attention that joins her to Simonides and to Celan, keeping them "from settling" and keeping her attention strong, it is suggested, also joins her to her readers. The intimations of the "Note on Method," which assumes Carson's own binding to a community of recipients, readers, and addressees, ask us to suspend our disbelief as we move through the essay, to ground our attention to its own professed "aesthetic work" in what we might call good faith. Regarding this kind of intangible bond as a condition of possibility for critical reading, like the bond that joins Simonides and Celan for the duration of the essay: to borrow from Carson's store of economic metaphors, we either buy it or we don't. Yet the economy of attention Carson makes the case for here, grounded in the supposition of good faith, echoes some of her early remarks on the essay form and the action of what she calls "grace." As poetry, for Celan, yields its gifts to the attentive, for Carson, the essay is—and invites—a comparable offering: "When you write an essay, you're giving a gift, it seems to me. You're giving this grace, as the ancients would say. A gift shouldn't turn back into the self and stop there . . . you take that gift and you do something with it . . . and that keeps it going."[18]

In her review of *Economy of the Unlost* for the *Chicago Review*, Danielle Allen called Carson's book "an act of grace."[19] In what follows, we will see how *Economy of the Unlost*, an essay about the gratuitous "grace" of poetry in two very different eras, enters into the texture of exchange by reciprocating certain material and immaterial qualities of the poems Carson reads and passing them on, keeping them going, in much the same way she sketches out her remarks on the essay as gift. Her confessional "Note on Method" warns us that the book is an unorthodox one in the relation it embarks on with its objects. Although she responds to her two authors in different ways, we will see how her essay on the gifts that poetry gives "for nothing" keeps those gifts in circulation in ways that suggest a critical practice committed to the gift economy of poetry, a homage or courtesy (what George Steiner calls "lexical *cortesia*") paid to the objects and source texts of criticism.[20]

Carson's book begins by exploring the distinction between gift and commodity economies, where the former trades in immediate equivalents, objects of commensurable value, and the latter through the mediation of a currency, breaking the through-line of relation from "you to you." A result, perhaps, of the hermetic ("windowless") relation she professed to sustain with her objects, the critical economy of Carson's reading is one in which the original "gift" is acknowledged, preserved, and reflected back in her response. The Marxian arguments she sets out in the book's opening chapters would suggest, by extension, that to dispense with the original gift by responding in an alien conceptual jargon—reading, as it were, for profit—would count as alienated reading. For Carson, Simonides changes the economy of poetry almost beyond recognition. The vocation of poetry has clearly proved a profitable one for Carson, yet the poetic economy of her reading turns the pre-Simonidean gift economy into a surprising expressional possibility for the relationships of criticism.

Xenia and Critical Economy

Carson's "you and I," a gesture of complicity appearing at several points in the book, is tied to a single, very specific moment of address. Like Celan's description of the channeling of voice from "you to you," delivered to an audience at the German Academy for Language and Poetry, Carson's address to "you" was first written for a time-bound occasion of public address. The text of *Economy of the Unlost* is a revised and significantly expanded version of Carson's Martin Classical Lectures, delivered at Oberlin College in 1992.[21] The Lectures in their original form were titled "Greed: A Fractal Approach to Simonides," a fact that makes two things immediately clear to readers of *Economy of the Unlost*. First, that the book's argument about grace and salvation is teased out of an argument about greed—the famed "stinginess of Simonides," as she puts it in chapter 1 ("Alienation," 10). Second, that Carson's reading of Celan, in the context of the book's backstory, starts out life as a reading of Simonides.[22] If one poet is placed so that the other comes into focus, it is Simonides who, through Carson's original lectures, becomes the backcloth or sounding board for Celan. And if Carson's reading of Simonides was given voice, a voice addressed to a listening public, at her Martin Classical Lectures, then it is curious that the palpable sense of voice in the expanded text—the distinctively rhythmic prosody of her prose writing—is significantly heightened in her readings of Celan. Reading Celan, we will see, Carson is more attuned not only to her own tonal poetics and vocal intonations, but more involved in and directly responsive to Celan's.

Carson's discussion of the advent of money in the gift economy of the Ancient Greek sixth century BC situates Simonides of Keos as the first "professional" poet—the first, that is, to charge money for his compositions. Simonides, Carson tells us, knew his price only too well: a character in Aristophanes's *Peace* exclaims "That Simonides would put out to sea on a bathmat for profit!"—just one example of Simonides's swift conversion into a comedy "stock type for avarice" following the poet's death in around 468 BC.[23] Carson grounds her presentation of Simonides's commodification of poetry in a Marxian disquisition on the "alienation" of objects, labor, social relations, and, in the new commerce of poetic composition, the gifts of *poiesis*: "To use Marx's terms, a commodity is an alienable object exchanged between two transactors enjoying a state of mutual independence, while a gift is an inalienable object exchanged between two reciprocally dependent transactors" (12). As Carson explains, objects in a gift economy are a kind of "connective tissue" between these reciprocally dependent transactors. The reciprocity of this connection, she says, is preserved in the "reversible terminology" in the Ancient Greek: "in Greek the word *xenos* can mean either guest or host, *xenia* either gifts given or gifts received" (18). The continuity of the gift given in the gift received, the recognition of the one in the other, recalls Carson's understanding (with its ethical overtones) of the essay as gift. Carson quotes Pierre Bourdieu on this form of mutual guarantee, which he calls "an act of communication":

> "Considered as an act of communication," says Pierre Bourdieu, "the gift is defined by the counter-gift in which it is completed and in which it realizes its full significance." Such an object carries the history of the giver into the life of the receiver and continues it there. (18)[24]

In the typical *xenia* economy, the gift given accrues a directly commensurable debt, producing a "connective tissue" of equity and identification between giver and receiver. Gifts exchanged between giver and receiver, guest and host, Carson says, create a direct equivalence expressed neatly in the reversible significance of *xenos*, a word whose two complementary functions are expressed under the same sign (as J. Hillis Miller famously explored in his defense of "the critic as host").[25] *Xenia*, likewise, refers interchangeably to gifts given and gifts received—gifts that, though materially different, are effectively worth the same. In spite of the required equivalence between parties in the *xenia* economy, the particularity of the gift itself—as Bourdieu's description suggests—is preserved: not only that; it is "completed," it "realizes its full significance," in the counter-gift. As an "act of communication"—as a *conversation*, we might say—the gift generates a refrain, a thread of continuity that the introduction of legal tender abruptly snaps.

Further into the essay, Carson discusses the customary use of *symbola*, equal halves of a single piece of bone cut in two and exchanged as a token between friends in certain *xenia* relationships. Symbolizing the relationship of equity, the *symbolon* allows the parties entering into the contract of *xenia* to renew and recapitulate their obligation.[26] "A gift" given under such a contract, Carson explains, "is not a piece broken off from the interior life of the giver and lost into the exchange, but rather an extension of the interior of the giver, both in space and time, into the interior of the receiver" (18). Symbol of this continuum—and what better than a piece of bone to signify the unspoken interior common to both parties?—the *symbolon* is by nature an incomplete object whose meaningfulness is conditional on the participation of another. Carson describes the *symbolon* in terms of what the exchanges under a monetary economy take away from it: "money denies such extension, ruptures continuity and stalls objects at the borders of themselves. Abstracted from space and time as bits of saleable value, they become commodities and lose their life as objects" (18).

Where *symbola* express the direct commensurability of obligations and of gifts—where one is a direct recognition of the other, the sign of a direct, unmediated connection in which the object's value and "life" are maintained—commodification is the process of substituting that value for another with little or no essential relation to it (the interior "life" of bone for a beaten piece of metal). The implication is, Carson argues, that what is extinguished along with this form of life is "its power to connect the people who give and receive it: they become like commodities themselves, fragments of value waiting for price and sale" (19). While the bone *symbolon* is still a *symbol*, a mediating sign like the metal coin in the monetary economy, its specificity of meaning travels directly between two—unlike the impersonal, universal grammar of coinage. Like two equal *symbola*, in the *xenia* economy the gift is recognized and preserved in the counter-gift as the recognition of debt and bond; rather like the way language (*langue*), an objective system of mediating signs, can in its mode of address (*parole*) preserve the intimacy of private conversation (and with it, in Carson's words, the "non-objective life of objects"). It is tempting to imagine—if again we suspend our disbelief—that words in the pre-Simonidean gift economy were always such gifts.[27] We have only to think of Odysseus, whose way with words gets him payment in kind, in the form of words of praise, fame, and feats of belief.[28]

Carson's argument draws its notion of the gift and its reciprocity in the *xenia* economy from Marcel Mauss's seminal study, *The Gift*, and from later anthropological works by Pierre Bourdieu, M. M. Austin and Pierre Vidal-Naquet, and Ian Morris.[29] The gift is a concept Jacques Derrida sought to destabilize in his Carpenter Lectures, published as *Given Time* in 1992, by arguing that the gift is locked in an impossible bind: as the gift is pulled into a circuit of exchange and restitution—as it creates a debt—it can no longer be understood as a gift. To be a gift, that is, the given object must remain outside the order of the gift, for its recognition as such immediately creates the expectation of a counter-gift and the tension of indebtedness.[30] The gift is destroyed, for Derrida, by the demand it creates for reciprocity: as such, the genuine gift would require the giver to remain anonymous, to give in the abstract with no hope of profit or direct return. Yet if we think about the kinds of gift both Celan and Carson invoke in their remarks on the poem and the essay, respectively—gifts in the form of written words and inner or spoken voice—we can see how such gifts might be gratuitous in this absolute and necessary sense. Directed to readers beyond number, the address of these gifts is anonymous: the gifts of authorship, intimate but impersonal, bring with them the "destruction of every voice, every point of origin," in Barthes's well-known expression.[31] (On the gift, Barthes says "any ethic of purity requires that we detach the gift from the hand which gives or receives it.")[32] To read is to pick up the echo of an original, in an anonymous exchange with its author and point of origin. Like the relationship Carson stages between Simonides and Celan in her book, author and reader, likewise, have no claim on one another. No actual "conversation" occurs; rather their "encounter" takes place by way of a great, un-chartable detour of voice from "you to you." For Mauss, the lapse of time between the gift and the counter-gift was its fundamental structuring principle; for Derrida, this delay or deferral is the condition of possibility for the genuine gift—the gift released from its bonds. A gift of language comes with this delay inbuilt. This intimate, impersonal system of symbols makes for gifts unbound, addressed to particular and universal recipients at the very same time. As Celan's continuous "you to you" suggests, the impossibility of final, total direct address makes the poem the gift that keeps on giving.

When the poem's gift is received in a critical reading, what kind of relation—what kind of "economy"—is set in motion? Carson explains that Marx compared the monetary economy not to the function of language but to that of translated language: "ideas which have first to be translated out of their mother tongue into a foreign language in order to circulate, in order to become exchangeable.... So the analogy lies not in language but in the foreign quality or strangeness (*Fremdheit*) of language" (28). Carson makes this the foundation of her reading of Celan in Part I of *Economy of the Unlost*, a poet who, she says, echoing John Felstiner's reading, "uses language as if he were always translating" (28).[33] Celan's poetry, that is, assumes something is lost in the exchange and plumbs it to express a loss inhering in all language. Translation is, of course, one of the principal routes by which poems arrive at new and unforeseeable destinies, together with a new strangeness in themselves; the distant closeness of the translated poem to its original is a complex form of self-relation that Carson's own translations tense to its limits. In Carson's version of events in the "Note on Method," her tendency is toward a hermetic, unmediated relation to her interpretive objects, copying down names and noting their activity, where copying down is a means of preserving the original terms, *symbolon* to *symbolon*, or, as Barthes wrote of the critic's task, orienting his language toward the language of his object ("*The symbol must go and seek the symbol*").[34] Translating Celan's poems is one way in which his original prosodic gifts are returned. His assumed German is given to Carson's English; her English is, in turn, made to preserve the powerful encounter with Celan's German: a preservation and a form of reversibility that Walter Benjamin called the task of the translator.[35] In her commentary on Celan's poems, Carson seeks to achieve just such a preservation—to extend his poem's gifts into those of her reading.

For both Simonides and Celan, as Carson sees it, the economy of a poem is its capacity to produce and sustain an extraordinary surplus of meaning in the shortest duration and out of the most reduced of material conditions. Where Simonides's poetic economy is a more literal measure of the space and time taken up by a composition, Celan's responds to drastic curtailment and immeasurable loss as the measure against which words, even single letters, are weighed.[36] The surplus value of the poem—its grace, so to speak—is both "given" and "possible," radiating as possibility in excess of written grammars. Simonides and Celan are thrifty poets, says Carson, because they squeeze more out of less. Where Simonides mostly relies on syntax, parataxis, and the juxtaposition of scenarios to sustain these excesses, limited by the constraints of lapidary space in the case of his epitaphs, Celan's more radical verbal thrift has consequences for the autonomy and integrity of individual words. The most vivid moments of Carson's reading of Celan are counter-gifts that, preserving the original, keep Celan's gifts in circulation. Out of an argument about poetic value and gift exchange comes a critical practice that reads "with" Celan, responding to his prosody in kind.

Prosody as Conversation

The final lines of the "Note on Method" offer a theory of the encounter staged in Carson's essay:

> Think of the Greek preposition πρός. When used with the accusative case, this preposition means "toward, upon, against, with, ready for, face to face...." It is the preposition chosen by John the Evangelist to describe the relationship between God and The Word in the first verse of the first chapter of his Revelation:
>
> πρὸς Θεόν

"And The Word was with God" is how the usual translation goes. What kind of withness is it? (viii)

The covenant between God and Word is evoked here as the most acute vibration of the preposition "with" in the mind of the author, who ends her impressionistic "Note" with a fleeting image of wild horses daubing up the banks of a train line. This particular vibration of "with," together with the idiosyncratic variant "withness," is significant not just in the context of the "conversation" staged in *Economy of the Unlost* but throughout Carson's work.[37] The Word *with* God describes a relationship in which difference and identity—the Word both *with* God and *was* God—are not paradoxical. Her exploration of "withness" has a curious history prior to its appearance here, including in the early poem "God's Christ Theory," as André Furlani has shown.[38] We can add to these iterations the term's later appearance in *Decreation*, where Carson riffs on Marguerite Porete's idiosyncratic use of the preposition "with" (discussed in Chapter 6 of this book), and her recent "Short Talk on the Withness of the Body," published in the *Float* pamphlet series.[39] Furlani notes the proximity of Carson's "with" in *Economy of the Unlost* to Celan's *Begegnung* (encounter) and perhaps also, through Celan, to Heidegger's *Mitsein* or Being-With.[40] Carson reads Simonides "with" Celan, her book's subtitle tells us. Yet in the many precarious forms of difference and identity that emerge in her readings, scholarship, and translation, the following chapters propose that Carson seeks out other forms of writing "with" her objects—thinking of Emily Brontë in "The Glass Essay," John Keats in *The Beauty of the Husband*, or Catullus in *Nox*. So, if one aslant, ahistorical "conversation" joins Simonides with Celan, "what kind of withness" (as Furlani has asked) joins Celan and Carson?

Carson's readings of Celan, I'd like to suggest, preserve and answer the refrains of Celan's contracted verse in remarkable ways. Amplifying the forms she attends to in Celan, the surplus value of Carson's prose—its immaterial, paralinguistic qualities, with and against its verbal materiality, and its elaborate symbolism—responds to Celan as sound, image, and rhythm, radiating and expanding beyond the syntactic measure of her sentences. In what Steven Willett calls "a sort of metaphysical trial by poem," Carson's opening reading of Celan's "Matière de Bretagne" jettisons "the normal meanings of words," Willett says, in favor of intersecting allusions that respond to or play along with her principal preoccupations in the essay: "what exactly is lost to us when words are wasted? And where is the human store to which such words are gathered?" (3).[41] Willett's is a fair judgment, assuming that what we—and Carson—are looking for in poetry, and looking to track down in poetry criticism, are "the normal meanings of words." If Carson's readings invite us to suspend our disbelief (as her "Note on

Method" seems to suggest), it is in order that we might credit that what interests Carson is the "waste" product of words: the excess of "normal meanings" gathered up and returned in the gifts of poems, redoubled in the symbolism and stylistics of Carson's reading.

Willett critiques *Economy of the Unlost* on several grounds, largely philological, but he also nurses a particular dislike of Carson's prose: "there is no thought in this book to justify the prose," he says, "which no one could confuse with poetry."[42] The philological and biographical weaknesses Willett points out in Carson's essay would certainly weaken its case, were her case for poetic economy built on an appeal to fact; were *Economy of the Unlost* a theory of the trafficking of tangible elements in poetry and its material history. Yet as we saw in the "Note on Method," in place of facticity, Carson appeals instead to what "vibrat[es]" in the absence or aftermath of facts. At key moments, such as the excerpt below, instead of meticulous exposition of the poem's philological facts, Carson's impressionistic prose daubs its colors and tonalities in a close reading that serves more to echo and reproduce how she sees and hears a poem than to tell us what *the poem* does and has done historically. Writing *with* Celan, Carson critical poetics preserve the tonal, rhythmic, and syntactic afterimage of his writing, responding on his poem's terms and, as an excess function of criticism—reading to "realize" his original gifts.[43] In this, we will now see, the prosody of the essay certainly can be "confuse[d] with poetry."

Celan's "Matière de Bretagne" zooms in on the dénouement of the romance of Tristan and Isolt (Carson's spelling), the moment Carson calls the "false sail." In this classic *Trauerspiel* of signs, whose central trope is first employed by Simonides of Keos, Carson tells us, there is an agreement between Tristan and the ship's helmsman about the color of the sails to be flown: white if the ship carries Isolt (or, in a variant on the legend, "for Isolt prospering") or black if it sails empty ("a black sail for her catastrophe," as Carson has it).[44] In the event, however, the color reported to Tristan by his jealous wife is the wrong one: this "false sail" is "blacker than a mulberry" (7). As Carson points out, the question of whether the catalyst twisting the tale toward tragedy is a deceitful act of telling, or simply a case of the wrong sail flown, remains unresolved in the Old French version of the romance, to which Celan's title clearly alludes. Taking up the old legend, Celan's poem reroutes its signifiers, its symbolic *matière*, through the terrain of a dream: "there is blood in the old French version but only dreamblood," says Carson, whose compound noun harmonizes and pays homage to Celan's signature contractions (*Sprachgitter, Tausendwort,* etc.) "As Tristan lies dying, Isolt out at sea recalls dreaming that she held in her lap the head of a boar that was staining her all over with its blood and making her robe red" (7). In an image appearing in the first and penultimate stanzas, Celan charts the course of a "bloodsail" [*Blutsegel*], ineluctable in its rhythmic progress as in the destruction it heralds. The poem's opening stanza, reproduced below in Celan's original and Carson's translation, pulls us into the whorl of the ship's approach to land:[45]

MATIÈRE DE BRETAGNE	MATIÈRE DE BRETAGNE
Ginsterlicht, gelb, die Hänge	Gorselight, yellow, the slopes
eitern gen Himmel, der Dorn	suppurate to heaven, the thorn
wirbt um die Wunde, es läutet	pays court to the wound, there is ringing
darin, es ist Abend, das Nichts	inside, it is evening, the nothing
rollt seine Meere zur Andacht,	rolls its seas toward devotion,
das Blutsegel hält auf dich zu.	the bloodsail is heading for you.

An earlier translation of this stanza by Michael Hamburger opens with the same line in English, and his version of Celan's inland call, *es läutet / darin* ("bells ring / within"), holds phonetically close to it, and provides a more concrete reference for the church where the "service" (*Andacht*, Carson's less tangible "devotion") is being held.[46] Yet what Carson's translation preserves that Hamburger's sometimes surprisingly dispenses with is the rhythmic progress that gives sensible form to the ship's approach. Hamburger's "the thorn / woos the wound" (*der Dorn / wirbt um die Wunde*), compared with Carson's "the thorn / pays court to the wound," drops the dactyl, the momentum that holds this, as well as earlier and later lines in the poem, on the same impervious course of destiny. It is a metrical stroke that cuts along some of the darkest moments in Celan's verse, thinking of the opening strains of the "Death Fugue" ("Todesfuge"): "Black milk of daybreak we drink it at sundown . . . / we drink and we drink it" (*Schwarze Milch der Frühe wir trinken sie abends . . . / wir trinken und trinken*).[47] As we move through the poem, the significance of the approaching sail finds itself "run aground," Celan's poem suggests, in its own human consequences: "Dry, run aground / is the bed behind you, caught in rushes" (*Trocken, verlandet / das Bett hinter dir, verschilft*). Out of this stuck semaphore, Celan directs a single, repeated question to the body and its labor to understand and be understood; in the third stanza, "Did you know me, / hands? . . . / did you know me?" (*Kanntet ihr mich, / Hände? . . . / kanntet ihr mich?*). These are labors that pass, in Hamburger's and Carson's translations, from one poet's hands to another's. The poem, as if regardless, labors its own ineluctable course, with Celan's dactyls relentless on the trail of human error (*Trocken, verlandet / das Bett hinter dir . . .*).

Carson introduces the poem as a story of signification gone awry, a semaphore lost in the translation of fact into apprehension. Beyond her translation of the poem, responding to Celan, Carson also draws the poem's errant semaphore into her reading. Her remarks on the poem cling close to its verbal facts, its mythic and symbolic economies, but they also seem guided by those facts' radiation in rhythm and tonal color. Benjamin insisted that translation give voice "to the *intentio* of the original not as reproduction but as harmony."[48] His observation, too, that "a real translation is transparent, it does not cover the original, does not block its light" offers us a way of thinking about Carson's prose as a secondary act of translation, with the same "transparency" she aspires to in *If Not, Winter*.[49] For Celan's prosody shines through in Carson's close readings, which seek apparently to harmonize with his original. Or, to extend Carson's own metaphors in the reading, her prose is stained through with the poem it presses against ("the redness of [Celan's] red sail stains fact deeply," 9). Carrying the impression of Celan, her writing reads like its translucent afterimage, whose sound vibrates after the end of the poem. Reading the lines "But what sails toward devotion is the Nothing" and "All these fluent traditions run aground . . . dry, stuck on land, lodged in rushes, bushed up, jabbering mud" at the start of her response to "Matière de Bretagne" (6), we might have to pinch ourselves to wake from the poem's own gorse-lit dream. Carson's reading also buoys on Celan's meter, along the iambs that pull against the central dactylic current, which she sends pulsing out in her prose: "the poem has the rhythm of a bloodsail, sailing forward in waves from gorselight to gorselight to you" (6).[50] Rolling on the poem's metrical current, Carson's prose recapitulates and halts at the composite nouns "dreamblood" and "bloodsail," performing a verbal coagulation after Celan's *Blutsegel* and the lambent *Ginsterlicht* (Gorselight), with which the difficult ebb and flow of "Matière de Bretagne"—the catching, jabbering, and eventual running aground of its symbols and refrains—begins:

Hände, die dorn-	Hands, the thorn-
umworbene Wunde, es läutet,	courted wound, there is ringing,
Hände, das Nichts, seine Meere,	hands, the nothing, its seas,
Hände, im Ginsterlicht, das	hands, in the gorselight, the
Blutsegel	bloodsail
hält auf dich zu.	is heading for you.

In a remarkably vivid sense, then, Celan's poem seems to "happen again" in the prosody of Carson's close reading. It is a form of reading that asks us, Carson's readers, to stake a certain faith on its iterations of Celan, its economical harmonies, and its transparency: for the very closeness to Celan that allows Carson to perform the sensations of his prosody in her own, is also where reciprocity and performance come closest to imitation. To be sure, while a risky move for most academic critics, echoing Celan is a seductive way for another poet, a poet-essayist, to read him. It also raises important questions about what these prosodic harmonies achieve that other forms of critical textuality ignore or avoid outright: identification, sensual affect, self-relation, but also a reckoning with their own authority, grandiosity, and desire. Celan's poem ends up appearing momentarily to read itself—to read itself aloud, at any rate—inside the impressionistic echo of Carson's writing. What are the desires moving this return of the poem's gifts? A desire to keep Celan going, as Carson wished to do with Proust? A desire to participate more fully in—rather than to record, comment on, or even short-circuit—the "conversation" of reading? Carson's sensible forms make for a mode of reading that depends on the reader and his solitary sounding of her prose; whose echo of Celan depends, like his original, on any number of tonal, material, and psychic contingencies. Where a descriptive exposition of Celan's poem might aim to enumerate its gifts and track them to an acute textual point of origin, the harmonically close reading is, at the same time, perhaps, intended to amplify an original sensation of the poem: its imitation crafted as a performance in which the poem's score is played ("happens again") in a series of variations on the original, in which the original continues to scan.

Inside Celan's aural palette and still plumbing its dactyls, Carson remarks: "the redness of [Celan's] red sail stains fact deeply with the fixative of counterfact. Redder than red, redder than the blood of a boar in a dream" (9). The reading's job here is to pull us back once more into the poem's currents (as Carson hears them at the time of her writing): to hold us in the red so that we see only red. Carson's symbolism of the "blood of a boar in a dream" is a *symbolon* to match Celan's *Blutsegel*, a gift that reciprocates the original and bears it toward new destinies. A gift from "you to you," and through another conversation in which no conversation takes place, Celan's poem is realized anew in a counter-gift that amplifies and spreads its color, pulsing to the rhythms of its source.

In the context of Carson's writing to date, it might be reasonable to ask, finally, if this imitative counter-song is a form of pastiche, or even, at moments, a parody of Celan. (For Linda Hutcheon, in *A Theory of Parody*, neither form requires an intent to ridicule; where pastiche seeks similarity of tone, form, and genre, the critical métier of parody "allows for adaptation" and "transformation" of its model).[51] It is a question we might do better to leave open: better to enjoy the tonal ambiguity of Carson's relationship to Celan, which slides lyrically between intimate identification and critical distance. Hutcheon notes of parody that the word's etymology contains the same ambiguity. *Parodia*—a compound of *para* and *odos*—is usually understood to mean "counter-song," yet Hutcheon draws closer attention to the prefix *para*—as Carson does to the preposition πρὸς (*pros*) in the "Note on Method," whose rich connotation covers the same ground ("toward, upon, against, with . . ."). *Para* is "counter" or "against," from which derives the ironic, distancing capacity of the parody; but it is also "beside" ("there is a suggestion of an accord or intimacy instead of a contrast").[52] Singing with Celan is, here, a way of singing against the current: singing, that is, with a critical difference.

We, You, Us

Readers of her extraordinary essay will know that it is not only by extending his poems' tonal and metrical refrains that Carson writes *with* Celan. For all that her register and stylistics lean into Celan's, her thinking, too, circles inside and mimics the logics she perceives in his writing, beginning with his rendition of the "false sail" story. As Carson traces the structural geometries of "Matière de Bretagne," her reflections follow the contours of Celan's "circle of great lyrical beauty, lit by gorselight, around Nothingness" (8), around that vanishing point where the poem meets its destinies in the life of "you," the universal reader. Carson moves through the poem's "you" toward a "you" whom she addresses directly, appropriating Celan's abstract "you" as her own personal addressee. Celan's poem, she says, "gathers us into a movement—toward you—that sails to the end. But you, by the time we reach you, are just folding yourself away into a place we cannot go: sleep." Celan's "you" is elided into Carson's, who, too, is no sooner reached than folded into oblivion:

> We travel toward your crisis, we arrive, yet we cannot construe it—the terrible thing is, after all (and most economically!) we are the false sail for which you wait. (9)

The striking gesture here is Carson's positioning of herself among the "us" and "we" of Celan's readers, who are also, in this case, her own readers. "You" (the "you" of "Did you know me, / hands?" but also the final line of "Matière de Bretagne," "you teach your hands / to sleep") remains impersonal, a figure for the autonomous, unconscious course of writing, as well, perhaps, as its destiny in the abstract—a reader, "the" reader in waiting. At the same time, what begins to take shape here is a clear identification of the author of *Economy of the Unlost* with Celan, both of whom share this "you" as their delayed addressee. These rhetorical moves—which scan as both humbly confessional and high-flown—continue a refrain that begins in the essay's opening pages, where Carson throws down a more direct comparison:

> His biographers recount that when the poet Paul Celan was four years old, he took a notion to make up his own fairy tales. He went about telling these new versions to everyone in the house until his father advised him to cut it out. "If you need stories the Old Testament is full of them." To make up new stories,

> Celan's father thought, is a waste of words. This father's sentiments are not unusual. My own father was inclined to make sceptical comments when he saw me hunched at the kitchen table covering pages with small print. Perhaps poets are ones who waste what their fathers would save. (3)

Were the "Note on Method" not a clear enough confession of a poet writing criticism, these twin vignettes remind us in no uncertain terms that what we are reading is the response of one poet to another: poets whose adult thrift and childhood excesses with words are exercised under the conviction that something—though things incomparably different—needs to be saved, salvaged, even reinvented. On a superficial level, the gesture recalls what Carson does in "The Glass Essay" in relation to Emily Brontë, comparing and contrasting anecdotes from the two writers' lives in a reading that is also, at the same time, a scholar's confession; or in relation to Weil in the title essay of *Decreation*, where Carson recounts trying to eat the pages of her childhood copy of *The Lives of the Saints*.[53] If we were to speak of what Carson and Celan share that Carson and Simonides do not, beyond the obvious, more radical difference in historical contexts, perhaps it would be useful to speak of a belief that the economy of poetry, its destiny and ability to "save," lies somewhere outside the poem. Where Simonides stakes his poetry on the measurable material dimensions of its writing, Celan stakes his on their vanishing point, measuring off the written to give voice to something beyond it: in Carson's words, to "measure out the area of the given and the possible" (118). The poem is saved, for Celan, by being realized—its gifts continually received—elsewhere.

Returning to Steven Willett's critique of what he calls the "slapdash" quality of Carson's comparative essay: where Carson shows inconsistent concern for textual evidence and historical fact, as Willett has argued, or where her readings are arguably more "spurious" (his word) is, perhaps surprisingly, in relation to Simonides.[54] Carson the classicist is, Willett says, "much more careful about hewing to biographical fact with Celan, who is too near us in time for the same treatment [she gives Simonides]."[55] He proposes that behind this imparity, and behind Carson's speculative readings of unreliable ancient *testimonia*, apocryphal stories, or philological ambiguity, is "a Foucauldian game [played] with her readers: the poet as author is everything that the tradition says he is. We can, as it were, roll all the disparate traditions, both the true and false, the probable and improbable, into one lump and apply it en masse to the ancient poet."[56] As the accrual and transfer of "both true and false, the probable and improbable," the Foucauldian function of tradition in Willett's critique is temptingly close to that of the gift economy, in which "grace" (the intangible "life" of tangible objects) is accumulated and moved through words and deeds. Each act of "grace" carries the residue of those before it, bearing with it both things present and things absent, facts and apocryphal stories. Carson pretty much spells out in the "Note on Method" that her reading of Simonides with Celan will not only be about the relation of facticity to the vibration felt in its absence—about the negative dialectics Celan's *unverloren* was crafted to perform—but that her inquiry will be guided by "the immediate experience (*Erlebbarkeit*) of the self as self" and cleared "of what I do not know": a manifesto for the subjective lyricism excoriated by Willett in his opening remarks on Carson's essay. This "immediate experience" undoubtedly includes the excesses of autobiographical identification ("too much self in my writing") and the squaring of her own strictures as a poet with those of Paul Celan, "poet of nothingness" after Mallarmé.[57] The "Foucauldian game" that Willett describes is precisely how Carson constructs and stages her own relationship to tradition: the splaying of affiliations and identifications that makes Carson, in a sense, everything she says she is—both the true and the false. This self-situating performance, I suggested in the Introduction, is one we believe in if and because we want to. Its implications for our task as her readers will be followed through what remains of this book.

Carson's performance of a mind "locked inside its own pressures," its "best moments" addressed to "a listening you" or a "you" whose voice it returns and whose tradition it all but professes to continue, is a risky mode for the straight-up scholarly essay. That it keels to a "lyric" mode—as per Culler's "iterative and iterable performance"—almost doesn't need stating.[58] Yet *Economy of the Unlost* models qualities of attention and transmission that have much to offer the prevailing culture of academic writing, with its conventions of address, its sanctioned emotional and "conversational" range, and its unofficial locks on style and form. If Carson's "aesthetic work" models the kind of poetic license only granted to poets writing criticism, then it also holds a question mark over the kinds of textuality and interpretive gesture functionally excluded from mainstream academic criticism (tonally mimetic, passionately close readings; comparative formalism against watertight literary historicism, not to speak of confessional "notes on method"). The decision of Princeton University Press to publish the work, more than a decade after publishing *Eros the Bittersweet*, suggests its editors chose to take Carson at her word regarding the nature and aspirations of her essay:

> writing involves some dashing back and forth between that darkening landscape where facticity is strewn and a windowless room cleared of everything I do not know ... it would be a gesture of false consciousness to say academic writing can take place there. And yet, you know as well as I, thought finds itself in this room in its best moments—

Carson's gamble in *Economy of the Unlost* is to open a place for this precarious, interim form of academic writing, a writing conscious of the "back and forth" between *Erlebbarkeit* and "the landscape of science and fact where other people converse logically and exchange judgements." Her poetic exchanges with Celan perform the real-time experience of one poet appraising and identifying with another. Celan himself put poetry's work—intimate as well as historic—to the test like perhaps no other poet before him (his question, as Carson has it, is "do words hold good?"). In working this question from the beginnings of poetry as written medium to her own incomparably different present, and in staging this particular destiny of his poetic gift, Carson offers a window onto that "windowless room." Hers is a scholarly account whose confessional transparency—in order for the book to work—we must take at its word.

Toward the end of the essay, finally, Carson explains the difference between Celan and Simonides in terms of one key emotion.

> We have seen Simonides estranged from his fellows on account of this condition; we have seen him recognize, resent and negotiate his estrangement; we have seen him transform it into a poetic method of luminous and precise economy. We have not seen him despair. (121)

Simonides does not despair, Carson suggests, because in his poetic economy, Simonides himself is not at stake. Writing does not put him on the line—and putting yourself on the line, she says of the *xenia* relationship, is the true meaning of "piety" (20). She tells us at the top of the same page that "a poet's despair is not just personal; he despairs of the word and that implicates all our hopes. Every time a poet writes a poem he is asking the question, Do words hold good? And the answer *has to be yes*: it is the contrafactual condition on which a poet's life depends." The cycle seems to be intractable: the word is at risk because the poet despairs of it, and in turn, she claims, we ourselves are at risk because the word is. But the book's penultimate paragraph appears to throw us a lifeline:

> Every praise poem is a presentiment of itself—a neologism that throws itself forward into song to whoever will complete it by seeing and hearing it, by taking it into their mind or heart. A praise poet has to construct fast, in the course of each song, this community that will receive the song. (133)

So the praise poem is not realized ("complete") until it is seen, heard, and "taken into" whosoever returns its compliment. It is only a praise poem, not a presentiment of one, when the community it anticipates receives its grace. Yet it is also, emphatically, a community the poet has to "construct": to pre-empt and play to in ways we will see Carson do throughout this book; to address as well as hear in the textures of her song.[59] Carson's appraisal of Celan "with" Simonides assumes and awaits a similar community, to seal its work of praise and keep in circulation what it has salvaged. Carson confesses to her readers elsewhere in the book, "There is no evidence of salvation except a gold trace in the mind" (95). Reading by gold trace, reading by echo, residue, and radiance, glinting off personal memory, is a response to texts that, however pleasingly economical, flaunts its own absolute dependence on the reader. Like the true gift in Derrida's conception of it, criticism as counter-gift gives over its own immaterial gifts without knowing to whom they are passed on, or to what or whom exactly they are indebted. The gold trace spreads in the form of an incantation, a presentiment of something to come.

PART II
GLASS ESSAYS

3
On Not Being Emily Brontë

In his brief introduction to *Glass, Irony and God*, the poet and scholar Guy Davenport relates how Carson's 1995 collection first came into being. The founding editor at New Directions, James Laughlin, "saw Anne Carson for what she is: a real poet whose poems are unfailingly memorable," Davenport tells us. Memorable though the poems are, Davenport's introduction to Carson's book only exists, it turns out, because "Laughlin thought 'she needs explaining.'"*[1] Though Davenport will disagree with this verdict—"I don't think she needs explaining at all"—he couldn't have chosen a more suggestive opening appeal than the question of explanation. Whether or not we think her work does need explaining, we would be hard pushed to find a poet who *explains herself* more often, with greater rigor, and with greater irony than Carson: a poet whose poems hijack, and return transfigured, the expository purposes of the essay; whose writing models a critical register seamlessly turned back on itself; and a poet, for that matter, in whose work the power of what *resists* explanation—"what facts lack" or where language "goes dark"—is a source of painstakingly declared interest. Perhaps Laughlin felt that Carson's explanations were part, too, of what needed accounting for; that the relationship between poetry, scholarship, and self-reading in Carson, the concerted transparency that follows and frames her complexity, was itself far from straightforward.

Glass, Irony and God opens with the acclaimed narrative poem, "The Glass Essay," whose thirty-eight pages of unrhyming tercets and quatrains, divided into irregular sections of between three and seventy-six stanzas, interweave an account of loneliness and loss with passages and vignettes from the life and work of Emily Brontë. A winding lyric confession whose form and first-person voice bind it to poetry, "The Glass Essay" is also a reading of Brontë's biography, her writing, and her critical reception. It is an essay in the sense that D'Agata and Tall say the so-called "lyric essay," for all its poetic "shapeliness," bespeaks an "overt desire to engage with facts"; in the case of "The Glass Essay," to engage with the verbal facts and anecdotes of the Brontë oeuvre.[2] It also resonates with the way in which Carson says *The Beauty of the Husband* is an essay: "a reflection on [the] story" to which these facts are brought to bear.[3] Carson's poem-essay, in this particular sense, tells two stories at once, conflated, says Davenport, "with Tolstoyan skill": the story of a love affair's end and aftermath, where the narrator has traveled to stay with her mother (who, like Haworth-born Brontë, "lives on a moor

Anne Carson. Elizabeth Sarah Coles, Oxford University Press. © Oxford University Press 2023.
DOI: 10.1093/oso/9780197680919.003.0004

in the north"); and the story woven out of her reflections on Brontë's life and writing—Brontë, who is referred to and addressed in the poem as "Emily."[4]

In "The Glass Essay," critical, biographical, and autobiographical impulses pull together in the transcribing of this unlikely accompaniment. As Carson explains at the start of the poem-essay, this is a reading arising from a deep personal identification, an involuntary analogy between Emily and the narrator that leads the latter to announce: "I feel I am turning into Emily Brontë" (1). Facts from Brontë's life and writing, recovered and pored over by the narrator, are summoned during the work against a long-standing tradition of reading Brontë as a case of creative subjection heedless of its scope, origins, and violence; an author stricken by a poetic impulse that, in Carson's paraphrase, "she could neither understand nor control" (10).[5] Weighing these facts against her own dilemmas of subjection, the narrator is interested in a Brontë in full possession of the "liberty"—not subjection—she finds in writing: in Brontë's case, a liberty won at the expense of lived life. In their convergence and, more importantly, in their differences, the stories of the two women's authorships are, like those of Simonides and Celan in *Economy of the Unlost*, "aligned and adverse," the one sounding a sidelong disquisition on the other.[6] In its comparative-confessional texture, "The Glass Essay" anticipates later examples of Carson writing "with" other authors—with Virginia Woolf on the question of time, with Keats on beauty, and with Catullus in the elegiac mode.[7] Similitude (an analogy struck up between two often very different authors or scenarios) does the work that verisimilitude seems unable to do. As "The Glass Essay" glides its focus between the narrator and Emily, each has the effect of rendering the other non-identical with herself, exposing the contradictions of one in the struggles of the other. A similitude, then, that places a hovering interrogative around the possibility of verisimilitude at all.

What is perhaps most striking about "The Glass Essay," read alongside *The Beauty of the Husband* as I attempt in this part of the book, is the way it performs and reflects on a critical reading of Brontë in what feels and sounds like real time. As the narrator talks her way through facts—intimate, textual, or paratextual—present-tense autobiographical commentary binds critical commentary to a precise set of circumstances and exacting emotional demands. Carson's reading of Brontë occupies the full swell of the poem's present tense, up to the point where, in its final pages, something in or about Brontë refuses to be read. There is an impasse at this sudden resistance to assimilation that brings the analogy—and the dramatic identification, "I feel I am turning into Emily Brontë"—to an abrupt end. Though it begins with the two women converged, the poem pursues precisely these qualities of resistance and liberty: first, in Brontë's errors and orthographical liberties in the handwritten fascicles of her work, and in her robust rejection of bodily and sexual life; then more fully in the question of Brontë's relationship with the mysterious figure she addresses as "thou," an interlocutor-muse the narrator describes as Brontë's "true creation." It is here, on the question of "thou," that the poem-essay leads into some of the wider concerns of *Glass, Irony and God*, anticipating those of *Decreation* a decade later: Where does self-sensing end and relationship begin? "What kind of withness" is compassion (a question posed in the poem "God's Christ Theory")?[8] These concerns gather in the earlier volume around the status of mystical experience and its documents—the "faked" photographs of St. Teresa in "Teresa of God"—and other dilemmas of faith, nomenclature, and difference that mark the poems of the "Book of Isaiah" and "The Truth About God."[9]

What Carson, or her confessional narrator, seems to want from Brontë is not a seamless literary analogy for her loneliness, but the thrill of resistance to such a project that comes from relation to an object or source that is *not* her "true creation"—the sensation of addressing a woman, reading an oeuvre, whose inscrutability and failure to be grasped are apprehended in and alongside features that can be seen and readily accounted for. Brontë's resistance to the ways she has been read—what Carson's poem fashions as her "liberty"—takes different forms in the poem. Among these are the idiosyncratic spellings, vocabulary, and verbal marks customarily excised from published editions of Brontë's writing or dismissed in tendentious editorial annexes; her relationship to the unbridled and unsignified forces of nature; and another, more difficult liberty of the imagination to conjure scenarios of violence or fantasies of intimacy, including the fantasy of total subjection to "thou." The tensile, explanatory lyric voice of Carson's poem-essay expresses commitments to both intimacy and liberty in the relationship of reading. Intimacy with Brontë and her story is found easily enough. It is in not being able to read or follow Brontë—in not *becoming* Emily—that the poem's narrator finds her own, also difficult, forms of liberty. As the "glass" of Carson's title suggests, it is possible to perceive an object and feel accompanied while being unable to grasp or hold it still. Transparency can mean the scrupulous revelation of failures of decipherment, being or reading "with" a work without cleansing it of its troubles.

Moving through the chapter, I will be concerned with how Carson's poem conforms—or doesn't—to the shape or ends we might associate with an "essay": an essay by a literary scholar, but a scholar who is, like the object of her identification, a poet and a writer of fiction. Carson's text, in which, for John D'Agata, "literary criticism" and "poem" speak in "one consistent voice," performs an argument about Brontë that unfolds via coarse- and fine-grained textual analysis, historical and biographical detail, and meta-critical commentary on the emotions of reading.[10] At the same time, this argument exposes its own intimate backstory in a way that binds it to the kinds of self-centered performance we normally associate with autobiography and, in particular, with the lyric mode.[11] "Time in its transparent loops . . . passes beneath me now" (8), the narrator explains, and the time of recollection is transparent to the time of reading, the time of reading to the time of loving. Carson's programmatic transparency is exacting in its expression of what she reads, as well as how, when, and where she is reading. Her attention to details of biography and text is where the demands of scholarship and lyric, with its "intimate and interior space of retreat," most compellingly converge.[12]

"Whaching" and Reading Brontë

"The Glass Essay" is a portrait of the unlikely forms of companionship that writing, in "the most awful loneliness of the poet's hour," can offer. The loneliness of Emily and its "rationale" in the address to her poems' interlocutor, "thou," are explored in parallel to the loneliness of Carson's "I," whose interlocutor is Emily herself. Carson's poem-essay is a testament to the complexity of literature as an analogue and companion to individual life, but it is one that renders the individual lyric voice an emotional impossibility. When the narrator asks about Brontë's "thou," about "the messages that pass / between Thou and Emily" (33), she is also asking about the origins of literature: about Brontë's writing and the myth of muse-given inspiration that surrounds it, and about the origins of this particular work. At the start of "The Glass Essay," the narrator's and Bronte's "need," the preconditions for their writing and inspiration, are collapsed in the narrator's first direct address to Emily: "what meat is it, Emily, we need?" (2). Channeling Brontë's strident, searching loneliness in her own, Carson's narrator parses these questions in Brontë's terms and addresses Brontë in hers, pushing the work's rationale of loneliness and identification as far as it will go.

As "The Glass Essay" takes us from "three silent women at the kitchen table"— mother, narrator, Brontë—to the hostile landscapes of tundra and moor, we follow Brontë and the mystery of "the little raw soul [that] was caught by no one" (6). Carson tells us: "She didn't have friends, children, sex, religion, marriage, success, a / salary / or a fear of death," and "spent / most of the hours of her life brushing the carpet, / walking the moor, or whaching" (6). At several points, the poem homes on the question of what exactly Emily was "whaching" (Brontë's idiosyncratic spelling of "watching"). "Whaching . . . taught Emily all she knew about love and its necessities— / an angry education that shapes the way her characters / use one another" (10). Brontë's lessons in "love and its necessities" derive, in this account, from the rough uses of nature and from the elation of a *physis* beyond her control. Those of the narrator, by contrast, are learned under the strain of erotic necessity, the troubles of *bios* or the events of the body and emotions, and the powerlessness of the mind to master them.

This early picture of Emily is where Carson begins to situate her reading. On page four of the poem in the 1995 New Directions edition, in the section titled "WHACHER," Carson introduces us to "Emily's habitual spelling of this word," one of a handful of distinctive Brontë errata listed in the index to the first published edition of Brontë's *Poems*.[13] Carson accounts for the eye-catching error with a striking exemplum, arguing by "example" being a typical gesture of essays:

> For example
>
> in the first line of the poem printed *Tell me, whether, is it winter?*
> in the Shakespeare Head edition.
> But whacher is what she wrote.
>
> Whacher is what she was.
> She whached God and humans and moor wind and open night.
> She whached eyes, stars, inside, outside, actual weather.
>
> She whached the bars of time, which broke.
> She whached the poor core of the world,
> wide open.
>
> To be a whacher is not a choice.
> There is nowhere to get away from it,
> no ledge to climb up to— . . . (4–5)

This passage is a statement of commitment to Brontë's singular vocation and a scholar's manifesto for reading and preserving her orthography. It introduces us indirectly to the narrator's own subjection to vision, whose description is almost identical to this description of Brontë. Like Brontë, for whom "to be a whacher is not a choice," the narrator, too, is condemned to watch "the poor core of the world, / wide open" (4)—glancing to the visionary "dark world and wide" of John Milton—in the form of the graphically violent visions she calls "Nudes."[14] Recounting a conversation on these visions with her psychotherapist, "Dr Haw," she recalls being asked: "When you see these horrible images why do you stay with them? / Why keep watching? Why not // go away? I was amazed. / Go away where? I said" (18). The same idea is reprised shortly after, repeating the metaphor for Brontë's predicament almost exactly: "I stopped telling my psychotherapist about the Nudes / when I realized I had no way to answer her question, // Why keep watching? / Some people watch, that's all I can say. / There is nowhere else to go, // *no ledge to climb up to*" (19, italics mine). Watching is a condition of subjection and an involuntary exposure, but it also models a form of transparency between its fraught subject and the world. As the narrator tells us, for Brontë, "the work" of whaching "has no name. / It is transparent. / Sometimes she calls it Thou" (5). A nameless and transparent condition, "whaching" is a mode of extreme openness in which the subject finds herself seamlessly coextensive with the objects she sets her mind to ("God and humans and moor wind and open night," etc.). Nameless and transparent, there is nothing in "whaching" to distinguish or protect its subject from the assaults of vision. In the narrator's description, "the work of whaching" is sometimes called "Thou": the whacher's transparency is such that she all but becomes someone else.

"The Glass Essay" threads much of its lyricism along the recurring motif of transparency. "Time in its transparent loops" exposes the poem's prismatic order, one of the most intimate expressions of Carson's dictum "all time is now."[15] Looped into its imagery are other examples, centering on glass as a medium in which relation and its constraint, or sameness and difference, are worked out. Carson's narrator reflects on the ambience at her mother's kitchen table: "it is as if we [narrator, mother, and Emily] have all been lowered into an atmosphere of glass. / Now and then a remark trails through the glass" (2). Ian Rae has written suggestively on the presence of a bilingual pun in the poem-essay on the English "glass" and its homophone, the French *glace* (ice), zooming in on the images of black ice and frozen ground that Carson has said inspired early reflections toward "The Glass Essay."[16] Images such as this one, "[t]he swamp water is frozen solid. / Bits of gold weed // have etched themselves / on the underside of the ice like messages," might, if we extend Rae's reading, echo the remarks that "trail through the glass" in their apprehension of a medium the narrator expects to be readable—or audible—but which she finds to be illegible, isolating, or opaque. Opacity is a recurrent quality in images of a natural world hostile to the narrator's efforts to read for "messages," messages addressed to the erotic psychodrama surrounding the narrator's former lover, "Law." Theirs is an opacity that offsets the poem-essay's frank, confessional register compellingly. Yet the lucid and open observation of opacity also feels all of a piece with the experiences of Emily. While "*watching*" makes an argument for the metaphysical origins of poetry, where transparency to the world means openness to the influence of "thou," "*whaching*" in its orthographically errant form does something quite different in "The Glass Essay."

What is so compelling about Carson's sustained attention to Brontë's orthographical error in the handwritten manuscript of the poems is how, in Carson's hands, it becomes the sign not of metaphysical influence but of a robust singularity of authorship. Reading for this robust singularity and against the metaphysical argument is, in simple terms, the broader critical function of Carson's "essay" as it moves through Brontë's texts and paratexts. Where the textuality of regulated typescript affirms the anonymity of writing, the unregulated orthographical error emerges as a vital and unextraordinary sign of individual life.[17] This intimate trace of the subject also erases her as its point of origin. Its resistance to editorial regularity becomes, for Carson's narrator, a cipher for Brontë's simultaneous presence and personal unreadability. To come across "whacher" for the first time is to come up against the familiar unfamiliarity of a foreign language, whose half-dark nouns float apart, their moorings in the syntax obscured. Not a nonce word, as several readers have characterized it, "whacher" is an example of what Charlotte Brontë called Emily's "little failings," as Carson's narrator drily recounts.[18] Other such "failings" include Emily's profanities—"foul language" whose uncensored reproduction in the published edition of the work Charlotte Brontë vindicates in her Editor's Preface to *Wuthering Heights*. Carson quotes Charlotte: "A large class of readers, likewise, will suffer greatly / from the introduction into the pages of this work // of words printed with all their letters, / which it has become the custom to represent by the initial and final / letter only—a blank / line filling the interval" (20). Carson also highlights the "small adjustments" made by Charlotte "to the text of Emily's verse" and listed in the annotations to the poems' posthumous publication: "*Prison* for *strongest* [in Emily's hand] altered to *lordly* by Charlotte" (21).[19] Such interventions substitute Emily's handpicked diction for one in line with Charlotte's more amenable poetic sensibility. In these and other instances in "The Glass Essay," Carson is drawn to the wayward sign, the recalcitrant sign—the one, as it were, that got away. Recalling her personal attachment to Virginia Woolf's cross-outs in "Appendix to Ordinary Time" (2000), here, the register that has been suppressed in the making of the published version becomes a "language of the unsaid" (21) as well as a cipher for death, "hid[ing] right inside every shining sentence we grasped and had no grasp of" (as in *prison* substituted by Emily for *strongest*, both subdued in the end by Charlotte's *lordly*; or the editorial suppression of *whacher* and other idiosyncratic spellings).[20] The recovery of such a language, and the liberty it represents, becomes a proxy for the narrator's own resistance, to the subjection she describes to a grieved erotic "Law." Her recollection, "Love is freedom, Law was fond of saying," works the complex dependencies of liberty and subjection into a profoundly ironic syntactic arrangement (20).

It is also significant in the extract above that the first line of the poem Carson reproduces is an editorial mistake, a misattribution, and a misreading of Brontë. "Whether," Carson signals, is a substitute for Brontë's original "whacher," yet "whether" is itself an orthographical eccentricity—"whether," instead, as Carson says, of "actual weather" (4). This is a case of an error mobilized to cover an error, and constitutes an imposition of poetical law on the part of a well-meaning editor. Carson's keen interest in the minutiae of handwritten textuality and its editorial suppression becomes a language for the problems of liberty and subjection. Her interest finds a strong parallel in the scholar-poet Susan Howe's passionate commitment to recovering similar minutiae in the fascicles of another Emily—Emily Dickinson. In her writings on Dickinson, beginning with her 1985 study, *My Emily Dickinson,* and continuing in *The*

Birth-mark: Unsettling the Wilderness in American Literary History (1993), Howe refers to a similar editorial intervention in the marks, errata, and punctuation of the original Dickinson fascicles as "Lawlessness seen as negligence is at first feminized and then restricted or banished."[21] Howe sees the editorial determination of official textuality as an assault on an entire order of residues of the physical body and—most importantly to Howe—the voice, whose recovery drives a significant part of her critical and poetic project. The understanding of errata as "unconscious talking," and often as stylistic choice, is at the center of Howe's commitment to the material singularity of Dickinson's originals, and, in common with Carson, lends to her recovery project an intimacy rarely seen in scholarly work: in Howe's words, "the heart may be sheltering in some random mark of communication" that editors deem "textually irrelevant."[22] Resistance to these editorial efforts in the case of the Emily Brontë oeuvre is infused in Carson's poem with the same kind of intimate hope, staged in the trials and attachments of her narrator. Carson, too, makes a comparable case for revising the received "ontology" of her own Emily's texts.[23] Yet Carson's poem also points, like Howe's readings of Dickinson, to the importance of such resistance in challenging a wider, remarkably persistent notion of female authorship—one that winds up defenestrating their difficulty, idiosyncrasy, or "lawlessness"—in the critical history of both Emilies.

In one of the most darkly humorous sections of "The Glass Essay," Carson marshals Charlotte Brontë as a critical interlocutor, suggesting Charlotte's reading of her sister's work has roundly missed the point. Paraphrasing Charlotte's own preface to *Wuthering Heights* (which Carson describes as like "someone carefully not looking at a scorpion / crouched on the arm of the sofa"), the poem-essay parses a reading of Emily set deep into her work's paratextual apparatus from its earliest publication. We are told of "Emily's total subjection // to a creative project she could neither understand nor control" (9–10)—an Emily, Carson explains with mock high-octane solemnity, "in the grip" (10). Carson's point in this section of "The Glass Essay" is that Emily has been subdued by a myth of involuntary authorship: that for more than a century and a half, Emily has been displaced from the center of her own work by a reading that casts her as inspired and self-justifies a series of dubious editorial interventions. Charlotte Brontë speaks for this long century, for which Emily has served as a figure of Romantic subjection to the muse. For Charlotte Brontë, Emily could neither "understand nor control" what she was writing.[24]

This metaphysical reading, as well as its contrast with the narrator's argument for Emily Brontë's authorial liberty and self-possession, matters in Carson's poem-essay for two reasons. First, as an interpretation of textual and—as the narrator reads it—spiritual intentionality: where the idea of Emily "in the grip" seeks to defenestrate the author, Carson's narrator seeks to affirm Emily Brontë's errant and erratic act of literary creation, including her own distinctive fantasy of subjection, with which the condition of "whaching" is loaded. It is also significant because, from the narrator's point of view, the question of Brontë's agency as a writer also intercedes in the all-important question of "thou"—specifically, the fact that Brontë's figure of influence and inspiration is gendered male.[25] If the suppression of her awkward handwritten textuality equates to a suppression of liberty, then the question of "thou" concerns not only the suppression of the feminine in Brontë's critical legacy, but how she—how the woman author in the age of the male pseudonym—interprets her own power.

Margaret Homans offers a compelling reading of Brontë's poetry as "troubled by the apparent otherness of her mind's powers, which she imagines as a series of masculine visitants who bring visionary experience to her."[26] Homans imagines Brontë in an impasse of potency, caught between "visionary experience offered by male figures" whose influence is necessarily exogenous, and an endogenous *poiesis*, historically devalued, implies Homans, because its *poiesis* is governable (hence subject to failures of governance like errata).[27] Brontë's work, Homans suggests, honors two very different myths of poetry's origin: involuntarism and the masculine muse on the one hand, and on the other, the woman writer committed to the rendering of human necessity as literature. Brontë was, in a sense, caught between these myths from the first: an avid writer and storyteller since childhood, her authorial identity, we should remember, first presented itself to the public under the sign of a man—the pseudonym, Ellis Bell. Brontë herself seems undecided on the issue. Her poem "My Comforter" speaks of and to "thou" but insists, in an audacious direct address, that "Thou hast but roused a latent thought," staking claim to a self-originating *poesis* in a subtle affront to her muse.[28]

"The Glass Essay," I have suggested, reads against a tradition of reading Brontë that more or less proposes casting aside what Brontë wrote to get at what she *meant*. It is a tradition steeped in a form/content opposition that reads Brontë's language as a stumbling block, claiming "real" meaning to be accessible by way of biographical, historical, anecdotical, and paratextual means. We find this mode of reading in Q. D. Leavis's "A Fresh Approach to *Wuthering Heights*" (1969), where Leavis separates the novel's written form from its "real" content. She speaks of "rhetorical excesses, obstacles to the *real novel* enacted so richly for us to grasp in all its complexity."[29] In speaking of the "real" novel as something other than the text Brontë wrote—even imagining the novel as its own obstacle—Leavis seems to argue for a kind of Ur-*Wuthering Heights*, a novel, or the conceit of a novel, of which the *Wuthering Heights* we read today is an awkward iteration or epilogue.[30] Frank Kermode critiqued this assumption of a "real," almost metaphysical anti-text when, in *The Classic*, he outlined Leavis's working conceit: a "hierarchy of elements [created] by a peculiar archaeology of her own, for there is no evidence that the novel existed in earlier forms which are supposed to have left vestiges in the only text we have."[31] This metaphysical reading of Brontë says the "real" poem, the "real" novel, is somewhere other than its written marks, and somehow other than Brontë penned it to paper. So-called obstacles to meaning are precisely what Carson's poem-essay covets in Brontë, as residues of the ultimate liberty of the little raw soul "caught by no one." That is: at one and the same time, Carson's text seeks to catch the intimate singularity of Brontë as an author and a woman in loneliness, and seeks the failure to be caught, the errancy, and the freedom, that guarantee such singularity.

"My Own Nude": The End of the Poem-Essay

The relationship between the intractable *whacher*, the critical and editorial rejection of Brontë's errors, and the intimate dilemmas chronicled by Carson's narrator, can help us to understand the need for "Emily" as a simile on the point of collapse with the narrator's experiences. Emily is, nonetheless, a difficult and recalcitrant object whose contradictions refuse to accommodate this similitude, and whose "messages"—not least her errata—often prove illegible. Among the eye-catching idiosyncratic spellings of the first published edition of Brontë's *Poems* are "buissy" (busy), "kichin" (kitchen, referenced on page 15 of Carson's poem), "majic" (magic) and "vally" (valley).[32] While its retention is a form of resistance to editorial normalization, I suggested, the erratic spelling fuses semantic associations to the correctly spelled word with semantic nonconformity and the material verve of a nonce word. Before we translate *whacher* or *buissy* into their established forms, these words are enigmatic messages, objects we don't quite know what to do with or where to place but that, in their readiness to sound, act—and act upon us—in undecipherable ways. Appropriable in ways "watcher" is not, the sounding capability of *whacher* is plumbed by Carson when she says of Brontë, "Whacher is what she was," reprising the sibilance of *whacher* in "what she." Knitting the two trochees into a dactylic lilt, Carson lends her line a latent, nursery-rhyme musicality. A sensible reciprocity mimics and entertains Brontë's singular vocabulary, arguing for it in ways an unlilted critical prose might advocate or explain, but would itself be unqualified to perform.

As the narrative progresses, the immediate enigma of the Brontë errata comes to occupy the same order as Carson's many representations of natural phenomena in the poem-essay, the bleak, illegible *physis* in which Brontë sets her novel, and through which Carson's narrator strides in search of insight and release. As the narrator wanders the moor, she comes across the resistance to decipherment we encountered earlier on:

> The swamp water is frozen solid.
> Bits of gold weed
>
> have etched themselves
> on the underside of the ice like messages. (33)

Immediately following these lines, Carson quotes Brontë's poem "I'll Come When Thou Art Saddest" in full, before announcing that "the messages that pass / between Thou and Emily" are "[v]ery hard to read" (33). The mirroring of "messages"—those the narrator observes and those exchanged between Thou and Emily—marks a convergence of purpose between Carson's scholarship and her intimate lyric response. Attention turns in both to the problem of loneliness. In the union of Thou and Emily, Carson wonders, what does relationship sound like—what relationship is there to speak of—if Thou is a "rationale" for the poet's loneliness? Her narrator wonders, in turn, what ice and moorland have to say to her—what relationship there can be—under Law's regime of meaning. The assonantal rhyme of psychotherapist "Dr Haw" with "Law" (and, in a Canadian-accented reading, Rae suggests, a near rhyme with "Ma," "Pa") turns Carson's portrait of erotic enthrallment into a delirious family romance, in which the lover's desire sets the terms for relation with just about everyone.[33] Yet what Carson's "I" finds in the unreadable, unaffiliated signs of nature, a *physis* uncontaminated by *bios*, is an irreducible nonsignifying force that refuses this symbolic law and hampers the pursuit of "messages" by lover and scholar alike. It is here, in the encounter with acknowledged illegibility, that the narrator begins to diverge from Emily. Here she first glimpses a hard-won liberty of her own.

The narrator/Emily analogy reaches a crisis toward the end of the poem-essay, just after the narrator's disquisition on the Thou/Emily relationship. Carson has, at this point, reproduced Brontë's disquieting poem "I'll Come When Thou Art Saddest," in which the lyric "I" ("I'll come") addresses a lowercase "thou" directly. "I" instructs "thou" to "Listen! 'tis just the hour, / The awful time for thee: / Dost thou not feel upon thy soul / A flood of strange sensations roll / Forerunners of a sterner power, / Heralds of me?" In this remarkable sequence, it is not the poet who addresses her muse—the traditional etiquette of the epic mode—but vice versa: this lyric subject ventriloquizes the muse and speaks, apparently, to herself, becoming a "thou" to his "Thou." Carson reads this vignette as a reversal of roles, in which we find Brontë "speaking not *as* the victim but *to* the victim" (Carson's emphasis). The narrator offers a reading of what happens in Brontë's poem when the poet, speaking as "Thou," addresses herself to "thou":

> It is chilling to watch Thou move upon thou,
> who lies alone in the dark waiting to be mastered.
>
> It is a shock to realize that this low, slow collusion
> of master and victim within one voice
> is a rationale
>
> for the most awful loneliness of the poet's hour. (34)

What is being watched here is a reversal of "roles," says Carson; no power game, we are told, but an effort to provoke pity in the poet "for this soul trapped in glass, / which is her true creation." Carson's lines describe a reversibility that means two different things for Carson and Brontë. For Brontë, the reversal of roles guarantees the reciprocity of the relationship with "Thou" and confirms His reality. For Carson's narrator, the same reversal is the symptom of nothing more than a "collusion" of self with self in "one voice." As the narrator reads it, Brontë's assumption of the voice of "Thou" to achieve self-address is an uncomplicated sublimation of her loneliness ("One way to put off loneliness is to interpose God," 31). Yet God is a question the narrator puts off, turning her interest instead to the dynamics of self-relation in the poem: the "soul trapped in glass," the self addressed as if from without, is the poet's "true creation." This is a climactic moment in Carson's poem-essay. It produces a reckoning in the narrator regarding her own collusion with Emily, as well as a louder reckoning with the larger, metaphysical other—the Old Testament "Thou"—who looms aloft the Brontë poem. The work done by Carson's versification, and in particular by rhyme, is central to her exposition of the collusion, but also suggests how her poem's narrator has, perhaps, come to replicate the very rationale she describes. The realization comes as a "shock." In the lines where the Thou/thou collusion is represented, sudden metrical regularity around the repetition ("Thou move upon thou" and "reversed the roles of thou and Thou"), together with the striking assonantal rhyme, "low slow collusion," perform the smooth coextension, the perfect immanence, of subject and interlocutor, exposing the intimate mechanics of the "rationale."

"But for myself," the narrator abruptly announces, "I do not believe this, I am not quenched—/ with Thou or without Thou I find no shelter. / I am my own Nude" (35). It is an announcement that marks a conscious break with Emily and an abrupt end to the analogy—the "rationale" of "I am turning into Emily Brontë"—that up to now has sustained the poem and offered solace to its narrator. The affirmation that will replace it—"I am my own Nude"—describes the narrator's confrontation with an uninvested, un-artful loneliness. In the final pages, having arrived at the limits of her literary-critical imagination and exhausted its emotional events, the narrator is left alone with what she calls the "difficult sexual destiny" of "Nudes" for the first time in the work.

The final pages of "The Glass Essay" announce the need for a change in key, following the exhaustion of its sometime rationale. "I want to speak more clearly," the narrator states: "Perhaps the Nudes are the best way" (35). The "Nudes" are a series of thirteen inset allegorical visions in which the narrator imagines a woman's body subjected to sometimes grotesque, Boschian violence at the behest of natural forces. The first four of these are recounted earlier in the poem in the section titled "Liberty," marking an early paratactic shift from the narrator's readings of Brontë's poems, the accounts of her life, and the present-tense autobiographical thread. In Nude #1, a woman stands alone on a hill, pitched against the wind:

> Long flaps and shreds of flesh rip off the woman's body and lift
> and blow away on the wind, leaving
>
> an exposed column of nerve and blood and muscle
> calling mutely through lipless mouth. (9)

The imagery conjured by the "Nudes" is vivid and various, but what it invariably stages is the female body or landscapes analogous with its interior. The female subject of the "Nudes" ranges from cautious and inward in her activity to battered under assault by foreign objects and natural elements—eviscerating winds, thorns, "bluish black" pressures in space. The body in Nude #1 is reduced by such an assault to a simple failed attempt to communicate, "calling mutely through a lipless mouth." Yet Carson summons the Nudes at the end of the poem-essay as a way of speaking "more clearly." What can the body say that reminiscences of words and transparencies of memory cannot? No analysis of these late listed "Nudes" is offered. Nor is there any repeat of the work's earlier strategies of collage and embedding of registers, quotations, biography, and analysis.

What the final "Nudes" perform is the narrator's gradual abandonment of the poem-essay, which up to this point has been a vehicle for analogy and identification, critical reading and self-reading. Carson's relinquishment of commentary on the images, with their vindication of a wordless affliction, seems to signal an end to the devices and sublimations accrued around "Law" and to the unhappy identification with Emily. The thirteen "Nudes" strip down the language of loss and betrayal to simple physical gestures, a ritualistic simplicity remembering the fourteen "Stations of the Cross." In doing so they perform the denuding of the poem-essay, its resources and its scholarly apparatus. In this final change of tack, what appeared earlier on to be the redemptive solace of scholarship is left oddly high and dry: a sort of anti-poem is staged, after the registers and reflections that sustained the work have been cut away. The final "Nudes" emerge into what the narrator tells us is empty space: in spite of her hope "to trick myself into some interior vision," "I saw nothing . . . but still—nothing. No nudes. / No Thou" (37). When they do return, the "nudes"—now referenced in lowercase—approach the "meaningless legs" of Carson's later poem, "Stanzas, Sexes, Seductions" (2005), whose jaded subject longs for an unsignified body in place of one saturated with erotic significance; for an end, too, to the performative sexuality that leads her to ask, "who does not become a female impersonator?"[34] In their vindication of *physis* over *bios*, the final "nudes" imagine the unwriting of the body as the seat of sexual history and biographical life, bound and shaped by inescapable hungers: including, in this poem, a scholar's compulsion to rationalize and close-read them.

The final "Nude," which arrives unexpectedly, marks a decisive end to the rule of "Law," for Nude #13, she says, "arrived when I was not watching for it." It reprises Nude #1 and yet is "utterly different." This Nude is a human body,

> trying to stand against winds so terrible that the flesh was blowing off the bones.
> And there was no pain.
> The wind
>
> was cleansing the bones.
> They stood forth silver and necessary.
> It was not my body, not a woman's body, it was the body of us all.
> It walked out of the light.

The body in this final scene walks away a "cleansed" cipher. In this last ritual "station," the exposed form high on the hill—"the body of us all"—is no longer an object of masochistic identification ("it was not my body"): as the narrator disentangles herself from Brontë and the drama of "thou"—a drama of sovereignty, muses, and literature—this cleaner, clearer imagery cannot help but deliver the biblical "Thou," whose exit from the world cleanses and purifies ("'In Thou they are quenched as a fire of thorns,' says the psalmist," 34). The scene carries with it a surplus of meaning accumulated around the "Nudes" and marks a poet's disassociation from the poem-essay. The reduction of its functions signals an end to "turning into Emily," yet its gnostic ambivalence toward the body is something the poem-essay actually shares with Brontë's poetry. A concordance of Brontë's poems counts only one occurrence of the word "body" in the form of an injunction to relinquish it: "the heart is dead since infancy / Unwept for let the body go."[35] In poems such as the "Prisoner" fragment, Brontë seems to refuse the material substance of poetry while continuing to mine its lyric capacities, using her poems to sound a desire for silence.[36]

"The Glass Essay" is a scholar's poem. Its chronicle of the consolations of literature and literary scholarship—reading for our own emotions in the study of another's reading of hers—ends with an eviscerated cache of imagery in which emotion, sex, *bios*, are ritually cleansed.[37] Yet Carson's poem-essay is all too conscious—her analogy with Brontë a fail-safe expression—of the limits of *poetry*. For all that the "Nudes" "speak more clearly," and for all that their archetypal ore—"silver and necessary"—plumbs the universally sexed phantasmagoria of dreams, they speak as images in a poem, iterations of other images in other poems, and iterations of Christian symbolism. At the end of this poem, an odd reverberation of the different functions and needs brought together in the work casts its final resolution into doubt, holding a question mark over what—if anything—has been redeemed. Poetry has made a claim for its own abandonment. Autobiography has made plain the attachments of scholarship, and, in the end, close reading of her verse—a key "essay" function here—has allowed Carson's narrator to disentangle herself from Brontë, her proxy in the emotional event called liberty.

The solace of "turning into Emily Brontë" is as urgent as it is unsettling. The story of that solace brings the speculations and emotive demands of reading into clear view, and in doing so, creates a curious side effect. It is easy to identify with Carson, candid as she is with her emotions and emotional limits as a reader, but the same candor—we might call it presence or personality—holds us back from "turning into" Carson ourselves. This is the limit sought by the American scholar Sarah Chihaya, whose recent response to Carson's poem-essay, titled "A Glass Essay," reads for what *doesn't* submit to her identification with Carson.[38] "The Glass Essay" is an early window onto the "windowless room" of Carson's work with other authors and literatures: that sealed-off consciousness where, she tells us in *Economy of the Unlost*, thought's "best moments" are to be had. Carson's poem-essay is a reflection on its private conditions of possibility: what led Carson to read Brontë, what drew her to—and what she sought to salvage from—the errata, the destructiveness of eros in Brontë's novel, the myths surrounding her authorship. "Essay" is little more here than a reflective tense, holding facts, examples, reflections, and memories in a running real-time present. In this present, there is no useful distinction to be made between the facts and fictions of literature and the facts of autofiction and autobiography, a mode she will push to extremes in the "fictional essay," *The Beauty of the Husband*.

4
Lyric Transparency and the "Fictional Essay"

"I feel it's a kind of fervour of mine," Carson has said, "to get away from whatever body of information I rest on when I give opinions. And I think poetic activity is a method for doing that," she continues: "—*you leap off the building when you think poetically.*"[1] The products of Carson's "fervour" are notorious: anachronism, parody, improbability, and fiction are the "errancy" she gathers into a rogue critical method, where "to get away from" information sets her against the grain of historicism and the academic essay form.[2] It is the same fervor Carson turns back on herself as a matter of course, setting her writing on the trail of its own implausibility. What she presents as a method for self-estrangement (unsettling the ground she "rests on") is at its clearest and most complex when its disciplined precarity is an approach to other works. One "body of information" preserved in the contours of another can defamiliarize and renew both, as the Brontë oeuvre offered Carson a language for writing her way out of a story gone stagnant, with Brontë revised and recolored along the way. At other times, the "body of information" appears to have vanished without a trace, her source texts transformed almost beyond recognition.

Carson's admission recalls a later mise-en-scène for her methods. It is the scene with which I began Chapter 1, in which Carson compares the "perilous activity" of freeform lecturing to the perilous choreography of Elizabeth Streb, whose dancers fall "straight down from a height of thirty-two feet," looking, as they leap, "like gods for an instant."[3] There, what interested Carson was an abrupt disorganization of desire brought on by these two very different simulations of accident, in which choreography and scholarship perform what the radical estrangement of their methods might look like. Here, though, talking about her fervor to "get away," Carson draws her own desire into view. A sudden, perverse symmetry emerges between the forsaken "body of information" and the body that "leap[s] off the building" in the name of poetic thinking. How are these bodies—textual facts and intimate history, knowledge and self-knowledge—bound together in Carson's activity? Does "thinking poetically" mean exposing more than just "information" to danger?

Another admission replicates the mise-en-scène and gives us some leads. Several pages into *The Beauty of the Husband: A Fictional Essay in 29 Tangos*

(2001), a semi-autobiographical narrative essay in irregularly lineated verse, Carson's narrator describes herself sitting "at a window (restaurant) high above the street, / married a little more than a year," and the moment when her husband ("with shy pride") slips out a photograph of his mistress:

> Quick work I said. Are you going to be arch he said.
> I broke the glass and jumped.
> Now of course you know
>
> that isn't the true story, what broke wasn't glass, what fell to earth wasn't body. (16)

No sooner is this fiction offered than it is exposed as such and withdrawn. "I" glances in complicity at "you," addressee of the palinode, who knows what it is to think poetically and grasps how compelling its leaps can be. The narrator then explains that "when I recall the conversation it's what I see—me a fighter pilot / bailing out over the channel. Me as kill." *The Beauty of the Husband*, a long-form disquisition on "the true lies of poetry" (33), makes the case early on for metaphors truer than the "true story" and, driving them, an almost fatalistic compulsion to fiction: fatalistic because the narrator's exposure of her metaphors—a favorite essayistic tic—leaves her compromised by the same "true lies," the same fatal attractions, she excoriates in "the Husband." Her brief self-exposure does a lot of work, for the betrayal of metaphor gives away both her medium and its seductions; its confession and retraction—its transparency, its history—is as much a part of the case being made for fiction as the fiction itself. Throughout *The Beauty of the Husband*, the thinking and feeling owed to metaphor, analogy, metonymy, the devices of poetry and fiction, are confessed repeatedly and at length. Carson's *Fictional Essay* offers a dramatic emotional backstory for "the true lies of poetry" and for the sustained scrutiny of poetics as a problem, seamless and simultaneous with its performance.

The Beauty of the Husband tells the story of a marriage in the *longue durée*, from adolescent love and serial infidelity to divorce and attempted reconciliation, drawn through philosophical asides, "reflections on [the] story," and uppercase title sequences addressed to the reader in the narrative present.[4] In what she calls "A SPIRIT OF UNASHAMED DIS-/CLOSURE" (123), the narrator interprets the dilemmas of her story with the help of the ancients (Homer, Plato, Parmenides) and the moderns (Keats, Barthes, Beckett, Proust). Chronicling her "seduction" by a man's "beauty" and way with words, a man who "liked writing, disliked having to start / each thought himself" (9), the narrator's most pressing dilemma is her ongoing enthrallment to the capacity of words—his and hers, borrowed and original—to "shine" (5), to "explode" (34), words that "showed up on all the walls of my life" (41). Critical comment on poetry and imitation, and exposés of the husband's uncreative writing ("Used my starts to various ends," 9), are thrown into relief by real-time interpolations to the "you"—"fair reader" (5)—who is both witness and accomplice to her own composition. Who reads it from without as she reads it from within.

We have seen how thinking in Carson is often inseparable from its lyric performance. We have seen her languages of exposure range from autobiographical asides, direct address, and scholarly statements of intent, to mimetic argumentative structures, performative forms, and drafts that expose her thinking and reading to scrutiny. In the concerted transparency of "The Glass Essay," Carson's reading of Brontë happens in a raw dream sequence, confessional, time-bound, and site-specific. In *The Beauty of the Husband*, which also claims the status of an "essay," the reading—the *critical* essay—is almost entirely eclipsed by the confessional narrative. What the book's blurb describes as "an essay on Keats's idea that beauty is truth, and . . . also the story of a marriage" is a provocation. It provokes us immediately into querying its form, but it also tells us that the functions of "story" and "essay"—in a leap of poetic thinking—are coterminous, their dimensions matched and their course intertwined. It is in Carson's self-scrutinizing "story of a marriage" that the putative "essay on Keats's idea that beauty is truth" emerges as an analogy to the story, buoyed along by it, held afloat by various means, but never broached directly. This is an essay caught in dense textures of lyric performance that stand in for the analysis of Keats, yet are dedicated in the uppercase "TO KEATS" in the work's opening line. The essay *on* Keats, the critical essay we might be expecting, remains a fiction of its own making.

What, then, is the *Beauty of the Husband*? In formal terms, Carson's *Fictional Essay in 29 Tangos* is a series of twenty-nine numbered verse compositions of irregular lineation and length, followed by a final, unnumbered entry and a list of "Notes." Each composition begins with a sparsely punctuated uppercase title sequence, which can be read continuously across the numbered entries, and each is preceded, on an otherwise blank page, by a short fragment of verse, errata, or marginalia from Keats. The book contains one near-quotation and no other mention of the "Ode on a Grecian Urn" in which "Keats's idea that beauty is truth" famously appears, though iterations of the poem's scenes and figures occur throughout, alongside scattered allusions to the poet and a small number of marked quotations and unmarked paraphrases from other works, several (not all) of which are referenced in Carson's "Notes." No direct commentary on this material is offered. The material is recalled, rather, in the narrator's account, alongside other recollected readings, quotations, and inquiries, love scenes, letters, close readings of letters, and staged compositions such as a series of inset "elegiac couplets" recording her daily observation of a branch (123; 123–125).

Addressed to "you," this iterative performance brooks little or no distinction between the textual facts of quotation and paraphrase on the one hand, and the textures of reflection and commentary on the other. Carson's fictional essay is transparent, indistinguishable from the rehearsals that give rise to it.

On the intimacy of writers and their texts, Rachel Blau DuPlessis quotes Virginia Woolf's remark that she (Woolf) saw "no reason why one should not write as one speaks, familiarly, colloquially." "Letters, journals, voices are sources for this element," says DuPlessis, "expressing the porousness and nonhierarchic stances of intimate conversation in both structure and function."[5] *The Beauty of the Husband* swaps a surface/depth hermeneutic for continuous lyric texture, in which story, source material, commentary, and meta-critical aside speak in the same voice. In this, the work shows strong affinities with the "horizontal discourse" of Roland Barthes, whose interpretive figures in *A Lover's Discourse* "always remain on the same level"—"no transcendence, no deliverance, no novel (though a great deal of the fictive)"—and in which quotation and reference are summoned and plundered as if from memory under the author's "piratical law."[6] Barthes called his "horizontal discourse" the expression of a "'dramatic' method," reproducing the lyric discourse of "its fundamental person, the *I*, in order to stage an *utterance*, not an analysis."[7] The digressive shape of Barthes's utterance offers a "simulation" of the lover's discourse in lieu of description.[8] Carson's nonhierarchic "conversation" with the Keats oeuvre, fused with the discourse of a searching former lover, rejects analysis of his work, reproducing instead events of "primordial eros and strife" in the face of which it is "useless to interpose analysis or make contrafactual suggestions" (20, 49). If the lyric is "the iterative and iterable performance of an event in the lyric present," as Culler suggests it is, then we might think of Carson's "fictional essay" as an extreme form of lyric essay, whose lyric present has become the main event.[9] The intimate and continuous disclosure of thoughts, memories, quotations, and feelings—a full-spectrum lyric transparency—has taken the place of analysis.

It is this transparency I will be trying to describe in what follows. Carson's transparency, distinct from the transparency of reference and process in the traditional scholarly essay, invites us to consider the performative textures of lyric voice against what we might expect (or demand) from the "reading" voice of criticism. Transparency is a method in Carson's essay on "Keats's idea that beauty is truth," but the method and its exposure form a targeted response to the "Ode on a Grecian Urn." Where Keats's poem is a hymn to "quietness," inscrutability, and the "unheard," Carson's reading turns this principle on its head, countering the urn's "silence and slow time" with all-out exposure and real-time commentary. The figure of glass—"I broke the glass and jumped," etc., but also Marcel Duchamp's *The Large Glass* (better known as *The Bride Stripped Bare by Her Bachelors, Even*), which makes an appearance in Carson's opening lines—is the essay's counterfactual proxy for Keats's "still unravish'd bride of quietness," object of the "Ode on a Grecian Urn." Carson's essay responds to an opaque metaphysics of presence with self-exposure and transparency, an account penetrated on all sides by sources, intertexts, myths, and voices. Like the exposed metaphor early on, its claim to "fiction" deliberately unsettles the text, for it also claims complicity with the narrator's principal object of suffering: the terrible beauty of imitation and lies.[10]

Drawn through this chapter is a series of questions around how it feels to read a transparent, "horizontal" discourse of this kind. Carson's fictional essay offers a sustained confessional exposure that hijacks and reroutes the traditional expository functions of the literary-critical essay. In place of a so-called symptomatic reading of Keats is the narrator's own intimate symptomatology, in which Keats is summoned as a series of reminiscences, confessional anecdotes, and a device of lyric address—"(IS IT YOU WHO / TOLD ME KEATS WAS A DOCTOR?)" (5). In place of the much-scorned "paranoid reading" is the jealous close reading of lovers—what in her recent poem, "The Keats Headaches," Carson calls "*oulipo* jealousies"—who steal and remix one another's metaphors and whose letters "pull libidinal devices into a new transparence" (37).[11] What Eve Kosofsky Sedgwick called criticism's "drama of exposure"—revealing in the text what the text doesn't know about itself—becomes, in Carson's essay, an exercise in designed and dramatic *self-exposure*. The fictional essay is a case of extreme meta-critical consciousness, whose essaying is marked at the outset as a fabrication, and whose analytical sensitivity to its own moves (to borrow from Keats) "tease[s] us out of thought."[12] Carson's performance of the histories and fantasies brought to bear on "Keats's idea," and into which Keats has been absorbed in turn, I suggest, speaks to a wider fictional practice in her writing. Between post-critical sensibility and the anti-art aesthetics of Dada, Carson's pro-fictive scholarship has sought ways to "get away" from bodies of information—listless philological facts, established histories, canonical versions—by making fantasy, desire, and unashamed subjectivity into radical determinants of textual interpretation. Her versions of the facts perform an imaginative life supremely capable of remaking objects in its own image—a long-established function of poems, but still a decidedly errant function of criticism and translation. Its example is a form of attention that brooks radical estrangement, where the bearings of the "essay" are thrown off course.

Dedication

The Beauty of the Husband opens in a strident, uppercase lyric mode with a dedication of the work and an exposure of its rationale that runs across the first three title sequences. In the first of these, "YOU," Carson's reader, are addressed in a barely punctuated live-stream declaration that begins with the performative utterance "I DEDICATE," and invokes "YOU" as both a past-tense interlocutor and potential accomplice in the present:

> I. I DEDICATE THIS BOOK TO KEATS (IS IT YOU WHO
> TOLD ME KEATS WAS A DOCTOR?) ON GROUNDS THAT
> A DEDICATION HAS TO BE FLAWED IF A BOOK IS TO REMAIN
> FREE AND FOR HIS GENERAL SURRENDER TO BEAUTY (5)

The declaration holds Carson's book between the parameters of subjection ("SURRENDER") and liberty ("IF A BOOK IS TO / REMAIN FREE"), parameters in which we saw Carson read Brontë in "The Glass Essay." Carson offers that the dedication to Keats is itself the flaw that, perhaps like the formal anomaly of the subtitle, *Fictional Essay*, releases the book from the bondage of conformity to its own apparent constraints—as though the indeterminacy regarding how exactly the book is dedicated, devoted to, or about Keats, is what guarantees its freedom to read Keats on new, or at least uncertain, terms.

The dedication continues to be theorized across the following two title sequences, where a dedication, "AN ESSENTIALLY / PUBLIC SURRENDER," "IS ONLY FELICITOUS IF PER-/ FORMED BEFORE WITNESSES" (9, title II.);

> III. AND FINALLY A GOOD DEDICATION IS INDIRECT
> (OVERHEARD, ETC.) AS IF VERDI'S "LA DONNA È
> MOBILE" HAD BEEN A POEM SCRATCHED ON GLASS (15)

The dedication, it turns out, only takes effect before witnesses—in this case, before the "YOU," whose complicity is rallied in support. Carson's opening *argumentum* reminds us, as several of the title sequences do, that the work's "DEDICATION" to Keats—indeed, its relation to Keats at all—is "INDIRECT," and little more than a declaration (as the *Fictional Essay*, the "essay on Keats's idea," is an essay principally because it says so). In the narrator's comprehensive commentary, the reading of Keats is made by analogy, occurring elsewhere than the site of its apprehension ("OVERHEARD, ETC."). Carson's final remark here—"AS IF VERDI'S 'LA DONNA È / MOBILE' HAD BEEN A POEM SCRATCHED ON GLASS"—extends out of one of the book's most striking image sequences, the imagery of glass, though it plays, too, on the kinds of exposure afforded by dedication. "Dedication [*Dédicace*]," observes Barthes, always runs the risk of betraying "the delirium [*délire*]—or the snare [*leurre*] in which I am caught" at the moment of making it.[13] *Dédicace*: from the Indo-European root *deik*, to show, becoming Latin *dicare*, to proclaim; its delirium [*délire*] can be all too readable [*lire*]. Its betrayal of emotion makes the dedication a performative, "giving away" the subject and giving, therefore, something in excess of what the dedication intends. (The later poem, "The Keats Headaches," has no such qualms about betraying feelings or being "given away": "Would Keats have liked me, I wonder?," asks Carson's narrator.)[14]

Dedication brings with it a crisis of dependency, an intimate as well as public surrender that makes the dedication a question posed about freedom and bondage in the use of language: the possibility (or impossibility) of dominion over what we say and what is said to us. This is a question posed directly or indirectly in almost all of Carson's twenty-nine tangos. In words she attributes to her lyric "you," and which recall the emotional mathematics of *erōs* and *aidōs*: "How do people / get power over one another? is an algebraic question" (38).[15]

Just how, then, is Carson's fictional essay an inquiry into "Keats's idea that beauty is truth"? What *is* Keats in the work, beyond a framing device for another of Carson's eros variations, in which erotic dependency is a part of our negotiations with the written and spoken word? And what is the "Ode on a Grecian Urn," here, beyond a proverbial, barely legible "poem scratched on glass"? In addition to the title sequences that invoke him (I quote from several others below), Keats enters the essay's field of vision in several remarks, recollections, and confessions during the course of Carson's story. The most dramatic of these, toward the end of the work, is also the moment of most direct engagement with the "idea that beauty is truth":

> ... let's just finish it.
> Not because, like Persephone, I needed to cool my cheek on death.
> Not, with Keats, to buy time.
> Not, as the tango, out of sheer wantonness.
> But oh it seemed sweet.
>
> To say Beauty is Truth and stop.
> Rather than to eat it.
> Rather than to want to eat it. This was my pure early thought. (139)

This last of the *29 Tangos* begins by explaining, in a shift to the third person, that "[t]o get them out of her the wife tries making a list of words she never got to say." To "finish it," as per her proposition above, is to say these words, to end their circulation by giving them definite form. By this point, Persephone has already made an appearance in *The Beauty of the Husband* in a brief commentary on the *Homeric Hymn to Demeter* (41–42). Condemned to live between the underworld inhabited by her husband, Hades, and the upper world of her mother, Demeter—between "seduction" and "production," as Carson characterizes her own affiliations to husband and mother (37)—Persephone crosses from the signifying field of fertility and filiation to that of desire and death.[16] "Not because, like Persephone . . .": dipping into this story of eros and violence, the negatively coupled simile draws to the surface the fatalism driving the narrator's seduction by the beauty of the husband. "Not, with Keats, to buy time. / Not, as the tango . . .": her denials play with apophasis, the kind of saying that can only get close to its motives by refusing their likeness. To synthesize her story and the poetic and philosophical yield of decades, the narrator indexes some of the work's most memorable figures—"Words, wheat, conditions, gold, more than thirty years of it fizzing around in me—." She does so, she says, in order to "lay it to rest," a wish she will qualify in the lines that follow: "After all the heart is not a small stone / to be rolled this way and that. / The mind is not a box / to be shut fast. / And yet it is!" (140–141)—more saying by naysaying. These final lines negotiate the "[t]errible risks" (141) of emotion by organizing words and figures, rolling them around, contradicting them, end-stopping a sequence. It is a messy affirmation, one that performs the ordeals of its pursuit, as though parsing words and images always expressed a desire to exclude them.

"Finishing" the story of enthrallment to these words to "buy time" remembers the urgent vocation of Keats's last months of illness, in which finishing and not finishing must both have seemed to him impossible. It picks up strongly on the lyric consciousness of the "Ode on a Grecian Urn," to which I turn in more detail below, where the "heard melodies" of the writing—its metered, sensible time—tense against what Keats calls the "those unheard"; the "slow time," the "history without footnotes" (in Cleanth Brooks's terms), of the Grecian urn.[17] The scenes of love and sacrifice danced around its frieze—Keats's "Cold Pastoral"—are simulations, unconsummated approaches, tangos frozen in time: "Fair youth, beneath the trees, thou canst not leave / Thy song, nor ever can those trees be bare; / Bold lover, never, never canst thou kiss, / Though winning near the goal."[18] To buy time, beat-by-beat or word-by-word, is to bring this song to life, but it is also, eventually, to bring it to an end. The unconventional essay that emerges out of the Keats/Carson encounter sketches a panorama not dissimilar to Keats's in the "Ode": some fictions are fatalistic, timeless, and disembodied—made to "cool my cheek on death" (Keats's "Cold Pastoral")—and others are bound to the moment of their making, preserving the *mania* of metaphors that have composed and undone a desiring life. Carson's early reading of the *Phaedrus* in *Eros the Bittersweet* flashes up once more here. Between words that pin desire down and words that betray its delirium in real time is the difference—or one way of measuring it—between death and life.

Carson's final confession in the above—"it seemed sweet. // To say Beauty is Truth and stop. / Rather than to eat it. / Rather than to want to eat it. This was my pure early thought"—is where essay and story, as it were, finally meet. At the famous final couplet of the "Ode" and the "idea" to which Carson's essay is dedicated:

> "Beauty is truth, truth beauty,"—that is all
> Ye know on earth, and all ye need to know.[19]

Carson's "pure early thought"—"to say Beauty is Truth and stop"—echoes a part of the sentiment of Keats's final lines: that the equation "Beauty is truth" quenches and consumes the desire "to know" anything beyond itself. Yet in its emphatic quotation marks, Keats's couplet proffers a metaphor ("Beauty *is* truth") that it claims to be reversible ("truth beauty") as well as inexorable ("that is all / Ye know on earth"). In her interview with McNeilly, Carson calls the equation of beauty and truth in Keats "a mistake," and an axiom that falls on the modern ear "with a tired thump": "You can't think into something you've heard that many times."[20] It is an act of language that, over the course of citations innumerable, has become oddly transparent: "obvious yet invisible," the literary cliché—which the Keats couplet has now become—"works best" and "self-perpetuates" (to borrow Namwali Serpell's words) when it "goes *unnoticed*."[21] It is not only overuse that has taken the edge off Keats's phrase, but something else, perhaps, in the aesthetic drama circling inside that final couplet. For "Beauty is truth/truth beauty" is a metaphor that conceals or cancels out what, in the "Essay on What I Think About Most," Carson calls metaphor's "error" and "mistakenness": the fact that beauty is *not the same as* truth, and vice versa. The full reversibility of Keats's proposition renders it symmetrical in a way that closes out all mediation, so that the second iteration ("truth beauty") can squeeze out the "is" of the first. ("The metaphorical 'is' signifies both 'is not' and 'is like,'" Paul Ricoeur observes.)[22] Its reversibility makes Keats's metaphor a tautology, collapsing the comparison and erasing its essential flaw: beauty eats truth, truth eats beauty, the one is a devouring metonym for the other.[23] Moreover, this totalized metaphor, Keats says, is "all / Ye know" and "all ye need to know." Absolute fulfillment of the desire to know, be all and end all of poetic thinking, it expresses a wish—a wish Carson shares in the above—for the *end* of metaphor. Interesting in this regard is Carson's description of her book as "an essay on Keats's idea that beauty is truth," occluding the second part of the formula, as her above confession suggests she wished to: "to say Beauty is Truth and stop."

Carson's narrator has been snared, she suggests, because beauty and truth do not fit together as cleanly as her "pure early thought" had envisaged. Truth eats beauty, but it leaves unknown quantities behind, accruing in the "true lies of poetry." In her efforts "to eat beauty," or "to want to eat it," Carson's narrator— "IMPURE AS I AM (FOODSTAINS AND SHAME AND / ALL)" (139)— seeks this surplus "out there with purposiveness, with temples, with God," understanding only later, she says, that "the beautiful when I encountered it would turn out to be / prior—inside my own heart, / already eaten" (140). There is an analogy here, surely, with the way Carson's text has "eaten" and digested the Keats oeuvre, which, like Emily Brontë in "The Glass Essay," has become a symptom of the narrator's tribulations and her interlocutor in a "fictional" argument. Yet more interesting and urgent here are our feelings as readers on engaging a work with such profound, intricately theorized ambivalence toward its own medium. We will see Plato's critique of writing and poetry in the *Phaedrus* and *The Republic* make an explicit appearance in Carson's thinking on poetic imitation in *The Beauty of the Husband*. At a certain point in the essay, the compulsive course of metaphor, analogy, and self-reading is reined in by an anti-poetic sentiment of the kind we see more faintly outlined in "The Glass Essay" and explicitly formalized in *Decreation*. There, in the poem "Stanzas, Sexes, Seductions," the wish whose utterance both clinches and wishes away the essence of lyric is "I want to have meaningless legs." The poem continues:

> My personal poetry is a failure.
> I do not want to be a person.
> I want to be unbearable.
> Lover to lover, the greenness of love.
> Cool, cooling. . . .
> Drink all the sex there is.
> Still die.[24]

To be "unbearable" is imagined as a full secession from meaning, the meaningful body that mediates between lover and lover. The fatalism tingeing *The Beauty of the Husband*, and the final scenes of "The Glass Essay," could not be clearer in this poem. For it doesn't matter how much sex you "drink," or how much beauty you "eat" ("beauty," she says in the first pages of the fictional essay, "makes sex sex," 9). "Personal" poetry cannot capture the immanence—the "cool" inside "cooling"— her narrator wants from love.

For and Against Poetry

It is striking that the rich anti-poetic lyric that emerges across several of Carson's "personal" poems and essays, and which she theorizes with the aid of Plato's *Phaedrus*, Simone Weil's decreation theology, even Paul Celan's drastic antimetaphoric economy, has gone unnoticed by readers who use the term "antipoetic" to Carson's discredit.[25] The resistance to poetry has a history as long as the history of poetics, though the tensions such resistance generates in poems comes to a head in and after twentieth-century modernism.[26] Marianne Moore's "I too dislike it" and W. H. Auden's more ambiguous "poetry makes nothing happen" declare what in later poets—Carson included—seems a more complicated reluctance. (In Carson, for example, the Dada-esque remodeling of what a "poem" or "essay" can look like rubs along with some of the most traditional poetic forms.) What I have been calling lyric transparency in Carson's essay, a thoroughgoing exposure of device and the disappearance of the reading of Keats into its intimate conditions of possibility, is by no means the only instance of this reluctance. "The Glass Essay" works something similar into its project for the essay, as do Carson's formal inquiries in *Decreation* and the early minimalism of *Short Talks*. The "fiction" in "fictional essay" can be understood as all of a piece with the ascetic drive of these compositions. Calling it "fictional" sets the extreme susceptibility of her reading—to emotion and to the art of lying—against the rationale "beauty is truth" with unsurpassable economy. Calling it a fictional essay also makes Carson's author-narrator all the more compelling. For the confession of unreliability, not a statement of scholarly integrity, is what makes this particular reading believable. It is also, perhaps, just the kind of susceptibility we want from a mimetically involved, creative-critical, or post-critical reading of Keats.

Following the subtitle, *The Beauty of the Husband* exposes its devices from the opening page ("Fair reader I offer merely an analogy," 5). Around two-thirds of the way through ("Tango XXIV"), the narrator pledges her commitment to an event of overhaul (at the "edge" of transparency), set out in uppercase in the title sequence: "AND KNEELING AT THE EDGE OF THE TRANS-/PARENT SEA I SHALL SHAPE FOR MYSELF A NEW HEART / FROM SALT AND MUD" (111). "Easy to say Why not give up on this?," she says of herself, a wife "in the grip of being," recalling Emily "in the grip" in "The Glass Essay"; but poring over and paranoid-reading the husband's speech is a métier difficult to abandon. This "NEW HEART" of unrefined, if not unsignified, material is of the order of the "meaningless legs" of "Stanzas, Sexes, Seductions," a poem in the spirit of the late ascetic turn in *The Beauty of the Husband*. "Not a bird not a breath in sight," the Tango concludes: no redemptive symbolism and no *pneuma*, the breath and life of poems.

It seems important to say here—though I hope it has so far come across—that Carson's metafictional exposures are not strictly "outside" the fictions of the fictional essay. That these exposures express ennui or profound disheartening in the face of poetic artifice, the husband's cryptic letters and beautiful lies, does not set the lyric voice of *The Beauty of the Husband* above or beyond device, as an essay in its documentary function might be styled. Rather, it sets device squarely at the center of the dilemma. The work's acutest moments of disclosure reach, with some urgency, for poetic artifice. The title sequence immediately following the staged rite above reads: "PROVIDED IN A SPIRIT OF UNASHAMED DIS-/ CLOSURE OR AS KEATS MIGHT SAY STITCHING THEIR / THROATS TO THE LEAVES SOMETHING TO MAKE TIME / PASS" (123). The mood is ambivalent as the narrator, in the verse following the title, catches our eye: "You see me, you see my life, see what I live on—is that all I want? / No. I want to make you see time." "KEATS," too, we have seen, is "what I live on" and rehearsing his "idea" in and through the events of a life makes us "see time" in the work. Carson has said, in a recent essay, that Keats's poem is "about the pathos of time."[27] Reading Keats, reading Plato, Parmenides, lends relief to the real-time narrative texture (as "CATULLUS" "makes time itself visible" in Twombly). Autobiographical exposure ("you see my life") is a performance of affiliation ("see what I live on"), and both are moved by a commitment they share with the spirit of critical inquiry. In Fredric Jameson's terms, "making time appear" is part of the "mimesis" due from criticism.[28]

Exposure and disclosure make us see the time of the lover, the time of a reader, as it moves, and the time of lovers and readers, we saw in *Eros the Bittersweet*, is sharpened by its sensible movement. An oblique allusion to Keats's "Ode to a Nightingale," and one of precious few direct invocations of the poet, "AS KEATS MIGHT SAY STITCHING THEIR / THROATS TO THE LEAVES" displaces the onus of disclosure onto Keats's icon of lyric song, whose sounding is—is sutured to, coextends—his natural habitat. Keats's nightingale sings of leaves, not scorned lovers: "Fade far away, dissolve, and quite forget / What thou among the leaves hast never known"; though it is his immanent song that Keats would imitate, carried aloft "on the viewless wings of Poesy."[29] Poetry "TO MAKE TIME / PASS" might seem to be the opposite of making us "see time." Yet as the narrator lists the elegiac couplets she composes, meditating daily on a branch, what we see is time passing in figures, time metered out, in a sample of the "5820 elegiacs. / Which occupy 53 wirebound notebooks" (125). This is poetry that both makes time pass and makes us see it. Reproducing its present tense in ours, Carson's exercises in "lyric mimesis" perform her daily meditations in "the lyric present": "Brighter than Bite / it bangs March Light too tight" (124).[30] Tin-bright assonance, too-tight rhyme, and bangy meter offer the narrator a song close enough—almost transparent—to the leaves. Her elegiacs, in their bare, subjectless testimony, seem to aspire, too, to the immanent poetry of the nightingale, in whose pure sounding is the promise of lyric without an "I."

In her reading of Plato in *Eros the Bittersweet*, Carson argued that where the written word effaces the time and time-bound crises of eros, playing games with the temporality of reading, the spoken word plants you right there in the heat of its circumstance. *The Beauty of the Husband* revives the dilemma of the *Phaedrus* in a play on the difference between language that is "true" to those circumstances and language that errs and strays. Hence between two kinds of betrayal: betrayal as the exposure of emotion, the kind of betrayal performed, for Barthes, by dedications; and betrayal as the cumulative lie of infidelity. On the one hand is what Carson calls the "enriched pattern" of "myth": the "two-faced proposition" that allows "its operator to say one thing and mean another," "the true lies of poetry" (33); and on the other, the voice as performative presence, language used "in the way that Homer says the gods do" (33), contra the language of mortals. The Husband speaks in the former key, where "not much" connects words and things. But he "flip[s] the switch at will" (33), she says, between the mortal, shared meaning of words, and another field of reference—Elysian, celestial, unbound to time or place:

> [I] went out to meet him
> in the ravine, traipsing till dawn in the drenched things
> and avowals
>
>> of the language that is "alone and first in mind." I stood stupid
>> before it,
>> watched its old golds and *lieblicher* blues abandon themselves
>> like peacocks stepping out of cages into an empty kitchen of God. (23–24)

These "drenched things and avowals" are the pure matter and gesture of words: vowels still wet on the tongue, a language of promise that seems to remember the promise of the very first language.[31] "The language for which we have no words," says Giorgio Agamben, to whom the unattributed inset quotation "alone and first in mind" belongs, is the mother tongue (Agamben is paraphrasing Dante, for whom the mother tongue is "the one and only thing first in mind").[32] "The language for which we have no words, which doesn't pretend, like grammatical language, to be there before being, but is 'alone and first in mind' is our language," says Agamben: "that is, the language of poetry."[33] The phenomenal force of this language can stupefy. It—the language of Dante—emerges from the "old golds and *lieblicher* blues" of illuminated text and passes quietly into a new, unpeopled stratum of sense: "like peacocks stepping out of cages into an empty kitchen of God."[34]

The husband's language at first claims this primordial force, but with hindsight the narrator comes to shed her illusions—"My husband lied about everything" (33)—and to ally him with a disorienting metonymy; a language for which we have all too many words. An "operator" of myth, he led "a double life" (33), spoke a language "always double, triple, caught up in the infinite recession of metalanguages" (so says Agamben of the grammatical language "that forever presupposes words").[35] Agamben/Dante's embedding here is one of several instances of critical and philosophical literatures consumed by the narrative, with stray phrases appearing as recollections in passing, remains of "what has seduced," and symptoms of an exacting self-analysis.[36]

The "Ode on a Grecian Urn," too, is invoked indirectly—"overheard"—in this account of the young narrator's stupefied gaze. The *lieblicher* (sweeter) tones of the language "alone and first in mind," the language wandering its own celestial vicinity, are those melodies Keats's second stanza calls "unheard"; a primordial, spectral language whose meaning stands outside of time:

> Heard melodies are sweet, but those unheard
> Are sweeter; therefore, ye soft pipes, play on;
> Not to the sensual ear, but, more endear'd,
> Pipe to the spirit ditties of no tone:
> Fair youth, beneath the trees, thou canst not leave
> Thy song, nor ever can those trees be bare;
> Bold Lover, never, never canst thou kiss, . . .

The "Bold Lover" traipsing the frieze of Keats's urn is stranded in a representation of love that binds him to the extemporal "nonlover" of the *Phaedrus*, the lover not *in* love but love's master. This nonlover's discourse (the speech of Lysias), in Carson's reading, plays not to the urgent, "sensual ear" of the lover's spoken word but to a kind of screen-grab to which he can return again and again—or rather, as for the "fair youth" of the frieze, which he "canst not leave," doomed to love unconsummated for eternity. The unheard melodies of this *lieblicher* language are "no tone" tonalities stranded in the imagination—and in words, before their speaking—, unmoored from the matter and melody of vocal music.

The "sweeter" melodies of verbal mimesis and their theorization in the *Phaedrus* are summoned at several points in the fictional essay. The following title sequence is Carson's most explicit allusion to Plato, which she references in the "Notes":

XI. MAKE YOUR CUTS IN ACCORDANCE WITH THE LIVING JOINTS OF THE FORM SAID SOCRATES TO PHAEDRUS WHEN THEY WERE DISSECTING A SPEECH ABOUT LOVE.[37]

The sequence is immediately followed by the narrator's first sight of her future husband in a high school Latin class: "for some reason I turned in my seat / and there he was. / You know how they say a Zen butcher makes one correct cut and the whole ox / falls apart / like a puzzle. Yes a cliché // and I do not apologize because as I say I was not to blame" (49). These two iterations of the "cut" combine to suggest that what Socrates's incisions in the "speech about love" aspire to—to locate and coincide with the "living joints of the form," exposing its rhetorical anatomy—is accomplished at the mere sight of the beloved, the unlocking of a puzzle without the slightest cognitive effort ("Useless to interpose analysis / or make contrafactual suggestions"). The vignette is moving, her exposure is moving, and it draws attention—intentionally or otherwise—to her sustained rhetorical analysis of the husband's dissimulating discourse of love, in lieu of analysis of "Keats's idea that beauty is truth" or even the recognition that it is Keats's (after it is Plato's) idea.

Carson has described the fragments of quotation separating her twenty-nine compositions as pieces of "bad Keats," interesting ("shiny") because of their aslant reflections on the principal story.[38] These fragments of marginalia, errata, and juvenilia derive mostly from the minor works *Otho the Great: A Tragedy in Five Acts*, Keats's only full-length play, and *The Cap and Bells; Or, The Jealousies*, a satirical fairy tale in Spenserian stanzas, first published under the ludic pseudonym Lucy Vaughan Lloyd of China Walk, Lambeth.[39] The convoluted plots of these works turn on the erratic course of a betrothal and/or marriage, deceit, and impersonation (starting with the authorial pseudonym, which Carson includes), scorned lovers, the delirium inspired by letters, and, in *The Jealousies*, a magic book.[40] Other fragments come from the "Ode on Indolence," marginal notes to *The Jealousies* and on Keats's copy of *Paradise Lost*, and finally, preceding the husband's closing interpolation, the phrase "O Isle spoilt by the Milatary [sic]" with the attribution "[words found by John Keats scratched on the glass / of his lodgings at Newport on the night of April 15, 1817]" (143).[41] This final fragment plays on the husband's penchant for war games ("Why play all night. / The time is real. It's a game. / It's a real game," 10) and the encroachment of their "real" simulations on the narrator's marriage.

The words found by Keats are ironic as they are serendipitous. Yet it is their material circumstances that, like the annotations to *Paradise Lost*, interlace most intriguingly with what Carson does in her fictional essay. These words, noted in the margin of a book or found scratched on the window at an inn, attest to the time-bound affects and attention of a reader. They attest, too,—or expose—the intimate speech of a writer writing unobserved, through whom the world of his sources, and his geographical and physical circumstances, is momentarily made visible. This is the "Emily" of Carson's "The Glass Essay" (like the "Emily" of Susan Howe's *My Emily Dickinson*), whose disposition and moods might be overheard, less in the cadence of vowels than in the minor contingencies of annotation and transcription.[42] Carson's description of these minutiae is minimal, but it is sufficient to suggest that, in Howe's words, "the heart may be sheltering in some random mark of communication":[43]

> a sort of delphic Abstraction a beautiful thing made more
> beautiful by being reflected and put in a Mist
>
> JOHN KEATS,
> note on his copy of Paradise Lost, I.321
>
> [there is a faint mark after *beautiful* read by one editor as a dash,
> by another as a slip of the pen, while a third does not print it] (103)

It is tempting to read intention into the content and placement of these fragments; to embark on the kind of jealous, paranoid reading that is the benighted task of Carson's narrator, sifting through the Husband's remarks, gestures, "faint marks," in search of signs meant for her. Yet the avid and devouring hermeneutic of jealous lovers is not one that *The Beauty of the Husband* recommends. On the one hand, the book provides precisely the kind of backstory in which Carson seems interested in Keats—the intimate circumstances and contingencies that turn scratched marks into signs and signs into wonders, as per the lover's hungered reading. On the other, the Keats fragments themselves are no clues to the "true" logic of Carson's thinking. Elements in a collage, the fragments' relation to the "idea that beauty is truth" is what we might call a relation of passive reading, in which they simply offset, augment, or unsettle the equation of beauty and truth without any explanation as to how this happens or any leads or remarks on the analogies they suggest with Carson's narrative. To go chasing after such signs in search of what Barthes called "transcendence"—the lover's "horizontal" discourse promised "no transcendence, no deliverance, no novel (though a great deal of the fictive)"—feels as fatalistic as Carson's book suggests by example.

To the degree that the narrator mimics our critical scrutiny by reading the essay's vignettes and motifs from within, and in a reading style that might justly be called paranoid, *The Beauty of the Husband* places our task as its interpreters in an odd light. The work sets us up as its accomplice—"Shall we sharpen our eyes and circle closer to the beauty of the husband-" (115)—but the same "story of a marriage" is a stark warning against suspicious hermeneutics and reading for truth. It is, after all, our complicity in a "fictional" essay that is invited, and as much as it asks us to sympathize with its analytical zeal, Carson's essay also cuts it aslant. A reading of autobiographical facts and autofictions is a proxy for the very reading of Keats these facts and fictions have made possible—a critique of "beauty is truth" addressed from wife to husband. The narrator's exacting attention to her story and its literary and philosophical resonances matters for our task, but not because it obliges us to out-read her or beat her at her own game.

Rather, her transparency invites us to look again at our position: at what it is we're accustomed to doing with literature that we can't do—or can't do as exhaustively as Carson does—here. How it feels to be told a story, told what it means, given analogies and even supporting quotations, by a single, self-compromising narrative persona.

World Not Art

Lyric transparency in *The Beauty of the Husband* exposes the "essay on Keats's idea" to some serious questions, beginning, I suggested, with the whereabouts of the "essay" itself. A thoroughgoing disclosure of motive, emotion, readings, and sources replaces that other expository work proper to an essay. Lyric transparency renders the essay a fiction of its own making; expressed differently, its confessional agenda seems to have made the entire, putative essay transparent. For in the absence of the exposition we expect, Carson's "INDIRECT" reading of Keats can make us feel we are looking through it to the personal story and private conditions of possibility from which it has arisen: that the essay has disappeared into its generative occasion. The transparency of Carson's fictional essay is acknowledged in the declaration "You see me, you see my life, see what I live on," but it is also implicit in suggestions that what her narrator says is self-evident, guileless, a story we know almost better than she does ("You know I was married years ago" . . . "You if anyone grasp this," 9). Should we misrecognize it in the telling, the narrator exposes her methods and tics along the way—"Fair reader I offer merely an analogy. // A delay" (5).

This last confession, the work's sixth and seventh lines following the opening title sequence, is immediately followed by an illustrative quotation to explain what Carson's narrator means by "analogy":

> "Use delay instead of picture or painting–
> a delay in glass
> as you would say a poem in prose or a spittoon in silver."
> So Duchamp
> of *The Bride Stripped Bare by Her Bachelors* . . .
>
>   What is being delayed?
>   Marriage I guess. (5)

Carson will revisit Duchamp in the work only by indirect allusion. Here, in this striking opening vignette, the quotation and the artwork it describes seem placed in order to expose the operations of her essay. Her quotation is one of the most widely cited phrases from *The Green Box*, a sheaf of loose papers with no determined order of reading, which Duchamp published as an accompaniment to *The Bride Stripped Bare*.[44] When the artwork famously shatters and Duchamp refuses to repair it, this is, he states, because he had always envisaged the work as open to contingency, a fact he sought to reflect in *The Green Box*—as Carson seeks to in *Float*—by establishing no order of reading.[45] "Delay," Carson's "analogy," happens for Duchamp by a trick of form—"a delay *in glass* / as you would say a poem *in prose* or a spittoon *in silver*"—and in place of representation: "Use delay *instead of* picture or painting." The trick of form is to expose the viewer, his beliefs, customs, morals, and expectations, to his own scrutiny. This is what "silver" does in Duchamp's second example: its simultaneous proximity and jarring mismatch with our idea of a spittoon makes us witness to our own surprise and manages to illustrate what a spittoon is without illustration. Silver, here, is an optic for the mind to observe its own activity. Glaring incongruity in Duchamp's famous "readymades," where this viewer-oriented, exposing function of art is most rigorously rehearsed, makes these works prime expressions of the Aristotelian idea of metaphor as a poetic mistake—the Carsonian reading of "error"—where the mind catches itself processing sense and cognitive dissonance in the same "aha!" moment.

"A poem in prose," Duchamp's first example, moves us closer to Carson and to the "fictional essay" that has, at this point, only just begun. Carson is a master of the literary "readymade," with her found material and Duchampian tricks of form. Like *The Beauty of the Husband*, many of her *Short Talks* are "about" their professed subject matter in name only. Consecutive translations of Ibykos fragment 286 in "Variations on the Right to Remain Silent" use "the wrong words" (readymade content from six restricted vocabularies) to throw its constative structure into relief, as it is supposed Duchamp's "prose" reveals the pure form of his "poem."[46] Carson's lecture in sonnet form, we saw, does something similar by using verse to address, and derail, our expectations of the lecture, which is then freed up for new imaginative work. Poems in prose are of course a commonplace, but Duchamp's "delay" is simply about presenting one form in the guise of another—a lecture caught in the weft of verse, an essay parsed through the twists and turns of a story. If prose is an instrument for asking the question of poetry, then perhaps a story is well placed to inquire after an essay: where it comes from, what drives it, what we expect from it, and where it takes its subject matter. *The Beauty of the Husband*'s narrative verse opens up a rift between the text and its designation, making the form itself an act of address: "Form is what is between the thing and its name," says Barthes: "form is what delays the name."[47]

Is Carson's fictional essay, then, "merely an analogy"—a clever use of "delay"? What does the Duchamp example suggest about the lyric transparency of Carson's essay? And what is delayed, finally, in a "delay in *glass*"? To respond to these questions, I turn once more to Keats, the dedicatee of Carson's book, who is mostly missing in action from the body of the text. Here is the opening stanza of the "Ode on a Grecian Urn":

> Thou still unravish'd bride of quietness,
>   Thou foster-child of silence and slow time,
> Sylvan historian, who canst thus express
>   A flowery tale more sweetly than our rhyme:
> What leaf-fring'd legend haunts about thy shape
>   Of deities or mortals, or of both,
>   In Tempe or the dales of Arcady?
>   What men or gods are these? What maidens loth?
>   What mad pursuit? What struggle to escape?
>   What pipes and timbrels? What wild ecstasy?[48]

Keats's scene sets one imitation against another. On the one hand, the urn: the "still unravished bride of quietness" and the pastoral love scene of its decorative frieze. On the other, the "Ode" and its tradition: "our rhyme." The urn has the quiet composure of an "unravished bride." The story told around its "leaf-ring'd legend" is all the more compelling, all the sweeter, Keats suggests, for what it withholds. This is where the "Ode" itself comes in, and by singing of the sweetness of the unsung, of melodies unheard and the delight of perpetual delay, puts itself in an awkward position. The "Ode" is a hymn to elusiveness and opacity of the kind the verse itself will not match, for Keats's "Sylvan historian" is as much a chronicler of fantasy and imaginative possibility as of irrecoverable moments. The intactness of his "bride" is its—the urn's—non-penetration by the circumstances of its making and refusal to divulge its meaning. The bride's eternal chastity is echoed in scenes from the frieze evoked in later stanzas: "Bold Lover, never, never canst thou kiss" . . . "For ever wilt thou love and she be fair!". . . "Cold Pastoral!" The love frozen in its scenes is one that never can, and never will, take breath. As Cleanth Brooks wrote of the "Ode," "all human passion does leave one cloyed; hence the superiority of art," yet this superiority leaves us cold and unconvinced: for, says Brooks, "*the beauty portrayed is deathless because it is lifeless.*"[49]

We can contrast this immediately, as I sought to above, with the desire of Carson's narrator to "make you see time," the streamed real-time of recollection, disclosure, address, and analysis. We can contrast Keats's "Cold Pastoral" with Carson's hot bucolic scenes at the house of the Husband's grandfather, where the young couple crush grapes under their feet and lick off the juice. The unconsummated love scenes of Keats's poem return us indirectly to Plato and the "nonlover" of the sophist Lysias, who would rather write a speech about love than risk getting his hands dirty, freezing love out of time rather than live with the threat of its ending. Carson summons Keats's "unravished bride of quietness" against her own "UNASHAMED" account of a bride given to speak (and apparently loath to stop). Yet she also positions *The Bride Stripped Bare* from the start as a strong formal counterpoint to the urn and as an optic through which the fictional essay begins to expose its inner mechanics.

Also known as *The Large Glass* (*Le grand verre*), Duchamp's *The Bride Stripped Bare by Her Bachelors, Even* (*La mariée mise à nu par ses célibataires, même*, 1915–1923) is a large-format plate-glass structure featuring several distinct scenes, etched and painted onto the glass in oil and lead. An aluminum frame divides the work horizontally, creating two sections: "The Bride's Domain" occupies the upper section; "The Bachelor Apparatus" the lower. The catalog of the Modern Art collections of the Tate Gallery describes the work as "a diagram of an ironic love-making machine of extraordinary complexity in which the male and female machines communicate only by means of two circulatory systems, and without any point of contact."[50] The work was intended by Duchamp to be freestanding, exhibited in the middle of the gallery space, where the glass becomes an optic for its surroundings. What for Octavio Paz is "one of the most hermetic works of this century" and "the very negation of the modern notion of [art]work" is also, for Umberto Eco, the prototype of the *open work* of Modernist aesthetics.[51] For Eco, the "open work" calls on the viewer to make sense of a work whose formal and symbolic boundaries are yet to be fixed, offering a free-for-all of possible affinities.[52] The open work is an artwork whose formal constraints potentially include the place of its exhibition and/or the circumstances surrounding its production or selection: the *objet trouvé* or the readymade whose purpose is to convert art into a performance, not of its manufacture—its madeness—, but of its interpretability. *The Bride Stripped Bare* is a symbol machine that, at the same time, for Paz, confronts us with the nihilistic destruction of the symbolic, a bride ravished from below by "her bachelors," and from without by the circumstances (and viewers) of her exhibition.[53] What is Duchamp's "story of a marriage," *The Bride Stripped Bare*, doing on the first page of an essay on "Keats's idea that beauty is truth"?

Keats's "Ode on a Grecian Urn" and Duchamp's *The Bride Stripped Bare* offer two radically different visions of the relation between art and the world. Where Duchamp's anti-art would have world and interpretation supplant the work, Keats's hymn to the urn's mysteries would have it remain just as it is, still quiet, timeless, unassailed by critics and well-meaning readers. *The Bride Stripped Bare* is contingent in the extreme on the circumstances of its exhibition, whose contours and colors determine its body, depth, and mood; the bride and bachelors etched onto the plate glass incorporate the exhibition scene and metabolize it—destroy and remake it—as though their union were meant to dramatize the insatiability of looking and to make this drama—the viewer's—the object of the work of art. Considered to mark the end of the autonomy of the work of art, *The Bride* claims final indivisibility from its surroundings, swallowing time and place into its formal parameters. Keats's hermetic "bride," on the other hand, keeps her secrets. Her sealed lips are the source of a lyricism sweeter than lyric: "Heard melodies are sweet, but those unheard / Are sweeter." (The "ditties of no tone," two lines down, might be those we imagine as we listen across time, as well as those elements of verse we don't "hear" but that speak to us all the same.) Where one work's drama of interpretability derives from its reticence, the other's derives from its transparency and radical permeability, which cedes the work's meaning (its consumption, its destruction) to the viewer.

Allusions to Duchamp and his glass crop up throughout Carson's essay. Her narrator, for example, calls the Husband "one of those 'original machines' that brings libidinal devices into a new transparency" (a listed reference to Baudrillard's *Forget Foucault*, on "original," "desiring machines" of libidinal energy, but also invoking Duchamp's *machine célibataire*, the "bachelor machine" that courts and exposes the viewer's desire).[54] The work is also alluded to through the Husband's friend, partner in "war games" and colluder in "mysteries," Ray (Man Ray, collaborator in Duchamp's optical experiments?): "his curiously crystalline little body / did set up a wise and fleshy relation / between world and retina" (105). The relation between world and retina, and the effects produced by artwork in the internal workings of the eye, were explicit preoccupations of Duchamp's and driving concerns behind the transparency and allegorized relation of *The Bride Stripped Bare*.[55] Reflecting on her own writing at the top of the same page, Carson's narrator asks: "What can save these marks from themselves. / What if we drop a little more solvent / on the seam // between foreground and background," concerns proper to *The Bride*, whose seam between foreground and background, work and world, is so difficult to pin down.

In a sense, then, what we might call Duchamp's "fictional" artworks, heralding the end of autonomous art and art created rather than "found," are a sort of prototype for Carson's fictional essay. What Carson provides, I suggested at the start of this chapter, is a detailed confessional backstory, a time-bound world that the essay's transparency brings into the foreground: this is to say, the background *becomes* the foreground; the world becomes the work, and the essay, invisible as such, becomes a provocative fiction.[56] Yet this, as Carson knows—and as Keats knew of his "rhyme"—, catches her book in a quandary. As Jay Bernstein has written of Duchampian "anti-art": "The anti-art moment of modernist works ... enacts art's desire to be world and not art; but only *as art*, as semblance, can art evince that desire, perform it."[57] Only as a "fictional essay" can Carson's book perform a desire for transparency—a desire to bring imitation and its analysis to an end.

The desire "to be world and not art" runs through much of Carson's writing. Not just the claims of *Decreation* to a version of Simone Weil's desire "to disappear," nor Carson's declaration at the start of *Economy of the Unlost*—"There is too much self in my writing"—but a claim made, rather, in the name of literary form. We can safely say, at least by most academic standards, that there is "too much self" in Carson's translations and adaptations—from *Nox* to *H of H Playbook*—as well as in her lectures, freeform essays, and other performances of reading and thinking: "The Glass Essay," *The Albertine Workout*, *The Beauty of the Husband*, and so on. The claim made in the name of form is something different. The above works, and not only these works, are examples of the personal, time-bound circumstances of Carson's reading shaping or replacing a descriptive, critical account or faithful translation of the works she reads. Her experience of "the facts" of these works, even where that takes her into fiction and fake source material, is set firmly in the foreground. Brooks wrote of Keats's "Ode on a Grecian Urn" that its reticent object represented a case of "history without footnotes."[58] In certain of Carson's readings, what we get are footnotes without history—or at least without chronology and "scientific fact": supporting anecdotes, sources, and quotations, reflections like those she lets bloom in the appendices of *The Albertine Workout*, compressed into a single prismatic plane.

It might be possible, if not too far-fetched, to consider this approach to form as a "glass" mode after Duchamp's *The Large Glass*. In Duchamp, the medium of glass—conspicuous if not "treacherous" in its transparency—becomes a reflection on the mediating function, on its own status both as matter and threshold for other matter ("apparition" and "apparatus," in Angela Leighton's terms for the double capacity of form).[59] The transparency of Carson's writing to the personal history of her readings, and in her real-time commentary, exposures of intent, and interpolations to readers, brings the world and mind of Carson the reader into the same discursive plane, wrought of the same vocal texture as the works she reads. It is, in the most literal sense, a reflection of the fact of being a threshold for other objects: for the words, texts, and facts she handles in her readings of literature. But by the same token, Carson's "glass" essayism draws attention to its own form, facts, and objecthood, the new and irregular forms that come into view by being sidetracked, displaced, and fictionalized in her hands. Carson's transparency is an appeal to pay renewed attention to form, in terms of the thinking it is capable of performing, simulating, eliciting, and closing down.

"I broke the glass and jumped" was the true/false confession with which this chapter began. The fatalism of *The Beauty of the Husband* toward the never-ending story of metonymy, metaphor, and mimesis, we will find in a very different emotional key in *Decreation*, the subject of the following part of this book. In one of its early title sequences in *The Beauty of the Husband*, Carson refers to her writing as "MY PROPAGANDA, ONE ONE ONE ONE / ONEING ON YOUR

FOREHEAD LIKE DROPS OF LUMI-/NOUS SIN" (23). Her propaganda against Keats's self-effacing metaphor: beauty as fiction against "beauty is truth."[60] In this performative declaration, the freshly coined verb, to "one" ("oneing"), does its designated activity in four onomatopoeic nouns (or imperatives) and a gerund. This new, readymade verb "happens."[61] "Propaganda" is a word Duchamp used to describe the work of his readymades, which he envisaged as everyday objects emptied of signification and leaving only an impression on the surface of the mind. It is a vision of form we have seen Carson share in her aspiration to "sensible form," in the poetics of "Possessive Used as Drink (Me)," and a penchant in her writing for the visually performative (*opsis*), "an art of pure shape." Yet the endless "secession from systems of meaning"—Rachel Blau DuPlessis's words for the action of Duchampian, or Steinian, aesthetics—has something death-driven about it.[62] "A tango (like a marriage)," reads the blurb of *The Beauty of the Husband*, "is something you have to dance to the end." The abiding unease that outlasts the final page of Carson's essay is that the spin-off from modernist and postmodern secession from meaning, the endless irony of anti-art and *mise-en-abyme* fictional essays, is at least vertiginous, at most self-destructive, as meaning is consumed and exhausted in and by the work. Her 2005 volume, *Decreation*, envisages radically different forms of transparency and "annihilation"—ways to "leap off the building" and take language down with you.

PART III
SPECULATIVE FORM

PART III
SPECULATIVE FORM

5
Decreation, or the Art of Disappearance

In "Foam (Essay with Rhapsody): On the Sublime in Longinus and Antonioni," Carson compares the films of Michelangelo Antonioni to the "muddled," "tautological" prose of Longinus's "On the Sublime" (*Decreation*, 45).[1] His treatise is a heady "aggregate of quotes," Carson says, and she affirms that, as well as the sensation of groundless awe with which it is usually associated, "the Sublime is a documentary technique" (45).[2] She explains the comparison with Antonioni. The director, for example, places "a mirror in the middle of the scene so that you glimpse a stray piece of world there. Or he likes to give you two successive shots of the same portion of reality, first from close up, then a little further away, scarcely different yet noticeably not the same" (49). Seeing in Antonioni is tautological, doubled over on itself, as Longinus's text redoubles the Sublime, says Carson, by reproducing it as an effect of style. Something about this tautological vision captures the death wish that gives sublime experience its intense, almost horrific frisson. In Antonioni's cinematic syntax this emerges in "a procedure, called *temps mort* by French critics, whereby the camera is left running on a scene after the actors think they have finished acting it" (49). Under sway of this procedure, in Antonioni's words, "the actors continue out of inertia into moments that seem 'dead.' The actor commits 'errors.' "[3] The actor, Carson adds, does "unscheduled things" (49).

It is tempting to translate this double case of performative documentation—syntaxes that simulate psychic muddle and self-estrangement—into a case for what Carson produces in her concept volume and multi-form compendium, *Decreation: Poetry, Essays, Opera* (2005). Carson's "documentary" of her thinking around Simone Weil's difficult concept, if that's what *Decreation* is, does "unscheduled things" with it, approaches the idea from a series of tautological "shots," lending the book an "aggregate" quality and the thinking it performs a certain elegant discontinuity. Carson's tic for self-theorization and exposure, we have seen, offers us several ways to take her at her word. If, in talking about Longinus and Antonioni, she is also talking about herself, then the onus is on us to resist the flattening-out that this redoubling invites: to refuse to truncate and simplify Carson's project, first, by reducing it to a display of technique, and second, by reducing it to what she says it is. If the consonance between what Carson describes and what she does suggests some kind of "sleight of hand" (Solway)—a performance of cleverness, affiliations, and so on—then it is worth asking, as this book seeks to do, about the compelling situation that puts us in as her readers: how Carson anticipates or even short-circuits our tasks and desires, and what we want or need her writing (as literature and/or as commentary) to be.

There certainly is strong consonance between Carson's arguments on the Sublime and the formal aesthetics of *Decreation*, and several readers have emphasized the importance of "Foam" for grasping how Carson works.[4] The same might be said of other works in the volume, whose formal characteristics and approach to questions of language, description, or "telling" offer to speak for *Decreation* as a whole. (The book's final piece, "Longing: A Documentary," includes the most compact autopoetic performance of the entire Carson oeuvre: "Facts lack something, she thought").[5] *Decreation* certainly does work over Weil's theology of "decreation"—"undoing the creature in us"—and does so at the level of form. Individual compositions rehearse what this "undoing" might mean by performing or failing to perform it in writing, an effort in which the multiform, iterative structure of the book as a whole is complicit. Yet we can't ultimately say *Decreation* is a case of performing the idea of "decreation" without also saying it contemplates the end of such a performance—the end of performative form.

A brief glance at the contents list tells us that what *Decreation* is, beyond "Poetry, Essays, Opera," is a series of variations on a theme. On the one hand, *Decreation* presents the kind of material and compositional modes we have come to expect in Carson: high-contrast or "stereoscopic" juxtapositions; versions and adaptations of other works; philosophical poem sequences; brilliant associative essays, and short, synthetic companion pieces in verse.[6] To cite a few examples: an essay on sleep in Virginia Woolf, Elizabeth Bishop, Homer, Plato, and Hamlet, and an accompanying eighteen-line "Ode to Sleep" (recalling John Berryman's eighteen-line "Dream Songs"[7]); the staging of sublime anachronism (e.g., "Kant's Question About Monica Vitti") in the "Sublimes" poem sequence; the "Decreation" essay/opera double act, the focus of the next chapter in this book; and an essay on chromatic and tonal "wrongness" during an eclipse (seen through "your spectroscope or bit of smoked glass," 149) in the writing of Emily Dickinson, Woolf, and Archilochos. "Drastic analogies abound in the literature of totality" (150), Carson says in the essay on eclipse, and it is easy—again—to see in her untimely combinations, as across the totality of the book, the staging of drastic analogy, analogies in sequence, and what she calls "incongruous ideas" set together in "a poetical kinde of a march, by friskes, skips and jumps" (so the book's epigraph from Florio's Montaigne).[8] If Carson is an analogist by technique and sensibility, then *Decreation* is the work that both showcases the technique in its maximum expression, as an inquiry conducted through iterative parallels, and tells us it is *not enough* to understand it as form and *technē* alone, its stakes confined to literary experimentation.

The "friskes, skips and jumps" of analogy have a special place in mystical literatures—and not just Weil's, as the following chapter discusses—because there of all places, where the object of desire and attention is absent, straight-up description is out. In the literature of divine absence, as in the "literature of totality," all we have are likenesses to the possible, sensations that fix possibility momentarily in the mind and body (and fixing her object is precisely what Weil wants to avoid). Jessica Fisher quotes Carson's remarks on "ecstasy" (*ek-stasis*) for the Ancient Greeks, one of Carson's analogs for "decreation," as "being up against something so that it bounces you out of yourself to a place where, nonetheless, you are still yourself; there's a connection to yourself as other."[9] For Fisher, the reckoning of *Decreation* with what Carson names "another human essence than self" is continuous with Carson's early work on desire, in which the lover has the beloved to come "up against" or "crash into," in another of Carson's metaphors.[10] In *Decreation*, however, where Carson reads desire through Weil's scenario, there is an important difference. Where the lover's "crisis of contact" derives from "the fact that two are not one," Weil's dilemma is having no "contact"—no palpable "two"—to speak of.[11] Rather than "up against" divine love, Weil is up against herself, crashing into her own perception: "when I am in any place I disturb the silence of heaven by the beating of my heart," and "If only I knew how to disappear there would be a perfect union of love between God and the earth I tread, the sea I hear."[12] "Another human essence than self"—whatever it is that survives "undoing the creature"—is, in Weil, less the product of an encounter than of the desire for it, strong enough to move the "self" to dare all in its pursuit.

Given the extreme emotional traction of these ideas in Carson's book, and given the radical un-reason of "ecstasy" as a reckoning with self and God and the tasks of writing, to speak of *Decreation* as the execution of a semiological "strategy" or the expression of a cognitive "principle" can be jarring.[13] The "other" of *Decreation*—what Carson calls "a connection to yourself as other," but what the authors she studies call "Sublime," "FarNear," "poverty," "contradiction," "God"—opens up deep psychic and emotional fault lines that a strictly formal analysis offers to close up, reducing the drama of the "other" to a drama of language and a literary exercise. *Decreation*, in this key sense, not only performs acts of deliberate authorial displacement, but also accounts for and seeks to perform a mind not entirely in control of itself: "The things you think of to link are not in your control," Carson has said: "It's just who you are, *bumping into the world*. But how you link them is what shows the nature of your mind."[14]

What follows is an argument about *Decreation* from two angles that seem, at moments, to converge. On the one hand, Carson's compendium performs an inquiry around the concept of "decreation," which is explored in various nomenclatures and put through different rigors of reflection and composition. The result is a sequential shifting of key and perspective, a displacement of the conceptual center that not only reproduces her working process but engages a mimetic harmony with the self-shattering métier of decreation. Carson's book, if we follow this line of reasoning, comes up with a more or less *decreative* account of decreation—a performance of self-undoing by disoriented and decentered inquiry. One of the things that most interests Carson about Weil's "decreation," we will see in the next chapter, is the contradiction it entertains as a matter of course: between Being and its apprehension, for example, or between the self as part of Creation and as an obstruction to its enjoyment by God. Carson turns Weil's spirit of contradiction onto the question of how to *write* decreatively: "To be a writer is to construct a big, loud, shiny centre of self from which the writing is given voice and any claim to be intent on annihilating this self while still continuing to write must involve the writer in some important acts of subterfuge and contradiction" (171). The erratic line of inquiry that emerges under the title of *Decreation* links authors, concepts, compositions, and memories in a paratactic organization; each association to the decreation idea bumps up against the others, and a kind of "passive synthesis" (Edmund Husserl's term) is achieved.[15] Yet where the conceptual through-line is broken and inconsistent, the book's lyric thread remains more or less intact. From the "I feel" of the first poem, "Sleepchains," to the self-observing "she thought" of "Longing: A Documentary," Carson's inquiry points toward a single speculative center, who rehearses her placement and edges under constraints of thought, grammar, and form. *Decreation* is the portrait of a mind "bumping into" an idea in its intertexts and analogies, in her scholarly material as in her intimate life; a mind whose displacement the book enacts by force of lyric testimony. This *voluntary* art of disappearance, Carson knows, does not escape "subterfuge and contradiction": the "big, loud, shiny center of self" floodlighting the mystic discourse of annihilation (171).

On the other hand, perhaps this is to misconstrue the nature of what Carson calls "links"—the "friskes, skips and jumps" of her "poetical kinde of march." Chapter 4 began with a scene from *The Beauty of the Husband* in which Carson's narrator "jumped" from a building only to tell us the "jump" wasn't real. To confess the fiction seems to neutralize the risk. But elsewhere, we saw, Carson is clear that her metaphorical jumps *feel* dangerous: "you leap off the building when you think poetically."[16] What is it that threatens (and thrills) in this leaping and jumping—or in "bouncing," "bumping," or "crashing"—from one place, one source, one idea, to another? In this chapter's close readings of individual works in *Decreation*, we will see the dilemmas of decreation reproduced in and across different compositional forms and from different angles of reckoning, the tonal and conceptual "jumps" between them carried off by a through-line of lyric interest and a sustained emotional pitch—at times ascribed to "I" or "she," at other times notorious for its staged impersonality. What we will also see, in the discontinuity of her forms and analogies, is a broken expression of decreation that thrives as much on the links Carson makes as on the gaps over which she jumps, and that confronts the terror that gaps themselves can arouse. In the Beguine mystic Marguerite Porete's drastic analogies, where likenesses are drawn across an immeasurable breach, Carson calls the effect a "thrill"—a sublime vertigo as meaning disappears into the gap and writing runs, as it were, on dead time. As in the intimated death wish of her "leaps" of poetic thinking, or in what she calls the "perilous activity" of associative linking, what Carson's versions of decreation stage, then, is less the desire to describe or perform decreation under controlled conditions than a desire far more ambivalent: to succumb to undoing in unscheduled feats of thought and writing—an *involuntary* art of disappearance.

Exit/Entrance

Decreation begins with a series of fourteen short poems titled "Stops," a group of tentative elegies for Carson's elderly mother—mentioned or evoked in all of them—who has passed into an inscrutable ("shoutless," "shipless") final phase of life (13, 3). Immediately following the poems is a short prose essay on sleep, "Every Exit Is an Entrance (A Praise of Sleep)," whose title riffs on, though does not cite, a phrase from the German mystic Meister Eckhart: "God's exit is his entrance."[17] Carson considers sleep and its analogous states as forms of exit "inwards," approaches onto the world "through self," through the mind on "the very inside of its definition," a phrase from the essay "Decreation: How Women Like Sappho, Marguerite Porete and Simone Weil Tell God" (179). The text on sleep moves nonchalantly, as so much of Carson's writing does, between sources, exempla, and facts, grasping at what piques her and reflecting—in Adorno's words, quoted in a brief commentary on Carson's essay—"a childlike freedom that catches fire, without scruple, on what others have already done."[18] In one of the essay's most memorable images, whose color palette streaks through the book, a three- or four-year-old Carson dreams of being asleep and waking on the "sleep side" of her dream:

> I dreamed I was asleep in the house in an upper room. That I awoke and came downstairs and stood in the living room. The lights were on in the living room, although it was hushed and empty. The usual dark green sofa and chairs stood along the usual pale green walls. It was the same old living room as ever, I knew it well, nothing was out of place. And yet it was utterly, certainly, different. Inside its usual appearance the living room was changed as if it had gone mad.... So, as far as I can recall, I explained the dream to myself by saying that I had caught the living room sleeping. I had entered it from the sleep side.... (20)

The young Carson's explanation that she had caught the paraphernalia of ordinary life asleep parses Simone Weil's "dream of distance" ("If only I could see a landscape as it is when I am not there . . .") in the natural theology of a child. It is a dream drenched in philosophical history. Its central premise—the non-instrumental life of everyday objects—recalls Plato's famous questions about beds (Platonic "Form") in Book Ten of *The Republic*, as well as some of the most distinctive inquiry lines of phenomenology.[19] The dreamscape has strong resonances, too, with the gnostic fables of a dissenting material world invoked by Carson in the "Gnosticism" poems later in the book (87–93). The first essay in *Decreation*, then, begins by essaying some of the book's brightest associations to decreation theology, including a complex affinity that emerges—it is never broached directly—between phenomenological and mystical thinking.

At the same time, Carson's anecdote tells a very ordinary tale of the everyday life of the mind, capable of wandering off from itself in fantasy, sleep, and dreams. This "other" life, indivisible from "self," is measureless and unplumbable (*unergründliche*: Sigmund Freud's term for the "navel" of the dream, its "point of contact with the unknown").[20] The essay touches on a more extreme instance of un-dimensionable mental life in the ellipses cut from the above extract:

> Later in life, when I was learning to reckon with my father, who was afflicted with and eventually died of dementia, this dream recovered itself to me, I think because it seemed to bespeak the situation of looking at a well-known face, whose appearance is exactly as it should be in every feature and detail, except that it is also, somehow, deeply and glowingly strange. (20)

Madness and dementia—involuntary self-undoing—take their place in *Decreation* alongside more romantic forms of ecstasy and inward exit. While the "strange" familiarity Carson recalls is another analogy for decreation, alongside the stray angles of Antonioni's mirrors and unscheduled errors, there is something more deeply perturbing about the unwilled exile she describes: a "well-known face" locked out of its precincts, beyond the limits of philosophy and at a stretch from the speculative angles of *temps mort*. The recollection of Carson's father reprises the story of his dementia told in "The Glass Essay," and is echoed again in descriptions of her father's uncle Harry in "Uncle Falling: A Pair of Lyric Lectures with Shared Chorus," where dementia takes its place among a different series of analogies. There, alongside the controlled free-fall of Streb dancers and the "terrifically perilous activity" of associative lecturing, the "dark custom of dementia" is read among kinds of "human falling"; her questions around a mind "com[ing] apart" concern how to "deaden the blow" or at least "deaden the sound of the blow."[21] There, too, Carson points to a problem that arises in *Decreation*, as it does in a different form, we saw, in *Eros the Bittersweet*. "Streb and her dancers imitate real falling by falling according to plan," Carson says. Levering open the difference between controlled and uncontrolled vulnerability, even between the lover and nonlover in Plato's *Phaedrus*, madness—Plato's *mania*—is where falling into gaps, or "undoing the creature," is *not a choice*.

Dementia is the vanishing point of Carson's essay on sleep. It points off at an angle from the reflections that surround it—on dreams to be analyzed on waking, on sleep "as a blindness, which nonetheless looks back at us"—as a case of undoing in which there is no redoubling, no deliberation or reflexivity, and no performance.[22] Essayed here is a kind of decreation that doesn't observe itself: whose fall from selfhood is headlong and uncontrolled, and whose *ek-stasis* is ecstatic without knowing it. Rather than mastering this radical contingency, analogy and link-making are simply the lightest and most pleasurable of its symptoms. "What we call reasoning, an argument, a conversation," Carson's lecture on falling ends by suggesting, does not reflect the robust force of the mind but its precariousness and fragility: "what a terrifically perilous activity it is, this activity of linking together all the threads of human sin that go into making what we call sense.... How light, how loose, how unprepared and unpreparable is the web of connections between any thought and any thought."[23]

Carson's reflections on sleep and the inscrutability of old age begin in the opening poems of *Decreation*. The first poem, "Sleepchains" (3), imagines a mother-daughter bond unspooled across a distance.

> Who can sleep when she—
> hundreds of miles away I feel that vast breath
> fan her restless decks.[24]

Carson's broken first line, left ajar at "she—," opens the poem with a sudden shift of angle. At the line break, the poem's lyric center slides out into an ecstatic proximity in distance, miles out at sea, to an improbable ship on a "shipless ocean." Both women, we understand, are awake ("who can sleep," "her restless decks"). Like a stray piece of world glimpsed in reflection, in what follows this break, the poem's inner mechanics are seen from without, redoubled by an image that performs itself in the rattle of metrics and the sibilance and clink of consonants: "Cicatrice by cicatrice, all the links rattle once." Links in the chain connecting "I" to the vanishing point at "she—": these are the involuntary thoughts and memories that keep "I" awake at night, but that suggest, too, the waking, voluntary links made throughout the book between facts from Carson's life and her reading material. All these links—from her "incongruous ideas" and interlocutors to the wounds of her biography—run together on a single chain of thought: what moves one is replicated across the others. What rattles "all the links" in the poem, as it happens, is a sublime sensation—"that vast breath"—streaming out the end of the second line. The heft of ocean breeze and the suggestion of an oceanic Creator breath reaches (and rattles, unrests) both women: as one pities the other's loneliness, loneliness of the ocean, it is herself she pities, herself who is moved.

"Sleepchains" could not be more intimate in its conjuring of what is phrased later in the book as the departure of self from its own center. Its scene dramatizes a concern that Carson first voices in the early poem "God's Christ Theory" for the "kind of withness" engendered by compassion (*com-passio* or feeling-with).[25] When she returns to "withness" in the "Decreation" essay ("Withness is the problem," 169), it has become an inquiry into what prevents her mystics from being "with" God: in Carson's summary, "I cannot go towards God in love without bringing myself along. And so in the deepest possible sense I can never be alone with God" (169). *Decreation* is full of iterations of this logic, from the masochistic wish for total erotic intimacy in "Stanzas, Sexes, Seductions" to the gnostic readings of language in the "Gnosticisms" sequence. As well as refracting her inquiry across multiple formal and contextual centers, another way in which the book as a whole "reads" Weil's decreation—a reading in which the "Decreation" opera plays a starring role—is the return of so many of Carson's texts to situations that redress what the philosopher Gillian Rose called Weil's failure to "bring the sublime into the pedestrian," scenes that humanize or even banalize decreation, as the chapter to follow discusses.[26] Carson's versions of decreation refuse to renege on the world of everyday objects and emotions, the everyday travails of the body desirous, sleepy, and infirm, that Weil's discourse of desire and decreation would sublimate out of existence.

It is in the "Decreation" essay and opera libretto that Carson's links and analogies are anchored, finally, in a specific devotional and philosophical canon. Weil's concern is that desire gets estranged from its source by the "false" objects it comes to rest on:

> Descend to the source of desires to wrench the energy from its object. It is there that desires are true insofar as they are energy. It is the object that is false. But there is an unspeakable wrench in the soul at the separation of a desire and its object.[27]

Weil's solution to the problem of desire is to "empty" it: "to desire in the void, to desire without any wishes . . . to wait."[28] Waiting (*attendre*) in Weil is an evenly suspended attention, disposition without aim or argument. One of the most striking poems in *Decreation* offers an exercise in precisely this form of suspended reading, product of an interpretive desire "without any wishes." In the case of this poem, the object—a sketch by the Canadian artist, Betty Goodwin, reproduced in the book—is present, and read without its reader settling on or sealing any one line of inquiry.[29] This poem asks, rather, about its *own* presence: the force, substance, and color of its attention.

The Color of Attention

Below are two short excerpts from "*Seated Figure with Red Angle* by Betty Goodwin (1988)," an ekphrastic poem in response to a work by the Canadian painter and printmaker, Betty Goodwin.[30] Carson reproduces the work facing the first page of the poem (Figure 1).

> If red is the color of italics.
>
> If italics are a lure of thought.
>
> If Freud says the relation between a gaze and what one wishes to see involves allure.
> ...
> If there is no master of allure.
>
> If conditionals are of two kinds allure and awake.
>
> If no matter how you balance on the one you cannot see the other, cannot tap the sleep spine, cannot read what word that was.[31]

Carson's poem is a sequence of open-ended inquiries. Its lines consist, grammatically speaking, of a series of conditionals (protasis) with no projected consequence (apodosis), no "then" to their searching "if." Reading these inconclusive stabs in the dark consecutively, each conditional qualifies the last, shifting (sometimes abruptly) its angle of reflection. In the continual substitution of unfinished propositions, what gradually accumulates, as though off-camera or out of earshot, is the vertigo of a subject whose thinking continually cedes its own ground: "If objects are not solid. / If objects are much too solid," an example from later in the poem. In their five pages or seventy-two sentences of guesswork, Carson's lines approximate the evasive *sfumato* and awkward inwardness of Goodwin's drawing, caught between momentary definition and a reluctance to define the figure. The body of the "Seated Figure" in Carson's poem is insinuated

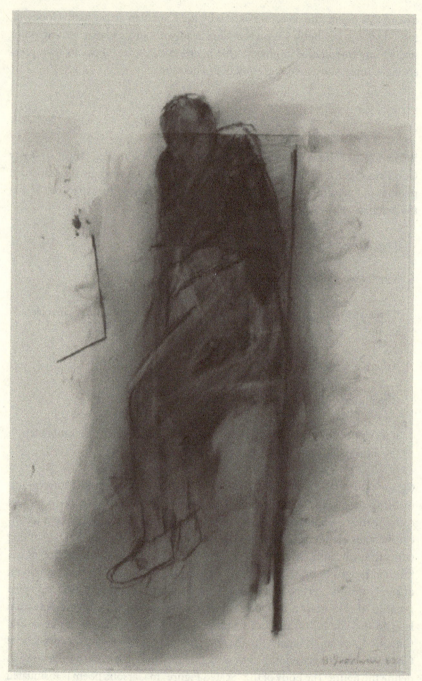

Figure 1 Betty Goodwin, *Seated Figure with Red Angle* (1988). Used with permission.

in lines that equivocate, digress, and retire from definite contour, such that the result, red-hued, brittle, and ambiguous, describes a process of association to the figure in lieu of the figure itself.

The poem's opening sets an equally ambiguous tone, but its speculation around the figure is distinctly uncomfortable, with images of coercion and violence emerging in the very first lines:

> If body is always deep but deepest at its surface.
>
> If conditionals are of two kinds factual and contrafactual.
>
> If you're pushing, pushing and then it begins to pull you.
>
> If police in that city burnt off people's hands with a blowtorch.
>
> If darkly colored or reddish (bodies) swim there.
>
> . . .
>
> If the seated figure started out with an idea of interrogation. (97)

If the poem begins with an intention, it is perhaps to weigh its own iterative inquiry against the weight and proportions of this "other body," the introverted figure of Goodwin's sketch. For even in these perturbing beginnings, it is unclear whether what is being reproduced in the associative sequence of conditionals is the thinking (the "idea of interrogation," for example) of the narrator and viewer of Goodwin's *Seated Figure*, or the inferred thinking of the figure him/herself ("If the seated figure started out with an idea of interrogation," shifting two lines down to "If *you* had the idea of interrogation," my italics). In any case, the poem starts to look like an exercise in Carson's performative form, mimicking an uncertainty or undefinition that is both inferred in the mind of the figure and experienced in the mind of the narrator/viewer. A repeated push-pull between conditionals "of two kinds factual and contrafactual" gives Carson's lines of inquiry their hesitant, discontinuous internal structure. (Later iterations of this phrase describe as well as perform the difference: "If conditionals are of two kinds allure and awake" and "If conditionals are of two kinds now it is night and all cats are black" pitch the poem's spare facts—it is night, conditional thought is alluring—against counterfact or logical syllogism.) A similar, more obvious structure of hesitation characterizes the move from line to line, as a proposition is ventured, almost affirmed, and then modified or abandoned in the next non sequitur.

"*Seated Figure with Red Angle*" is a poem that holds its thinking work in suspense as it moves, if not forward, then between disjunctive "ideas." The poem's conditional syntax is a striking formal decision in a poem that presents, from its title to its reflections on "the seated figure," as ekphrastic. The practiced inconclusiveness of its phrases describe the Goodwin sketch without, as it were, actually describing it, venturing an action of interpretive approach without exactly arriving at a reading. The non-sequitur movement between associations performs not only inconclusiveness but inconsequentiality, a quality Carson ascribes in the "Decreation" essay to the logic of mystics, for whom inconsequence—one thing not leading to another, or, in Carson's own essay structure, a three-part essay turning out to have four parts—is a language of apophasis: the affirmation of God through negation or, closer to Carson's aesthetics, through deliberate error. Carson's poem isn't quite a poetics of negation, nor do its associations to the figure form a cumulative or aggregate picture of what the narrator thinks about the figure (or thinks the figure might be thinking). Each line of approach offers an angle or analogy that, over the course of the poem, produces a dispersed subject of attention whose reflections arrive from a multiplicity of angles, as per Antonioni's redoubling cinematic vision. At the same time, though, each of these analogies or approaches to the figure dissolves as the next is arrived at. Something seems to fall away in the gaps between them—as one line suggests explicitly: "If the feet cross in a way that sucks itself under, sucks analogies (Christ) under" (98). It is the gaps that, sucking each analogy down, starting with the blood of Christ at Goodwin's "red angle," perform the radical de-authorization that Carson seems, uncomfortably, to be after here.

Carson's ekphrastic poem is attuned from the start to a certain violence stalking its edges: the un-primed shock of the "blowtorch" and a disquieting proposition regarding the provenance of this gruesome imaginary (to whom exactly "the idea of interrogation" and its associations belongs). Monique Tschofen has written persuasively on the presence of torture, forced disappearance, and state-sponsored atrocity as themes in Goodwin's work, which Tschofen finds reflected in the poem's more diffuse exploration of interrogation as a means of extracting knowledge and procuring certainty.[32] Such certainty—and the force from which it is historically inseparable—is refused by the poem in its hesitant grammar and the continually displaced sovereignty of its approaches to the artwork. Yet the poem does not entirely elude the violence at the edge of its associations. Carson's question of where the "idea" of violence originates seems to recognize that there is something coercive about interpretive projection per se, a sort of violence by association; an idea that is consonant with Simone Weil's thinking on interpretation and attention—"try to love the object naked and without interpretation. What you love then is truly God"—and even with Freud's notion of evenly suspended attention: "If Freud says the relation between a gaze and what one wishes to see involves allure," above.[33] The poem's impersonal, almost imperceptible narrator replicates the undefinition of Goodwin's figure—both might be understood as notionally "decreated" or undone—but many of his/her associations are to forms of violence: animal experimentation, bomb, "how many were killed by David" and "how many were killed by Saul," an elusive "art pain," and so on. In this, he/she becomes an anonymous, unconsenting accomplice to violence by the mere "perilous activity" of analogy and association. In the above lines, just as conditionals can be "factual and "contrafactual," so the thinking they perform moves between coercion and freedom, voluntary and involuntary ("If you're pushing, pushing, and then it begins to pull you"). The question of to whom the associative violence of the "blowtorch" belongs is a question that never goes away in the poem. The narrator both exposes and sublimates its violence in his/her associations to the brief red intrusion in the image: the "red angle" of its title, to the left of the seated figure.

To glance back briefly to Weil, for whom, we saw, "desires are true insofar as they are energy. It is the object that is false." One of the most striking things about the Goodwin reproduction in Carson's book—as opposed to the original *Artforum* publication of Carson's poem—is that it appears, as it does in the print edition of this book, in black and white. The color red is present only by association, with the poem's rogue talk of red speaking only to the "red angle" of the title. For the insinuated red of the poem as we read it, there is, in a peculiarly literal sense, no object beyond the "true" desire for one. As the product of perception mediated by imagination, the object "red," in this case, is false.

In a book concerned with what Carson calls the "big, loud, shiny centre of self from which . . . writing is given voice" and "the brilliant self-assertiveness of the writerly project" (171), "*Seated Figure with Red Angle*" is both an attempt to reflect on this center of self as a point of origin for assertion/coercion, and to mitigate its force by suspending commentary at the edge of each syntactically incomplete line. Weil's "energy" of desire, we saw, is an energy that moves toward objects without ever grasping or settling on one. It is pure approach: *erōs* held in suspense by *aidōs*, the "voltage of decorum" that, for Carson, reins in the desire to possess.[34] Cropping her syntax at the hinge between "if" (protasis) and "then" (apodosis), Carson coins a grammar for pure interpretive energy in the form of deliberately inconsequential, often counterintuitive perceptions. Denying readers the extension (enjambment) of sense from one line to the next, the docked syntax of "*Seated Figure with Red Angle*" encourages us to tarry in the unfinished statement, inviting inquiry to accrue awkwardly inside each line, or to flash up symmetries and recall between lines. A neat example from the excerpts with which I began is what happens to the word "allure" under pressures of Carson's verse:

> If italics are a lure of thought
>
> ...
>
> If there is no master of allure.
>
> If conditionals are of two kinds allure and awake.

Tschofen has noted that "allure" picks up resonances from Husserl, who uses the word to refer to "the particular pull that an object given to consciousness exercises on the ego," "relaxed when the ego turns toward it attentively."[35] For Husserl, this pull can be weak: its "affective rays of force," then—as Carson all but quotes—"do not actually become an *allure* that *awakens*."[36] Where Carson's "italics" refer us to Goodwin's title, and to the targeted lure of titles in general, "allure" suggests a different kind of traction of objects on the mind. "Allure" has "no master" to begin with, but under certain conditions—certain kinds of conditional, is Carson's suggestion—"allure ... awakens" and "the self of the object"— not the associative subject—is disclosed.[37] This poem puts the conditions for disclosure, for a Husserlian "passive synthesis" or "transcendental association" on the part of the speaker, whose speculations snapped in half then reproduce it in the reader.[38] Reading closer to the words here, we hear how "a lure" picks up the glint of its cognate "allure." "Allure," too, changes hue next to "awake," the noun disoriented by an unscheduled affinity with the adjective, the "factual" tipped by the "contrafactual." Carson reflects on the value of such disorientation in the "Essay on Error" and "Essay on What I Think About Most" in terms of the fresh, unexpected insights the sensation of momentary mistakenness brings about.[39] In the final chapter of this book, we will see Carson attribute her interest in syntaxes with sensible effects, syntaxes that mime and induce distinctive processes of thought, to her early encounters with the fragments of Ancient Greek lyric. Producing a deliberately denatured syntax like that of "*Seated Figure with Red Angle*," in which sound and association accrue without direction, compels in us the deconstructed perspective and decentered center of its subject. The poem works in this way as a case of decreative writing, a deliberately performative form.

I have so far suggested that Carson's reading of decreation probes the limits of this idea of form and the construal of mental life behind it, wondering whether "undoing the creature" is an effect to be induced, an imperative of form, or something more improbable and difficult to master. For Carson, and for the women mystics at the center of her book, "decreation" (or "ecstasy") is at once a question of will and its renunciation: a voluntary and involuntary disappearance of self.

Carson's own take on this complexity comes through in the idea of "perilous" link-making and, above, transcendental association, but also, we saw, in the drastic psychic undoing of madness and old age. In a lecture on "Chairs" given at the University of Chicago in late 2019, Carson discussed her poem's response to the awkward posture and ambiguous mood of the seated figure, speculating whether he/she might have "forgotten to exhale, as people with dementia often do."[40] What changes, finally, if we read the poem as performing an unscheduled "undoing [of] the creature," the solitary speech of a mind that *does not know* it is "undone"?

> If afterwards she would sit the way a very old person sits, with no pants on, confused.
>
> If you reach in, if you burrow, if you risk wiping in. (97)
>
> . . .
>
> If you want to know why you cannot reach your own beautiful ideas.
>
> If you reach instead the edge of the thinkable, which leaks.
>
> If you stop the leaks with conditionals. (99)

The poem's cropped lines plot out this "edge of the thinkable" and the leakage the poem surmises might be stopped with conditionals. The poem, these lines suggest, follows thoughts pushed to the edge of the thinkable, not by pursuing their logic to its unsound end, but by having logic stopped dead in its tracks. Carson's conditionals do not set the limits of the thinkable—their incompletion is a refusal of precisely that—but this "edge," these "leaks" call us back to the gaps between her inconsequent phrases, gaps down which meaning and possibility pour and pool. Resisting definite contour, identifying with the openness of "if," Carson's response to the Goodwin sketch continually cedes its own center, or—never far from this secession—keeps losing its own mind.

The shattered pane through which we observe Carson's image of an image—her disfiguration of a figure—ventures an exercise in decreation with a difference.[41] For this is no decreation in the abstract. Rather, the poem meets the cooler, more aloof spirit of decreation theology by imagining "undoing" in relation to ordinary mental confusion and its barely sublimated violence. We can call it Weilian in its spirit of withdrawal, refusing to fix its object under a single or direct gaze, or a form of looking without a gaze to speak of. The suggestions of torture also bring up resonances of Weil's stunning essay, "The Iliad, or The Poem of Force," which describes a brutal form of creatural "undoing"—the conversion of person into thing—under conditions of war.[42] Thinking about how it invokes and tries to sideline personhood, we might also observe that Carson's poem is also one of the most Carsonesque of the volume. The studied incongruities and flatline tonality courted by the clipped lineation not only recall other poems by its author—"The Life of Towns" sequence is the most obvious example—but remember Carson's distinctive modes of public recital. Assuming we've heard her perform her work, we would be hard pressed to read this poem without hearing Carson's dry, wry recital monotone, a vocal style that cultivates counter-intuition, insouciance, and inconsequentiality. Carson's is a voice that plays its nonchalance off against a cultivated errancy, the far-fetched logics of her forms, conversations, and comparisons.[43]

The problem of *performing* subjective undoing, which begins in poems like "*Seated Figure with Red Angle*" to look like a performative contradiction, is picked up in several other works in the book that pitch the controlled abandon of authorship against other forms of self-undoing with higher personal stakes. The following poem, one of the book's most majestic, charges language—and specifically poetry—with complicity in decreation's problem of impossible intimacy: "If only I could see a landscape as it is when I am not there...."

"It's Good to Be Neuter"

When Simone Weil laments the impossibility of union with creation, she lays the blame squarely at the door of *bios*. Bodies make claims, and bodies claim a singularity that for Weil is simply incompatible with union:

> If only I could see a landscape as it is when I am not there. But when I am in any place I disturb the silence of heaven by the beating of my heart [or: "by my breathing and the beating of my heart"].[44]

The body and its vital metrics—breath and beating heart—are expressions of being that prove troublesome to Weil, and that find themselves translated, Carson proposes, in the "big, loud, shiny centre of self from which writing is given voice" (171). But the body, as Carson understands it, poses another problem. The body is meaningful, signified; the body saturated, scripted, and mediated by words. Carson's poem, "Stanzas, Sexes, Seductions," speaks from a desire to bypass the body's significance and to achieve an intimacy with the beloved that runs off-script. In spite of this wish, what the poet calls her "personal poetry" is named as her proxy in a failure of relation.

DECREATION, OR THE ART OF DISAPPEARANCE   141

           My personal poetry is a failure.
            I do not want to be a person.
              I want to be unbearable.
                Lover to lover, the greenness of love.

      Cool, cooling.

      Earth bears no such plant.
        Who does not end up
          a female impersonator?
            Drink all the sex there is.
    Still die.[45]

This is a poem—these the third and fourth of its seven stanzas—whose extraordinary sensual presence and charisma is the not un-ironic source of the poet's discontent. Unlike Auden's more famous and ambiguous disqualification, for this poet, "poetry"—her own, accomplice of her personhood—makes too much happen. The poem is jaded with whatever success we, its readers, might admire in it. Under sway of a desire for unmediated relation, any such success as poetry means "failure" as relation. To be moved by this poem, whose métier moves against its own form of life, is almost to betray it on its own terms.

This counterfactual lover's complaint, already compromised by its own making, sends its song out in stanzas that drift to the right-hand margin, approaches to an object whose distance is at least partly guaranteed by the poem as a source of "meaning," "impersonation," and "seduction." The poem ends despondent of its enterprise, and in the gestures, syntax, and sound of the final lines (reproduced below), pares itself down to a diminished inventory of moves. What we can't miss about the poem's mise-en-page is that each drift of the stanzas rightward is pulled back to degree zero at the left-hand margin, domain of the following lines: "Then you die" / "of dying" / "Cool, cooling" / "Still die" / "Legs die" / "spin." Each counter-pull to the left resets the poem until its final rightward drift, a thinner stream than the stanzas before:

           some ballet term for it —
                fragment of foil, little
spin,
  little drunk,
    little do,
      little oh,
        alas.

The degree zero of the poem's stanzas, sexes, and seductions is death—"die," "of dying," "still die"—though it imagines another form of reset beyond biological death: a symbolic zero at which the meaningfulness of the body is stripped back; "to be neuter," "to have meaningless legs." It is this form of neuter life, non-symbolic life, *physis* or life impersonal, that the poem's lyric subject pursues.

The self-defeating desire at the heart of "Stanzas, Sexes, Seductions" is sexual as much as it is creative, and sex for the poet (or the poem's poet persona) is what drives the defeat home.[46] "Drink all the sex there is. / Still die": all those drifts of lover to lover, what this poet calls lovers' and poets' "little size of dying," signal the simple mortal facts of bodies, not the unsignified erotic immanence the poet seems to crave.[47] The poem's final stanza is ambiguous in this regard. It stages a series of involuntary gestures, signs of the body and its failure ("some ballet term for it—": even uncoordinated movement, it turns out, is meaningful). The poet seems then to search for this "ballet term" or otherwise define the body and its movement: "fragment of foil, little / spin, / little drunk, / little do, / little oh, / alas." But the effect of her series of descriptors—all diminutives—, each of which carries an excess of potential meanings, is not what we might have expected. *Little spin*: [a] little spin, a turn, or a bit of spin, a seduction, and picking up the indictment of their relationship by Carson's ex-lover in "The Glass Essay": "not enough spin on it."[48] *Little drunk*: [a] little drunk, or little [has been] drunk. *Little do*: [a] little do, a small affair, doing little, little ado. *Little oh*: a sigh, little "o" for a "little death." Their meaning short-circuits in this surfeit. A fatigued language is one that means out of control and so stops being meaningful: the opposite of the limpid and unassuming "Lover to lover, the greenness of love."

What does the poem offer against this tide of disappointment? First, an intuition of what pure relation and total intimacy might *sound* like. The smooth metric regularity of the wish "I want to have meaningless legs" reaches a kind of rhythmic symmetry with Carson's evocation, two stanzas down, of an intimacy without caesura: "Lover to lover, the greenness of love." A momentary plateau in the poem, this dactylic line sounds out a euphony that catches in its refrain other tonalities of "green": the living room of "Every Exit Is an Entrance," "sunk in its greenness, breathing its own order"; Sappho's image of ecstatic immanence, "greener than grass I am and dead," one of the centerpieces of the "Decreation" essay; even Andrew Marvell's vision, several centuries earlier, of another kind of decreation: a drastic emptying of nature and a thought continuous with its immediate surroundings—"Annihilating all that's made / To a green thought in a green shade."[49] The poem is decided its denial that this vivid, total intimacy is anything more than a fantasy: "Lover to lover, the greenness of love. / Cool, cooling. // Earth bears no such plant." The imaginary of erotic immanence is performed in a smooth, co-extensive slide of "cool" into "cooling," before a slapdown of spondees—"Earth bears no such plant"—tells it like it is.

The vision of relationship and version of decreation offered in "Stanzas, Sexes, Seductions" is one in which self-undoing or mystical-erotic annihilation is only possible through union. Its suggestion is that more language, more failed "personal poetry," only deepens the rift between lover and beloved. The very first line, "It's good to be neuter," sets the poem in a place of equivocation between the linguistic and the erotic, positing a grammar to navigate from logos to eros. On the one hand, there is the neuter gender: "it" or "its," the pronoun of things and of "meaningless legs"; on the other, neuter sexuality, the unsexed or the (voluntarily or involuntarily) undefined. The thinker who navigates most fluidly between these fields of possibility is Barthes, an interlocutor to whom we have seen Carson return, from *Eros the Bittersweet* to *The Albertine Workout*, where she describes his commitment to a "third" language "in which we would all be exempt from meaning" ("appendix 15 (b) on adjectives"). Barthes's famous essay on the "death of the author" includes the remark I quoted above: writing means "the destruction of every voice, every point of origin. Writing is that neutral, composite, oblique space where our subject slips away."[50] For Barthes, writing undoes the creature who writes, but does so whether she likes it or not. The destruction of "every point of origin" is what guarantees the possibility of destination, insofar as writing, unbound from the author, can belong momentarily to all readers. Writing, that free-for-all of meaning and desire, guarantees a strange kind of universality at the expense of the lyric subject: a loss for the individual voice—the disappearance of individual desire—is a gain for the desiring many.

The "neutral" space of writing and its claim to universality mean several different things in Barthes's own work. His lecture course, *The Neuter*, defines its approach to texts as "anecdotal," guided by intuition and desire. The rationale of *The Neuter* is the production and performance of a theory by freeform associative linking, the disorderly pursuit of what "shines by bursts."[51] *Decreation* keeps its own idea of the risks and attractions of the freeform close to the emotive surface of the book. It is in association, incomplete approach, and iterative drafting that an involuntary disappearance of the subject is imagined, even while the book's analogical links "show the nature" of the mind doing the thinking. Carson's chain of thought and testimony forms a lyric through-line even in the absence of personal pronouns—or the presence of a neuter pronoun—to own them. For Barthes, "Neuter" is also androgyny. Neither sexlessness nor "meaningless legs," the grammatical neuter hints at another possibility—what we might, glancing up to "Stanzas, Sexes, Seductions," and anticipating this book's next chapter, call "impersonation": the hypermobility of (sexual) identity and a thoroughgoing defiance of difference.[52]

Carson's inquiry into the neuter voice and the arts of authorial disappearance does not end with *Decreation*. The struggle "to get every Me out of the way," a phrase she cites from John Cage, has taken Carson from the "scholarly hesitation" of her early research, through fragmentation, variation, and collaboration, to the edges of "uncreative writing."[53] There is the "freefall" organization of *Float*, which unlooses the writing from a predetermined order of reading, but there are also her experiments in constrained writing techniques, aleatory poetics, and randomization software, used in "By Chance the Cycladic People" and *Red Doc>* to produce chance lineation and formatting patterns.[54] This "literature in the conditional mood" takes the conditional "If" of "*Seated Figure*" and turns it into a compositional mode, where "if"—chance, contingency, *hasard*—decides the formal arrangement of the words.[55] "Uncreative writing," as Kenneth Goldsmith calls it, continues the inquiry into *decreative* writing, but without the unapologetic sublime of decreation theology.[56] "Unoriginal genius," in Marjorie Perloff's expression, asks about origins and about "I," but its questions rebound inside a drama of textual culture: language and literary form, intertextuality, creativity, and influence.[57]

Uncreativity plumbed to its extreme is not perhaps so far removed from the promise of a "decreative" writing. If the uncreative author "bumps into" or "bounces off" an "other," it is, in the first instance, the "other" of other texts, whose otherness is defused in the act of appropriation, or the "other" of algorithm, automation, and artificial intelligence. This post-human "other," as Colin Burrow has shown, is adept at imitating authors and imitating authorship.[58] Yet in its most acute incarnations, the questions of origin, creation, and difference raised by post-human poetics—where the machine definitively supplants human authorship, or where lines of verse implanted and reproduced in a genetic code generate new "uncreative" poems[59]—share something in common with Carson's arts of disappearance in *Decreation*. They, too, run the blurred line between the performance of controlled technique and an opening to vertigo when we sense in the subjection of language to non-human laws the annihilation or radical exposure of human culture. These anxieties are channeled in the "Gnosticisms" sequence in *Decreation*, which riffs on early Christian gnostic fears of rebellion of the created world against God, and of art and names against man.[60] In the first of these poems, it is the word "bird" that rebels by performing *bird*—as Harold Bloom, in an essay on gnosticism, argued Blake's loping verse in "The Tyger" conjures and fears the phenomenality of the beast. Carson's dreamer-narrator is decentered by the spectacle, "Astonishment inside me like a separate person": "For some people a bird sings, feathers shine," she concludes: "I just get this *this*" (87).[61] Language in the "Gnosticisms" poems knows and acts autonomously.[62] "Bird" announces its own law and, by the end of the poem, insubordinates the poet by the sheer force of its tautology. For this "bird" does not sing, it *birds*. Her deictic "this" points only to "*this*."

The questions of *Decreation*, finally, are questions Carson is still asking. In her recent essay on "Stillness," derived from the same lecture series as her lecture on "The Chair," Carson asks how the "I" of Emily Dickinson's famous poem, "I heard a Fly buzz—when I died," can embody the stillness (and hear the noise) simultaneous with her own death.[63] She talks about Virginia Woolf's last novel, *Between the Acts* (1941), as the climax of Woolf's experiments with what Carson calls "techniques of reticence." These techniques, she says, are Woolf's attempts to "draw back a little further from the authorial surface in each novel, replacing the "damned egotistical self," as she called it, with the pronoun "we," or with phenomena like furniture or moonlight, or with humanity as a whole."[64] Describing the distinctive textuality of *Between the Acts*, Carson touches the question of who it is that speaks (or who it is we hear) in the autonomous, "neuter" voice of language: "there are voices, words, and phrases slipping in and out of different consciousnesses and behind them someone called 'third voice' or 'another voice' or 'that was nobody.'"[65] Crashing into and bumping up against the voices of other writers—as Carson does in the "Decreation" opera to spectacular effect—or procuring this "other" voice under strict formal constraints, as in "*Seated Figure*," are just some of the ways in which *Decreation* rehearses its fantasy of "nobody" speaking, its voluntary/involuntary art of disappearance. Yet the works that emerge from these ideas—randomized formats or an increasing preference for performance-driven, collaborative working, getting the lyric "Me" out of the way—show Carson's growing interest in what is produced (as she says of Antonioni's actors) "out of inertia": in what happens by chance, and in the shared, unmastered potential of live collaboration.

Analogy is often used to show an absence of contradiction. In traditions of scriptural exegesis, an analogy can quash controversy around different accounts of the same event, or procure agreement between texts of different origin. Carson's "friskes, skips and jumps," in *Decreation* and elsewhere, invite another understanding of analogy, one we can illustrate with the word's etymology. *Analogia* is a traversal, a through-movement, that posits a gap by traversing it in words.[66] Gillian Rose writes of an analogy of her own that "the 'ana' expresses the gap, while the 'logy,' the logos, makes it possible to speak, to propose to raise the difficulty of knowing or not knowing the relation."[67] All analogy gestures to this difficult openness, exposing a leap whose landing may or may not be safe. Bumping into the world, or into and between the work of other authors, can produce dizzying effects, as it so clearly does in Carson: voluntary can become involuntary, truth become fiction, the "fake" a discomfiting index of the real.

6
Fake Women

"This," Carson begins," is an essay about three women and will have three parts."[1] The title essay of *Decreation: Poetry, Essays, Opera* (2005) begins on a lie, confident of its invisibility until Carson announces, in the undeclared fourth part of the work, the presence of "some inconsequentiality" (171). The essay, "Decreation: How Women Like Sappho, Marguerite Porete and Simone Weil Tell God," approaches a wish Carson says joins the three women of its title and places unreasonably high demands on their writing. Their wish is for an intimacy that seems, on the face of it, to be not only unreasonable but impossible: for nearness to God, or to a personification of divine love, whose price is the annihilation of self. In the fourth part of this three-part essay, inconsequentiality (also called "subterfuge or contradiction") is Carson's theme. Any writer intent on "annihilating" the "big, loud, shiny centre of self from which [her] writing is given voice" cannot write, Carson argues, without performing a sizable contradiction (171). What's more, in her three women's reckoning with this contradiction—not just daring the self "to leave itself behind" (162), but daring to examine what it means to express such a wish—is a recognition that there is something essentially *performative* about decreation: something that is "done," voluntarily or otherwise, and that language, written or spoken, must find a way of doing too.

"Decreation is an undoing of the creature in us—that creature enclosed in self and defined by self. But to undo self," Carson's essay concludes, "one must move through self, to the very inside of its definition" (179). What kind of writing does a self on the "inside of its definition" produce? Not, it seems, a writing with claims to true likeness, where the writer is truer to or more "like" herself, her "telling" any closer to the sound or image of divine love. At the end of her essay on decreation, rather than laying the question of self, telling, and writing to rest, Carson explodes its possibilities. The decreative writer, she announces, is an out and out "fake" (180). Sappho, Porete, and Weil are, all three of them, "fake women."

Carson's surprising term is a translation of one of the accusations leveled at the Beguine mystic Marguerite Porete at her trial and indictment for heresy in Paris in 1309–1310. Porete, a woman "filled with errors and heresies," is condemned in the proceedings of her trial as a *pseudo-mulier*—a sham, phony, or imitation of woman.[2] The implication was, perhaps—and if so, the judgment of her inquisitors would prove surprisingly resilient—that a woman (a "real" woman, at any rate) could not have written a work of the theological complexity and imaginative daring of Porete's *The Mirror of Simple Souls*, a text finally attributed to Porete in 1946, before which point it was assumed to be the work of an anonymous (male) mystic.[3] Carson's first response to the "fake woman" indictment is a coolly noncommittal disqualification: "Society is all too eager to pass judgements on the authenticity of women's ways of being but these judgments can get crazy" (180). Then, a paragraph down, she appropriates its terms:

> Love is also a good place to situate our mistrust of fake women. What I like best about the three women we've been studying is that they know what love is. That is, they know love is the touchstone of a true or a false spirituality, that is why they play with the figure of jealousy. As fake women, they have to inhabit this figure gingerly, taking a position both near and far at once from the object of their desire. The truth that they tell from this paradoxical position is also fake. (180)

By the end of Carson's essay, it doesn't seem to matter whether or not we trust these women or find their ways authentic. Love—*agapē*, but also *erōs*, desire and jealousy—is where the paradox of true and false, near and far, is sustained as a matter of urgency. Carson describes what her three women do here as "play[ing] with" or "inhabit[ing] a "figure." Theirs is no active hermeneutic, but a "position" from which even "the truth that they tell" is undermined. This is "telling"—and writing—with the potential to expose itself in scandalous ways, and whose self-exposure performs its integrity as a metaphysics of love. "Telling" from this position, Carson says, generates a "ripple of disbelief—a sort of distortion in the glass" (176), in which testimony and artifice move as one. What they say never manages to remain identical with itself, never quite converges with its own purposes.

Equivalences between the "fake" and the feminine, between "the wiles of woman" and literary artifice, are at least as old as the theory of mimesis.[4] This chapter does not seek to give an account of these equivalences, or to situate Carson's reading in a history of reading women as imitators or imitation as feminine. Nor am I interested in speculating about the femininity or femaleness of Carson's trio. (Weil, as numerous critics have noted, signed letters to her parents as "your son, Simon").[5] What I do want to address here is how Carson appropriates the *pseudo* of Porete's indictment as a capacity for revelation and dissent; as a name for women whose conversancy with paradox disorients but, in disorientation, gifts us a language for the most intimate of contradictions: that we *are* and *are not* what we think we are. In the words of Weil, for whom Being and personality are non-identical, "I, too, am other than what I imagine myself to be."[6]

Carson's "fake women," who understand "I" as a fiction of its own making, are women who, one way or another (as she says of Aeschylus's Cassandra), expose "a site that has no business being underneath."[7] In the "Decreation" essay, with which this chapter begins, Carson's three interlocutors make a surprising collective case for the "fake" and its unorthodox reckoning with self. Their "paradoxical position" might condemn their writing to a certain logical inconsequentiality, but from where each of them is standing, such inconsequentiality not only comes with the territory of imagination, desire, and telling; it is, for Porete and for Weil particularly, a continuous performance of "undoing the creature," presaged more than 700 years earlier in Porete's "s'abandonne la creature" (unaccented in the original).[8] Where Porete and Weil seal their writing under the covenant of non-identity, where it is obliged to embody certain contradictions, is not only where they are most interesting—their thought its freest and most liberatory—but where the decreative text becomes a ritual text: the performance of a rite.[9]

I focus here on Carson's reading of Sappho, Porete, and Weil, beginning with the essay, "Decreation: How Sappho, Marguerite Porete and Simone Weil Tell God," then crossing to Carson's performance-driven reworking of the essay's source material, "Decreation: An Opera in Three Parts." A "thought opera" in an emerging tradition that includes Charles Bernstein's libretto for the opera *Shadowtime*, which reads and remixes the writings of Walter Benjamin, Carson's libretto employs a mix of citation, imitation, and invention to produce a critical performance based on the essay's arguments.[10] The libretto is Carson's imitation of "what the facts are doing," a "form for the form" for the paradoxical position of her "fake women" and their own orientation toward performance, whose defining action is saying—or not quite saying—"I." The opera in three parts, which does in fact turn out to have three, is composed of a series of fantastical scenarios that dramatize the lines of inquiry of Carson's essay, but, unlike the essay, the opera's interpretive work happens by *divergence* from her sources. The libretto's scenarios reproduce the dilemmas of Carson's "fake women." Yet the precise fate of her source material—which is, variously, reproduced verbatim, reprised aslant, or transformed almost beyond recognition—makes this compelling text an active participant in Carson's case for the "fake."

The libretto is extraordinary in the "paradoxical position" it occupies vis-à-vis Carson's sources, and, as such, in the profound ways it comes to perform some of her most searching questions around decreation. Reading near and far from them at once—the "distant closeness" she so often achieves—, the libretto iteration both *is* and *is not* faithful to its sources. It impersonates, quotes, and ventriloquizes them, imitates their concepts, vocabularies, and deepest concerns;

indeed, the versions of *imitatio* on display in Carson's text make it a test case for just how dizzyingly flexible literary imitation—a form of "faking it"—can be. As Colin Burrow has written, *imitatio* is alluring precisely because of its complex overlap with other practices and "rebellious doubles" such as "parody, forgery, and mimicry," as well as paraphrase and translation.[11] Shifting between faithful rendering and rebellious doubling, Carson's *imitatio* of the three decreatives amounts to a strong close reading of decreation that finds its form in the forms and structural dilemmas of its sources. The problem of "telling God" is parsed in a striking, sometimes shocking retelling.

This book has sought to map Carson's preference for mimetic and performative reading styles: forms that imitate or reproduce the strictures, sensations, or models apprehended in other works.[12] The "Decreation" libretto and its scripted aesthetics of performance reproduce the dilemmas of decreation as Carson reads them. But they are also consonant with some of the most distinctive aspects of the textuality of Christian mysticism, a textual history without which Weil's "decreation," not to speak of Porete's *Mirror*, is difficult to come to grips with. The "mystic fable" described by Michel de Certeau is a discursive orientation toward the fictive—Certeau's "fictions of the soul"—, as well as toward performative orality and song.[13] What Alois M. Haas terms the *Appellstruktur* or dialogic structure of call and answer, speculative appeal and invocation, common in Christian mystical texts and immediately obvious in Porete's *Mirror*, is a structure that characterizes much of Carson's libretto.[14] It is a tradition of writing whose textuality takes on a ritual function: Eucharistic in its staging of absence, vocally driven in its forms—sermons, poetic songs, or canticles—and an invitation to "go through" an experience, as well as, or in lieu of, its description.[15] Weil's writing has a complex relationship to this tradition. Sappho's "kletic" hymns and epithalamia share its spirit of invocation and erotic image repertoire (*thalamo*: the nuptial bedchamber; *epithalamion*: literally, before the bed). Yet Porete's *Mirror* might be called exemplary.[16] The performance-orientation of *The Mirror of Simple Souls* is a model for the "Decreation" libretto on several fronts. Carson's libretto form, as an imitation of "what the facts are doing," seems to emerge first and foremost from a reading of Porete.

To add one more reflective angle on the *jeu de miroir* of "telling," I propose we bring Carson herself into the picture—Carson, whose essay on "How Women Like Sappho, Marguerite Porete and Simone Weil Tell God" leaves us in no doubt as to whom it ventures as a likeness. It is perhaps unsurprising that the accusations leveled against Porete at her trial—*pseudo-mulier*, a fake, a sham, an impostor, "full of errors and heresies"—map onto the most belligerent critiques of Carson's writing. Carson is, after all, an aficionado of the fake: of impersonating authors (Euripides in *Grief Lessons*, Stesichoros in *Autobiography of Red*) and adapting, imitating, or otherwise miming their writing; of "heresies" against the conventions and forms of academic scholarship; of error and mistake, not just a poetics in Carson, but one of her most distinctive critical grammars. Carson's play with dissenting forms of likeness, including her writing's frequent non-coincidence with either scholarly decorum or recognizable poetic constraints, notoriously provoked the scorn of Canadian poet and literary hoaxer, David Solway:

> Carson may be our newest pedestalized inamorata but the fact is—and I say this unabashedly—she is a phony, all sleight of hand, both as a scholar and a poet.[17]

Solway hoped to prove iconoclastic in his takedown of an idol of contemporary Anglophone poetry. Especial indignation is reserved for Carson's techniques of quotation, imitation, and copying, modes of reproduction whose wider trend in contemporary writing have been garlanded with the terms "uncreative," "iterative," "citational poetics," and "unoriginal genius."[18] As Ian Rae has discussed, Solway coins a whole host of terms for the object of his tirade: lines "*conceptually* downloaded from Akhmatova" (25, Solway's emphasis), or ideas absorbed by "negative biomimicry" (26).[19] The crux of Solway's argument, Rae summarizes, "is that Carson ransacks the canon of Western poetry and is therefore a literary impostor."[20]

The consonance of this critique with historical anxieties around literary imitation is also unsurprising. We saw in the Introduction how, for Jacques Derrida, "sleight of hand" is the art of the imitator of philosophy, who invokes its "monuments (*hypomnēmata*), inventories, archives, citations, copies, accounts, tales, lists, notes, duplicates, chronicles, genealogies, references," throwing down the gauntlet to philosophy and its claims to "science."[21] (Speaking to John D'Agata, Carson's acknowledgment of her precarious knowledge of English literature—as opposed to literatures in Greek and Latin—is disarming: "it's fake. Totally fake").[22] We might be surprised, though, to find a correlative to imitation anxiety in Carson's early essay on the "feminine" as a locus of contamination, "Dirt and Desire: Essay on the Phenomenology of Female Pollution in Antiquity" (1990), reprinted in *Men in the Off Hours*.[23] Carson traces "the image of women as a formless content" to Plato's remarks on "the matter of creation" as a mother: a receptacle "which is 'shapeless, view-less, all receiving,' and which 'takes its form and activation from whatever shapes enter it.'"[24] Carson's own "genreless texts" (in the words of a nonplussed reviewer) concentrate unease around a writing whose form and activation absorbs the shapes of others; writing concerned with the consequences and derivatives of whatever Carson is reading.

The term "fake women" resonates across Carson's canon of iconic women: Cassandra, Phaidra, St. Teresa of Ávila, and the hybrid Helen of Troy/Marilyn Monroe are my examples here, though others might be cited. What does their capacity for revelation and dissent suggest, I ask, about the difficult liberty of Carson's writing—liberties taken with form, scholarship, translation, and autobiography? For this liberty to "work" requires a certain suspension of disbelief. In both Carson's writing and the lives and work of her "fake women," revelation and dissent are accomplished, as it were, with our consent. We are asked to become their accomplices and collaborators—to allow ourselves, at least momentarily, to be taken in.

Decreation as Performance

"Decreation: How Women Like Sappho, Marguerite Porete and Simone Weil Tell God" and "Decreation (An Opera in Three Parts)" are among the final works collected in *Decreation*. The titles of both texts and the tripartite structure they announce immediately suggest a form of mirroring and rehearsal that is borne out by their shared source material. The essay begins with Sappho fragment 31, one of the feature lyrics of *Eros the Bittersweet*—where Carson read the poem as staging a "mise-en-scene," a "geometrical figure" (the triangle), and "a dance in which everyone moves."[25] Carson reprises her reading of the poem's "geometry" in the "Decreation" essay, and seems to stick to her convictions in *Eros the Bittersweet* that "it is impossible to believe [Sappho] is representing herself as an ordinary lover" and, more importantly, that the poem is "a disquisition on seeming" ("He seems to me . . . I seem to me").[26] What changes as we move from *Eros the Bittersweet* to *Decreation* is that "seeming" changes from a gloss for "the lover's mind in the act of constructing desire for itself" ("a single consciousness represents itself"), to a reading of the non-identity of self with self, where "ecstasy" is "a spiritual event."[27] The "deeper spiritual question" Carson now finds in fragment 31 hangs on her reading of the poem's final line—the first line of the otherwise lost fifth stanza—"But all is to be dared, because even a person of poverty . . . ," which encodes an act of "consent" to love's impossible demand: "*Love dares the self to leave itself behind, to enter into poverty.*"[28]

Substitute "self" for "soul" and this cursive last line—Carson's—could be lifted from *The Mirror of Simple Souls*, with its dramatic declarative style, or from the drastic aphorisms of Weil's notebooks. Part Two of Carson's essay crosses into a parallel between Sappho's poem of daring and Porete's late thirteenth-century allegorical dialogue—full title, *The Mirror of simple and annihilated souls and those who only remain in will and desire of love*—in which the "annihilated soul" (*l'âme anéantie*) is a soul "carried outside her own Being," Carson says, by the "absolute demand" of divine love (163).[29] Carson quotes lengthy passages from Porete's devotional tract, attributed to her authorship by the Italian medievalist Romana Guarnieri, who went on to establish what is now considered the authoritative text.³⁰ Porete's *Mirror* stages a debate between personifications of Reason (*Raison*), Love (*Amour*), the Soul (*Âme*) and other minor characters, around the nature and stages of love.

The book belongs to a genre of medieval *miroir-livres* whose designation picks up on St. Paul's remarkable image in the first letter to the Corinthians: "For now we see through a glass, darkly [or "through a mirror dimly"]; but then face to face: now I know in part, but then shall I know even as also I am known."³¹ While on earth, says St. Paul, we are condemned to see our own obscure (and inverse) reflection in all things. "Then face to face" with God, he imagines, we will see and know as God himself apprehends us. The looking "glass"/"mirror" image (*esoptron* in the Ancient Greek, *speculum* in the Latin) elegantly disqualifies mortal perception, including self-perception, as misleading. Yet the figure of the mirror is also a way of confirming the text's interest in itself and its fictions. Carson quotes Porete: "for everything that one can tell of God or write, no less than what one can think, of God who is more than words, is as much lying as it is telling the truth."³² Writing under the sign of the mirror, Porete instills in every word of her tract an admission of its inaccuracy, making it mimesis and a critique of mimesis in the same gesture. Hers is a writing that, in the act of telling, tells us it is not what it claims to be.

Porete's *Mirror* celebrates its fiction as a robust affirmation of the truth of which it falls short, much as, Carson writes, "she recognizes her poverty [of the soul] as an amazing and inexpressible kind of repletion" ("absolute emptiness which is also absolute fullness," 164). "Dialectical but ... not tragic," says Carson, Porete's logical inversions are at no point explained by their author and not always explicable after the event. In fact, the refusal of explanation extends, with tragic consequences, to the circumstances of Porete's trial, at which she declined to clarify her "errors and heresies" or to speak in her own defense. "How are we then to understand the relationship between Marguerite and her *Mirror*," asks Manuela Ceballos, "when Marguerite's own response to this demand was silence?"³³

The *Mirror* offers its logical inversions not as a topsy-turvy scholastic treatise but as acts of invocation and performances of desire. Carson reads the most brilliant of these by admitting her failure to read it:

> Marguerite Porete invents a word: *le Loingprès* in her Old French, or *Longe Propinquus* in the Latin translation: English might say "the FarNear." ... At the end of her book she returns to the concept one last time, saying simply:
> "His Farness is the more Near."
> I have no idea what this sentence means but it gives me a thrill. It fills me with wonder. In itself the sentence is a small complete act of worship, like a hymn or a prayer. (176–177)

Carson reads Porete's phrase alongside Sappho's "kletic" hymn—"a calling hymn, an invocation to God to come from where she [Aphrodite] is to where we are" (178)—whose function is to mime the difference between these places and "decreate" ("not to destroy") that difference by sustaining distance and proximity in unison. On the trail of its incomprehensibility, Carson gestures toward the place of Porete's expression in a Christian literary tradition that spools out of the Song of Songs' complaint, "I sought him but I did not find him."[34] The song or canticle of absence in this tradition cannot be constative—cannot "tell God"—and so seeks, instead, to perform its desire. The furthest port of call from the textual hermeneutic traditions of Judaism, the song's simple address to God is an act of worship; similes, likenesses that replace one another in sequence, form a syntax that enacts its extreme longing. Where we have "no idea what [a] sentence means"—remember Carson's wish to leave an impression in the mind "no matter what the words mean"—its cyclical appeal and yield of neologisms tell us that "meaning," at least of the kind we can reliably return to, is not where we should be looking. Certeau's *fable mystique* is a discourse bound to orality and fiction: its interweave of sighs and cries ("a response in search of that to which it responds"), its "turns" of language, and its "fictions of the soul" are ways of inventing a textual corpus that wills its own sacrifice (*le sacrifice du langage*) from the start.[35] Not quite knowing what she means, feeling the "thrill" at the expense of the language, is what Porete's performance seems to be inviting. ("Thrill," we have seen, is a word with an interesting history in Carson, a gloss for words "imitating" experience without explaining it).[36] "FarNear," Porete's sharpest "turn" of language, is Carson's "sensible form" in the most compact and economical of proportions. A message is embodied in the thrill of its form, a communion performed at the taste of the words.

In the longest of Carson's quotations from the *Mirror*, she zooms in on "its personnel," the interlocutors who rotate and exchange their positions:

> ... and I pondered, as if God were asking me, how would I fare if I knew that he preferred me to love another more than himself? And at this my sense failed me and I knew not what to say....[37]

Echoing the allegorical conversations of the *Mirror*, Porete performs an *Appellstruktur* in miniature. In this imagined dialogue with God, says Carson, Porete pictures herself in her own place, in God's, and (as God sees her) in another, second place of her own. Porete figures this triangle "consisting of God, Marguerite and Marguerite" in tautologies—"the brilliance of divine being, by which I have being which is being"[38]—and in a compelling use of quotation marks around the word "with": "And so long as I was at ease and loved myself 'with' him, I could not at all contain myself or have calm: I was held in bondage by which I could not move."³⁹ Her logic is complex and evasive. Porete cannot contain herself in a single being—cannot get "to the very inside of [her] definition"—so long as she is held in bondage to herself, split by self-love from a true being equal and returnable to God. Carson speaks of Porete as her own confessor in the *Mirror*, yet it is important to note that Porete's "I" is not the lyric "I" whose testimony and song derives from a single, personal center, but an allegorical one, mouthpiece for "Simple Souls" in the plural and displaced across several personifications. Who speaks of bondage in the above is "the Soul," but it is Porete who has wrought a form for decreative testimony, devotional confession through the looking glass. Porete's "fiction of the soul" is a mirror in which she who speaks (or writes) does not coincide with herself and, in any case, finds her condition of possibility in dialogue. Her quotation marks around "with," which Carson reads, stunningly, as the sign of a heartbeat or a quivering embodied breath, are also, in this sense, something rather simpler. They lend her intimacy with God the status of a citation, an ironic and irreverent proposition and a parody of genuine union. (For Mihkail Bakhtin, Linda Hutcheon notes, the language of parody is always placed in "cheerfully irreverent" quotation marks.)⁴⁰

Porete's dialogues, both those staged in the present tense and those fantasized and recalled, presage what Niklaus Largier has called the "hermeneutic performance" of the sermons of Meister Eckhart—Porete's contemporary and a potential reader of the *Mirror*—where a declarative "I," staged in conversation, exposes the conjury of thought in "real time" and involves the listener in the interpretive process.⁴¹ Carson's own modes of reading, this book has proposed, tend toward the performative in similar ways: from artless self-exposures, deictic address, disclosures of process, and "arts of pure shape," to writing in "conversation" with other writers. Porete's compressed logic—the tautological "being . . . being . . . being" or the "FarNear," above—is a rhetorical performance that learns its arts from Plato and the Neoplatonists, but there is something specific in its compression that reminds us of Carson. Squeezing out the possibility of paraphrase, Porete's logic celebrates the single occasion of its expression, in which meaning and form are indivisible. The form of its utterance is the sole, undisputed site of a "thrill" replacing comprehension.

I suggested at the start of this chapter that Porete's *Mirror* occupies a special place in relation to the "Decreation" opera libretto. Carson's libretto has an antecedent, a sort of proto-version, in "The Mirror of Simple Souls: An Opera Installation," performed in New York in 2001, of which Porete's *Mirror* was the sole source text.⁴² Quite apart from the "Decreation" libretto's play on the conceit of the mirror, reflecting and distorting the material in the essay, Carson's choice of a performance-oriented form for her reading—in both the earlier and later librettos—might also lie with Porete. In chapter 58 of the *Mirror*, where the dialectical compound *Loingprès* appears out of nowhere, Porete makes a sudden appeal: "I pray you, understand these words divinely, hearers of this book!"

(*Entendez ces motz divinement, par amour, auditeurs de ce livre!*).[43] This direct address tells us in no uncertain terms that Porete's book was written with vocalization and performance before an audience (*auditeurs*) in mind.[44] Its sudden shift into verse in Chapter 120—including a striking mise-en-page resembling Carson's "Blended Text" in *Decreation*, its central mid-line split cueing the *locuteur* to perform an exaggerated pause—would have registered as sound, rhyme, and an unambiguous case of literary artifice, rather, perhaps, than truth-telling or sermonizing.[45] What Carson adapts from Porete, marking a turning point in her work more broadly (coinciding, too, with her creative partnership with Currie), is a performance-oriented form in which dialogue, dialectical compounds, shapely tautologies, non sequiturs, and turns of language are apprehended in the instant and without explanation. Porete also provides Carson with a profound justification for *imitatio*—for pastiche as well as parody—as a means of performing, amplifying, and sending up the dilemmas she encounters in her sources. Feats of logic and language in the original cannot always be explained, admits Carson. But sometimes, "approaching a mystery"—she quotes Giorgio Agamben, at the end of a recent essay—"one can offer nothing but a parody."[46]

Imitatio and Mirror

"Decreation: An Opera in Three Parts" mirrors the essay's putative three parts and the dilemmas shared by Carson's three "fake women," the last of whom—Simone Weil—I turn to in a moment. A glance at the opera's opening part suggests this particular "distortion in the glass" has warped Carson's source material at times beyond recognition. *Imitatio*, Burrow reminds us, does not have to mean direct verbal connection between the new text and its source: "It might display instead deep analogies to its form, in a variety of senses ranging from the 'idea' of the author imitated, through syntactic and rhetorical structures, right down to the appearance of the poem on the page."[47] What plays out across the three parts of the "Decreation" libretto is a form of *imitatio* that blends together different kinds of textual and authorial mirroring—transcription, impersonation, rhetorical and verbal pastiche, parody, analogy, and preserved "ideas" or *paradeigmata*. The essay's central ideas remain more or less intact, as do the contradictions and inconsequentiality argued for in the essay's final part. Were their intactness achieved by simply rehashing her sources, either verbatim or in paraphrase, the "Decreation" libretto would make for a decidedly un-thrilling read, and an even less thrilling live performance. It is in *how* Carson imitates her "fake women" that the work becomes significant as the staging of reading and misreading. The performative fakery of the *Mirror*, with its allegorical sung dialogues, verse interludes, and calculated self-exposures, ghosts the libretto as an interlocutor, blueprint, and Ur-text.

Part One, "Love's Forgery," reprises Carson's reading of Sappho fragment 31, with its triangular geometry of jealousy and extreme desire, which Carson glosses in the essay in relation to Sappho's cult-worship of Aphrodite (162). In the libretto, the same triangle goes full mythic. As described by Homer in Book 8 of *The Odyssey*, the love triangle in which Aphrodite is caught features her husband, Hephaistos (Carson's "god of the forge—god of fire, art, craft, igneous eruptions and technological cunning") and her lover, Ares. A "Volcano Chorus" of "7 female robots built by Hephaistos" provides accompaniment in the libretto (187).[48] This mythic iteration of the Sapphic triangle picks up Carson's reading in *Eros the Bittersweet*, which arrives by way of Plato's *Phaedrus*. In the essay on eros, we saw, it is the artifices of writing (poietic craft, forgery, mimesis) that grant "nonlovers" the means to tame and instrumentalize erotic desire, and to bypass the jealous dance of displacement that is its consequence. Reining in or capturing desire—producing, for Socrates, a failed *erōs* and a failed philosophy—is here the goal of Hephaistos, who hopes to catch Aphrodite and Ares in the act of love and then force her compliance. Hephaistos forges a net of fine chains to trap the lovers, while, in Carson's version, the chorus of automata cheers him on. Carson's "New Chorus: Love Is Always New When It's You," sung by Hephaistos and his robots as they install the trap, moves through associations, synonyms, and analogies for Hephaistos's coercive renewal of his and Aphrodite's love: "Newly caught. / Newly watered. / Neological. / Newborn, new-flayed, newly enfranchised, anew, of late. / Fresh curdled" (194). An associative, synonymic displacement performs his fantasy of renewal, but gets caught up in the net of signifiers and flounders as eros.[49] Carson's parody of the Sapphic rationale of desire strays wide in all features save her poem's triangular geometry and love's dare to the self to abandon its artifices ("how true love can / ever avail // against forgery," 204).

The trials of Hephaistos in "Love's Forgery" are a pastiche of Sappho's ecstatic ordeal that opens Carson's libretto on an unmistakable note of camp. The beginning can feel disorienting after the solemnity of the "Decreation" essay, whose weighty intonations include "undoing the creature," the "metaphysics of love," "problems with eating," and the indictment and trial of "fake woman" Porete. In her "Notes on Camp," Susan Sontag picks out as its essence "its love of the unnatural: of artifice and exaggeration," qualities it is easy to alight on in Carson's operatic pastiche: big, loud, shiny anachronisms of staging and tone—"Aphrodite waiting by a phone" and "Ares in the back of a taxi," Ares singing "Easy Sugar"— or the conversion of philosophical hauteur into kitschy chorus lines and burlesque stage directions ("the Chorus of the Void tapdance around [Weil]").[50] At their most extreme, these conversions move the libretto into the impertinence of parody—parody, that is, whose tonalities do not belong where we find them. In her reckoning with the analysis of camp "sensibility," Sontag highlights the importance of what she calls a "sharp conflict" in her own: "I am strongly drawn to Camp, and almost as strongly offended by it."[51] "To name a sensibility, to draw its contours and to recount its history," she proposes, "requires a deep sympathy modified by revulsion."[52] Carson's modes of *imitatio* in the "Decreation" libretto require a similar modification—sympathy/revulsion, inspiration/bathos—in her readers and/or audience. In fact, the modification brings the concept and emotional stakes of decreation into sharper relief, in the libretto's final part especially. There, dramatization of a sympathetic dilemma of passion, longing, and belief in Weil resounds along the edge it shares with a blind self-destructiveness, what Sontag would read as Weil's fanaticism.

The libretto's second part, "Her Mirror of Simple Souls," performs an altogether different relationship to its principal source text and a different permutation of *imitatio*. Arias sung by Porete begin and end this part, separated by mock-interrogative exchanges on Porete's vulgate text with the Latin-speaking "Quidnunc Chorus," and a Duet of Outer and Inner Space where Porete, in an ingenious mise-en-scène, shares the stage with herself. Where Part One includes no direct quotations from Sappho, Part Two features transcriptions of the Porete material as it appears in the essay, as well as pastiches of ideas and phrases from the *Mirror* that do not. Unlike Carson's essay, the libretto contains neither notes nor references, so to distinguish between verbatim quotation, paraphrase, and pastiche in the Porete and Weil sections requires us to return to the essay and, in some cases, to the sources themselves. That is, it requires a reader "in-the-know" in order to function fully as pastiche or parody (Linda Hutcheon's "imitation with a critical difference," which I return to below).[53] On the immediate textual surface of the libretto—its citational poetics—the question of fiction and mirroring in Porete's "problem of telling" manifests as a problem of how it is retold.

An example of the ambiguity around citation opens Carson's "Chorus of the 33 Questions [recitative by the Quidnunc Chorus]," which bold-types the letters "J-A-L-O-U-X" in errant acrostic mode: "Jesus should be put into a mortar and pounded with a pestle / so much that no one may any longer justly see or taste the Person put there: do you say this?" (217). As far-fetched as this material might sound—Carson makes no reference to it in the essay—the metaphor is genuine Porete.[54] In the light of moments like these, the questioning of Carson's Quidnunc Chorus is aimed not just at Porete's "fake" writings, but at Carson's "fake" adaptation and its fidelity or not to Porete ("do you [—*does she*—] say this?"). Other phrases sung by the Chorus preserve stylistic dissonance from *The Mirror* while summarizing its insights—"Love liberates you from Reason, / love releases you from Obedience, / love replaces the Law," and so on (217). As Porete's and Carson's voices blend together and apart, the core insight of "fake woman" Porete regarding the self's difference from itself, its hosting of a *mimēma* of whom God is jealous, is played on and performed by the restaging of her work. Porete's "errors and heresies," her willful falsifications, are suddenly also Carson's.

Carson's version of Porete's life and writing is what we might call an "intimate" reading in two connected senses. First, in the instances where *imitatio* moves into actual citation: in the "Chorus of the 33 Questions" above; in the "Swimming Aria," which begins as a pastiche and then, part way through, picks up quotations from Porete that are reproduced in Carson's essay; or in the "Song of the Most High Jealous One," whose opening strophe is verbatim Porete, and whose later riffs on darkness and nothingness pick up elements of the *Mirror* not quoted in the essay.[55] This mixture of true citation and fake version proves a faithful performance of Porete's idea of telling—"as much lying as it is telling the truth." The "Duet of Outer and Inner Space [sung by Marguerite Outer, who wears headphones and listens to Marguerite Inner projected behind her on video]" stages a different combination of verbatim quotation (Marguerite Inner's long solo) and interpolation (Marguerite Outer's "[recitative whisper]: It makes me so nervous to listen to it," 221).[56] The intermedia mise-en-scène enables Carson to mime Porete's split self in "sensible form," reproducing the drama of "withness" that, in *The Mirror*, is expressed as an effect of grammar. Here, the *auditeurs* of Porete's original performance scenario are herself.[57]

This pattern of far-nearness makes the libretto an intimate record of something else too. The whole text offers a kind of screen-grab of Carson's reading of decreation as a reckoning with writing. For all its deference to the imitated source or exemplum, *imitatio*, Burrow suggests, is also the portrait of a reading, a record of what the imitating author believes makes her exemplum worthy of imitation and/or recognizable in the new text.[58] It is nonetheless, and by the same token, a performance of virtuosity by the imitator, as impersonator, composer of dramatic verse, and/or as close reader. Carson's iteration of her three authors is "fake" and knows it, but uses its likeness and non-likeness to bring the emotive rationales and rhetorical strategies of their work into new clarity. Many of Carson's works record her reading of "what the facts are doing" in similar ways, raising questions about the difference between adaptation, imitation, parody, and pastiche in her versions of other works, including two yet to be discussed in this book: *Norma Jeane Baker of Troy*, a version of Euripides's *Helen*, and *Antigonick*, a rendition of the *Antigone*. These versions see her develop a trademark tonality of pastiche—ironic, bathetic, untimely, artificial—that, in her responses to other works, risks becoming imitable itself.

Faking Weil

Porete's performative and self-compromising position offers a model for Carson's experimental reading of her "fake women." The earlier "opera installation" on *The Mirror* is not, however, the first time the themes and sources of

"Decreation" make an appearance in Carson. We know that the history of Carson reading Sappho goes back to her very earliest scholarly writing. Simone Weil, too, has been a long-standing interlocutor on the question of desire. Carson's 1981 PhD thesis, "Odi et Amo Ergo Sum," features a striking chapter epigraph from Weil, whose terminology of "consent" and "distance" forms the axis of the "Decreation" essay: "To soil is to modify, it is to touch.... To love purely is to consent to distance."[59] In *Eros the Bittersweet*, the revamped thesis, Carson looks to Weil for what she calls an "analog" of desire in hunger. Here is Weil:

> All our desires are contradictory, like the desire for food. I want the person I love to love me. If he is, however, totally devoted to me, he does not exist any longer and I cease to love him. And as long as he is not totally devoted to me he does not love me enough. Hunger and repletion.[60]

Weil ventures an analogy that, following her death, would come to leave a permanent mark on her critical reception. Weil's notes on desire and hunger are copious and disorganized, but they are too easily given false coherence by their elision with her own complex relationship with food, now commonly understood, along with other elements of Weil's life, as a kind of real-time performance of her philosophy.[61] This trend in reading Weil begins in the wake of Simone Pétrement's monumental biography, but it is Sontag's better-known remarks that popularized the elision of Weil's philosophical commitments with her emotional life. Sontag attacked a "fanatical asceticism" in Weil that made her life, in Sontag's words, "excruciatingly identical with her ideas."[62] What perturbs us about Weil, says Sontag, is less her ideas—which few readers "really share"—than her fierce, uncompromising consistency with them.[63] Weil can be pitiless and unrelenting, exacting in her diagnostics of the maladies of her times, and stringent in what Sharon Cameron calls the "minimalist economy" of her philosophical writing (a "performance of impersonality").[64] Yet to see the events of her life as the consummation of her thinking is to impoverish that thinking by literalizing it, an oversimplification Weil herself would not have supported. A literal reading has already dismissed decreation as a philosophy of masochism.

Carson talks about the consonance between Weil's life and writing toward the end of the "Decreation" essay, where she glosses Weil's practical "arrange[ments] for her own disappearance" (173) and "a problem with eating all her life" (175). Carson's Weil is not the fanatically consistent Weil of Susan Sontag; nor does she argue for a philosophy of decreation completed by its biographical analogues. What Carson finds in Weil is a theorist—and, to a certain degree, a practitioner— of contradiction. In Part Three of the "Decreation" essay, Carson introduces Weil as "a person who wanted to get herself out of the way" (167), picking up the resonance of John Cage's struggle "to get every Me out of the way" with which Carson says she identifies. As with Porete, however, getting self "out of the way" is no mean feat. Nor is this complex desire, so simply expressed, the whole story. In one of Carson's first quotations, Weil refers to "the power to say 'I'" as "what we must yield up to God." Carson continues the thought: "[Weil] feels herself to be an obstacle to herself inwardly" (167). "Jealousy is a dance in which everybody moves," she says, returning to Porete's tautological triangle, "because one of them is always extra—three people trying to sit on two chairs" (169). Decreation, as Carson suggests, is not willed self-destruction but a radical reconception of self that begins with its exposure as a cover story for Being; a recognition that "I" (or "Me") thwarts and blocks access to itself. Self, in this model, is a conflict of interest.

The paradox of the self that is not itself stalks Weil's thinking. If "I" truly is "other than what I imagine myself to be," then self-knowledge begins with the knowledge of self-difference: "'know yourself' means," she explains, "Do not identify yourself with your thoughts."[65] Carson quotes expressions of longing from Weil that call upon the promise of St. Paul that knowledge will one day be possible without mediation, a mediation so intimate we might almost miss it: "If only I could see a landscape as it is when I am not there. But when I am in any place I disturb the silence of heaven by the beating of my heart" (168–169). When Carson approaches the "subterfuge and contradiction" of decreative *writing* in the essay's fourth and final part, it is Weil she turns to for her theory: "Contradiction alone is the proof that we are not everything. Contradiction is our badness and the sense of our badness is the sense of reality. For we do not invent our badness. It is true" (171).[66] When Carson speaks of "being placed at the crossing point of a contradiction, which is a painful place to be . . . but mystics love it" (175), "So Simone Weil" is her end-stop.

For Weil, contradiction—and being contradictory—is the touchstone of the real. The contradictory in us, "our badness," which "we do not invent," is the foil to all fantasies of self-control, self-knowledge, self-invention, and possessive love. In fact, Weil says elsewhere, "This need to be the creator of what we love is a need to imitate God."[67] This Weil committed to contradiction, the Weil at the center of Carson's reading, might come as a surprise to readers who, in good company, associate Weil's philosophical writing with cold-limbed axiomatic abstraction, the unfriendliness of what Carson calls her "punchy passages" (174);[68] with a preference in the French for the impersonal *soi* ("one" or "oneself") over the confessional hesitancy of *je* ("I");[69] and with an aggressive ideological purism that fails as ethics when, in Gillian Rose's words, it "claims . . . violently that violence is cultivated elsewhere."[70] There are striking exceptions to the pushy axioms of her theological prose. Weil's essay on *The Iliad* ("The Iliad, or The Poem of Force," 1939) lends an astounding lyricism to describing the affliction of individuals dehumanized by force. The victims of force, she says, become a living contradiction—both person and thing—whose soul is obliged to "imitate nothingness."[71] In its unflinching revelation of force, *The Iliad*, she says, is "the purest and loveliest of mirrors."[72] What emerges in many of Weil's notes and letters is an idea of thought and writing bound by obligation to reflect and reproduce the humanity they encounter. Writing on the tasks of the historian, she critiques the "so-called historical spirit [that] does not pierce the paper to find flesh and blood; it consists in a subordination of thought to the document."[73] Her own writing, she suggests, should and will be transformed by its readers. In a letter to Gustave Thibon, which Carson quotes in the "Decreation" essay, Weil bequeaths him her notebooks in the hope that they might "find a lodging beneath your pen, whilst changing their form to reflect your likeness."[74] Valuing contradiction as she does, it would come as no surprise to find Weil genuinely comfortable with the emergence of contradiction in her own writing, owing to the close attention of her readers: "attention fixed upon something reveals the contradiction in it," she writes: "a sort of unsticking process takes place."[75]

Carson is precisely this kind of reader of Weil. The first iteration of her response—the "Decreation" essay—concludes with the importance of contradiction in Weil's thinking. The second—the libretto—performs it under the equivocal, rebellious sign of the mirror. In the final part of the libretto, "Fight Cherries," Carson turns her attention to the "subterfuge and contradiction" of Weil's letters to her parents. Carson's dramatization makes these letters a means of exposure: not only of what is disavowed in decreation and in the making of decreation theology, but of the fact that both the theology and the filial relationship are determined forms of psychic organization. For all that Weil is not what she imagines herself to be, and for all that her philosophy declares itself against imagination, Weil still has to deal with what *others* imagine her to be; with the emotional demands of their imagination, and with the physical demands of a desire that slips the net, exposing human contradictoriness outright.

That desire, here, is "hunger." The "Argument" of Part Three sets out Weil's dilemma as follows:

> Simone Weil's life was caught in the net of her parents' care. . . . She took lunges through the net—into Descartes, into Plato, into trade unions and communism and Homer and theology and the arts of hunger. She did not want to be a woman. She wanted to disappear. Certain aspects of the disappearance had to be concealed from the parents so her many letters to them are repetitions of the one same glowingly factitious postcard that every good daughter sends home— *Dear people what splendid weather thanks for the chocolate I'm making lots of friends here kisses to all*—meanwhile she was dying.[76]

The six movements of "Fight Cherries" include duets between Weil and Monsieur or Madame Weil, two solo arias, and a "Chocolate Chorus" in which "Simone and the chorus measure hunger." Several of these scripts suggest that Weil not only took "lunges through the net" but that she also sought to reinforce its weave. Her philosophy, in Carson's reading, finds itself pulled out of shape by human attachment and attachment to the world. The third movement, a "Duet of the Sleeveless Sports Blouses," stages Weil's correspondence with her mother on what Carson calls "the rules of life." The duet performs, with a literalism both satirical and elegant, what Carson describes above as "repetitions of the one same glowingly factitious postcard." It begins with a pastiched letter from Weil to her mother that undergoes an "unsticking process" as its phrases and grammatical parts are remixed to revelatory and comic effect:

> Chère Maman I have bought two sleeveless sports
> blouses Today a street fight between Nazis and
> Communists No I was not there! Please send
> me *special post* what I asked for last
> letter (the Hegel) Kisses.
>
> . . .
>
> Chère Maman I asked Hegel to send
> *special post* kisses what less.
> sleeves I have Communists fight
> blouses last! Please no sports
> today I was bought (between
> two and the Nazis)
>
> . . .
>
> Chère Maman I was *special* there I
> bought less Hegel Please Today have
> Nazis send blouses between sports
> I asked what Communists kissed
> me for (two fight sleeves)
> No not last *post*! . . .[77]

The fictional letter "cites" images from several of Weil's actual letters to her parents.[78] The consecutive iterations give us Weil's letters through the looking glass. They turn phrasing whose original intention was to "conceal" into a means of revelation. These performed "repetitions of the same one glowingly factitious postcard" employ a technique of phrasal remix to explode Weil's tightly governed prose into a permutatory "potential literature."[79] Putting the same constrained vocabulary to new uses, Carson's remixes release alternative logics and associations inside the poise of Weil's writing, from which even her correspondence offers no let-up. The move decreates Weil, displacing her from the putative center of her writing and producing a hybrid text of ambiguous origin; but it does something more than that, too. In an exchange in which Mme. Weil's lines consist mainly of injunctions and imperative prohibitions—"Do not leave your money lying by the bed / Do not run on the mountains when they are icy. / Do not forget a card to us as soon as you arrive at the war"—Carson's iterative pastiche makes of Weil's concealment a fine-grained form of dissent. For though Carson de-authorizes Weil, she also makes her speak out of turn. Where Weil's correspondence turns euphemism and concealment into arts of impoverishment, Carson makes her fake letter a free-for-all of meaning, possibility, and contradiction. In the last of her remixes—ending "*Chère Maman* out of my way!"—an unexpected, aggressive claim to selfhood is made.

Weil's protection by her parents is met in her letters by reciprocal (and hostile) protection of them by Weil. "The Weils themselves were perfectly aware of their role," writes Toril Moi: " 'If you ever have a daughter,' Selma [Weil] said to [the poet, Jean] Tortel, 'pray to God she won't be a saint.' " When people expressed sympathy for her parents, Simone would reply: "Another member of the Society for the Protection of my Parents!"[80] Yet her correspondence, as Carson reproduces it, might have us believe Weil was this Society's most stalwart member. What Carson performs in the remixed letter is the pull of loyalties to her parents and to their idea of Weil, her self-relation mediated by theirs.[81] It exposes the bind of decreation theology and its principal theorist to the world and the most unassuming of its currencies. It shows up the loss of innocence of objects (the "sleeveless sports blouses"), whose accumulation of meaning across Carson's verses involves them in an off-scene drama of destructiveness, as "Nazis send blouses between sports." The effect is to humanize Weil and her prose. The sublime hauteur and the relentless poise are gently, and with a self-conscious artifice, exploded.

The libretto opens straight into Weil's signature declaratives—"Grace can only enter where there is void to receive it"—, reproduced verbatim alongside imitation Weil lines in the "Duet of What Is a Question avec Papa."[82] It is here that Carson begins her inquiry into just what decreation dispenses with to accomplish its program of self-undoing (not only "What Is a Question," then, but what exactly is refused in order to answer it). In her critique of Weil, Gillian Rose rebukes her discourse for its distance from the world, which it leaves "untouched supernaturally," and its failure to "suspend and resume the ethical with its features of modern state and society."[83] Weil fails, for Rose, to "bring the sublime into the pedestrian," and the consequence is a rejection of both the world and the demands of political life.[84] Carson parses Weil's declaratives by forcing them into a parodied confrontation with this "pedestrian"—the everyday mundanity of which M. Weil acts as spokesman:

> M. WEIL: What does she mean, void?
> What about shoes and fruits and winecorks, many things exist, they have colour and duration, they bear down on us.
> What does she mean?
>
> SIMONE: Winecorks are not a question.
> Power is a question.
> Not to exercise power is to endure the void. (225)

As in each of Weil's responses to her father's disavowed questions, the final line of this fictive exchange is an actual quotation from Weil. Weil's philosophy of saying "no"—Weil: "God allows me to exist outside himself. It is for me to refuse this authorization"—is forced, in each, into negative dialectics.[85] Carson renders a broad spectrum of disavowals implicit in Weil's refusal, from the haughty to the ridiculous: "Neither Mme Trotsky nor Mme Weil is a question"... "Chairs are not a question. / Worldly need is a question" (226). These are strong interpolations. Where the libretto includes verbatim and adapted quotations from Weil among inventive variations and paraphrase (e.g., "like an unwelcome third between two lovers" (235), adapting Weil's "the unwelcome third [*le tiers importun*] who is with two betrothed lovers"[86]), the question is again raised—as it was in the Porete iteration—as to what kind of *imitatio* is being practiced and what exactly is the point of its divergence. "Quotation," notes Hutcheon, can be "a form of parody": exposing the source text not to ridicule but, by virtue of the new—in this case, irreverent—context, to a critical distancing.[87] Agent of this distance, Carson interposes something between Weil and her readers. What kind of "third" is Carson's text between them? Or rather, who is it that speaks in this "third" or "other" voice, not quite Weil and not quite Carson?[88]

Carson's *imitatio*, whether she intends it to or not, parodies a certain pomposity in Weil's attachment to the gravitas of decreation. For Hutcheon, parody is "imitation with a critical difference," or "repetition that includes difference"; its "dialectical synthesis" of source and imitation shakes up meanings that have, through familiarity or cliché, simply stopped meaning.[89] Parody, Judith Butler says in her essay "Merely Cultural," expresses the refusal of subordination to a unity that "domesticates difference": parody, there, is a form of "resistance to unity," claiming the capacity not only to distinguish itself from a true, original version, but to reveal the *internal* difference of the version being presented.[90] Always provisional and ready to be replaced by the "true," uncaricatured version, parody expresses the desire for what Butler calls "an intimacy" with the position or object being parodied:

Parody requires a certain ability to identify, approximate, and draw near; it engages an intimacy with the position it appropriates that troubles the voice, the bearing, the performativity of the subject such that the audience or the reader does not quite know where it is you stand.[91]

What Butler calls the "deconstructive play" of parody exposes the hidden or contradictory desires of this original "position." But it also appropriates and acquires that position's desirousness—in the case of Weil, the desire to participate in creation, not only by decreating herself, but by loving, desiring, and imagining objects as they desire and are desired by others. Butler's logic would suggest that to get close to—to close-read—this contrary position, you would do better parodying it than trying to explain it. That an incongruent tone or untimely context (Butler's "destructive play") can reveal more about an object than any attempt to accurately pin it down. Parody's distance from the original position—the longing inside parody, let's say—makes for new forms of intimacy and proximity. Its "farness," to borrow Porete, "is the more near."

Fake Women

What Carson does with Weil in the "Decreation" libretto, then, is to "unstick" her thinking from itself by performing more or less subtle estrangements of her writing. Faking Weil, imitating, citing, and parodying her prose, reveals its capacity for internal non-identity and dissent; but the appropriation, unsettling as it is at moments, produces its own drama of ambivalence. Glancing back to Butler, we are never quite sure where it is that Carson stands on Weil (and not just on Weil, of course).

The libretto's final scene stages Weil in the Kent sanatorium where she passed the final weeks of her life. "Aria of Last Cherries" is, following the stage directions, "sung by Simone Weil from a hospital bed, the Chorus of the Void tapdance around her." Weil's philosophy of desire—desire without an object, "desire in the void"—is adapted as a confessional psychodrama, with hunger playing the part of desire.[92] In Weil, the desire that knows what it wants is invariably a fiction: "desires are true insofar as they are energy. It is the object that is false."[93] But Carson's Weil is staged in extreme fear and tension around what Carson calls "failing not in my life but in my death" (238). Failure in death, for Weil, is to die on terms that are not her own.

There is, here, alongside the voluntary "death" of decreation, an involuntary one stalking Weil's pursuit by the Chorus, who taunt her with involuntary claims of the body. In "Fight Cherries," the choice of cherries as Weil's provocateur picks up on another of Weil's "glowingly factitious" letters, sent to her parents from

London, as well as hosting a deliberate sexual euphemism.[94] A cover for the fantasy of annihilation in union, desire in the void is suggested in Carson's libretto to be capable of changing places with the eroticism and corporeality it eschews:

> SIMONE: ... Take all my food away, I cannot lift the spoon.
> I must finish this letter to my parents
> about the blossoms here
> in London all is joy and very happy! perfectly happy!
> Also I must ask the chaplain of the Free French
> whether, despite the fact that I—
> CHORUS: Come cherries come.
> Come close.
> Come tingle.
> Come tease a saint.
> Come cherries
> continue: we'll discover where you sweat. (238–239).

Carson's scene remixes Weil with Thérèse of Lisieux who, dying and unable to eat, was famously tormented by images of feasting. Toward the end of the aria, Weil hesitates: "Perhaps I would like some cherries. / There is nothing else I want" (240). Imagination can be blindsided, the scene suggests, but the body isn't so easily quelled. In fact, hunger is where the voluntary—decreation, and Weil's consistency with it here—meets its limits. To quote Hephaistos in the libretto's opening "Hunger Tango," "Hunger / looks like me / but it is not original with me" (189): hunger is where the self meets its rebellious double face to face. Hunger, too, by this account, is also a cipher for appropriative or "unoriginal" poetics, the consumption of others' writing that preserves origin along with its devouring—something we also see in *The Beauty of the Husband*. (In *Economy of the Unlost*, Carson calls "Delay, disappointment and hunger" "experiences catalytic for poets").[95] She remarks in the "Decreation" essay on Weil's fantasy of "a state in which to look is to eat." Merely looking gets you what you want, she notes. A devouring gaze—like a text of desire, the *erotikos logos* of Plato's *Phaedrus*—bypasses the claims of the body. It "need not end in perishing."[96]

The actions that in her lifetime might all too perfectly have performed decreation are, finally, where Weil's position slips into contradiction. Her disavowal of her own body ended up drawing even greater attention to her: Jean Tortel described her as "a kind of bird without a body, withdrawn, in a huge black cloak which she never took off and which flapped around her calves."[97] Likewise, her writing, whose conspicuousness and otherworldly abstraction, for Rose, suspends it as ethics, betrays its paeans in its own philosophical hauteur. For all her desire to disappear, Weil seems to have been incapable, wrote her friend Gustave Thibon, of "pass[ing] unnoticed."[98] Yet tension and resistance in Weil are not only where her writing is most interesting, as Cameron eloquently argues, but where her project evinces the sharpest mix of emotional responses.[99] This difficult mixture can be hard to swallow in Carson's camped-up rendition of Weil's final hours. We may indeed feel sympathy and revulsion at her portrait of Weil's self-starvation, especially when starvation for Weil was inextricably linked to those with whom she identified: the striking factory workers whose strife she sought to reproduce in herself. It is impossible to feel at ease in the final scene of "Fight Cherries." Yet perhaps this unease is Carson's point. Through parody and the conflict of emotions it produces—the internal dissent it throws into relief— we might just "get" decreation in all its troubled, humanized complexity.

Going on Carson's "Decreation" essay and opera, "fake women" are women who, under pressures of strife and longing, push their thinking to exalted, sometimes unpalatable extremes. Finding themselves on the edge of paradox, they follow this "position" to its most radical consequences and stay there. The "truth" produced at this outlier position, Carson explains, is "also fake." Out of this self-compromising "truth" comes an unexpected case for the fake—for *miroir-livres*, an ecstatic lyric "I," or voluntarily de-authorizing authorship—that is also a justification for *imitatio*, pastiche, and parody; for preserving the contours and contradictions of a source text by reproducing as well as transforming them. As well as pulling the weight of paradox and contradiction, "fake women" pay the price for the strong emotions—the sympathy and the revulsion—it can provoke. We look to them for coherence, then critique them when it is missing, or else slam them for fanaticism, for cohering that bit too much.

Decreation is where Carson brings together three such women and produces a double act of form to express what the "fake" can do. Yet *Decreation* also lends its reading to other "fake women" making cameos of various kinds in Carson's work. Beyond *Decreation*, Carson's writing to date is full of revelatory misrecognitions at the hands of women, from the Sappho of "TV Men" to *Norma Jeane Baker of Troy*. Writing on Euripides' Phaidra, whose story "came in as a free wave and crashed on your beach," Carson alludes to a complex set of relations between the real, the fake, and the feminine that provoke sympathy and revulsion in the *Hippolytos*.[100] Phaidra's outlaw love for Hippolytos exposes a desire that is, necessarily, never identical with itself. Though not "fake," Carson insists:

> Truth is often, in some degree, economic. Which isn't to say [Phaidra's] passion for Hippolytos was fake. Women learn to veil things. Who likes to look straight at real passion? Looks can kill. I would call "feminine" this talent for veiling a truth in a truth.[101]

...

There was a shame in her but not the kind you wanted to see, not woman's modesty... "What do we desire when we desire other people? Not them. Something else. Phaidra touched it. You hated her for that."[102]

Writing on Cassandra—"nonlinear, nonnarrative and the most beautiful of Priam's daughters"—Carson describes another gesture of unveiling, this time associated with the disclosure (*alētheia*) of prophecy:

> Is it possible to believe something truly unbelievable? . . . Is there an edge of light all around the dark mass of your life up to this moment? Can you see the dark mass as a veil? Can you want it gone? Can you say *flic flac it's gone*? Cassandra can.
>
> . . .
>
> Aeschylus would like us to see the veils flying up in Cassandra's mind, would like us to be wondering at what level of herself she is translating some pure gash of Trojan emotion into a metrically perfect line of Greek tragic verse and what that translation has to do with the arts of prophecy.[103]

Cassandra is a prophet, purveyor of unbelievable news and circular reasoning, and a translator, Carson says, of "some pure gash of Trojan emotion into a metrically perfect line of Greek tragic verse." Cassandra's imitation of this verse enables the characters and audience to comprehend "Trojan emotion" (as rather a lot like Greek emotion), but it also unveils "a site," Carson says, "that has no business being underneath."[104] Trojan emotion is made Greek by an act of translation, but "Greek metrics inside a Trojan silence" also sound out the psychic and linguistic profile of conquest, revealing who speaks for whom and into whose silence that speech encroaches. The power of "fake women," a power that renders them objects of both fascination and hatred, lies in their revelation of the unseeable and inaudible (Troy), their touching of the untouchable (Phaidra's love), and their inspiration of belief in the unbelievable (prophecy and mystic fable). Belief—or the radical suspension of *disbelief*—is what the "fake" seems to demand. In her remarks on Phaidra, incidentally, Carson is impersonating the character's author, Euripides, in a species of epilogue on "Why I Wrote Two Plays About Phaidra," signed "by Euripides." Not a fake woman, then, but a fake male tragedian speaking sympathetically about the wiles of woman.

Closer in sentiment to Carson's "Decreation" trio is Teresa of Ávila, who appears in "The Truth About God" sequence in *Glass, Irony and God*. A poem about Teresa's testimony, the truth or fiction of her sensations and stigmata, "Teresa of God" ends with a different dilemma of testimony:

> To her heart God sent an answer.
> The autopsy after her death revealed it was indeed rent.

> Photographs of the event
> had to be faked (with red thread and an old gold glove)
> when the lens kept melting.[105]

Faking here is a mechanism that responds to the unbelievable, whose representation incapacitates (melts) the representational medium. This "fake woman," who lives in a "personal black cube" (or "interior castle," in Teresa's famous image), forces her self inside its own definition. The *morada* or dwelling-place she finds there requires a whole repertoire of fictions, neologisms, and new names.[106] Carson argues in the "Decreation" essay that "ecstasy" has a knock-on effect on writing that forces it into contradiction. (Julia Kristeva diagnoses Teresa in more extreme terms: "Teresa's ecstasy is no more or less than a writerly effect!").[107] The anxieties aroused by "fake women" carry over onto the medium of testimony, hyper-charging questions of imitation, forgery, doctoring, fiction, and falsification. Carson's own reception, we saw, suggests similar anxieties might still be at large.

This brief survey would not be complete, finally, without Carson's reading of surely the first "fake woman" in Western literary history. The figure of Helen of Troy comes replete, in Carson's words, with "an adjectival tradition of whoredom already old by the time Homer used it. When Stesichoros unlatched her epithet from Helen there flowed out such a light as may have blinded him for a moment."[108] This unlatching—recall Weil's "unsticking"—occurs in the Palinode that Carson reproduces among the paratexts of *Autobiography of Red*: "No it is not the true story. / No you never went on the benched ships. / No you never came to the towers of Troy."[109] In her adaptation of Euripides's *Helen*, Carson reproduces the Helen unlatched from Troy that Euripides chose to stage; the Helen whose *eidōlon*, likeness, or "breathing phantom" in the Loeb translation, goes to Troy in her place, while the real Helen is in Egypt.[110] The Helen who doesn't go to Troy—Helen under the sign of the fake—is excoriated in Euripides with no less fervor than the Helen who, in Homer's account, does.[111] Carson's subtitled "version of Euripides' *Helen*" not only unlatches Helen from Troy but, in the same stroke, unlatches Helen from her mythic person. Carson's Helen is, as the title of the version suggests, displaced onto her fellow idol of female beauty, "fake woman," and object of sympathy and revulsion, Marilyn Monroe (née Norma Jeane Baker), in the spoken and sung performance work, *Norma Jeane Baker of Troy*.

If Euripides's *Helen* is a play about fictive versions, likenesses, and *eidōla*, *Norma Jeane Baker of Troy* at least doubles its fakery. Carson's version brings the play's central paradigm of imitation into focus by transposing its context and condensing its characters into a complex monologue, woven of impersonations, identifications, and imaginary conversations ("Enter Norma Jeane as Mr. Truman Capote," or, announced by Norma Jeane herself, "Enter Norma Jeane as

Mr. Truman Capote to join Norma Jeane as Norma Jeane,'" 10, 46). In Carson's alternate version of the play's facts, Norma Jeane—like Helen—anguishes over the afflicted of Troy, and—unlike Helen—reproduces imagined conversations with a psychoanalyst and with "Arthur [Miller] of New York and Sparta" (Carson's Menelaus). This "fake" version of the *Helen* sings and dances its own redoubled artifice, and sets out its rationale in a series of mock lesson plans. In the first of these "Lessons," complete with "Case Studies," keywords, and "Teachable Moments," Carson describes the action and the interpretive strategy that mirrors it: "Managing optics cleverly will generate an alternate version of the facts, which then stands alongside the facts like a cloud in the shape of a woman, or a golden Hollywood idol in place of a mousyhaired pin-up girl from Los Angeles" (5). The "keyword" here, Carson's "Lesson" indicates, is "εἴδωλον [*eidōlon*] 'image, likeness, simulacrum, replica, proxy, idol'" (5). Where Helen's simulacrum exposes the false dossiers on which wars are waged ("WMD in the forked form of woman!," 6), Norma Jeane's is the "decoy"—Jacqueline Rose's word—who absorbs the shock of desires stoked, disavowed, and disappointed in the making of a Hollywood idol.[112]

The fantasies that Helen of Troy/Norma Jeane Baker is made to answer for run the full length of Carson's text. A later "Lesson" begins with the keyword ἀπάτη (*apátē*), whose definition is performed as a rant: "deception illusion trickery duplicity doubleness fraud . . . subterfuge ruse hoax shift stratagem swindle guile wile wiles The Wiles of Woman" (31; this last, capitalized definition is a quotation from the *Helen*).[113] Carson's gloss on the list is delightfully to the point: "In war, things go wrong. Blame Woman" (31). Norma Jeane reflects on "doubleness" in some of the play's wittiest asides. "One thing I learned from psychoanalysis," she says, "is how to fake it, with men," describing a case of psychoanalytic transference in which she hones her descriptions of Arthur to match the sexual tastes of her analyst, whose enjoyment she then finds gratifying:

> Psychoanalysts call it triangular desire. But it's not what most people mean by faking it. They just mean acting. Well, in the first place, acting is not fake. And, number two, acting has nothing to do with desire. Desire is about vanishing. You dream of a bowl of cherries and next day receive a letter written in red juice. (22)

The mimetic desire of Sappho's fragment 31 returns here, its passion dependent on the interpolated desire of a "third." In the logic of Euripides's Phaidra: "What do we desire when we desire other people? Not them. Something else." The same geometry of desire is shared, we have seen, by Sappho, Weil, and Porete who, like Norma Jeane Baker, come to perceive themselves from a "fake" angle of self-relation. What Baker seems to mean by "faking it"—performing to the other's desire, which demands the occlusion of hers—is not altogether different from the "vanishing" desire Carson imputes to Simone Weil (and which comes, in the "Decreation" libretto, with its own "bowl of cherries"). Each woman "vanishes" so that others can "really be together" (Weil) with their own desires. So that when we dream of a bowl of cherries, we are allowed to believe, so to speak, that the cherries are real. The price of our desires' fulfillment, in this particular American "dream," is the woman's disappearance.[114]

Inviting Greece—as Euripides's Helen does—to reckon with its own destructiveness, Carson's Norma Jeane Baker also exposes Hollywood's need to make "fake women" in its own image.[115] In an interview, Monroe spoke of her own struggles with this need, struggles that place her in a paradoxical position: "You try to be true, and you feel it's on the verge of a type of craziness, but it isn't really craziness. It's really getting the true part of yourself out."[116] Carson has spoken in similar ways about her method of translating and adapting source texts: "I generally try to work first and most attentively out of the grammar, syntax, allusions of the original while keeping the language alive in a way that interests me, then later crazy it up if that seems appropriate."[117] Negotiating what it means to be "true" to oneself or true to "the original," Carson suggests, can mean working on the verge of "a type of craziness." What is "appropriate" there is to stray wide from your bearings, to stretch credibility almost to breaking point.

PART IV
OPEN TRANSLATION

PART IV

OPEN TRANSLATION

7
Grief Lessons
(Two Stories of Translation)

"Why does tragedy exist? Because you are full of rage. Why are you full of rage? Because you are full of grief."[1] In the opening lines of Carson's preface to *Grief Lessons: Four Plays by Euripides* (2006), tragedy exists because you cannot get a straight answer to a question about yourself. Tragedy's grief lesson, triangulated through rage as if by force of magnetism, is that a human life seldom recognizes itself head-on. Were grief to be seen for what it is, Carson's reading suggests, perhaps the thrashing and raging that is tragic violence simply wouldn't need to occur. But while grief struggles to recognize itself inside its own story, *someone else's story*—even a thinly disguised version of our own, as in Hamlet's play-within-the-play—can recognize it for us. Carson describes something similar in the experience of watching actors onstage. Though she claims to have "never understood catharsis,"[2] her remarks offer a quirky approximation of the theory of using "other people's emotions (*allotria pathē*)."[3] Stripped of the requirement to make an object lesson of grief and rage, it is couched instead in terms of the acquisition of a story:

> Do you want to go down to the pits of yourself alone? Not much. What if an actor could do it for you? Isn't that why they are called actors? They act for you. You sacrifice them to action. And this sacrifice is a mode of deepest intimacy of you with your own life. . . . The actor, by reiterating you, sacrifices a moment of his own life in order to give you a story of yours.[4]

Acting "for you," the actor, giver of stories, allows you to recognize yourself—"a mode of deepest intimacy"—in a time, place, and circumstance different from your own, and through a "sacrifice" that leaves both of you more or less unharmed. In 1916, in the middle of the First World War, Sigmund Freud described a similar sacrifice to action on the tragic stage. Returning from his performed death unscathed, the actor, Freud wrote, "makes it possible for us to reconcile ourselves with death: namely, that behind all the vicissitudes of life we should still be able to preserve a life intact."[5] Both accounts would have it that this reiterative "other" life not only makes our own lives more bearable, but that its fiction is a form of intimacy with truths we have come to disown. The stage for sacrifices of various kinds, then, tragic theater offers up its stories to be used and appropriated with no holds barred. The point of the spectacle is not just to offer us something we can make our own, but to return to us something that was already ours.

Carson's remarks on the emotive exchanges of Greek tragedy introduce her translation of four lesser-known plays by Euripides—*Herakles*, *Hekabe*, *Hippolytos*, and *Alkestis*. One thing that is immediately striking about Carson's idea of Greek tragedy as an iterative exchange of stories is how it squares with her distinctive modes of studying, interpreting, and translating classical texts, and how it jars—as we might expect it to—with traditional rigors of classical philology. In her freeform essay, "Variations on the Right to Remain Silent" (2013), Carson tells us that "as a classicist I was trained to strive for exactness and to believe that rigorous knowledge of the world without any residue is possible for us. This residue, which does not exist—just to think of it refreshes me."[6] She continues:

> To think of its position, how it shares its position with drenched layers of nothing, to think of its motion, how it can never stop moving *because I am in motion with it*, to think of its shadow, which is cast by nothing and so has no death in it (or very little)—to think of these things gives me a sensation of getting free.[7]

Carson has spoken often of the demands of what she calls "the texts I deal with," in particular the demand on classicists—whose discipline includes the measurement of aporia, the canon's "drenched layers of nothing"—to stick to the verbal "facts."[8] In *Economy of the Unlost*, the published version of Carson's Martin Classical Lectures, she talks about the struggle this demand has caused her:

> My training and trainers opposed subjectivity strongly, I have struggled since the beginning to drive my thought out into the landscape of science and fact where other people converse logically and exchange judgments—but I go blind out there.[9]

These two sets of remarks suggest several things about Carson and the field of her academic training. The opposition to subjectivity Carson describes is perhaps particularly strong in classics because of the discipline's distinctive relationship to textual "fact." Nowhere are concordances more widespread and meticulous, intertextual connections more painstakingly mapped, than in this field whose primary texts can be so difficult to establish; where the history of its texts' reception and quotation has in some cases—Sappho is an obvious one—directly determined which, or how much, of those texts has survived.[10] The history of the Ancient Greek and Latin canons is a history of appropriation and transposition of stories, determined and accidental preservation, distortion, pastiche, parody, and staged intertextuality.[11] While this history might give ground to the idea that deliberately distortive, flagrantly intertextual, and creative readings like Carson's aren't really anything new, in practice, her translations, versions, readings, and riffs on classical texts have been received at times with a hostility usually reserved for deconstruction and other disciplinary iconoclasms. The exhaustive spirit of classics, which Carson's appropriative and interventionist spirit seems to offend, responds to a certain *inexhaustibility*: the fact that so much of its original canon is lost and therefore unmappable—and the fact that its two principal languages of study are dead languages—means there is so much "residue" around its facts that, in a sense close to Carson's, it can conceivably "never stop moving," unstoppable, she says, *"because I am in motion with it."* It is only to be expected, then, that willfully subjective and inventive reading be looked on, at best, as a kind of alt-classicism—an "erudite *in*discipline," in the words of Laura Jansen: invigorating, impish, potentially reckless in spirit, and founded on those precise elements to which the academic classicism of Carson's training is opposed.[12] At worst, as an anti-discipline whose "antipoem[s]" (as Carson calls the gaps in Sappho) or "anti-book[s]" (as Stephanie Burt calls Carson's *Nox*) radically abridge or distort philological facts, forging meaning out of what is simply not there.[13]

Carson positions herself from the start, then, as a classicist with a difference. If her professed interest in the "beyond" or "residue" of facts gives her a clear rationale for creative composition, its relation to translation and academic scholarship is far less easily defined and far higher in its stakes. "The empty place that a garland of fragments surrounds is a precise drawing of the contours of the work," Philippe Lacoue-Labarthe and Jean-Luc Nancy have written.[14] In her production of *new work* out of these contours, Carson performs this observation—makes its empty place "happen"—like no other living writer or translator of classical texts.[15] Yet as we saw in the first part of this book, the blurring between scholarship and invention so characteristic of Carson's work, seems, for some, to cross a line. Readers of *Eros the Bittersweet* will recall Carson's opening image of the "spinning top" taken from Kafka's short story, "The Top." T. J. Sienkewicz's accusation, we saw, is that Carson gets caught up in the "spinning top she creates," falling "into an illusion of fragmentary wholeness, a temporary delusion that the fragmentary state of Greek lyric is structurally intentional."[16] Kafka's story, Carson wrote, "is about the delight we take in metaphor" and its "impertinent," "fantastic motion."[17] Carson gets carried away—is *in motion*—, if we follow Sienkewicz, with the sublime metaphoric potential of the "empty place" at the heart of classics. Rather than slowing her motion and attenuating her delight in metaphor, error, emptiness, and the negative, if anything, in recent years, Carson's intrepidity with her Greek and Latin source texts has gone up a gear. New work emerges out of gaps found and gaps rent in these texts. The question of what precisely this new work is—translation, transcreation, critical rewriting, strong misreading, or a refusal of the difference between them—not only confronts translation and its critical imaginaries.[18] It leads us to ponder what it is we ask of the texts of antiquity, and of tragedy in particular: what lessons of destruction and redemption we still require of their stories, and what moral exemplarity we demand be left intact.

The chapters in this final part of the book pursue what Carson does with her source texts in some of her best-known works of translation. "Translation" is easy to say—and two out of three of the works addressed in these chapters do call themselves translations, while the other charts and contains the translation of a single text. The loudest question on most reviewers' lips is usually how to go about classifying such works, but this is a question the works goad us into asking. For where Carson involves her sources in purposes, formal organizations, textual and emotive dramas beyond their immediate scope, the *sensation* of involvement—the traction of these texts in a given moment—is often part of her inquiry. So when we ask what the work is, what has occurred, and what it means for Greek tragedy or for translation, we are often asking along with Carson.

This chapter reads two such works together. Both are accounts of stories to which an original source text has been bound. Both open their translator's working to scrutiny in the texts' structural, citational and/or material form, and in direct exposures of process, thought, or wider reading. Both are works of striking visual as well as textual interest, both the fruit of collaborations that extend acknowledgement or collaborative intent to the reader/audience (the "exchange of action" we have seen Carson bind to the performative).[19] The resulting works, both strong performances of compositional artifice, stage a process of inquiry into their source, its central story, and the stories and purposes for which it has come to speak.

The first of these works is *Nox* (2010), the high-quality facsimile of a scrapbook produced by Carson as an epitaph or elegy for her brother. The book contains a semi-autobiographical essay, handwritten notes, photographs, scraps of correspondence, and a glossary of the individual words of another elegy, Catullus's poem 101—an elegy composed for *his* brother—, whose attempted translation by Carson is the work's unifying thread. The second is *Antigonick* (2012), a handwritten and vividly illustrated adaptation of Sophokles's *Antigone*, of which Carson published a more orthodox translation, staged to international acclaim, three years later.[20] Running through both works is a story of grief and its misrecognition, and of the fraught recognition or inscrutability of others' lives and motives. Both depart from the untimely loss of a brother and the performance of mourning rites in the respective forms of elegy and burial. In both works, these rites come up against their partial or total limitation, producing an inquiry that turns on the mutual inscrutability of minds and languages.

The visual artist, Bianca Stone, Carson's collaborator in the production of *Antigonick* alongside Carson's husband, Robert Currie, reflects on their work together. She describes Carson's "collaboration with another work of art," referring to the translator's use of Sophokles, Beckett, Hegel, Woolf, and others, in the composition of her text: "Carson is less about borrowing or interpreting from her sources," Stone concludes, "than she is about breaking and rebuilding the possibilities of her art."[21] This chapter pursues Carson's "collaboration" with her sources and the working premises, valencies, or abuses of translation, that give rise to this striking conception of her work. We have seen Carson reproduce a theory of desire and a reading of Plato, a reading of Proust and an appraisal of pronouns, inquiries and staged complicities with Paul Celan, Emily Brontë, and Simone Weil, and an unblushingly personal critique of Keats, as *effects of form*. Form in Carson is an act of approximation—measuring, likening, miming—that wants us to go through the motions of an idea, rather than simply hosting its description. The translations I read here, whose approximation of their source texts is both more and less obvious, are both performative theories of the art. *Antigonick* presents an *Antigone* transfigured: not by changing the story, but by importing into its present tense a long and complex history of appropriation—of which, we might say, Carson's staged "collaboration" is merely the most recent. *Antigonick* critiques what Judith Butler has called the "representative function" of the *Antigone*: how the story, in its elevation to the morally exemplary, has become a cover for its own violence and "political possibility."[22] *Antigonick*, on the contrary, is a tragedy that inhabits its own wound, radically capable of reading violence and refusing its organization into the representative lessons of the play's future—*our* philosophical history. In *Nox*, with which I begin, Carson borrows Catullus's "last gift" of elegy: not to extract from it lessons in grief, but to join in its pursuit of singularity; to expose its most difficult work, open, unorganized, unfinished.

Nox

In Carson's translation of Euripides's *Herakles*, Theseus speaks for the audience when, witnessing the fallen Herakles hide his face in shame, he asks: "what if I came to share his grief?"[23] To share another's grief is a strange and difficult proposition. Maybe it is only possible if what has befallen him also happens to you. Maybe it requires you to have words for what happened, or perhaps its proper recognition demands you have no words for it at all. The sharing of grief, in this last case, occurs in the recognition that it cannot ever be shared completely. While for Celan, we saw, a poem is a gift bearing immeasurable destinies to innumerable addressees, the epitaph is a gift whose destiny (the epitaph itself seems to recognize) can never be fulfilled. Addressed to his infant son, Celan's "Epitaph for François" is a gift neither received nor reciprocated by the "you" it ventures, but which remains pending, this side of the twin doors Celan sees slam shut behind the child. Shutting, they seal off the shape of this last gift from the eternity that belongs to François: they "carry the thing that's uncertain / and carry the green thing into your Ever" (*tragen das ungewisse, / und tragen das Grün in dein Immer*).[24] Reading such grief, Carson says in *Economy of the Unlost*, "we watch helplessly as the green adjective of life (*das Grün*) disappears into an everlasting adverb (*dein Immer*)."[25] She describes epitaphs there as "an act of attention shared between poet and reader, which moves out from the reader's voice through all the surfaces of the poet's language" (87). And yet, she says, the epitaph "makes one spare fact explicit: the privacy of grief" (89). The formal contours of the epitaph measure the near edges of a measureless content. But the gripping of epitaph to these edges, Carson suggests, isn't always fair to the dead:

> The responsibility of the living to the dead is not simple. It is we who let them go, for we do not accompany them. It is we who hold them here—deny them their nothingness—by naming their names.[26]

In 2010, Carson publishes *Nox*, a concertina-format reproduction of the scrapbook she produced as an epitaph for her brother, Michael, who died in Copenhagen in 2000, following a long period of estrangement from his family.[27] *Nox* is presented in a solid dark gray box with a light gray spine and a faded photograph of Michael on the lid. The book inside is a high-quality facsimile of Carson's original epitaph, made up of whole and partially intact photographs, fragments of correspondence, sections of typed manuscript, handwritten notes, scribbles, scrawls, and other interventions, on unnumbered pages. "Originally," Carson says, "it was simply a hand-made book (at first empty) that I filled with stuff and thoughts."[28] This "multimodal" work is the scene for two textual projects that are mutually dependent and reciprocally incomplete.[29] One, a prose commentary on translation, history, and loss that veers in and out of the biographies of Anne Carson and her brother, and whose numbered installments run throughout the book; the other, a piecemeal translation of "Poem 101" (CI) by the Roman poet Catullus, an elegy for his own brother, which appears in the Latin at the start of Carson's book and whose individual words are glossed throughout it in a series of lexicographical entries. Catullus's poem is composed in elegiac couplets, a poetic form Carson has called "the acoustic shape of a perfect exchange."[30] The rhythmic pattern it performs, she says, "resembles a pendulum: it moves out, moves back, by its own momentum, wasting nothing. Economy of breath in motion."[31] A form, then, whose metrical physiology reaches into and beyond itself; whose outreach Carson extends to meet in an unscheduled response to its call.

The short text of Catullus "101" is reproduced on the first page following the hand-produced title page of *Nox*. Three instances of named direct address—*frater* (brother)—reach from the poem toward one who will never hear them spoken:

> *Multas per gentes et multa per aequora vectus*
> *advenio has miseras, frater, ad inferias*
> *ut te postremo donarem munere mortis*
> *et mutam nequiquam alloquerer cinerem.*
> *quandoquidem fortuna mihi tete abstulit ipsum,*
> *heu miser indigne frater adempte mihi,*
> *nunc tamen interea haec, prisco quae more parentum*
> *tradita sunt tristi munere ad inferias,*
> *accipe fraterno multum manantia fletu*
> *atque in perpetuum, frater, ave atque vale.*[32]

It is not until prose instalment 7.1, more than halfway through the book, that Carson acknowledges the elegy into which her translation-by-glossary seeks to make inroads:

> I want to explain about the Catullus poem (101). Catullus wrote poem 101 for his brother who died in the Troad. Nothing at all is known of the brother except his death. Catullus appears to have travelled from Verona to Asia Minor to stand at the grave. Perhaps he recited the elegy there. (7.1, n.p.)

Catullus 101 was written for a brother who, like Michael Carson, died far from home.[33] Carson's speculative vignette imagines a poem performed only once, whose unique moment of address gathers the singular intensity of a rite. "Elegy," the poet-critic Angela Leighton has written, is "a literary form defined by the body-form which lies somewhere within the container or reliquary of the text."[34] Recital of the poem at the grave empties this container or reliquary. The literary form is discharged—becomes superfluous—in the presence of the body-form that is its true content.[35] Carson plumbs the question of what to do with the bewildered biographical "content" she is left with: "No matter how I try / to evoke the starry lad he was," Carson says of Michael, "it remains a plain, odd / history" (1.0, n.p.). Yet the problem of evoking, a problem that gives contour to the loss, is approached in *Nox* through the task of translating another poet's poem of loss.

Carson has said that the book itself "is not about grief" but "about understanding other people and their histories as if we are all separate languages."[36] There are no *grief lessons* here—no moral-of-the-story and little apparent consolation in the making of elegy (a "last gift" from the dead to the bereaved, offering reconciliation, comprehension, wanted or unwanted closure).[37] What there is, in *Nox*, is the performed scrutiny of "residues" of the two sets of facts in which her work deals: the facts of Michael's life, and the textual facts of "101." Cutting into the "slow surface of a Roman elegy," what Carson comes up against, surrounding each of these facts, is darkness (7.1, n.p.); yet it is in darkness that their "residues" find a store. The synthetic, symmetrically enclosed "*NOX / FRATER / NOX*" (Night / Brother / Night), pasted over Michael's hand-scrawled name at the start of Carson's book, holds "Brother" in a syntax—cartouche, container, reliquary— that secures his loss and his history between the unlit words of a dead language.

No form of verse, Carson wrote, eleven years before *Nox* and one year before her brother's death, "is more profoundly concerned with seeing what is not there, and not seeing what is, than that of the epitaph."[38] Carson wrote these lines in an argument for the self-effacement of epitaph, a form interested not in calling attention to its artistry but in diverting attention to an emphatic elsewhere. Carson uses the terms "elegy" and "epitaph" interchangeably in *Nox*, though she suggests in an interview that, where elegy is "a difficult form" in which "it's hard to keep the dignity of the subject without getting your fingerprints all over it," the "epitaph" (her preferred term, appearing in the book's blurb) is a compellingly un-self-interested form of "making."[39] Epitaphs economize not just on material—less is more, and less, very often, is cheaper—but on mediation. The point of the epitaph, she argues in *Economy of the Unlost*, is to cancel itself out. Yet Carson's "epitaph," in the first instance, does anything but cancel itself out. Its immediate vindication of the book as object—a striking object, conspicuous in form—poses a straight-up question about memorialization and the monument, the pull of artifice against human effacement. It reminds us, too, of Carson's ambivalent relationship to printed, what we might call "nondescript," textuality and her long-standing identification, proclaimed on numerous occasions, with visual artistry.

The material singularity of the original handmade scrapbook, which the industrial-scale, "un-Kindle-izable" print reproduction both approximates and misses, does a certain amount of thinking for us regarding the loss of unique being and the possibilities for its commemoration in the epitaph.[40] While the reproduction replicates the texture and visual density of the original document on its smooth printed pages, calling constant attention to the fact that there is—or was—an original, it sets up a glaring contrast with the fact that Michael is, of course, irreplicable: there is no "original" because there can be no "copy." The boxed book-object of *Nox*, as several readers have noted, is akin to a headstone, offering its inert material in place of a body and gestures once saturated with meaning.⁴¹ Carson's glossary exercise adds to the book's material drama a performance of translation as the search for an impossible original. A monument to "what is not there," this commemoration happens in the negative, in the space opened for missed encounters—for speculation, association, not affirmation—between languages. Not "about" grief, *Nox* pursues the stuff of grief's shapeless trafficking. The unnamed because unnameable; that which "does not exist."

It is in the analogy between Carson's inquiry into Michael and her experience of translating the Catullus elegy that the book produces a critical reckoning with translation. The prose commentary, divided into numbered sections, is intercut on almost every other page with the glossary entries for each word in the Catullus elegy, including examples of usage, etymology, grammatical variants, and semantic associations. With no pretention to exhaustiveness, these entries stage the presence of the sister and translator "in motion" behind them.⁴² Out of the piecemeal dismantling of one elegy come the expressive terms of another:

> *manantia*
>
> *mano manere manavi*
>
>> [dubious] to flow, pour, run; to exude, be shed, run out; to leak in or away (of liquids); to allow water to penetrate, leak (of containers); to be wet, run, drip; *manantia labra saliva* lips dripping with saliva; to pour forth, shed; to extend, spread; *poetica mella manat* he distils poetic honey;
>
> ...
>
>> *omne supervacuum pleno de pectore manat* the whole pointless night seeps out of the heart.

Carson's glossary splays out Catullus 101 in its barest facts. Her explosion of the poem is the exposure of a process, less of translating—though her definitions, concordances, and exempla are a translator's working materials—than of organizing the residues accrued for Carson around the "night" that is her brother. These residues include typical exempla, unattributed and often untypically translated: *omne supervacuum pleno de pectore manat* ("all that is superfluous overflows the heart"), rendered in the above entry as "the whole pointless night seeps out of the heart," is from the *Ars Poetica* of Horace, while *poetica mella manat* riffs on a line from his *Epistles*.[43] As we follow her associations to each word, the vanishing points of one language and one action of elegy—Catullus's Latin verse, Carson's English prose—become a measure for the opacities of the other. The lexicographical "entries" confess the mutual dependency of translation and elegy, and the missed encounter that, here, binds them together. Carson's "open" translation needs the negative—the residues, the inscrutability, the "night"—to fulfill its destiny as elegy.

Like an extraordinary facing-page translation, then, Carson's prose account of "prowling" Michael is placed in parallel to the itemized lexical facts of Catullus 101, as though to elucidate not so much one another as one another's resistances.[44] "Muteness" is the word Carson favors, from Catullus's *mutam*, a quality she glosses—not without irony—at several points in the prose instalments:

> Note that the word "mute" (from Latin *mutus* and Greek μυειν) is regarded by linguists as an onomatopoeic formation referring not to silence but to a certain fundamental opacity of human being, which likes to show the truth by allowing it to be seen in hiding. (1.3, n.p.)
>
> ...
>
> I am looking a long time into the muteness of my brother. It resists me. He refuses to be "cooked" (a modern historian might say) in my transactional order. To put this another way, there is something that facts lack. "Overtakelessness" is a word told me by a philosopher once: *das Unumgängliche*—that which cannot be got round. Cannot be avoided or seen to the back of. And about which one collects facts—it remains beyond them. (1.3, n.p.)

In *Economy of the Unlost*, reading Celan's use of a nonsense word coined by Hölderlin, Carson describes what she calls a "problem of pure origin: you cannot get behind the back of it." Such a word is "its own clue," she says, opaque in its reasoning and mute in its claims.[45] In *Nox*, Carson pursues expressions of muteness—of truths "seen in hiding," a certain transparency around the opaque—in the book's twin stories of loss, like a "storydog," she says, that collects "bits of muteness like burrs in its hide" (1.3, n.p.). And this "storydog" knows her stories: apocryphal or fictive; interpolated, like the unattributed quotations that bring other texts into her performance of working: versions of muteness and resistance overlay and out-speak one another in *Nox*. Where *das Unumgängliche* is Heidegger's, "overtakelessness" is a coinage of Emily Dickinson's, used in a poem of her own to describe "those / Who have accomplished Death."⁴⁶ (A quick Google search reveals Carson's phrase for Michael, "the starry lad he was," is part unacknowledged citation from an earlier translator of Catullus).⁴⁷

We have seen Carson use Emily Brontë's life, work, and errata to confess and configure loss of a different kind in "The Glass Essay." In the "Appendix to Ordinary Time," the belated conclusion to the essay "Ordinary Time: Virginia Woolf and Thucydides on War," she relates how crossed-out passages from the text of Woolf's diary offered a register for loss following the death of Carson's mother: "Crossouts sustain me now. I search out and cherish them like old photographs of my mother in happier times. . . . Now I too am someone who knows marks."⁴⁸ Both are examples of acquired "residues," traces of another's writing life that provide Carson with a way of comprehending a key moment in her own. Theirs, then, is the story of an anti-discipline prowling the rigors of literary scholarship: of unruly, unspoken attachments accruing around critical attention; of critical attention making its way into autobiography and lyric testimony. They bring into the vocal and textual foreground the backstory—another story reading itself and comparing notes—to Carson's encounters with her sources.

Carson has explained her use of the term "essay" to describe *The Beauty of the Husband: A Fictional Essay in 29 Tangos* as the signaling of a double function: "calling it an essay," says Carson, "means that it's not just a story but a reflection on that story."⁴⁹ Ever more striking as we turn the pages of *Nox* is a sense that translation and elegy together are more than just reflections on one another's stories of homage and pursuit. They have become inseparable, and are bound together by necessary failure. Carson's translation of the elegy does fail to some extent—or so she suggests—but she finds in this shortfall a new way of conceiving her task: "I never arrived at the translation I would have liked to do of poem 101. But over the years of working at it, I came to think of translating as a room, not exactly an unknown room, where one gropes for the light switch" (7.1). *Nox* grants us access to this room—as *Economy of the Unlost* pointed us toward a "windowless" room for "aesthetic work"—by documenting what Carson does and what she recalls in its unlit corners. Carson doesn't leave the room with a satisfactory version of Catullus "101," but what she does get is a performative theory of translation.

Each of Carson's glossary entries enacts "groping for the light switch" in its presentation of cognates, literary examples, sample syntaxes, and associations to the word in question, and in each entry's inexorable journey toward "night": *nox, noctis, nocte, noctem*. An exposure of the tendentiousness and deep personal interest driving the translation, it is also a brilliantly literal rendering of the fact that searching inside the source language brings the translator—as the elegist—up against darkness. (Carson admits, as is evident in the text, to having "manipulated" the glossary "to put in more *nox*").[50] The book's prose commentary begins with a curious statement to the contrary: "I wanted to fill my elegy with light of all kinds." To fill with light in this context is to *throw light on* the dimensions of night, the darker corners of words, the unlit passages of Michael's life, so as to give shape to darkness, the formless and residual, not to cancel it out. "Night" is where Michael is—"NOX / FRATER / NOX"—and where he is sought, between the decomposed units of another elegy in another language:

>   *vectus*
>   ...*per*
> *noctem in nihilo vehi*: to vanish by
> night into nothing; *quod fugiens semel*
> *hora vexit*: what the transient hour
> brought once and only once.
>
> ....
>
>   *miseras*
>   ...*nocte fratris quam ipso fratre*
> *miserior*: made sadder by the brother's
> night than by the brother himself.
>
> ....
>
>   *donarem*
>   ...*ego te*
> *quid donem*? what would I give you? *nox*
> *nihil donat* nothing is night's gift.
>
> ....
>
>   *mutam*
>   ... *silentia*
> *muta noctis* deep speechlessness of
> night.

A record of process, fantasies, and encounters in the concordance—*quod fugiens semel hora vexit* is from Horace's "Ode XXIX"—, the glossary makes the pursuit and the errancy of words a proxy for "prowling" the residues of another life. Foiling the exactitude and exhaustiveness of classical concordance, the glossary exposes the personal claims stalking so much of Carson's scholarship, and affirms claims to creative liberty that have long stalked Carson's relationship with Catullus. The alt-Catullus of "Catullus: *Carmina*," her sequence of freehand translations in *Men in the Off Hours*, shows us how far classical translation can run with its remit. What Carson does with the lyric poem "Odi et Amo"—the poem from which her PhD thesis takes its title—is a limit case, turning his famous statement of erotic ambivalence into a combinatorial concrete poem consisting of the words "hate," "love," "why," and "I," repeated in symmetrical sequence.[51] Carson's poem, an abstract impression of the original, offers a snapshot of how extreme lexical reduction works as a reading, a "strong misreading" that appraises/destroys the original.

The openness of *Nox*—its exposure of process, its open-endedness, even an implicit invitation to share in its task—takes its place in a tradition of performativity, theatricality, and invitation to complicity in Carson: from sustained address to her readers (in "The Life of Towns," "the position you take on this may pull you separate from me"), through the alluring hermeneutic minimalism of *The Albertine Workout* and her lectures in sonnet form, to recent "interactive" versions of the *Short Talks*, and the aleatory format of *Float*.[52] Carson's move toward collaborative intermedia work and site-specific performance, discussed in the Postscript to this book, is inseparable from her creative partnership with her husband, Robert Currie, credited for the design of *Nox*. The work's concertina format and unboxing, rather than simply opening at the first page, invites readers into a certain iterative complicity with Carson's project of lexical "entry." Carson and Currie even report how, in one of their many workshops on creative collaboration, they had a class of eight-year-olds draw on the blank backs of the pages of *Nox*.[53] Divergence from its customary purposes is what gives rise, in *Nox*, to the critical agility of Carson's translation and its openness to the reader, an openness that permits Carson's "epitaph" to perform and reprise the structural outreach of elegy. Out of the remains of one kind of work, the purpose and the rituals of another begin to be defined.

"Unlike a work of literature," Walter Benjamin wrote in his much-cited essay on the task of the translator, from which Carson quotes in her edition of Sappho, "translation finds itself not in the center of the language forest but on the outside facing the wooded ridge; it calls into it without entering, aiming at that single spot where the echo is able to give, in its own language, the reverberation of the work in the alien one."[54] As a performative account of translation, *Nox* offers to stage this action of address and attempted entry into an impossible interior. Benjamin continues: while "the intention of the poet is spontaneous, primary, manifest; that of the translator is derivative, ultimate, ideational."[55] Carson's translation of Catullus is certainly not ultimate, as she herself admits, and is, for obvious reasons, both derivative and proudly ideational. Yet it is derivative to the degree that the version of translation on display in *Nox*, out of which a new and very different work is produced, is a performance of its own derivation. Rather than simply a "copy" or faithful rendering—possibilities raised by the book's material ontology, the perfect copy of a hand-creased and fingerprinted original, a simulacrum of aura—Carson's translation splays open the distance between itself and its "alien" original.

When we finally reach the full translation, we find a poem incapable of closing the gaps that have emerged between the source, printed on Carson's notional first page, and its accommodation in the target language. Questions and wounds remain open for the translator:

> *Many the peoples many the oceans I crossed—*
> *I arrive at these poor, brother, burials*
> *so I could give you the last gift owed to death*
> *and talk (why?) with mute ash.*
> *Now that Fortune tore you from me, you*
> *oh poor (wrongly) brother (wrongly) taken from me,*
> *now still anyway this—what a distant mood of parents*
> *handed down as the sad gift for burials—*
> *accept! soaked with tears of a brother*
> *and into forever, brother, farewell and farewell.*
>
> Catullus 101

Like Celan's "Epitaph for François," the Catullus elegy sends its call out "into forever," offering up a "last gift owed to death" (*ut te postremo donarem munere mortis*). Invoking its unreachable destination and imploring its addressee to "accept!," the elegy in Carson's translation hangs back in a series of asides, spoken in a spirit of inquiry and lament that binds it to the present: "(why?)," and "poor (wrongly) brother (wrongly) taken from me." These interpellations sustain the frustration of "entry" and address that the glossary has staged throughout. As there, this final affirmation of a heedless, speechless region beyond the poem's speech ("night," "mute ash") is what makes the poem's lexical facts burn. It is also what makes the proclaimed unsatisfactory, unfinished translation a monument to the edgeless condition of mourning a brother: "I guess it never ends," says Carson. "A brother does not end. I prowl him. He does not end." This monument, at once creative and derivative, makes the edgeless or endless something we encounter at every turn, as residues spread and accumulate, sources go unacknowledged, and elegies—brothers—blur into one.

I have said little about the photographs in Carson's book, an area to which existing material scholarship on the work attends amply.[56] The photographic fragments of *Nox* sustain the same dilemma as the glossary by virtue of their fragmentation: "The more you cut, the more story they gather," remarks Carson on the fragment's facilitation of a larger "empty place" to work with.⁵⁷ They also sustain it by some essential logic of photography. Speaking of a photograph of his mother in the posthumous *Mourning Diary* (*Journal de deuil*), published in French the year before *Nox*, Roland Barthes remarked that "whatever it grants to vision and whatever its manner, *the photograph* is always invisible: it is not it that we see."⁵⁸ Like the epitaph, the photograph directs our attention elsewhere, to an object sensible by the notoriety of its absence. In this invited and avidly desired diversion, the photograph—again, like the epitaph—sacrifices itself, reverts to pure medium, in the service of another object.

Both photography and translation sacrifice themselves in this way. Laboring among ruins, Benjamin saw, both offer strange forms of resurrection. In entry 8.4 of *Nox*, Carson talks about Lazarus of the Gospel of St. John as, like her brother, "an example of resurrection or as a person who had to die twice." "Mute throughout his resurrection," she says, "[e]ven in the painting of it by Giotto, notice the person with raised hands and no mouth (perhaps his sister) placed behind Lazarus to load this space with muteness." It is this sister's obligation, the suggestion is, to carry the muteness that is owed to death; her obligation to live with and comprehend her brother's two deaths. This is where Jacques Lacan famously placed Sophokles's Antigone—between two deaths: one psychic and judicial, the other physical. Antigone, sentenced to live burial, can never leave the cave in which she is walled. Carson speaks of Catullus 101 as a room she can never leave, an unlit, dimensionless space between two languages. The clamor and the residue that fills this "between" is the object of inquiry of these two very different translations.

Antigonick

In Carson's remarks on tragic violence, one of tragedy's hardest lessons is that grief seldom recognizes itself as such. Grief's apprehension as rage means that inside the story of a tragedy is another story that must wait until the tragic denouement to be told, claimed by chorus and survivors as the version to be carried forward. At a speaking event in New York in 2014, Judith Butler quoted the same remarks from Carson: "Speaking from rage," Butler began by saying, "does not always let us see how rage carries sorrow and covers it over."⁵⁹ Instead, she says, sorrow gets "shouted down" by rage, turning mute and inscrutable, barely recognizable in its most intimate consequences.

In the *Antigone*, Sophokles's play about one form of law "shouting down" another, inscrutability is a malady to which few of its characters are immune. His heroine Antigone is muzzled in her grief, compromised in her honor, by the prohibition on performing burial rites owed to her brother Polyneikes. Antigone's defiance of the prohibition by decree of her uncle, Kreon, unleashes a story of rage and violence that—we can only fantasize—might have been avoided, had Antigone's grief for her kinsman been recognized and the natural justice of burial and mourning rites been allowed its exercise. The problem of inscrutability famously precedes the *Antigone*. In *Oedipus at Colonus*, Antigone leads her father-brother to a reckoning with his own tale of failed self-knowledge (*gnōthi seauton*), which his self-blinding ruthlessly performs. Carson's acclaimed 2015 translation of the *Antigone*—a sharp modern-vocabulary version premiered in Luxembourg in the same year, starring Juliette Binoche as Antigone under the direction of Ivo van Hove—preserves the throughline of inscrutability and sudden, smarting exceptions to its law: "you're the only person in Thebes who sees things this way," says Carson's Kreon. Her Antigone: "no actually they all do / but you've nailed their tongues to the floor"; a lucidity she applies to herself, confessing to Ismene "you chose life I chose death . . . my soul died long ago."[60]

Tragedy is the ultimate test for philosophy, Philippe Lacoue-Labarthe has written.[61] Yet the extreme pathos of the *Antigone* is where philosophy's moral drive gets derailed, and where "the possibility of philosophy, the opportunity of its reassurance and its accomplishment," hits a wall.[62] Sentenced to be buried alive, to a death that "crosses over into the sphere of life, a life that moves into the realm of death," Antigone, in Jacques Lacan's words, "crosses the line."[63] Her father-brother has already crossed the lines of kinship, opening a "caesura" or "non-site" in social intelligibility, Butler writes, a non-site Antigone occupies long before her banishment to the tomb.[64] Her speech in the play seems to call from this non-site, the other side of a crossed line where we, her audience, cannot follow. Her resolve and her tragic sublime—much like those of Simone Weil—are intractable and otherworldly, perfect and alienating in their perfection. In her translator's note to the 2015 text, Carson highlights a single line spoken by Antigone before she exits to her death, a line that, for Carson, isolates her perception of a moral virtue impeccable beyond scrutiny: "I was caught in an act of perfect piety [*eusebia*]."[65] Antigone's "perfect piety" shouts down all expressions of doubt. Inscrutability joins fatal consistency in Sophokles's drama, and Carson's *Antigone* sustains the near-unsustainable tension produced at this juncture. Neither Antigone nor Kreon sees the cracks in their story until it is too late to pull back.

Three years earlier, Carson published a very different translation of the *Antigone*. *Antigonick* (2012) is a facsimile reproduction of a graphic novel of the play, discontinuously illustrated and penned in scrawling, uppercase script, a format reprised in her translation of Euripides's *The Trojan Women* (2021) in collaboration with artist Rosanna Bruno.[66] The irregularly spaced handwritten text of *Antigonick* appears in black and red ink—the alternating colors of Greek epitaphic verse documented in *Economy of the Unlost*—where red picks out not only the dramatis personae but pronouns, interpolated allusions ("*To the Lighthouse*"), keywords ("*law*"), and sharp phrases ("*nick of time*"), signalled using italics in my quotations from the text.[67] The text is punctuated at regular intervals by Bianca Stone's heavy-lined color illustrations, printed on translucent vellum paper so that the text on the facing page overleaf shows through. (The arrangement recalls the extraordinary "tri-colored play with music" and proto-graphic novel, *Life? or Theatre* (1942) by the German-Jewish artist, Charlotte Salomon, composed in gouaches with text commentary and dialogue painted onto translucent overlays.)[68] Though Stone has suggested the role of her drawings is structural, not illustrative, these images depict a mixture of domestic scenery, including furniture and hung paintings, and sublime, untamed landscapes, featuring animals, anodyne figures or isolated body parts, and abandoned outbuildings.[69] In certain images these registers encroach on one another, structuring-in a mood of disquiet and disarray. Stone tells us that the images' order of appearance was determined in collaboration with Currie using a random integer generator, so as not to lead the reader of Carson's material. "My hand is in the book but never pointing," Stone says.[70]

Antigonick, then, is a text attuned to power, domination, order, and consistency at the level of its form, which seems to have been designed expressly to counter these. The handwritten text of irregular lineation gives an impression of reading a series of notes to the play, a "playbook" or "found" text of the tragedy, transcribed by a single reader together with her interpolations, recollected texts, and notes toward a philosophical history of the *Antigone*, "one of the enduring and canonic acts in the history of our philosophic, literary, political consciousness" (George Steiner).[71] Penned in a single continuous hand, the transcription leaves us in no doubt that these interpolations are functionally inseparable from the play script; another way of saying that the characters and Chorus who speak its lines have laid claim to the history of their story—their future, our past—in a single discursive present. Shattering the Aristotelian unities, they reflect on the absurdity of their destiny, but they also exchange literary analogues, philosophical quips and quotations, anecdotes from the performance history of the *Antigone*, and observations on one another's speech and stage directions ("why do messengers always exaggerate / exit eurydike bleeding from all orifices // [eurydike does not exit]").[72] Where the lyric transparency of "The Glass Essay" or *The Beauty of the Husband* has Carson's narrative subject perform the collapse of orders—commentary into narrative, the citational into the lyric—it is the characters of *Antigonick* who bear the task, in the wake of a more drastic collapse, of reading themselves. Transparency here redoubles tragic irony. For this is a tragedy that knows its own script—its own unredeemable outcome—only too well. Versed in permutations of their story, conversant with the critical literature,

Carson's cast are no longer mutually inscrutable. Escaping inscrutability (to borrow Lacan's translation of a line from the play) "*into* impossible sicknesses," they are wretchedly conscious, powerlessly lucid.[73]

A "Philo-performance" of *Antigonick* at the Sorbonne in 2014 cast Butler as Kreon, the philosopher Avitall Ronell as Antigone, and invited the audience to share the composite role of the Chorus.[74] In one of several jokes, whose critical function needs no explaining, Carson's Chorus asks "how is a greek chorus like a lawyer," responding "They're both in the business of searching for a precedent / finding an analogy / locating a prior example / so as to be able to say / this terrible thing we're witnessing now is / not unique you know it happened before."[75] In Sophokles's original, reflected in Robert Fagles's classic translation, the Chorus does appeal to precedent, recalling the fate of Danaë who, like Antigone, is buried alive.[76] Carson's 2015 translation summarizes the appeal to Danaë as one of "three examples / of people who lost access to the light." Her story is told, as it is in the original, and the Chorus wonders aloud, "what does this tell us?"[77] In *Antigonick*, the example of Danaë, like the examples that follow her, is replaced by a description of its function: "the business of searching for a precedent." Parsed from within, the play's critical description becomes another affirmation of the law, with its precedents, analogies, witnesses, and inexorability. Tragedy exists, here, because you know your griefs inside out, yet are powerless to stem their consequences.

As the interactive Sorbonne performance seemed to pick up on, then, this is no ordinary tragic chorus, the traditional representative of our "outside" consciousness of the play. The Chorus of *Antigonick* has its boundaries breached, its edges nicked, and tragic consciousness and consequentiality saturate the entire script. Antigone, Ismene, Haimon, Kreon, and Eurydike not only comment on their utterances as they happen, but are disposed to edit them in real time. Here is Haimon to Kreon on hearing of the fate of his future bride: "I could not would / not do not know how to say you are wrong / it may be some other way, I don't know, might / turn out, I delete this line, I am your defender / I'm yours."[78] *Antigonick* tracks its precedents and points of moral contention, but it also interweaves them with echoes and case histories in the play's aftermath, the iterative and iterable history of reading the *Antigone*. (Lacan opens his seminar on "The splendor of Antigone" by asking, "Is there anyone who doesn't invoke *Antigone* whenever there is a question of a law that causes conflict in us . . .").[79] As Butler writes in *Antigone's Claim*, the play's famous critique in Hegel's *The Phenomenology of Spirit* "continues to structure appropriations of the play" within philosophical discourse.[80] Hegel, whose appraisal of the *Antigone* is reproduced among the back matter of *Antigonick*, is one of the play's many examples of use and hijack of the Antigone legend, an intellectual history whose reckoning falls to the characters themselves.[81] In this simple fact alone,

Antigonick offers a rebuttal. For Hegel's reproach of Antigone for her suffering (*pathein*) without self-consciousness—an *unethical* pathos—is answered by Carson, not only in Antigone's explicit remarks on it (several of which I quote below), but with the devastating self-consciousness that saturates the speech and action of the drama. Echoing Carson's aslant take on catharsis with which this chapter began, here is Antigone on the staging of her story: "Hegel says people want to see their / lives on stage look at me people."[82]

Barely three lines into *Antigonick*, Carson has Antigone broach her own philosophical history in conversation with her sister, Ismene. Their conversation is about sources and correct citation, situating the play not only among different authorships and competing stories, but between the before and after of its events. Antigone's opening line, like her entire story, the play suggests, has become a citation. Not only that: it is a citation whose origin is uncertain and whose sense has been misplaced by paraphrase. This opening presents the terrible determinism in tragedy along with a determinism in the way it is read. Something about the story's iteration, appropriation, and paraphrase proves as inexorable as the story's events:

> [Enter Antigone and Ismene] *Antigone*: We begin in the dark and birth is the death of us *Ismene*: Who said that *Antigone*: Hegel *Ismene* Sounds more like Beckett *Antigone*: He was paraphrasing Hegel *Ismene*: I don't think so *Antigone*: Whoever it was whoever we are dear sister ever since we were born from the evils of Oidipous what bitterness pain disgust disgrace or moral shock have we been spared...[83]

In the *Antigone*, the sisters' opening dispute hinges on the act Antigone proposes to commit—the burial of Polyneikes forbidden by decree. In *Antigonick*, the same dispute concerns the phrasing of their destiny and to whom to attribute its precise expression—Hegel or Beckett.[84] The problem returns later to absurd effect: "*Ismene*: Quoting Hegel again / *Antigone*: Hegel says I'm wrong / *Ismene*: But right to be wrong *Antigone*: No / ethical consciousness *Ismene*: Is that how / he puts it."[85] More orthodox translations have Antigone reflect here on the wholesale disgrace fallen on the house of Laius: "There's nothing, / no pain—our lives are pain—no private shame, / no public disgrace, nothing I haven't seen in your griefs and mine."[86] In *Antigonick*, the same negativity ("no," "nothing") is applied to the historical effort to construe these griefs as a philosophical problem and a political exemplum. There is nothing that hasn't been said, no act unplumbed, no stone unturned—the message is—in our reading of the *Antigone*, an exhaustion it shares with the first of the Theban plays, *Oedipus the King*. Philosophy's Antigone joins the Antigone of psychoanalysis, the Antigone of post-Renaissance performance, of twentieth-century literature; even Simone Weil refers to herself, as unlucky as she was uncompromising, as "always Antigone."[87] Lacan's famous positioning of her "between two deaths"—buried alive and waiting to die, a reading Carson's heroine reflects on—is joined in *Antigonick* by a third tense of fatality.[88] Conversant with the "representative function" of her death before the sentence is issued—*avant la lettre* but *après coup*—Carson's Antigone carries death with her from the play's opening line. Pronouncing the words "I died long ago," she speaks for the shattered temporal order of the translation, where the play's discursive future is its past, the very flattening of time in which Lacan locates the death drive in the play.[89] The Chorus reads this exploding of tragic time as an explosion of consciousness, responding simply "Your soul is blowing / apart."[90]

Stone's reference to the work as a form of "collaboration" between Carson and other works of "art" (with Hegel's *The Phenomenology of Spirit* or Beckett's *Waiting for Godot*, for example) suggests that *Antigonick* not only reflects on appropriations and iterations of the *Antigone* but goes one better by producing an iterative and appropriative text.[91] "I put Hegel and Brecht into *Antigonick*," Carson has said, "because those readings of her are part of how she lives in our minds. I put Beckett in because Antigone would have liked him."[92] Our *Antigone* comes after Beckett, so *Antigonick* plays a Beckettian drama of paraphrase and misquotation in place of Sophokles's reminder of the sisters' iterative shaming. His play's intertextual affiliations have already "crossed the line," so Carson simply daubs them into the dialogue. This is a text for which "All time is now"—Carson's Augustinian rebuff, we saw, to the idea of anachronism. Yet these staged histories and affiliations, like the inquiries around citation, shoot a look not just at the reception of the *Antigone* but at its reader and translator. For this tragedy is not just post-Beckett, contemporary with Butler on kinship or with Giorgio Agamben, whose biopolitical epic *Homo Sacer* stalks the play's references to the "state of exception." Carson has Eurydike introduce herself with an unlikely comparison to "poor Mrs. Ramsay who died / in a bracket of *To the Lighthouse*." Woolf's Mrs. Ramsay—a woman of few words, whose death is announced in a square bracket of "Time Passes," the remarkable second part of *To the Lighthouse*—is Carson's association, and the object of reflection in several other of her writings.[93] Mrs. Ramsay and her death, whose bracketing makes it exceptional to the novel's time, is part of how the *Antigone* lives in Carson's mind.

We have followed Carson's performance of reading, with its underscored present and transparency of thought, process, and intertext, throughout the chapters of this book. What this performance lends to the adaptation of tragedy, and to the *Antigone* in particular, begins with the writing-in of its discursive fate, but it does not end there. The moral absolutism of Antigone's "perfect piety," like the imperativity of moral arguments in her name, gets diluted down by Carson's errant, non-positional, openly intertextual reading. For all its philosophical reference, the play is unforgiving in its treatment of philosophy—and of Hegel in particular—, an exposure of its impossible stringency (or simply its "impossibility," for Lacoue-Labarthe). Eurydike channeling Mrs. Ramsay, improbably but ingeniously, brings her into smaller scale and brings the play into a more speculative register, the marks of a reader thinking, and being moved, improbably.

Improbability of this kind is one of the principal modes of *Antigonick*. When Antigone is taken to have her sentence carried out, the Chorus reprises its search for precedents, citing a famous staging of the work by Bertolt Brecht:[94]

> *Chorus*   ... Remember how Brecht
> had you do the whole play with a door strapped
> to your back
>
> *Antigone*: Oh I don't want to talk about him
> or him or *him* all that plowing in the dark
> I go to them now, one final intersection O my
> brother you have despoiled me[95]

Antigone doesn't want to talk about the famous men who have staged and siphoned her story. Yet the work makes plain the preponderance of their gaze; the fact that she—we—can't quite get free of their readings. The shifts in tone in this passage are tremendous. The line that most closely approximates Sophokles's text and the tragic key of Fagles's English—"O my / brother you have despoiled me"—sounds and looks in the above like an interpolation, as though Antigone is quoting herself.[96] The exchange is pure critical parody of the kind theorized by Hutcheon: the dramatization of "difference" from the source text, but in which the "parodic foreground and parodied background" are compressed into one.[97] Butler has described the speech of Sophokles's heroine as an appropriative parody of Creon's language and law, and describes parody in general terms as dissent that does not "domesticate difference."[98] Bonnie Honig argues superbly for the ways in which Antigone's parody, mimicry, and citation—a language of what Honig calls "agonistic humanism"—mitigate rather than resecure the distinctions undergirding arguments for and against her ethical exemplariness.[99] Seen in this light, the controversy over citation at the beginning of Carson's translation simply caricatures the play's foundational logic.

If *Antigonick* does manage to slough off the moral exemplarity of the *Antigone*, it is not by changing the course of its events or the contours of its characters, but by reproducing the clamor of its conscription to diverse moral and ethical causes. Intransigent Antigone, here, is whatever Hegel, Brecht, and Lacan would have her be, and, what's more, she knows it. This history of competing claims is one of the chief objects of irony in the dialogues of Antigone and Ismene, and a source of an unsettling comic bathos. Indeed, among the smattering of criticisms of Carson's otherwise widely acclaimed translation, Steiner reproaches her text for introducing "vulgarity" and "populist witticisms" that fall dissonant, for him, with the "adult" grandeur of Sophokles.[100] Carson is clearly not the first writer to parody or distort the registers of Greek tragedy; in fact, it is now widely accepted that their appropriation and mockery begins in Old Comedy.[101] What is less well known is that the exchange runs both ways, and Greek tragedy unsettles its own "adult" hauteur by means drawn from comedy. Classicist Craig Jendza has shown that, far from unable to respond to comedy's mockery of the sensibility, tropes, and staging conventions of tragic drama, Greek tragedy does just that, including innuendo and obscenity in the texture of its dialogues.[102] "We have things in modern movies that are blends of tragedy and comedy," Jendza explains, "but we don't have a really serious drama that would co-opt costumes, dialogue or a scene from something like a Will Ferrell movie."[103] Perhaps Carson's adaptations are something approaching this missing equivalent: the lawyer jokes and anachronisms of *Antigonick*, or Euripides's Helen recast as Norma Jeane Baker (Marilyn Monroe), on the telephone or engaging in erotic transference games with her analyst.[104] The comic improbability of Carson's versions is not arbitrary, nor is it simple alienation effect, but the result, she suggests, of a philologically close reading: "I generally try to work first and most attentively out of the grammar, syntax, allusions of the original," she says, "while keeping the language alive in a way that interests me, then later crazy it up if that seems appropriate."[105]

Carson observes these same commitments to distance and closeness in the history of the *Antigone* and in a single translation event that, for her, explodes the complex obligations of translating to view. Her experimental lecture, "Variations on the Right to Remain Silent," takes up Friedrich Hölderlin's famous "mad" translations of Sophokles, specifically his 1804 text of the *Antigone*, which would become Brecht's principal source for his landmark 1948 adaptation. The improbability of Hölderlin's translation is the result of what Carson calls a "deadly literalism": "His translating method was to take hold of every item of the original diction and wrench it across into German exactly as it stood in its syntax, word order and lexical sense," so the verb *kalkhainein*, a verb for "profound and troubled emotion" which Carson traces to the purple sea mollusk (*kalkhē*) and an expression for its difficult capture, appears in Hölderlin as "to dye your words red-purple" (a Carson gloss for *Du scheinst ein rotes Wort zu färben*).[106] Carson rehearses variations on this form of structural imitation in her six translations of Ibykos fragment 286, immediately following the body text of "Variations on the Right to Remain Silent." What she also draws from Hölderlin is a feeling for the emotional obligations that make an improbable, "disfigured," or "unreadable" translation—some of the verdicts on Hölderlin's—an appropriate one.[107] Not just appropriate to the moral violence of the *Antigone*, Hölderlin's "vocabulary of excess" is absolutely consistent, for Carson, with a reasoned rage against the "gigantic cacophonous cliché" of "one's own language," and with an effort to keep that language "living (*lebendig*) enough."[108] Hölderlin's search for "livingness [*lebendigkeit*]" in the *Antigone* is met by Carson's quest to perform "how [Antigone] lives in our minds." But she meets him, too, in the sublime literalism of *Antigonick*, in which Haimon's shaken filial piety makes him edit his speech in real time, and the characters' parsing of their destiny—now a cliché—makes prophets of them all.

Carson's account of Hölderlin's *Antigone* joins several other accounts of translation, more or less contemporary with *Antigonick*, that offer to break with the sublimating work of tragedy by preserving in translation the violent unreason stirring in the original. Her "Cassandra Float Can," an earlier lecture that joins "Variations on the Right to Remain Silent" among the pamphlets of *Float*, introduces us to the character who gives her name to a "sensation" Carson associates with translating: "Whenever I am engaged on a translation project I experience continually, offside my vision, a sensation of veils flying up." Carson "call[s] the sensation Cassandra," she says, because it first emerged on reading the passage in Aeschylus's *Agamemnon* where Cassandra utters the searing cry, "OTOTOTOI POPOI DA!"—"untranslatable, yet not meaningless"—before delivering her prophecy on the fate of the house of Atreus.[109] Carson quotes some of Cassandra's most incandescent lines:

> *Behold no longer my oracle out from veils*
> *shall be glancing like a newly married bride but*
> *as brightness blows the rising sun*
> *open*
> *it will rush my oceans forward onto light—*
> *a grief more deep than me.*
> (1178–1183)[110]

This blown-open sensation describes the arrival of prophetic insight, a saturated intelligibility that explodes its source—"as brightness blows the rising sun / open"—and defies its subject's dimensions: "a grief more deep than me." The sensation is a "catastrophe" of the kind Carson claims as a method against the "cliché" of "one's own language" in "Variations on the Right to Remain Silent," and indeed translation and "the arts of prophecy" are compared directly in "Cassandra Float Can." Translating and prophesying share what she calls "some action of cutting through surfaces to a site that has no business being underneath," an action of mystics, prophets, and—in Carson's oeuvre—women, my previous chapter argued. The disclosures afforded by translation and prophecy can be "unbelievable," "tautological," and pry at "the edge of belief," though *Nox* provides us with an important caveat to the comparison. "I wanted to fill my elegy with light of all kinds," Carson begins there, but the exercise itself will downgrade her expectations: "Prowling the meanings of a word, prowling the history of a person, no use expecting a flood of light," but rather smaller, less glaring illuminations: "little kidnaps in the dark" (or "If light appears . . . we undo a bit of the cloth" in *If Not, Winter*).[111] The prophet enjoys no such attenuations. "Everywhere Cassandra ran she found she was already there," posits Carson. "What is the future doing underneath the past?"

This is the question Carson has us ask in *Antigonick*, for whose characters the play's future reception has already happened.[112] To be a prophet is to speak improbably and inconsequentially, only to see your speech translated into the devastating consequences it foretold. Intelligent of their significance and powerless to alter it, the characters of *Antigonick*—not least Antigone, whose "soul is blowing / apart"—share in the violence of the prophet's floodlit consciousness. Their struggle is also, if we follow her reading of Cassandra, a reflection on Carson's struggles as a translator: not with illumination, so much as with a language in which—her words—"Nothing has not been said before. The templates are set."[113] We have seen the artist Tacita Dean describe Carson's translations as "ripping" the classics "out of the past, shocking them back to life as if with electrical voltage," but this is not just a question of contemporary setting or shocking and awing with ultraviolence, as Sarah Kane has done with Seneca.[114] As she tells it, Carson's story of translation is the pursuit of an unwritten rawness in words; of *lebendigkeit* as something done to the target language by direct action on its "templates" (Hölderlin's translations she describes as "ripping the lids off words and plunging his arms in").[115] "Ripping" is one word for Carson's interventions. Others she lists in her lecture on Cassandra and the sensations of translation: "Cracks, cuts, breaks, gashes, splittings, slicings, rips, tears, conical intersects, disruptions, etymologies."[116] The presence of "intersects" (Antigone's "intersection"), cuts, and gashes, clearly marks *Antigonick*. First, in the influx of information that conventionally "has no business" in the script; the rupture of a boundary between the work and its critical environs. Second, in one of Carson's most striking divergences from Sophokles: her title, and the silent character it references—"Nick."

The word "nick" is scattered throughout Carson's script, from its most conspicuous showing in the cast list to the expression "nick of time," which several of her characters use. "Nick *a mute part [always onstage, he measures things]*" introduces us to a character who goes unreferenced until the direction for him to remain onstage at the end of the play— "[Exeunt omnes except nick who continues // measuring]." That "Nick" references the edgelessness of this particular play, the extension of its consciousness beyond the script and beyond the bounds of its performance, is suggested by his remaining onstage and by his designated task. "For each of us has his measure," reads Carson's epigraph from Hölderlin in *Economy of the Unlost*, a study of elegies and epitaphs, mute sounds, visible invisibles, residues, and language kept alive in the face of loss.[117] The epigraph heads Carson's paean to subjectivity and unlocked form in the essay, beginning with the mise-en-scène that puts Celan by Simonides of Keos, "side by side," as they live in Carson's mind. The measure of Antigone, still a moral benchmark and a site of moral scrutiny, is set and reset by reading, continuing under Nick's performative critical gaze beyond the end of *Antigonick*.

The single monologue spoken by Eurydike, almost double the length of the equivalent speech in Carson's 2015 rendition, points to the same ruptured criticism/literature boundary and concentrates its most powerful effects. In the 2015 text, Eurydike recounts how the intuition of things awry irrupts in her mind in "a voice like sorrow," overheard and only barely recognizable.[118] The Eurydike of *Antigonick* unspools her prescience. Her speech offers a backstory and rationale for what has happened to Antigone, the gist of which—as is hinted in Sophokles's text—she already seems to intuit. This Eurydike brings up Brecht ("that girl with the undead strapped to / her back"), describes her speech in the third person ("This is Eurydike's monologue it's her / only speech in the play"), and compares herself, we saw, to a character from Woolf. Eurydike steps in on the play's analysis: on Antigone's self-exclusion from the law, her "state of exception," and the darkened family romance to which Eurydike, via her husband and son, is also bound, and which she parodies in a therapeutic tableau—the four of them "on the staircase all on different steps"—to disentangle crossed lines in the house of Laius. Knowing she is too late, Eurydike asks us a question that has no equivalent in Sophokles: "Have you heard / this expression the *nick of time*." She follows it with another, which she repeats: "what is a / nick / I asked my son what / is / a / nick / I asked my son." "In the nick of time" is a stock phrase for something done at the last possible moment.[119] It has an obvious place in tragedy given the genre's concern with last possible moments, getting there in time to prevent disgrace and bloodshed. Here, in a script saturated with foresight, the "nick of time" is a nick *in* time—a "rip in spacetime" is Carson's expression from "Cassandra Float Can"—but this is also to say it is a wound. "Nick" marks an intrusion of content and a saturation of consciousness, and so signs the playtext with a knowing woundedness. Eurydike gives the final description of this damage, wrought by intelligence of its violence and the violence of the "state of exception": "Exit Eurydike bleeding from all orifices," she announces, though remains onstage.

"Nick" is not the first mute part to appear in Carson's versions of classical drama. In "Twelve Minute Prometheus (After Aiskhylos)," the character "Govt (formerly Zeus)" bears the standard of the law that is a state of exception to the law of the play.[120] This silent state of exception guarantees the play's non-identity. It holds questions open, as Carson's shorthand form does: a twelve-minute script in lieu of *Prometheus Bound* and in allusion to the *Prometheia*, a trilogy of which the play is speculated to have formed part. Mute parts, muteness, gaps, entries, cuts, fragments, radical abridgements, interpolations, and anachronism: Carson's interventions in the classical canon perform a position on what that canon is and the rich speculative life of what it is not. For each of her translations and versions enlists the presence of an anti-work, an ellipse or excess of the established text, that presents us with an essential speculativeness in the original. This speculativeness can be textual, as in the speculations surrounding the *Prometheia* of Aiskhylos, the fragments of Sappho, or the haphazard work of translation itself. But it is, in the main, a record of how texts live and a way of keeping them alive. *Economy of the Unlost* charted a similar journey of radical elision and the intuition of radical excess toward the affirmation of language when it most needed to be kept alive. *Nox*, we have seen, tells the story of Carson's own personal search for life among the ruins.

In 2018, Carson collaborated with Dean in the production of a one-hour film meditation on the destinies of a name, the name of the artist's sister, Antigone Dean. *Antigone* is Dean's inquiry into the "undramatized" gap between the Theban plays and an attempt, she says, at "scripting that fictional time" without fixing it to a single story.[121] Speaking with Carson in the film, Dean notes that Carson has already explored this gap, first in the poem "TV Men: Antigone (Scripts 1 and 2)," where she debuts the conceit that Antigone—Antigone bound to her history, Antigone who lives in our minds—knows her script.[122] Dean's film runs two synchronized 35mm anamorphic films on a single reel, splitting the screen in half and telling two stories at once. This split work, she has said, "was instructed by my blindness": "*Antigone* has taken form as a result of the inherent blindness of film. Using masking inside the camera's aperture gate, I filmed one part of the film frame before rewinding the camera to film another part. This meant that the film was composed without the possibility of seeing what was already exposed in the frame."[123] The scenes on one half of the screen couple and decouple from the other at random ("like a gambler in light").[124] Conversations between Dean, Carson, and others fall into dialogue with images of Antigone's father in exile, filmed on location in Thebes, and the ominous progress of a solar eclipse. The story of the house of Laius, a story of bound and binding destinies, is not completed, and its disquiet is not canceled. There is pain in the consequence of a name, Dean suggests, and in what it leaves unrestored.

Writing in 1908, Ulrich von Wiliamowitz-Moellendorff, a contemporary of Freud, scholar of Sappho and Simonides, and fierce critic of Nietzsche's *The Birth of Tragedy*, made the following remarks on what might be done with the troubled remains of Greek drama:[125]

> The tradition yields us only ruins. The more closely we test and examine them, the more clearly we see how ruinous they are; and *out of the ruins no whole can be built*. The tradition is dead; our task is to revivify the life that has passed away.[126]

What to do with the remains of a life, a language in disuse, a tradition now obscure, overread, or necessarily irredeemable, are questions threading the texts of *Antigonick* and *Nox* into Carson's personal story of translation. It is a story of performed speculation, but one that can't get away from—rather, is committed to staying in—the fray of emotion roused in her source texts. We can place Wiliamowitz-Moellendorf's remarks next to Carson's on Euripidean tragedy: it "breaks experiences open and they waste themselves, run through your fingers. Phrases don't catch them; theories don't hold them, they have no use. It is a theatre of sacrifice in the true sense."[127] What the tragedy pulls open stays open in Carson's porous rescripting of the *Antigone*. Spaces that open in the translation of an elegy stay open in *Nox*. There is little consolation and scant lessons in Carson's dealings with the texts of both genres. What there is, in *Nox* and *Antigonick*, is a performative openness that won't be resealed, and which expands as we watch or read. To seal or leave open what remains of the classical canon is a question faced by all its translators, but few more so than translators of the fragments of Sappho. The final chapter of this book reads Carson's acclaimed translation of this broken oeuvre, still unfixed, in *If Not, Winter: Fragments of Sappho*.

8
Sappho in the Open

If Not, Winter: Fragments of Sappho (2002) is not an obvious choice to conclude the chapters in this book. Carson's Sappho, a tour de force of translation, has been reviewed to almost unanimous acclaim and translated in turn into at least one other language.[1] Her edition presents Carson's English with the extant Greek text established by Eva-Maria Voigt en face, a series of brief introductory remarks, extensive and accomplished notes on the text, a "Who's Who," and an appendix of "Some Exemplary Testimonia."[2] *If Not, Winter* is something apart from the performances of working and interpretive "form for the form" that this book has charted up to now. It is an outlier, too, from the emotions commonly associated with Carson's work. She "makes people uncomfortable," writes a reviewer of her most recent work, *H of H Playbook* (2021), "for she has a hard time being categorized"; another way of saying that form, if only by affront to our expectations, never passes unnoticed in her work.[3] If the form of this translation is distinctive, it is a distinctiveness entirely proper to the source text, which Carson's facing page mirrors almost exactly. Reviews of *If Not, Winter* mostly note the fidelity of the translation and the plainness and elegance of Carson's English, as per her stated aim to use the "plainest language I could find" (x). Other readers are struck by how anomalous the unremarkability of this language is in Carson. The Classicist and translator Emily Wilson, writing in the *London Review of Books*, confirms that "Carson tries to translate nothing which is not in the Greek, and to follow the original word order and line breaks as far as possible."[4] Emily Greenwood notes what many readers of Carson's Sappho—at least those who go to it for *Carson*—will have been struck by: "Carson has kept her own poetry on a leash in the translation."[5] Meryl Altman goes further: "Given the art Carson [has] made before by taking liberties with the lives and lines of others, what she wants now, it seems, is to respect distance and difference."[6]

The benchmark for readers' expectations of what Carson might have done with a sheaf of fragments in Classical Greek is perhaps *Autobiography of Red* (1998), published and rave-reviewed (by Alice Munro and Susan Sontag, among others) four years before *If Not, Winter*. Out of the remnants of Stesichoros's epic, the *Geryoneis*, Carson produced a modern-day, novel-length prose poem complete with an introductory essay, renderings of the surviving fragments in English, and outlandish mock-scholarly paratexts. Contrast this outlandishness and scholarly errancy with the wishes Carson proclaims to be behind *If Not, Winter*: "I like to think that, the more I stand out of the way, the more Sappho shows through. This is," she admits, "an amiable fantasy (transparency of self) within which most translators labor" (x). "Transparency of self," we have seen, is a complex desire in Carson. On other occasions where she invokes transparency, "distance and difference" have appeared on the point of collapse: in the emotively charged citational poetics of "The Glass Essay," or in the "poem scratched on glass" that is her "fictional essay" on Keats, where the lyric foreground and scholarly working background of the reading are apprehended in a single, horizontal vocal texture. No reviewer has asked where Carson or her poetry is in these readings. None has spoken of leashed poetics or respectful distance in her translations of the *Antigone* or her versions of Plato's *Symposium* and Euripides's *Helen*.

What readers and scholars have asked, for more than two millennia, is where *Sappho* is. In Monique Wittig and Sande Zweig's *Lesbian Peoples: Materials for a Dictionary*, the entry for Sappho is a blank page.[7] The twelfth-century poet and grammarian Joannes Tzetzes lamented that the illustration of Sapphic meter was only possible using examples from other poets' work.[8] In Jeanette Winterson's experimental novel, *Art and Lies* (1994), Sappho herself leads the inquiry: "I have a lot of questions, not least WHAT HAVE YOU DONE WITH MY POEMS? When I turn the pages of my manuscript my fingers crumple the paper, the paper breaks up in burnt folds . . . I can no longer read my own writing."[9] As Margaret Reynolds notes, Sappho cannot read her own writing because "the writing is not hers."[10] Reynolds alludes to the widely known fact that Sappho has been quoted, misquoted, impersonated, imitated, bowdlerized, paraphrased, and fictionalized like few other authors in the history of Western literature.[11] A good deal of the very little Sappho we have—what Carson calls "stranded verse" and "*exempla* without context" (xii, xi)—comes to us in the form of citations, where Sappho's lyric song was used to illustrate points of grammar, meter, Aeolic dialect, and poetic sensibility. Carson describes "still more haunting instances" where context is supplied without the *exempla*, where anecdotes float unstrung from the songs they recall but fail to cite.[12] Given that "fictions of Sappho" are de rigueur, citational poetics part of her writing's history, it is easy to imagine why Carson chose not to give her fragments the *Autobiography of Red* treatment, or that of the wry anachronistic poem, "TV Men: Sappho" in *Men in the Off Hours*.[13] When the accidental ontology of the Sappho fragment asks loud enough questions of its own about form and authorship, why use a different form, an active "mistake" or a fictional interpolation, to mime or elucidate its power?

This chapter puts forward *If Not, Winter* as the unlikely work that best illustrates what form—in particular, mimetic or performative form—is for Carson, and what, at the level of emotion, interpretation, and self-relation, is at stake there. What follows is a reading of *If Not, Winter* as a translation whose shape on the page is a concentrated expression of the same mimetic instincts that drive form across Carson's writing. I return to Carson's early theorizations of mimesis to suggest that the idea of performative form in her work begins life as a theory of *lyric*—more specifically, as a set of close readings of *Sapphic* lyric. I return to these early texts by way of some of Carson's more recent writing on the subject of translation to ask, and hopefully respond to, the question of what Carson's Sappho is exactly, and what this thrilling translator of Ancient Greek hopes to achieve by reproducing the original material drama of the papyri on which Sappho's poems have been found as a drama of textual form at the very limits of textuality. Here, where textuality is used to transact the non-textual (the material, the sensible, silence), the word (*logos*) balances on the edge of its symbolic value and participates in the visual concretion of the image (*eikon*) that borders on semantic emptiness. These mimetic forms are given shape by their layout on—their radical conditioning by—the white space of the page. Carson's open translation hopes to put nothing between us and Sappho's work. To show us only what preservation, quotation, and accident have bequeathed to literary history. The "accidental" forms of mimesis that occur in fragments left open, broken sentences left unfixed, raise the stakes on what the young Carson theorizes as "lyric mimesis" and its dramatic exchange of action with the reader or listener. Its open spaces become the stage for our own dramas of interpretation, our own dizzying movements of mind.

White Paper and Lyric Accident

In an early essay, "Simonides Negative" (1988), Carson offers a speculative account of Simonides's invention of four new letters of the Greek alphabet. In a scene that remembers Plato's *Cratylus*, Simonides, Carson imagines, hears sounds being pronounced that were unaccounted for in the written language: "He sat down and filled in the absent presences, by means of his poetic mind. Simonides' is a mind that sees its poetic task clearly: the task is to reject absence wherever it occurs."[14] In a note on the text, Carson reproduces a short verse extract from the Chinese poet Lu Chi (AD 261–303) by way of comparison:

> Tax Non-Being to demand Being
> Knock on silence to seek sound
> Contain what is endless on a foot of white paper
> Utter what is boundless from the square inch of the heart.[15]

Not only do Lu Chi's lines share an image repertoire and a lapidary negative dialectics with Carson's reading of Simonides, both here and in *Economy of the Unlost*.[16] They also belong to an ancient form that, a decade on from her essay,

Carson would herself go on to produce—a theory of literature written in verse.[17] Several such premonitions of what would become the signature tics of Carson's thinking and composition appear in these first scholarly essays. The "Essay on What I Think About Most" in *Men in the Off Hours*, for example, a book of essays and poems in various draft forms, is one of several verse redrafts of the arguments and source material of the early essay, "'Just for the Thrill': Sycophantizing Aristotle's *Poetics*," whose reading of Aristotle on error leaves stray iterations all over Carson's writing.[18] On the Lu Chi stanza, Carson says very little, but what she does say is worth quoting: "A twentieth-century mind, by contrast, may recognize the task [of negative dialectics, sustaining being on non-being, etc.], but is inclined to lose heart in the midst of it: 'Nobody kept answering,' says Holden Caulfield, hanging up the telephone."[19]

The nobody (or the "nothing") that answers the poet's call is the subject of *Economy of the Unlost*, where Carson reads Simonides with Celan because both poets use sound in their poems to transact silence. Both, that is, find ways of saying "yes," of answering a call from language, without ceding the "no" that, in very different ways, underwrites their experiences of it. Poetry held good for Celan, Carson proposed, until one day it didn't, and he lost heart in the midst of the task he had set for himself: taxing non-being, knocking on silence, containing what is endless, uttering what is boundless, in the measured space of poems. Lu Chi's verse *describes* what Carson argues Celan and Simonides *perform* in the compact economies of theirs. This performative quality is one of Carson's chief objects of interest and among the chief delights of her work. Yet it is *what* Simonides and Celan perform—the weight of a presence that pivots on absence, forms of life given form by their cancelation, by death, non-being, or nothingness—that Carson will return to time and again: in *Nox*, in Virginia Woolf's cross-outs, Emily Dickinson's ecstatic "I heard a Fly buzz / When I died," Marguerite Porete's "FarNear," Simone Weil's "decreation," and Sappho's self-observing fragment 31 ("greener than grass I am and dead").[20] Or, in the most striking example, in her relation to the extant Sappho oeuvre.

Lu Chi's injunction to "[c]ontain what is endless on a foot of white paper" asks us to think about writing in terms of the page it is written on. The "foot of white paper" that both alludes to and limits what is endless, is ready to be pressed with marks that allude to and constrain the endless in a similar way: marks that are both features in an endless symbolic system of meaning and that potentially secede from that system, acquiring a kind of retinal relief—once decoupled, that is, from recognizable grammars and syntax. It is difficult, in the context of this chapter, to read Lu Chi's verse without thinking of the very large expanses of white paper that distinguish the mise-en-page of *If Not, Winter* at regular intervals; expanses that remind us constantly of what is missing and (the white paper alludes, just as it constrains) what is without limit. So much white paper is a significant formal decision. Meryl Altman confesses to having used the blank pages of *If Not, Winter* as a "workbook," filling in "its absent presences" in a way that recalls Carson's Simonides, inventor of letters, as it does Carson's anecdote of a class of eight-year-olds drawing on the blank verso of *Nox*.[21] The brackets littering the pages of Carson's edition of Sappho—its most distinctive formal element together with the abundant blank space—allude to lines whose original shape, tonal color, and extension are unknown. Carson justifies the brackets in the following terms:

> Brackets are an aesthetic gesture toward the papyrological event.... Brackets are exciting. Even though you are approaching Sappho in translation, that is no reason you should miss the drama of trying to read a papyrus torn in half or riddled with holes or smaller than a postage stamp—brackets imply a free space of imaginal adventure. (xi)

The "drama" Carson's brackets want to reproduce is a drama much like that of Lu Chi and his metrics for the endless. Formal constraint is—and has long been understood to be—a condition of imaginative possibility, as per Carson's confession to Peter Constantine that "I like constraints in general, there being no better freedom."[22] Earlier in the book I quoted an observation from Philippe Lacoue-Labarthe and Jean-Luc Nancy that the "presentation" of the fragment is such that it "does not pretend to be exhaustive"; that "the empty place that a garland of fragments surrounds is a precise drawing of the contours of the work."[23] This empty place has no dimensionable shape but that imposed (unexhaustively) by the remains of the poem, which measures the missing as Lu Chi's white page measures infinity. Looking at a fragment like 87D (p. 171; Voigt, p. 95) on the page, our "free space of imaginal adventure," conjuring the "contours of the work," has only one border, straight as an arrow in Carson's English text:[24]

```
          ]                    ]
     ]                         ]
     ]εσθα                     ]
     ]ρπον ἄβαν                ] youth
     ]                         ]
     ]εσθαι·                   ]
     ]                         ]
     ]                         ]
     ]                         ]
     ]                         ]
```

On one side of this border is "youth." On the other side (and, in fact, all around "youth") is non-being, timelessness, residue, longing, what you will. The single legible word Carson extracts from the combination of legible and partially legible words in Greek draws its revenue from the empty place to which it offers an edge, "youth" a lifebuoy on an open imaginal sea; "youth" becomes a kind of boast of legibility, measured against the holes in the Oxyrhyncus papyrus on which the fragment was discovered. Its legibility is serendipitous, falling, as it were, on the right side of death; but in its status as sole survivor of the poem it seems to embody a form of salvation, a small, pressurized promise of immortality. It is the "green thing" (*Das Grün*) of Celan's "Epitaph for François," carried over the threshold of "the two doors of the world" and "into your Ever," the doors slammed shut behind it. The accident by which this single legible word turns out to be "youth," so carrying an exorbitant poetic load, is a shining case of what we might call lyric accident: the accidental imposition of constraint provoking an accidental yield of personal imaginative freedom, the twists and turns of which give us unique insight into what we ourselves want from poems—perhaps especially lyric poems, with their promise of intimacy and emotional through-line. But the extant Sappho oeuvre is full of such accidents, just waiting for critics and readers to overdetermine their contingencies, as I have done here. Carson, we saw in Chapter 1, was accused of something similar by a reviewer of *Eros the Bittersweet*, who chided her book for falling "into an illusion of fragmentary wholeness, a temporary delusion that the fragmentary state of Greek lyric is structurally intentional."[25] *If Not, Winter* was criticized, in one of the few negatively tinged reviews of the book, for its reliance on white space, a mode, Daniel Mendelsohn suggested, of vindicating this kind of delusion: where Sappho the lyrist and composer of songs is out-sung by the lure of sheer possibility.[26] Carson's reading of fragment 105a, of which three suggestive lines have survived, states that "the poem is incomplete, perfectly."[27] That chance has made Sappho's original verse a better—even a "perfect"—poem.

Lyric accident is not only a symptom of our desire for the words that have survived, either as a result of historical contingency or the contingencies of citation (who quoted Sappho and why, and what didn't they quote). In her introductory remarks, Carson talks about another space of imaginal adventure, a drama in parallel to that of the "papyrological event." She quotes several instances of what she calls "context without citation," where what have survived are anecdotes unmoored from the poems that inspired them:

> Solon of Athens heard his nephew sing a song of Sappho's over the wine and since he liked the song so much he asked the boy to teach it to him. When someone asked why he said, *So that I may learn it then die.*
> —Stobaios, *Florilegium* 3.29.58 (p. xiii)

In her comments on this piece of context minus exemplum, she writes: "As acts of deterrence these stories carry their own kind of thrill—at the inside edge where her words go missing, a sort of antipoem that condenses everything you ever wanted her to write."[28] The Stobaios anecdote places Sapphic song, alluded to here in its complete form, on the cusp between life and death. This mythic song is given its sharpness in the anecdote, its metaphysical bite, by the suggestion that it transacts its own immediate reversal: as though the true métier of poetic song were to produce silence, not sound. For in the ambiguous consequentiality of Solon's pronouncement, the song becomes a siren song, luring us to learn it and then die, as though the former precipitated (rather than eased or brought resolution to) the latter. The story is lent "drama" by the fact that the song is now impossible to place, which can look, in retrospect—and if what we are looking for is "drama"—as though the song already carried fatality and loss within it. There, Carson suggests, is the deterrent and the thrill. Like the surviving single word "youth" in fragment 87D, the story of Solon of Athens comes to symbolize what Carson calls in *Economy of the Unlost* "the poetic life of an economy of loss."[29] Yet it does so entirely by accident.

Lyric accident may sound like something of a contradiction in terms—like choreographed chance or controlled falling—but in the sense in which Carson finds such accidents meaningful, it isn't. For she doesn't talk about the fragments in terms of what they say about Sappho, as performances of *her* (Sappho's—or even Carson's) mind moving. The "drama" Carson reproduces—papyrological damage mimicked by the gesture of brackets, white space, and stranded, synthetic words—quite simply has no author. The drama she wants you to participate in is that of your own mind provoked to thought and its stranding: moved by gaps and illegibility to acts of spontaneous composition, reasoning, sudden suspense, and unexpected emotion. The aim of Carson's mimetic translational form—insofar as it is a *lyric* form—is for your mind to overhear its own "iterative and iterable" moves in the present.[30] The onus of lyric in the fragment is passed, whether we like it or not, to us.

"An Open Force Field of Mimetic Energies"

To better understand the kind of drama Carson believes transpires at the outer limits of the fragment, and which her brackets are put in place to mimic, it is salutary to turn back to *Eros the Bittersweet*. The strongest imprint of Carson's doctoral thesis is felt in the book between chapters 1 ("Bittersweet") and 10 ("Alphabetic Edge"), chapters that deal with something Carson calls "logic at the edge."[31] Carson quotes from Bruno Snell, whose *The Discovery of the Mind* (1953) is a linchpin of her thesis: "It is the obstruction [of desire] which makes the wholly personal feelings conscious . . . [the frustrated lover] seeks the cause in his own personality."[32] Carson comments: "The self forms at the edge of desire . . . ('I am more myself than ever before!' the lover feels) . . . Nowhere in the Western [literary] tradition is that crisis [of contact] so vividly recorded as in Greek lyric verse" (39, 41). Carson presents her argument—from which she says Snell's thesis would have benefited—around the phenomenon of "alphabetic literacy": the fact that "the poets who invented Eros, making him a divinity and a literary obsession, were also the first authors in our tradition to leave us their poems in written form. . . . To put the question more pungently, what is erotic about alphabetization?" (41). Carson's "logic at the edge," deepening what she calls "an ancient analogy between language and love, implicit in the conception of breath as universal conductor of seductive influences and of persuasive speech" (55), takes several forms. One is the "special sensibility" of "edges" in the Greek alphabet (51): the limit imposed on the vowel sound by the consonant (and vice versa), which Greek phonetic script "imitates" (61). Another is the perceptual limits of textual composition on a page (and as Denys Page argues, the single words that replace the phrase as units of composition, following the transition from oral to written culture).[33] Finally, the "edges" of self, says Carson, contract under the constraints of written culture, where the self-control required by private reading replaces the "open conduits of the senses" in oral, often public recital (43). In short, edges of all kinds are sharpened by the private acts of imagination fostered and forced by alphabetic script. The first lyric poets to benefit from the "literate revolution," Carson argues, were given like no poets before them to describing and imitating the physiological assault of eros on the edges of body and mind (47). For them, too, she suggests elsewhere, language becomes an erotic object, a love interest in its own right.[34]

Among these lyric poets is Sappho, whose fragment 31, a textbook example of the Sapphic strophe, is an unflinching dramatization of the extreme effects of eros on the lyric subject of the poem.[35] The narrator of fragment 31 is moved by desire to an extreme state of being, "more herself" than ever before. So extreme, in fact, that she becomes the embodiment of a paradox: both a self on the "inside of its definition" (Carson's words in the "Decreation" essay) and a self able to apprehend itself from without ("greener than grass / I am and dead—or almost / I seem to me").[36] Carson's reading of the poem in the early essay " 'Just for the Thrill': Sycophantizing Aristotle's *Poetics*" sets it at the center of an argument about the "thrill" of "lyric mimesis."[37] Carson puts forward there how Ancient Greek lyric poems concerned themselves not only with describing complex sentiments aroused by time, death, eros, but with causing them "imitatively" in the reader.[38] Reading another Sappho fragment (55), she talks about the "reasoning process" provoked by the imitative microdramas of metrical license and a performative address to "you"—the poem's anonymous female addressee, and "you," reader, who process the address for her. Her use of the word "reasoning" is justified, she explains, by Aristotle's proposition that "all the affects produced by words fall under the category of reasoning or *dianoia*" (*Poetics*, 456a36–37).[39] By the time she reaches fragment 31, Carson is talking about "mimetic action" as something that transacts familiarity and strangeness, the distance and closeness of words, in the same gesture. The famous beginning of Sappho's poem—φαίνεταί μοι (*Phainetai moi*), "He seems to me"—reaches out to a third ("He"), and, in doing so, wrests open a space to feel and reason with this paradox of distance and closeness. Here, "His" closeness to the beloved measures out the narrator's distance:

> φαίνεταί μοι κῆνος ἴϲοϲ θέοιϲιν
> ἔμμεν' ὤνηρ, ὄττιϲ ἐνάντιόϲ τοι
> ἰϲδάνει καὶ πλάϲιον ἆδυ φωνεί-
> ϲαϲ ὐπακούει

> He seems to me equal to gods that man
> whoever he is who opposite you
> sits and listens close
> to your sweet speaking

"The rest of the poem," Carson says, "is a research through appearance to reality, beginning and ending... with forms of the verb *phainesthai* [φαίνεϲται, to seem] and framing a revelation at the core. The action of the poem is in a true sense spectacular."[40] As desire runs roughshod over the narrator's senses, what she is left with at the end of the poem as we have it—what she sees, what "seems" to her (*phainom' em'* [φαίνομ' ἔμ'])—is herself: "I" (*emmi* [ἔμμι]):

> ἐκὰδ' μ' ἴδρωϲ κακχέεται, τρόμοϲ δὲ
> παῖϲαν ἄγρει, χλωροτέρα δὲ ποίαϲ
> ἔμμι, τεθνάκην δ' ὀλίγω 'πιδεύηϲ
> φαίνομ' ἔμ' αὔται.

> and cold sweat holds me and shaking
> grips me all, greener than grass
> I am and dead—or almost
> I seem to me.

Carson uses Aristotle's description of "seeing" or "spectacle" (*opsis* [ὄψιϲ]) to understand what exactly has happened here. This drama of complete sensory subjection comes to us courtesy of a narrator in thrall; in thrall, that is, until the final line of the stanza, when she turns to observe herself "on the brightly lit stage at the center of her being." Where "seeming" starts out as something done by an anonymous other ("that man / whoever he is"), now it is the narrator who "seems" to herself.[41] This translation from sensation to seeming is, Carson understands, an effect of extreme desire known to the Greeks as *ekstasis* ("standing outside oneself"). Yet it is also, as Carson reads it through Aristotle, a compelling portrait of mimesis. Aristotle's terms for what happens in visual spectacle declare that it "kidnaps the soul" (*he de opsis psychagōgikon* [ἡ δὲ ὄψις ψιχαγωγικὸν, *Poetics*, 1450b17). "So too is Sappho's soul kidnapped by the spectacle of her own mimesis, or so it seems," Carson concludes.[42] This particular spectacle is double. Imagining the poem sung aloud at a public performance, we can picture how Sappho's stunningly visual account of acute physical sensation blends seamlessly into the performance of lyric virtuosity (even, or perhaps especially, one in which the narrator claims—against the evidence—that "no speaking / is left in me ... tongue breaks"). Visual and verbal mimesis is signaled and mimicked from within the poem by Sappho "seeing" and hearing herself, speaking and announcing her failure to speak, as though in mirror image. Another implication is that in the experience of erotic delirium is another experience inseparable from it at the point of expression: Sappho is carried away—as Socrates is in the *Phaedrus*—by the artful *mania* of the words that perform eros; by the compositional arts of seeming (*phainesthai, mimēsis*). Captured by the spectacle of the poem, this narrator sees and hears herself from without just as—and at the same time as—we do. Her lyric mimesis produces an exchange of action with us as she occupies our place as its spectator, and as we occupy hers while she "seems" to herself from without.

At the end of the essay, Carson will suggest that we, the readers of lyric, undergo a similar experience of "seeming" or self-observation as we experience the mimetic micro-dramas of poems that pull us into their emotional strictures, as in the above (Carson provides several examples in addition to fragments 55 and 31, including fragment 20 of Alkman, in which the poet commits a deliberate error with the aim, Carson suggests, of drawing our attention to our own "reasoning process").[43] This is her account of the inward attention transacted by poems:

> But the question of what exactly it is we enjoy ... at that moment when the soul turns to look at its own reasoning process like an actor upon a stage and intervenes just in time to forestall kidnap, seems to be a question fundamental to our understanding of Aristotle's understanding of what poetry is. "No brush can write two words at the same time," says the classical Chinese proverb. Yet Aristotelian mimesis is just such a brush, able to paint knowledge and error shaking hands with one another in a mirror.[44]

Similar arguments are rehearsed in *Economy of the Unlost* with regard to the "radical mimesis" of Simonides's synthetic sentences.[45] A means to render the visible and the invisible at the same time, she says, "[Simonides's] medium is words positioned so as to lead you to the edge where words stop, pointing beyond themselves toward something no eye can see and no painter can paint." Simonides's syntax is worked to provide a "picture" (not a description) of the ontology of which it speaks: binding *logos* to *eikon*, words to the immediacy of the image, Simonides's synthetic syntax is "mimesis in its most radical mechanism," performing but also eliciting in the reader a movement of heart or mind. The "little kidnaps in the dark" that Carson describes in her translation of Catullus "101" in *Nox* imagine in similar terms the mind's capture by something at once sensible and invisible, an afterimage (or after-word) that "no eye can see."[46] Mimesis, as Carson understands it, is "an action of the mind captured on a page" that, in turn, reproduces that action in the reader: "[reading, then,] is a movement of yourself through a thought, through an activity of thinking, so by the time you get to the end you're different than you were at the beginning."[47] Replicating the "mind captured on a page," the reader's capture or "kidnap" leaves her changed by the encounter.

Carson is not of course the only scholar to have ascribed these compact and compelling mimetic effects to lyric poetry. Jonathan Culler's formula, "the iterative and iterable performance of an event in the lyric present," suggests a kind of poetry with immediate and reprisable performative effects, poetry whose "event" is inseparable from the reader's present.[48] Helen Vendler speaks of comparable experiences that she says are "appropriate to lyric" in her reading of Shakespeare's sonnets. These are minutely perceptible changes in syntactic structure or topic as strategies that "mimic changes of mind"—as "[f]ormal mimeses of the mind and heart in action" or, in terms closer to Carson's, that "mimic the structure of thinking."[49] Yet it is in the obstruction or degradation of lyric in its complete form that Carson's ideas find their boldest exemplum; in the movements of mind provoked by the accidental and errant textuality of the fragment. Looking at her description of Simonidean syntax, it is not difficult to make the leap from the synthetic sentence to the fragment: "words positioned so as to lead you to the edge where words stop, pointing beyond themselves toward something no eye can see and no painter can paint." The radical imposition of line breaks in the fragment, the radical truncation of sentences, makes for an artificial synthesis and dialectical valency at least on a par with the most iconic (visual) of syntaxes or the most judiciously placed punctuation. If Carson's arguments about obstruction, alphabetic edges, heightened self-perception, and lyric mimesis gloss experiences that lyric poets are especially attuned to, then what (perhaps more readily universal) experiences of obstruction and fruition are aroused by the accidental, authorless edge of the fragment?

The following several examples from *If Not, Winter* show how fragmentation participates in the "radical mimesis" Carson locates in Sappho and Simonides. These fragments take their cache of meaning and desirability principally from the "edge where words stop." Several have a history of strong philological conjecture and fantasy (it is not just Greekless readers who run with the lures of the fragment). I begin with fragment 22, from which Carson's edition of Sappho takes its captivating title, reproduced here as per Carson's *mise-en-page*:[50]

]βλα . [	]
]εργον, . . λ ' α . . [	]work
]ν ῥέθος δοκιμ[	[face
]ησθαι	]
]ν αὐάδην χ . [	
δ]ὲ μή, χείμων[	if not, winter
].οιςαναλγεα . [	]no pain
]δε	]
.]. ε .[. . .] . [. . . κ]έλομαι ς . [	]I bid you sing
. .] . γυλα . [. . .] ανθι λάβοισα . α . [	of Gongyla, Abanthis, taking up
πᾶ[κτιν, ἄς ςε δηὖτε πόθος τ . [	your lyre as (now again) longing
ἀμφιπόταται	floats around you,
τὰν κάλαν· ἀ γὰρ κατάγωγις αὔτα[	you beauty. For her dress when you saw it
ἐπτόαις' ἴδοιςαν, ἐγὼ δὲ χαίρω,	stirred you. And I rejoice.
καὶ γαρ αὔτα δή πο[τ'] ἐμέμφ[	In fact she herself once blamed me
Κ]υπρογέν[ηα	Kyprogeneia
ὡς ἄραμα[ι	because I prayed
τοῦτο τῶ[	this word:
β]όλλομα[ι	I want

The mise-en-page of Carson's Greek text replicates that of Eva-Maria Voigt's standard edition almost exactly, and is identical in its placement of parentheses and ellipses. Reviewing Carson's version, Dimitrios Yatromanolakis has drawn a fascinating speculative history of the tantalizing phrase "if not, winter" (δ]ὲ μή, χείμων[, line 6 in the above), beginning with the fusion of two texts—fragments 22A and 22B—by Edgar Lobel in 1925, a fact neither Voigt's nor Carson's text indicates.[51] That Carson was lured by this particular "fragmented 'poetic' image" is apparently nothing new. The image's reconstruction by scholars almost as soon as the Oxyrhynchus papyri came to light (P. Oxy, 1231, printed as fragments 12 and 15 in Bernard Pyne Grenfell and Arthur Surridge Hunt's 1914 English edition) has its origins in a rendering suggested by Wiliamowitz-Moellendorff and reproduced in a conjectural note to the English edition. Yatromanolakis provides a genealogy of the image's adaptation and adoption as a convention in subsequent editions, in spite of the original line's grammatical ambiguity and our hampered knowledge of Sappho's literary dialect. In "if not, winter" (δ]ὲ μή, χείμων[) the first and last letters are inferences, the first being a conjecture that, for Yatromanolakis, doesn't quite hold up.[52] Yet the image "if not, winter" *has* held up, and is now, despite its conjectural origins, almost universally favored. The image, says Yatromanolakis, "was to be considered especially attractive (and appropriate for Sappho's aesthetics) by classical scholars and readers of archaic Greek literature. The fragmentary image was to endure time and even to become an integral part of Sappho's surviving poetry."[53] This history of conjecture and poetic value judgment is part of what Sappho is and, Yatromanolakis's account suggests, always has been. "[W]hat is Sappho's text, anyway?," he asks.[54]

I'd like to pose a follow-up question. Can we close-read fragment 22? Analysis of poetry in translation is an exercise apart from reading in the original. Yet the pool of conjecture through which Voigt, Grenfell and Hunt, or Denys Page have trawled to establish their Greek texts laps at the edges of any reading of the English, whose instability—and whose provisionality, for any reading of a fragment is provisional—must be recognized and even embraced. Margaret Williamson has written on what we *can*, with some degree of certainty, infer from the incomplete poem. Fragment 22 offers us an arrangement of "subject positions" not unlike the triangular tableau of fragment 31.[55] The poem has a speaker, an addressee ("you"), and a third ("Gongyla," whose praises our speaker asks Abanthis to sing). As Williamson notes, the song of Abanthis—the projected future tense of the poem—corresponds to the poem we are reading or hearing in the present.[56] No sooner does the narrator conjure Abanthis than she steps into her shoes, taking up her lyre "(now again)" in a deictically surcharged present tense. Carson's notes on the translation contain a reference to the performative "(now again)," including an interpolation which Carson also employs in fragments 1 and 130. "The parentheses are not Sappho's," she says,

> ... but I want to mark her use of the temporal adverb dēute [δηὖτε]. It is probably no accident that, in a poem about the cyclical patterns of erotic experience, this adverb of repetition is given three times.... *Dē* is a particle signifying vividly that some event is taking place in the present moment; it strikes a note of powerful alert emotion (sometimes a tinge of irony or skepticism), like [the] English "Well now!" (357)

Carson's interest in the "now" takes us from her early work on the lover's claims on time to her scholarship's compelling case against anachronism, summed up by her as "[a]ll time is now." Deictics and performatives, records and provocations of "alert emotion" and "event," are her own grammar of choice in exposures of a present moment of thought and reading that would exchange its action with ours in another present. Emily Greenwood notes the curious absence of any reference in this and other notes in the edition to Carson's own rich scholarly work on the erotics of the present tense in Sappho and on erotic temporality in Ancient Greek lyric in general (the chapter "Now Then" in *Eros the Bittersweet*, for example).[57] Yet her introductory text throws up a striking parallel between Sappho's temporal adverb, with its "tinge" and "note," and the sensations of translating her, which take their place alongside other descriptions by Carson of the emotions of handling texts. Carson describes hearing "Sappho's echo," picking up an earlier reference to Walter Benjamin's "echo of the original": "I am never quite sure how to hear Sappho's echo but, *now and again*, reading these old citations, there is a tingle" (xii). "Tingle" and "thrill" index a kind of understanding that brooks no description, like the "gold trace in the mind" left by certain verses of Celan.[58] The "tingle" felt "now and again" is where the poem stretches out of its deictic scheme, its cues and references to the imagined conditions of its performance, and reaches us, as we saw Celan imagine poems arriving continually at their destiny.[59] Carson's remarks in the McNeilly interview float once again into view:

> The ancient poets thought of the publication of a poem as the time of saying it, and the time of saying it is also the time of it being heard, and that's the time when there's *an exchange of that action*, that verb, whatever the verb is that's being described. The verb *happens*.[60]

Whether or not the "I" of a lyric or choral song is a definite, possessive "I," or an "I" or "we" with whom we are supposed to identify ("if those intense expressions of individual subjective yearning were written . . . for performance by large choruses of young girls who sang Sappho's songs at public occasions," as Daniel Mendelsohn wonders); whether or not the song allows for exchanges of action between the "creative" role of the composer-author and the ostensibly "recreative" role of the performer (as Gregory Nagy argues of Provençal lyric): perhaps "at the time of it being heard," these things don't matter.[61] When the verb "happens," it happens to us. Deictic cues like "you" and "we," even "I," whomever they are speaking to and for, speak to and for us. In fragment 22, "her dress when you saw it / stirred you"—and so we do see it, and so it does. The imperative to see without seeing or to see unwillingly—Elaine Scarry's "Imagine this. Now."—can itself be stirring.[62]

The final "I want" of fragment 22, final because the fragment breaks off legibility there, happens to us in the reading insofar as it accounts for the stranded, objectless desire of reading it. As Stephanie Burt says of *Nox* and *If Not, Winter*, "we encounter a book full of spaces where poems cannot be, spaces that say what we cannot have."[63] What Carson has professed to "value most" in translation is "the way meaning disappears into the gaps" between words in the source and target languages.[64] Where Carson's "apparatus" and "emptiness" (brackets and blank space) provide space for the experience of desire, fantasy, and their curtailment, we might say that what her translation achieves is a form that makes reading Sappho a close-up inquiry into what we want from her, and what we "cannot have," what "disappears." (This echoes the sentiments of Page DuBois's and Margaret Reynolds on the desire-provoking "body" of Sappho's work but doesn't share their terms for it: as Emily Wilson has noted, "textual bodies are not really much like physical bodies. For one thing, their gender is indeterminate.")[65] Any close reading of Sappho that hopes to be both responsive and responsible must recognize its reliance on lacunae; that its moments of definition are a product, not just of the words, but the uncertainties and rough edges of Sappho's poems. Carson's edition is transparent in this regard, reproducing its dependency on edges and white space for all to see.

Where Mendelsohn's critique of Carson's Sappho seems to be justified is in fragment 176, for example, which Carson reproduces as "lyre lyre lyre" (the original Greek reads "βάρβιτος. βάρωμος. βάρμος.," described in Carson's gloss as "cited by Athenaios [*Deipnosophistai* 4.182f] free-associating on different spellings of the word lyre" [*barbiton*], 349, 382). Here, the invitation to read the sequence of strumming dactyls, or three single strums in the English, as performing the music it describes—"lyre" imitating the lyre—clearly is a case of absence transacting presence, the loss of almost all of the original poem yielding a felicitous anti-poem in its wake. In "lyre lyre lyre" it is the noun that "happens." Postmodern aesthetics, Mendelsohn argues, give us our taste for poems like these—what Burt calls the "minimalist visual poems" of Carson's Sappho—in which repetition, empty signs, and performatives are sites of unreconstructed aura.[66] Similarly, fragment 118, where Sappho addresses her lyre—"yes! radiant lyre speak to me / become a voice" (241)—seems to ask the music, the medium accompanying its original performance, to carry forward into the medium of its reading in the here-and-now, in words and voice alone.[67] It is difficult to deny the fleeting charm of these accidental performatives. Yet the danger is—as Mendelsohn seems to warn—that they out-sing the lyricism that *has* survived in Sappho; not the lyricism of accident, but of well-tuned, expressly longing lyric song.

The charm of "if not, winter," then, is a compelling expression of what many of Carson's readers find in *If Not, Winter*. Not just the aesthetics of fragmentary syntax and the "open work," but the aesthetics of *Carson's* fragmentary syntax as modeled by her poems. Many of the shorter fragments, as well as longer ones such as fragment 22, have something unmistakably Carson about them. (Fragment 22, curiously, contains an exact phrase—"you beauty"—spoken by the narrator's lover in "The Glass Essay.")[68] This struck me on my first reading of the translation more than ten years ago. But the question of Carson's own poetics, obliquely "cited" or recalled in the edition, sneaked up on me again on discovering that the translation had been translated into a third language, creating a "trilingual edition" of Carson's Sappho. Whose poetry, I wondered, is being translated here? The obvious and likely answer is Carson's *and* Sappho's. Yet it bears considering that if Carson's aim in her English version is to stand out of the way, transparent so that Sappho shows through, then a trilingual edition seems to query, if not to trash, this aim: to suggest there is something in Carson's English—some "Carson" quality—that is not exactly in the Sappho; or that what we recognize in Carson's writing is an aesthetics profoundly influenced by the look and sound of uncorrected Sappho.

It goes without saying that, on the one hand, the poetic aesthetics of any historical moment bleed into its dominant aesthetics of translation, and, on the other, that the aesthetics of the fragment have long influenced the aesthetics of poetic composition—as famously in the case of Imagists Ezra Pound and H. D., both of whom wrote fragments after Sappho.[69] Bruce Whiteman has proposed that the prevailing notion of how Greek lyric poetry "should" sound is conditioned by a canonized aesthetics of Imagism, reflected in Mary Barnard's celebrated translation, just as the aesthetics of Modernist poetry are, to some degree, conditioned by the aesthetics of the fragment.[70] Yet *If Not, Winter* is no latecomer to the Imagist celebration of Sappho. Let's look now at what it is Carson seems to be celebrating in Sappho and her accidental lyric economy.

"No Sound": Lyric and Emptiness

In remarks made to John D'Agata, Carson describes what she calls the "enchanting white space" around the fragment prompting us to imagine "all the experience of antiquity floating but which we can't quite reach."[71] Fully formed narrative gives us "just too many words," she says: "too many other words that aren't just the facts."[72] Carson acknowledges in the D'Agata interview that her "painting notion" of writing, producing a mimetic shorthand of the kind she locates in Simonides, comes from "dealing with classical texts . . . like Sappho. . . ."[73] In the Introduction I quote from a different interview, in which Carson says she aspires to write so as to leave an impression in the mind "no matter what the words mean."[74] There is a considerable jump from descriptive shorthand to semantic emptiness. Yet both depend on—and make claims for—the power of mimetic syntaxes like Sappho's and Simonides's. The final part of this chapter explores some of the ways in which the pressurized forms of the fragment have left their mark on Carson's work.

The incomplete conditionals of the poem "*Seated Figure with Red Angle* by Betty Goodwin (1988)," first published three years before *If Not, Winter*, are expressions of the extreme constraints and imaginative efficacy of suspended syntax. Forcing poetic consequence out of grammatical inconsequentiality, the incomplete "If not, winter" is evoked in the docked syntax of "*Seated Figure*"—"If to care for her is night.", and so forth—where conditionality is an artifice, not a result of accidental damage.[75] Another strong example is the early poem sequence, "The Life of Towns," whose opening mock-scholarly preface begins, "Towns are the illusion that things hang together somehow, my pear your winter." In the poems of "The Life of Towns," the verse doesn't enjamb but end-stops paratactically like a torn papyrus, creating new and surprising units of sense: "Every day. / Opposed us like a wall. / We went. / Shouting sideways at one another. / Along the road it was useless." read the opening lines of "Apostle Town."[76] Carson picks up the elliptical pear/winter refrain later in her preface:

> What if you get stranded in the town where pears and winter are variants for one another? ... there is a place, I know the place, where you will stand and see pear and winter side by side as walls stand by silence. Can you punctuate yourself as silence? You will see the edges cut away from you, back into a world of another kind—back into real emptiness, some would say.[77]

The structure imagined here is one we have seen Carson read in the "radical mimetic economy" of Simonides and Paul Celan, in which compact, iconic syntaxes draw on a cache of invisibility and silence. We cannot speak of a deliberate "economy" of the fragment, but we can see the same kinds of pressure exerted on words by radical, if accidental, formal constraint. Pear and winter become variants for one another, the suggestion is, in a "place" where there is nothing else to crowd them out; where their contiguity becomes a distilled form of metaphor, a perfect "mistake" of the kind Carson theorizes in "'Just for the Thrill'" and "Essay on What I Think About Most," riffing on Aristotle's theories of literary and visual mimesis. Pear/winter become the proverbial impossibility of Carson's Chinese proverb in the "Essay on What I Think About Most": "Brush cannot write two characters with the same stroke."[78] While Carson's interest in Chinese proverbs, and in Chinese verse such as Lu Chi's, merits an essay of its own, it is significant that the Chinese ideogram is—as Ezra Pound understood—a form of visual mimesis that the Ancient Greek fragment sometimes comes close to approximating. (Pound had read the work of Hispano-American art historian

Ernest Fenollosa, whose *The Chinese Character as a Medium for Written Poetry* (1936) was edited by Pound following Fenollosa's death.)[79] The "real emptiness" promised by the ideogram—an Orientalist fantasy if ever there was one—is, in Carson's image of pear/winter, an emptiness bound to a "place" where we "stand," not a language we use.[80] Carson knows the place, we might say, because it is (or stands for) the place of her early academic training—the empty, echoing place surrounding all fragments of Classical Greek.

Below are the final broken lines of fragment 94, a poem whose first stanzas are complete ("I simply want to be dead. / Weeping she left me . . . ," and whose narrator ventriloquizes a beloved who addresses the poet from inside the poem ("Sappho, I swear, against my will I leave you").[81] Carson translates the poem's final broken tercets as follows:

κωὔτε τις[	οὔ]τε τι	and neither any[	]nor any
Ἴρον οὐδ' ὑ[	]	holy place nor	
ἔπλετ' ὄππ[οθεν ἄμ]μες ἀπέσκομεν,		was there from which we were absent	
οὐκ ἄλσος . [	] . ρος	no grove[	]no dance
	]ψόφος]		no sound
	]. . .οιδιαι		[

Taking Carson's rendition of these threadbare tercets, we can see that what has survived in the first is a set of negations stripped of two out of three of their objects: "neither any," "nor any / holy place," "nor." What is left of the remaining lines is yet more negation, whose objects are named in order to be ruled out ("grove," "dance," "sound," and another, illegible word in the final line of the Greek). As well as ruling them out, the naming of these places has an affirmative, deictic function: pointing to the performance of the poem itself, saying "this" place, "this" dance (. ρος is interpreted here as the remains of χόρος—*choros*, the circular dance accompanying ritual song in Ancient Greek celebration and performance).[82] All that you are now witnessing—even the song you are hearing—, it says: the poem's lovers were all of this. All groves, all dances, all sound, because absent from none.

The deictic invocation of place, dance, and song in fragment 94 registers as descriptive and sensory plenitude, but the plenitude is conjured by means of a sequence of negatives: *No grove . . . no dance . . . no sound.* The song seems to draw attention to itself in order to cancel itself out, dismantling its deictic world in the same gesture as it is invoked. It asks the listener to imagine the absence of place, spectacle, song, in order to grasp the plenitude of the lovers and the magnitude of the singer-composer's loss. Real and imagined empty space—including, as we read it, the missing words and verses of the original—are made to pull the beloved's weight here. In the poem "Epitaph: Evil," Carson imagines a comparable operation: "To get the sound" we must "take everything that is not the sound" and listen as it falls in a well, plumbing what the sound is not, for the contours of what it is.[83] The poem then asks us to drop the sound and to listen as the difference between sound and not-the-sound "shatter[s]." Lu Chi's Daoist theory of literature has it that writing trains us in the same negative discipline: "Knock on silence to seek sound / Contain what is endless on a foot of white paper." In what remains of fragment 94, the lovers' presence and their fate disappear (to quote Carson's essay on "Stillness") "into what Japanese poets call 'the silence between two thoughts' (*jikan*)."[84] This silence, like the nowhere, the "nor," "neither," and "no" from which the lovers were absent, is given sensible form by the fragment, with its unheard melodies and white spaces. As meaning pours into the gaps, the open structure—the unmarked paper—vibrates with its disappearance, to paraphrase *Economy of the Unlost*. Other sounds, other losses, might then install themselves.

Carson remarked to D'Agata, we saw, that narrative, as opposed to fragmentary forms, offers "too many other words that aren't just the facts." In a more recent interview, she describes her first encounter with the fragments of Sappho: "I had little interest in writing as a child and still seem to approach writing as a very complicated, rule-bound form of drawing . . . when I discovered Sappho at age 15 the physicality of ancient poetry (transmitted via the mystique of the fragment) fitted easily into this aesthetic."[85] It is not only that the letters of the Greek alphabet, as Carson says, "seemed to me fantastic drawings," but that the distribution of fragments in a layout like Voigt's and Carson's approaches the pure formalism of concrete poems. A recent collaboration of Carson's with artist Jenny Holzer (*Cliff Sappho*, 2013) brought this home, as Holzer carved fragments of Sappho (in Carson's translation) into the rocks at Ekeberg Park in Oslo. At a distance, these land-art interventions render the Sappho fragments monumental ideograms, concrete poems set into the landscape.[86]

Readers of the pamphlets of *Float* will know that the non-discursive visual mimesis of the fragmented papyrus is almost precisely how she describes what she has long been trying to say about translation. Here is her confession in the experimental lecture, "Cassandra Float Can," whose remarks on prophecy I discussed in the previous chapter:

> Sometimes I feel I spend my whole life rewriting the same page. It is a page with "Essay on Translation" at the top and then quite a few paragraphs of good strong prose. These begin to break down towards the middle of the page. Syntax

decays. Perforations appear. By the end there is not much left but a few flakes of language roaming near the margins, looking as if they want to become an art of pure shape.[87]

What Carson describes is the deliberate impoverishment of description, narrative, "good strong prose," in a writing that performs the decompositional journey of lyric poem to fragment. The "flakes of language" and "art of pure shape" that result are not only how Carson has experienced translation (translating Sappho), but a lesson in compositional artifice she has derived from translating an accidental "shape." The experience of deliberation and discipline has resulted, she also suggests, in a practice she can't quite control—that imposes itself like a tic or contingency ("I feel I spend my whole life rewriting the same page").

As it happens, Carson goes on to perform this rewriting, with its decompositional ebb, in the prose of the lecture. "Cassandra Float Can" is about forms of non-discursive shorthand. It begins with the sharp, untranslatable cry of Cassandra in the *Agamemnon*, moving to the shorthand of phenomenologist Edmund Husserl (an algebra that would "disrupt or cut through" what she calls the "usual sequence of conceptual and syntactic formation"), and ending with the architectural interventions of American anarchitect, Gordon Matta-Clark. Clark's work, she explains, consisted of cuts of various kinds in the surfaces and structures of buildings "to make volume visible" or turn the space "into an abstract of itself," interventions through which the building summarizes its own construction. The lecture is one of several strong expressions of Carson's commitment to mimetic or performative form (close to the "sensible form" of another lecture, "Variations on the Right to Remain Silent"), in which form transacts meaning immediately without having to spell it out. Each of these forms involves cutting into and excising material in order to extract a shorthand or "abstract" of the discourse in question—the architecture of a building, Cassandra's "grief more deep than me," and so on.[88] Beginning with several printed pages of block prose, "Cassandra Float Can" gets distilled down through several "cuts" of its content ("Original Cut," "Birthday Cut"), reduced in the "Final Cut" to the "few flakes of language" and "an art of pure shape" that Carson begins the lecture by describing. The "Final Cut" bears all the hallmarks of a lyric fragment: the vertical gash of its mise-en-page recalls Carson's English in *If Not, Winter*. Its "idea" of form, we have been told, is one of abstraction—producing an "abstract" or "shorthand" of the lecture's "good strong prose." The "Final Cut," reproduced below, purports to perform "just the facts"—the bone structure of Carson's lecture—excising "the usual sequence" of lecturers' syntax. The remaining words, a shorthand thriving on the emptiness around it, "vibrates" (as in *Economy of the Unlost*) with the "disappearance" of sequential exposition:[89]

>   If
>   gigantic
>   veils
>   bounce
>   silence
>   offside
>   screaming
>   these
>   etymologies
>   float
>   until
>   lunch
>   broke
>   alas
>   just
>   exit
>   !

We cannot reduce the drama of Sappho to visual mimesis, to "kidnaps in the dark" (*Nox*), arts of pure shape, and the semantic emptiness of "iconic grammar." What we *can* take from the formal choices of Carson's edition is a sense of its continuity with the constraints employed in her own compositions and the commitments expressed in her scholarship. Carson's "art of pure shape" has a long history in her experiments in lecture and talk formats, which it is the task of the Postscript to reflect on now in a form of conclusion. Carson's minimalist ending to the lecture draws on the performative force of abstraction and, on the page, concrete visual poetics. In doing so, it reminds us why the combination of non-expository, sensible forms with exposure of process or explanation—what Rachel Blau DuPlessis calls "un-transparent textuality" with the lyric transparency of Carson's scholarship—proves so compelling.[90] Abstract or fragmentary poetics can be understood as expressions of reticence and indifference to their readers, but they can also be seen, as I suggest we see Carson's, as an invitation to relation. The critic and art historian Michael Fried's much-cited essay on the theatricality of minimalist or "literalist" gesture in art asks us to recognize that their withdrawal from discursive or figural relation—the very little they appear to have to say—is these works' way of courting subject/object drama and its self-conscious duration.[91] "Interactive lectures" and other recent performance works at the center of my postscript court the relation of "action[s] of the mind" by means transparent and untransparent. They remind us, too, just how important the function of teaching remains to Carson's project; teaching that draws open rather than closes down the full emotional cache of working with letters, words, voices, and white space.

Facing a painstaking and interminable search for "true" or "original" Sappho, finally, perhaps love lyric as a genre has the last word. Vendler has some surprising remarks about the relation between how lyric "mimic[s] changes of mind" and what she calls "semantic emptiness."[92] Perhaps, the shape of Sappho's original lyric, too, is fairly simple, a shorthand for the lover's slim repertoire of claims:

> ... the wish of interpreters of poems to arrive at something they call "meaning" seems to me misguided. ... Lyric poetry, especially highly conventionalised lyric of the kind represented by [Shakespeare's] Sonnets, has almost no significant freight of "meaning" at all, in our ordinary sense of the word. "I have insomnia because I am far away from you" is the gist of one sonnet. ... The poet Frank O'Hara had a better sense for the essential semantic emptiness of love lyrics, when he represented them (in his poem "Blocks") as saying "I need you, you need me, yum yum."[93]

Postscript
Short-Talking

Taking to the stage for a lecture on "Corners" at the City University of New York (CUNY) in 2018, Carson offers to begin "with a 'short talk' of the interactive nature."[1] "A 'short talk,' when it's an interactive one," she explains, "is a thirteen-second lecture that has a part by me and a part by you, which come together to form a short meaning." The "short talk," two words Carson lilts into one in pronunciation, is a subgenre coined in the 1992 collection, with a few one-off exemplars appearing in her later writing.[2] The piece performed at CUNY turns out to be one of the shortest of the original *Short Talks*. The part by Carson is just over two lines long, reproduced below in standard typescript; the audience, whom Carson splits into what she calls "Chorus A" and "Chorus B," recite the final, cursive line as two consecutive strophes (A: "*let's buy it*," B: "*what a bargain!*").

> SHORT TALK ON THE SENSATION OF AEROPLANE TAKEOFF
> Well you know I wonder, it could be love
> running towards my life with its arms up
> yelling *let's buy it what a bargain!*[3]

In the brief collaborative event that is the result—"the most fun you're gonna have for an hour"—the audience perform the yelling onrush of love, a pantomime antistrophe to Carson's deadpan inquiry. Carson knows what this makeshift double chorus shares with the Chorus of Greek tragedy, the medium by which action is reproduced—rises to the surface of the drama—as knowledge. The Chorus, like Carson's improvised chorus here, interprets the performance in real time. This chorus is the guarantor of Carson's short meaning, whose coalescence, or at least the desire for it, is confirmed by laughter and applause.[4] The interpretation she manages to secure in these thirteen-plus seconds is double. For while we "read" what happens between us and Carson, between ourselves and other members of the audience, we are also the interpreters of a score—performers, actors, accomplices in ensuring an original "sensation," mimed in the textual event of the "Short Talk," happens again in the short space of the performance. Finishing Carson's thought, we become the punch line we have been expecting but which,

Anne Carson. Elizabeth Sarah Coles, Oxford University Press. © Oxford University Press 2023.
DOI: 10.1093/oso/9780197680919.003.0010

nonetheless, takes us by surprise: the sensation of unexpectedness on which the "Short Talk" stands or falls.

Carson's unassuming script could hardly place higher demands on the lecture form to which it lays claim. The three-line "interactive lecture," which she has elsewhere called an "interactive poem," depends on the kind of mimesis this book has sought to track throughout her work.[5] Instead of describing the "sensation of aeroplane takeoff" in a disquisition on high speed or the literature of vertigo, Carson's "Short Talk" dramatizes a scenario that *mimics* its mix of frivolity, fast, unpunctuated elation, and sublime panic. This textbook example of the performative in Carson marshals synthetic effects to imitate her sensation; an unbroken slipstream from lyric "I" into "you" and into the "yelling" voice of love, which our participation turns into a live crash of voices and intentions, a real-time *partage des voix*.[6] The way in which it is a talk "on" "aeroplane takeoff" recalls the "on" of Carson's "essay on Keats's idea that beauty is truth," a fictional essay, that, we saw, is "on" Keats to the degree that it talks us through a scenario whose stakes and questions are analogous to and aslant those of Keats. Remember the *pròs* of *Economy of the Unlost*: "toward, upon," but also "against, with, ready for, face to face, engaging, concerning, touching."[7]

The "talk" is mimetic, then, in the way Carson theorizes mimesis in her early writing: as an experience of *dianoia* or emotional reasoning thrown into relief—and reproduced in whoever witnesses it—by metaphor, grammar, meter; by the synthetic shocks, syntactic shifts, iconic presentations, and other "true mistakes" of poetry. In fact, the simplest way to read the "Short Talk on the Sensation of Aeroplane Takeoff" is as the activation of one of these "mistakes," so that one scenario resists and then unexpectedly converges with another—the Aristotelian "How true, and yet I mistook it!" moment of Carson's "Essay on What I Think About Most."[8] For this to work, "love running towards my life" must be "love running towards my life" *and* the exponential thrust, lateral smudge, and lifting inner rift of "aeroplane take-off," which in turn roars with the full-tilt landing of love. Coming just before what is billed as a lecture (on "Corners"), this small theatrical event offsets the main act in curious ways (querying the lecture form and the lecture as *performance* is just one of them). Yet it also invites us to scan back over Carson's trajectory in search of the "talk" and the "lecture" as a history of encounters between performative form and live, increasingly collaborative performance. To inquire into how what began as the intimate, text-driven form of the "Short Talk" has evolved into an unreconstructed academic "happening."[9]

This is where I'd like to situate these final reflections on Carson's work. Alongside her growing volume of translations and adaptations of Greek drama to date, with Euripides a clear favorite and collaboration a preferred method, Carson's mainstay in recent years has been the more-or-less experimental, more-or-less academic lecture. From her 2016 collaborative "Lecture on the History of Skywriting," a dark-toned cross-weave of Creation myths and "footnotes" with Carson in character as "the Sky," to her Clark Lectures at Trinity College, Cambridge, which included traditional lectern presentations and dance, Carson's lectures plumb a subgenre that emerges in her work in the first decade of this century with the premieres of "Possessive Used as Drink (Me): A Lecture on Pronouns in the Form of 15 Sonnets," "Cassandra Float Can," "Uncle Falling: A Pair of Lyric Lectures with Shared Chorus," and her first opera libretto.[10] Many of the most recent lectures are delivered at academic venues, the highlight of comparative literature or critical theory programs, and are a testament to an appetite in Humanities departments not just for Carson but for what her work has come to represent. Rather than read these recent lectures as a complement to Carson's writing or a phenomenon apart from her early, text-based "essays" and "talks," I want to sketch out a rough lineage between the constrained mimetic energies of the "Short Talk" and these recent, notably long-form presentations that deal—contra the "Short Talk" form—in exorbitance, multiplicity, free association, collaboration, and, in a compellingly straightforward sense, in Carson just "talking."

*

At the start of her lecture on "Stillness," later published as an essay in *Critical Inquiry*, Carson ponders:

> How to begin an essay on stillness. Insofar as an essay is a broaching, an interference, a disruption, a breaking in of me upon you—your mind a quiet lake, me jumping into it—we start with some discussion of quiet as disquiet. That is to say, Helen of Troy.[11]

So far, so Carson in two key senses. First, the transparency of composition, by which Carson's reflections on the lecture ("How to begin") provide both its argumentative structure and lyric through-line. Second, the performative non sequitur by which, in order to illustrate how the lecture should broach, break, and jump, Carson does just that—jumping from "quiet as disquiet" to Helen of Troy. Carson's inquiry into stillness travels from the *Agamemnon*, Sappho, Barthes, and Sapphic papyrology, to John Cage, Meister Eckhart, Emily Dickinson, Robert Rauschenberg, Willem de Kooning, Keats, Woolf, Cage again, Sappho again, the *Antigone* via Agamben, Derrida, and Proust, ending with the artist and Carson's collaborator, Jenny Holzer. This breathless summary is so because Carson's lecture—likewise her published essay—makes almost no pauses for air. It offers no cursory justifications or gestures at summing up, except to say, in the final paragraph, that "there are many stillnesses we didn't get around to in this essay [/ lecture]."[12] Instead of the "abstract" of a phenomenon or quality (as Carson says of Gordon Matta-Clark's architectural interventions, and as we might say of the emotional "shorthand" of *Short Talks*), Carson's lecture gives us a whole reading list, commented, close-read, and reflected on in the continuous texture of her discontinuous inquiry. In a recorded interview with the Argentinian poet, Maria Negroni, Carson offered that her work has always sought to put the mind's "mess of encounter" ("that same mess") "down on the paper," a haphazard, intimate discursivity she compares to the arrangement of books on a bookshelf at home.[13] The lecture is a performance of thinking, an exposure of working, that makes no attempt to peel her sources away from the order and tempo of their encounter, or, for that matter, from personal memories. In the lecture on "Corners," she relates that she cannot read certain scenes of *The Odyssey* without returning to scenes of her father during his years of dementia, "as if to collapse the two scenes into a single false memory."[14]

It is no great leap to suggest that one of the things Carson's work has come to represent, at least in academic circles, is the creative *un-constraint* of scholarship; the sabotage of structural prohibitions on experimental form, autobiography, chance procedures, and what Eric Hayot describes as "belle-lettrism" (or we might, carefully, call "essayism") in the contemporary academy.[15] In his illuminating *Scholarship and Freedom* (2020), Graham Galt Harpham cites Max Weber's 1917 lecture on "Science as a Vocation," in which Weber denounced "unmediated intimacy" with a source text, or the (quintessentially Carsonian) concepts of "sublimity, immediacy, and totalization" as "forms of Romantic or quasi-theological irrationalism that lay beyond the pale of any inquiry that claimed validity."[16] In a modern Humanities obsessed with replicable rigors and scientific outputs (Weber's "Science," *Wissenschaft*, is closer to "scholarship" or "research"), binding interpretation to chance—or (which is worse?) binding it to *form*—is likely to be received at best as quaint, "literary," or "artistic," all synonyms for the worst case scenario: speculative or unscientific work.

We have seen ample evidence for Carson's saboteur relationship with scholarship and its forms. What is surprising is Carson's embrace of another term, in relation to what she has called "Standard English forms" (having been trained not in English but Classics). This term, I noted in the Introduction, is the *amateur*:

> the thing about being an amateur is that it opens out that space for the third thing to happen. If I'm totally professional and locked in to my credentials as a professional, I can't let you have a thought about what I am telling you. I have to make you have my thought about what I'm telling you and I just don't like doing that. It's not teaching, it's closing off teaching.[17]

Guy Davenport hinted at something similar in Carson in his 1987 review of *Eros the Bittersweet*, where he described the opening of Carson's inquiry into eros with Kafka's short story, "The Top," as the mark of "a good teacher, enticing us."[18] This book has sought to make the case for Carson's writing as performative in the sense she expressed to McNeilly: reproducing or mirroring an original experience so that it might happen again in reading or recital. This is to understand her writing as an enticement or lure: a set of conditions of possibility for reading *closer* to the sensations and activity of words, facts, and ideas. What results can offer the sublime immediacy of Aristotle's "visual mimesis," the immediacy of *opsis* (*he de opsis psychagōgikon*—visual spectacle that "kidnaps the soul").

It is fitting, then, that Carson begins her lecture on "Stillness" with an image of stunning visual—or rather, synesthetic—clarity: "your mind a quiet lake, me jumping into it," where stillness is brought to us as silence (a "quiet" lake), and whose jump, then, is the sudden irruption of sound (the sensory "mistake" mimics and reproduces the impact). "Silence *noticed* is stillness," Carson says in her lecture, and, citing Cage, "Silence is not acoustic. It is a change of mind, a turning around."[19] What Carson finds in Cage's infamous performed silence—a transparent act of sabotage—has interesting resonances with her own project. There is their shared concern to mime and induce "changes of mind" (*metanoia*), but there is also the relation of both to the complex quality of transparency as it has been pursued here. Carson discusses Cage's desire "to silence personal taste, expressiveness, ego" using "chance operations," a proposition taken up by Carson and Currie's "EgoCircus" workshop in experimental collaboration, which asks participants to use "objects and gestures to perform ideas," and which one participant described as "a reinforcement of what I've learned ... about the Cage/Cunningham collaborations."[20] Carson's relationship to form, as well as to sources, collaborators, and influences, has striking affinities with Cage's, and her experimental lectures inherit clear features of his, such as the collaborative "Lecture on the Weather" performed in Buffalo in 1975.[21]

Cage's "Composition in Retrospect" includes the following mesostic (or medial-acrostic) on "DISCIPLINE":

> thoreau saiD the same
> thIng
> over a hundred yearS ago
> i want my writing to be as Clear
> as water I can see through
> so that what I exPerienced
> is toLd
> wIthout
> my beiNg in any way
> in thE way[22]

We know Carson's position on the "problem of telling," on "too much self in my writing," on the "amiable fantasy (transparency of self) within which most translators labor," on the lyric transparencies of "The Glass Essay" and *The Beauty of the Husband*, and so on. This last (Carson's own "POEM SCRATCHED ON GLASS") reminds us that her source/reading collapse exercises a transparency that might be called Duchampian in its aspiration to form as a drama of whatever is in front of it, a staging of interpretation less interested in itself than in mirroring or reproducing the world around it. In Cage's mesostic, as Jann Pasler has written, "the sympathy Cage feels towards a predecessor turns into an identity. When he might like to have said something similar, Cage takes on Thoreau's voice as if it were his own."[23] Where Cage's "water" is glossed as transparency or self-clearing ("wIthout / my beiNg in any way / in thE way"), what that "water" performs is the merger of voices—much in the way we have seen Carson's readings move between distance and closeness, separation, citation, *imitatio*, and iteration, self-withdrawal and intimate identification; the sharing of voices—a recognition that voice is always shared—as an alternative to description. The transparency of water, like that of glass, is testy (and, as Carson says, there are different "kinds of water").[24] Its aspiration here is the disappearance of work into world—or, as in Keats's famous epitaph, "Here lies one whose name is writ in water," the disappearance of the author's "I" altogether. It is also, then, an express commitment to plurality, collaboration, world. As Duchamp famously wrote, "* water writes always in * plural," or, as Susan Howe has offered, "Truth is water. Attraction makes it open."[25]

The kind of medium water is, mirroring and/or transparent, is one of the opening concerns of *Short Talks*, which, like *Eros the Bittersweet*, entices us by opening with a story. The "Introduction" to Carson's micro-lectures sets the scene for their drastic shortness—for something "missing"—with an elliptical narrative that begins "Early one morning words were missing. Before that, words were not. Facts were, faces were." Like one of Carson's Daoist proverbs, "words were missing"/"words were not" reflect one another back, not as opposites but as expressions of the same negativity. The narrator, we are told, "began to copy out everything that was said. The marks construct an instant of nature gradually, without the boredom of a story," recalling the model of "academic writing" announced in *Economy of the Unlost* ("I copy down the names . . . and note their activity," "fishing up facts of the landscape") and preparing us for an exercise in the making of "marks." It is well known that the *Short Talks* began life as a series of drawings—what was published in 1992 were simply augmented versions of their titles—but what follows in Carson's introductory mise-en-scène indicates that mimesis, transparency, the immediacy of *opsis*, are retained as the métier of the "Talks." "I am to imitate a mirror like that of water (but water is not a mirror and it is dangerous to think so)." What exactly is this double imitation (to mirror a mirror) that undercuts itself ("water is not a mirror") because of some danger in the idea of it? What is this danger?

*

Short Talks is a sequence of forty-five reflections, vignettes, and apocryphal anecdotes shot through with notes, quotes, and fragments of close reading from Carson's research. Each of these is delivered in the name of a wider phenomenon on which it claims the status of a "talk." The "Short Talk on Chromo-luminarism," for instance, is a sequence of oblique remarks on light in the paintings of Seurat. "Short Talk on Hölderlin's World Night Wound" talks loosely and obliquely about Hölderlin's encounter with Sophokles, to which Carson returns, thirty years later, in the lecture and performance piece "Variations on the Right to Remain Silent" and, obliquely, in *Antigonick*. Though the title/content relation of the talks is rarely so confidently far-fetched as the "Short Talk on the Sensation of Aeroplane Takeoff," each of Carson's exemplars of the form relies on a certain mechanics of risk that it shares in common with the live performance of the "thirteen-second lecture." Pending our complicity, the "short meaning" is sustained momentarily and without explanation. In place of a disquisition is a brief and elusive effect, the intuition of an inquiry that, in its text-bound form, lacks almost all of the means to see it through.

Carson's mirroring of the phenomena talked of by the *Short Talks* is located somewhere between the *mimēsis* of Plato's late reflections (preserving the "paradigm" or structural geometry of an object, not necessarily any of its details) and the "true mistakes" of Aristotle's visual mimesis, as theorized by Carson. The "Short Talk on Shelter" exposes directly both the thrill and the danger in this kind of imitation, for, it is announced, "I am writing this to be as wrong as possible to you." The "wrongness" of the scene, details unmoored that provide an automatic description of a poem's declared talking point, remembers Duchamp and reminds me of Susan Howe's early work, "Hinge Picture" (1974), whose poem-pictures—many shapely-small with justified margins—operate the Duchampian principle of the "hinge" as displacement of foreground and background, materiality and idea.[26] The risk of Carson's shorthand, with its performative gestures and far-fetched affinities, a risk of erring too far from the phenomenon she wants to reproduce, is that the "mistake" doesn't ring true, or simply doesn't get through to the reader.

For the sake of brevity, I discuss below just two of Carson's *Short Talks*, the first briefly and the second in some detail. The first, "Short Talk on Sylvia Plath," just over eight lines long and making no mention of either Plath or her work, concerns the emotive occlusion of Plath by the poet's mother. The "Short Talk" performs the occlusion by chronicling a television interview with "her mother," in which the unnamed Aurelia Plath speaks of her daughter's writing:

SHORT TALK ON SYLVIA PLATH

> Did you see her mother on television? She said plain, burned things. She said I thought it an excellent poem but it hurt me. She did not say jungle fear. She did not say jungle hatred wild jungle weeping chop it back chop it. She said self-government she said end of the road. She did not say humming in the middle of the air what you came for chop.[27]

What Aurelia Plath says pulls along with it a deep trawl of unsaying and not saying, a belied aggressivity the talk parses in the "jungle fear" refrain, cut back mid-flow ("chop"), and whose destructiveness is named as the saying of "plain, burned things." Conjured aslant in a one-off pronoun, Sylvia Plath's striking absence from the "Short Talk on Sylvia Plath" is not only a case of Carson's logic of errancy and "paradigmatic" imitation, which often does not *talk about* what is being observed, but also reproduces the psychic rationale it attributes to Aurelia Plath, in which exorbitant euphemism—a verbose art of *not* saying—does the talking. "humming / in the middle of the air"—what "you," we, "came for"—is the persistent vibration of chopped-back words and emotion; whether the hum of suspense around Plath or the hum hanging in her poems is what we came to this scene expecting, both are cut out of the picture. The drastic compositional constraint of *Short Talks*, its own function of not saying, likewise calls on its excluded faculties. Indeed, the "Talks" often access the imaginative possibilities of "talking"—and, in the interactive version, "lecturing" (*lectio*), with its traditional linear display of *expositio, quaestio,* and *disputatio*—precisely by virtue of not doing them. (The German *Vorlesung*, literally *reading forth*, whose etymological kin include the "gathering" of information, still enshrines this notion of display.)

Displaying what is not there by means of a strict compositional economy, the object of interest of *Economy of the Unlost*, is the work of most of the *Short Talks*. Knowing there were originally drawings to accompany Carson's forty-five short texts affects the way we think about their minimalism, for the texts, sans images, are charged with doing what was once a shared labor of approximation. Talks that are ekphrastic or which conjure the backstories and sensory affects of paintings—"Short Talk on Chromo-luminarism," "Short Talk on His Draughtsmanship," "Short Talk on the Rules of Perspective," "Short Talk on Van Gogh," "Short Talk on the Mona Lisa," "Short Talk on the End," "Short Talk on *The Anatomy Lesson of Dr Deyman*"—draw attention to just how much phenomenal as well as argumentative weight is being pulled by these small textual frames. "Short Talk on the End" is one of the most striking in this regard:

> SHORT TALK ON THE END
>
> What is the difference between light and lighting? There is an etching called *The Three Crosses* by Rembrandt. It is a picture of the earth and the sky and Calvary. A moment rains down on them, the plate grows darker. Darker. Rembrandt wakens you just in time to see matter stumble out of its forms.[28]

Also known as *Christ Crucified between the Two Thieves* (1653), the copperplate etching summoned up here is one of many vellum prints derived from Rembrandt's progressive alterations to a single plate.[29] While Carson does not exactly describe *The Three Crosses*, beyond the three marks of "earth," "sky," and "Calvary," her "Short Talk on the End" plots the course of several almost indivisible denouements. One is the scene pictured by Rembrandt in *The Three Crosses*—the climactic moment in the Passion of Christ. It is a "moment" whose weight of foreboding, whose momentousness, like a microclimate, "rains down on" the three crosses, and over earth, sky, and Calvary. Another is the material production of the etching. "A moment / rains down on them" is as much a description of the technique of dry point, the fine rain of hatchings that falls on the "moment" it captures; the doubled-down darkness ("darker. / Darker") elides the mood of ending at Calvary with the intensification of ink as it builds on the plate and, finally, saturates the print medium.

The scene of the "Talk" stages the disappearance of content into form and moment into artifice (recall *The Beauty of the Husband*, "I want to make you *see time*"). Its oblique commentary asks—the question with which Carson begins her "Talk"—after the difference between phenomenal experience and its imitation, between "light" (the photonic phenomenon, and "the light of the world"; Creation's "let there be light!") and its mimicry in "lighting" (compositional effect, creation, *technē*). Where Rembrandt "wakens you just in time" from this dream of the Passion, Carson spotlights the critical moment captured in the etching, its optimal rendering of shadow and luminosity, and the crisis of an inked-up plate lifted off the vellum to reveal "matter stumbling out of its forms": the chance resurrection of matter out of each individual impression.

Without saying as much, and in lieu of an argumentative process, Carson imitates a compositional one that, as it happens, played out over several years. As documented in examples of each stage of printing held at the Bibliothèque

Nationale de France, Rembrandt's darkening of the etching was incremental, culminating in the occlusion of almost all the "light"/"lighting" after which Carson inquires.[30] The "just in time" moment of this final stage of printing is also a "just enough" moment, a historical (not to mention theological) moment of time-bound urgency, with barely enough light remaining in the print to insinuate matter out of forms. The "Talk" hints at a compositional process that it mimics in its own "just enough" presentation, with a minimum of words (or "marks") and the intimation of a whole set of missing links, extrapolations, and arguments. Perhaps all this analysis is a case in point that Carson "needs explaining," in the words of James Laughlin of New Directions, likely in response to *Short Talks*: that cryptic, compelling arguments made of gesture and image will eventually—for better or for worse—be made somewhere in words.[31] Yet the "Short Talk" passes the onus of thinking, narrativizing, arguing, over to us. Talking to Will Aitken, Carson returns once again to what she called the "exchange of action" between performance and audience, explaining why she values it: "this capturing of the surface of emotional fact is useful for other people in that it jolts them into thinking, into doing their own act of understanding." In the lecture that doesn't "lecture" us (the transitive sense in which "lecture" is often used now), thinking—and not necessarily Carson's thinking—stumbles out of form as if by chance: the "starry, stumbling, chancing" of Carson's lecture on pronouns, and the "short kind of dance" she imagined the original *Short Talks* to be.[32]

Just what, then, connects the condensed mimetic gestures of *Short Talks* with the immersive long-form narratives of lectures such as "Stillness" and "Corners," which simulate a process of associative thinking so perfectly that it almost sounds off-the-cuff—as though Carson is literally thinking and talking as she goes along? Perhaps what joins them is a desire to imitate without artifice or mediation, to reproduce "that very jar on the nerves before it has been made anything" (spoken by Woolf's Lily Briscoe as she paints in *To the Lighthouse*).[33] In the first case, in the performative manner of a picture; in the second, as a performance of associative thinking as it happened, with no pretensions to either exhaustiveness or conclusion: the brilliant "mess of encounter" before it has been put into order. This is not to say that Carson's lecture is formless or without device. Rather, that its device is artlessness: a late style, following Adorno's characterization of late styles, whose work is in "the outer reaches of art, in the vicinity of document."[34] A documentary interest has always been there in Carson, traceable from "The Glass Essay," *The Albertine Workout*, and the paratexts of *Autobiography of Red*, through the scrapbook formats of *Nox* and *H of H Playbook*. Yet in these late lectures it is as though the documenting of process, the performance of thought, is the sum and total of the work. Their associations and idiosyncrasy move transparently, almost nonchalantly—as Barthes's lectures did, lured by "what shines by bursts"—, from one object to another, with little concern for whether the arguments hold water.

In *Scholarship and Freedom*, Galt Harpham reflects on what he calls the "mission" of scholarship: what it is that distinguishes scholarship from "argument" and "the approximations and illusions of received wisdom."[35] "The constant mission of scholarship is to bring about a change in the way the reader thinks," he says; it expresses a "capacity to create, to bring newness into the world."[36] Though we can be fairly sure the *Short Talks* do not figure on Galt Harpham's list of scholarly works, they, like Carson's long-form lectures, give themselves over fully to both of these aims—*metanoia*, a change of mind, and *poiesis*, creation. Where the long-form lecture spools out the process, the close readings and annotations, *Short Talks* capture the afterimages of study. Their mission, under Harpham's terms, is shared.

John D'Agata begins his 1997 interview with some remarks on Carson's "creative" work and a rationale for the scare quotes he hems around the word. He notes her distinction as a scholar of Greek, then invokes the c-word with some hesitancy: "We write 'creative' because Anne Carson's scholarship is as lucid as her poetry and essays, her essays and poetry as sharp as her scholarship. Indeed," he adds, "the two are, for many readers, indistinguishable."[37] Twenty-five years on from this, are we still to write "creative"? In the age of Performance Philosophy and Clark Lectures with dance accompaniment, what does "creative" cover for, and what conclusions do the quotation marks hold in suspense? Carson talks in that interview about her writing as an "approximation of what the facts are doing," of "their activity more than their surface appearance"; first seeing "that a fact has a form" and then "trying to make that happen again in language."[38] It is not just their lucidity and sharpness that causes the singular indistinction of Carson's scholarship, poems, and essays. Carson's "approximation" (unlike Harpham's "approximations and illusions of received wisdom") doesn't parse wisdom or retell stories. It produces a form, and form—as Carson, like few others, has sought to show—makes us think differently. It is useless, then, to talk of any of her forms in terms cut loose from these forms' occasion, the discoveries and demands about which Carson is always, though never simply, transparent. Why not talk instead about what these forms—their shapes, titles, internal theorizations—ask us to do, and whether we're willing to go along with it. To throw ourselves "off the building," to be broached and disrupted, or just to "look at this." To find here and there "a fragment of unexhausted time."[39]

Notes

Introduction

1. Carson alludes in her essay on Cy Twombly to several works invoking Catullus by name, including *Catullus* (1962), *Six Latin Writers and Poets: Catullus* (1976), and *Untitled (Say Goodbye, Catullus, to the Shores of Asia Minor)* (1994). She cites Barthes's "incomparable" reading at several points. See Roland Barthes, "Cy Twombly: Works on Paper" ("Non multa sed multum," 1979), in his *The Responsibility of Forms: Critical Essays on Music, Art, and Representation*, trans. Richard Howard (Oxford: Blackwell, 1986), pp. 157–176 (p. 163), quoted in Anne Carson, "The Sheer Velocity and Ephemerality of Cy Twombly," *LitHub*, October 22, 2020, https://lithub.com/anne-carson-the-sheer-velocity-and-ephemerality-of-cy-twombly/. The essay was previously published in *Cy Twombly: Making Past Present*, ed. Christine Kondoleon et al. (Boston: MFA Publications, 2020).
2. Barthes, "Cy Twombly," p. 167.
3. Ibid., p. 164. See Rosalind Krauss's compelling defense of Barthes's argument that Twombly's Latin is performative and not "to be consumed as erudition." Rosalind Krauss, "Cy's Up," *Artforum International*, September 1994, https://www.artforum.com/print/199407/cy-s-up-33352.
4. Carson, "The Sheer Velocity and Ephemerality of Cy Twombly." Carson's quotation is a paraphrase. Twombly's exact words, spoken during an interview for the Louvre, are: "Everything lives in the moment, that's the only time it can live. But its influence can go on forever." Marie-Laure Bernadac and Cy Twombly, "Interview/Entretien," *Cy Twombly—The Ceiling: Un plafond pour le Louvre*, ed. Marie-Laure Bernadac (Paris: Èditions du Regard, Musée du Louvre, 2010), p. 21.
5. Tacita Dean, "Anne Carson Punches a Hole Through Greek Myth," *Interview Magazine*, December 16, 2021, https://www.interviewmagazine.com/culture/anne-carson-punches-a-hole-through-greek-myth.
6. Melanie Rehak, "Things Fall Together," *New York Times*, March 26 2000, https://www.nytimes.com/2000/03/26/magazine/things-fall-together.html; and Will Aitken, "Anne Carson, the Art of Poetry No. 88," *The Paris Review* 171 (Fall 2004), (207), https://www.theparisreview.org/interviews/5420/anne-carson-the-art-of-poetry-no-88-anne-carson. Carson describes her working arrangements in several interviews. See, for example, John D'Agata, "A__ with Anne Carson," *The Iowa Review* 27.2 (1997), 1–22 (9); and Kevin McNeilly, "Gifts and Questions: An Interview with Anne Carson," *Canadian Literature* 176 (Spring 2003), 12–25 (14).
7. Dean, "Anne Carson Punches a Hole Through Greek Myth."

8. Anne Carson, *Economy of the Unlost: (Reading Simonides of Keos with Paul Celan)*, Martin Classical Lectures (Princeton, NJ: Princeton University Press, 1999), p. viii.
9. Ibid.
10. Sam Anderson praises what he calls the sensation of "distant closeness" in her juxtapositions. See Sam Anderson, "The Inscrutable Brilliance of Anne Carson," *New York Times Magazine*, March 14, 2013, https://www.nytimes.com/2013/03/17/magazine/the-inscrutable-brilliance-of-anne-carson.html. Robert Stanton, Laura Jansen, and Gillian Sze have each used the term "errancy" or "erring" to describe Carson's deliberate courting of surprise and mistakenness. See Robert Stanton, "'I am writing this to be as wrong as possible to you': Anne Carson's Errancy," *Canadian Literature* 176 (Spring 2003), 28–43; Laura Jansen, "Introduction," in *Anne Carson/Antiquity*, ed. Laura Jansen, Bloomsbury Studies in Classical Reception (London and New York: Bloomsbury, 2022), p. 5; Gillian Sze, "Erring and *Whatever*," in ed. Jansen, *Anne Carson/Antiquity*, pp. 63–74.
11. Harold Bloom, "The Breaking of Form," in *The Lyric Theory Reader: A Critical Anthology*, ed. Virginia Jackson and Yopie Prins (Baltimore, MD: Johns Hopkins University Press, 2014), pp. 275–286 (p. 276).
12. The remarks are Ernest Hilbert's in a review of *Men in the Off Hours*. See Ernest Hilbert, "On and Off Parnassus" [Review article], *Contemporary Poetry Review* (July 8, 2005), https://www.cprw.com/on-and-off-of-parnassus. In the light of this criticism, Carson's early poem "Now What?" (1990) reads like a reckoning with the question of where to go "after" the scholarly essay.
13. The remark was made by Michael Lista: "How many genres can you mix before your inventiveness waters itself down? Is there a limit to pretending there is no limit?" Lista's answer, of course, is "yes": "Carson's poems stopped singing; the essays stopped thinking. The cross-pollination that had made her writing popular was now running to seed." Michael Lista, "Is Anne Carson the Only Poet with More Fans than Readers?," *The Walrus*, October 2016, https://thewalrus.ca/audens-opposite/. In response to a question about the danger of her subject matter running dry, Carson responded: "As to the danger, wouldn't I be the last to 'know' this?" See Kate Kellaway and Anne Carson, "I do not believe in art as therapy," *The Guardian*, October 30, 2016, https://www.theguardian.com/books/2016/oct/30/anne-carson-do-not-believe-art-therapy-interview-float.
14. Charles Simic, "The Spirit of Play," *New York Review of Books*, November 3, 2005, https://www.nybooks.com/articles/2005/11/03/the-spirit-of-play/; and John Timpane, "Nox Is a Moving Story—and an Art Object," *Philadelphia Inquirer*, October 3, 2010, https://www.inquirer.com/philly/entertainment/20101003__quot_Nox_quot__Is_a_moving_book_-_and_an_art_object.html.
15. Charles Bernstein, *A Poetics* (Cambridge, MA: Harvard University Press, 1992), p. 1.
16. See McNeilly, "Gifts and Questions," 20.
17. Ibid., 14.
18. Anne Carson, *The Beauty of the Husband: A Fictional Essay in 29 Tangos* (London: Vintage, 2001). Carson was the first woman to win the T. S. Eliot Prize for Poetry (2001). Other major awards and prizes include: a Lannan Literary Award

(1996), the Pushcart Prize (1997), a Guggenheim Fellowship (1998), a MacArthur Fellowship (2000), the Griffin Poetry Prize (2001, 2014), a Princess of Asturias Award (2020), the PEN/Nabokov Award (2021). Carson has been widely reported to feature on the shortlist for the Nobel Prize for Literature (2019, 2020, 2021, 2022).

19. "Possessive Used as Drink (Me): A Lecture on Pronouns in the Form of 15 Sonnets," published in unpaginated pamphlet form in *Float*, was performed at the 92nd Street Y in New York, March 26, 2008. A recording of the performance can be viewed online: https://www.youtube.com/watch?v=j8y5SvhpbwU. Carson's *Autobiography of Red: A Novel in Verse* (New York: Knopf, 1998) brought her work to the attention of a wider audience, garnering the highest number of published articles and reviews of the whole Carson oeuvre to date. The book is currently taught on several university and college syllabuses in the United States, and eNotes and GradeSaver guides are available.

20. See Joshua Marie Wilkinson, ed., *Anne Carson: Ecstatic Lyre* (Ann Arbor: University of Michigan Press, 2015) and Jansen, ed., *Anne Carson/Antiquity* (2022). Wilkinson's multi-author collection brings together "a constellation of approaches" to Carson, in thirty-two short "appreciations, readings, investigations, experiments, and performances" by writers and artists (p. 5). Jansen's volume of scholarly essays approaches Carson's "engagement with classical antiquity" (p. 1), highlighting "the erudite *in*discipline of her classicism as it emerges in her poetry, translations, essays and visual artistry" (p. 2). A study by classicist Louis A. Ruprecht Jr. has approached "the role played by generic transgressions on the one hand, and by embodied spirituality on the other," arguing for Carson's refusal of the "tired (and falsifying) dichotomy that separates Classical and Christian learning." See Louis A. Ruprecht Jr., *Reach Without Grasping: Anne Carson's Classical Desires* (Lanham.MD: Lexington Books, 2021), blurb and preface. The submission of a full manuscript of *Anne Carson: The Glass Essayist* for review in November 2021 coincided with the publication of both Jansen and Ruprecht's books. The manuscript has been updated to reflect the new research landscape.

21. See Neil Hertz, "Lurid Figures," *Reading De Man Reading*, ed. Lindsay Waters and Wlad Godzich (Minneapolis: Minnesota University Press, 1989), p. 86.

22. "Sleight of hand" is an expression used by critic Robert Potts in relation to Carson's use of scholarly material in her work. See Robert Potts, "Neither Rhyme nor Reason," *The Guardian*, January 26, 2002, https://www.theguardian.com/books/2002/jan/26/poetry.tseliotprizeforpoetry.

23. Aitken, "Art of Poetry no. 88," 204.

24. Carson uses the term "interactive lecture" in recent performances of several "Short Talks," for example, preceding the lecture on "Corners" delivered at the City University of New York in 2018 (discussed in my Postscript). See Carson's discussion of the imitation of "affect" and "causal connection" in the grammatical organization of lyric verse: Anne Carson, "'Just for the Thrill': Sycophantizing Aristotle's *Poetics*," *Arion: A Journal of Humanities and the Classics* (Winter 1990), 142–154 (147).

25. D'Agata, "A__ with Anne Carson," 14, 13, 14.

26. Aitken, "Art of Poetry no. 88," 204 (italics mine). For Carson's approach to mimesis in classical lyric, see Carson, "'Just for the Thrill'" and *Economy of the Unlost*, pp. 51–52.
27. Susan Sontag, "Against Interpretation," in her *Against Interpretation and Other Essays* (1961; London: Penguin Modern Classics, 2009), p. 8; and Eve Kosofsky Sedgwick, "Paranoid and Reparative Reading, or You're So Paranoid You Probably Think This Essay Is about You," in her *Touching Feeling: Affect, Pedagogy, Performativity* (Durham, NC, and London: Duke University Press, 2003), p. 132.
28. Hilbert, "On and Off Parnassus." Hilbert describes *Men in the Off Hours* as "a dissertation on poetic possibilities. This can be invigorating but also a bit overpowering."
29. Christopher Ricks, "Literature and the Matter of Fact," in his *Essays in Appreciation* (Oxford: Oxford University Press, 1996), p. 286.
30. An early, nuanced discussion of Carson's "generic hybridity" can be found in Ian Rae's essay "Dazzling Hybrids." See Ian Rae, "'Dazzling Hybrids': The Poetry of Anne Carson." *Canadian Literature* 166 (Autumn 2000), 17–41.
31. Anne Carson, "Short Talk on Shelter," in her *Short Talks* (Kingston, ON: Brick Books, 1992, 2015), p. 70; Carson, *Economy of the Unlost*, vii; Carson, *Short Talks*, p. 24.
32. See Rita Felski, *The Limits of Critique* (Chicago: Chicago University Press, 2015) and Eve Kosofsky Sedgwick, "Paranoid Reading." This wide-ranging discussion touches questions of critical method (Anker and Felski, 2017; Felski, 2015; Hartman, 1976; Jarvis, 2002; Ulmer, 1983); descriptive attention and textuality (Love, 2013; Rooney, 2010); criticism's affective styles (Ruddick, 2015; Sedgwick, 2003; Serpell, 2014, 2017); critical culture as a determinant of literary style (Eve, 2017; McGurl, 2009); and hybrid and adaptive modes of scholarly writing (Bammer and Boetcher-Joeres, eds., 2015; Benson and Connors, eds., 2014).
33. Charles Bernstein, "Frame Lock," in Bernstein, *My Way: Speeches and Poems* (Chicago: University of Chicago Press, 1999), pp. 90–99 (p. 90). Rachel Blau DuPlessis has produced a fascinating survey of writers who have "loosened the tone and affect of critical ('academic') prose coming from a professional space they regard with some suspicion": from Susan Howe and Avitall Ronell to Alicia Ostriker and Jacques Derrida. See Rachel Blau DuPlessis, "f-Words: An Essay on the Essay," *American Literature* 68.1, "Write Now: American Literature in the 1980s and 1990s" (March 1996), 15–45 (19).
34. Sedgwick, "Paranoid Reading," pp. 130–131. In 1950, Lionel Trilling described the culling of surprise as one of the destinies of "liberal" critical culture: "there may come a moment when [art, literature] cannot satisfy one of our legitimate demands, which is that it shall surprise us." Lionel Trilling, *The Liberal Imagination* (New York: Scribner's Sons, 1976), p. 256.
35. Carson remarked on the origins of the "Short Talk" form in a reading of the work "We've Only Just Begun" at the European Graduate School, Saas-Fee, Switzerland, June 30, 2016 (0.45–1.02s), https://www.youtube.com/watch?v=3OazI4kygXQ.
36. Stephen Benson and Claire Connors, eds. *Creative Criticism: An Anthology and Guide* (Edinburgh: Edinburgh University Press, 2014).
37. See Lisa Samuels's Introduction to Laura Riding, *Anarchism Is Not Enough*, ed. Lisa Samuels (Berkeley: University of California Press, 2001), pp. xiii, xiv.

38. Sarah Chihaya, Merve Emre, Katherine Hill, and Jill Richards. *The Ferrante Letters: An Experiment in Collective Criticism* (New York: Columbia University Press, 2020); and, for example, Ann Lauterbach, "As (It) Is: Toward a Poetics of the Whole Fragment," in *American Women Poets in the 21st Century: Where Lyric Meets Language*, ed. Claudia Rankine and Juliana Spahr (Middletown CT: Wesleyan University Press, 2002), pp. 363–366. Juliana Spahr speaks of "awkward, bifocal moments" in her writing that are the result, she says, of feeling "caught between an academic scene and a poetry scene that are often antithetical in desires and intents." Juliana Spahr, *Everybody's Autonomy: Connective Reading and Collective Identity* (Tuscaloosa: University of Alabama Press, 2001), xi.
39. Charles Bernstein, *Shadowtime* (Los Angeles: Green Integer Editions, 2014); Stephen Collis, *Through Words of Others: Susan Howe and Anarcho-Scholasticism* (Victoria: ELS Editions, 2015).
40. Jan Zwicky, *Wittgenstein Elegies* (Kingston, ON.: Brick Books, 1986); and Jan Zwicky, *Lyric Philosophy* (1992; Edmonton and Calgary: Brush Education, 2014).
41. See T. W. Adorno, "The Essay as Form," in Adorno, *Notes to Literature*, Volume I, ed. Rolf Tiedemann, trans. Shierry Weber Nicholsen (New York: Columbia University Press, 1991), pp. 3–25. The "search for style" is the expression used by Gillian Rose in *The Melancholy Science: An Introduction to the Thought of T. W. Adorno*, Verso Radical Thinkers (1978; London and New York: Verso, 2014), pp. 15–26. Susan Sontag, "On Style," in her *Against Interpretation and Other Essays*, pp. 15–36 (p. 31). In *The Philosophical Disenfranchisement of Art*, Arthur C. Danto describes the history of Western philosophy as "a history of dialogues, lecture notes, fragments, poems, examinations, essays, aphorisms, meditations, discourses, hymns, critiques, letters, summae, encyclopedias, testaments, commentaries, investigations, tractatuses, Vorlesungen, Aufbauen, prolegomena, parerga, pensées, sermons, supplements, confessions, sententiae, inquiries, diaries, outlines, sketches, commonplace books, . . . and innumerable forms which have no generic identity or which themselves constitute distinct genres." Arthur C. Danto, *The Philosophical Disenfranchisement of Art*, foreword by Jonathan Gilmore (New York: Columbia University Press, 1986, 2005), p. 141.
42. See Jacques Derrida, *Dissemination*, translated and with an introduction by Barbara Johnson (London: Athlone Press, 1981); Gregory Ulmer, "The Object of Post-Criticism," *The Anti-Aesthetic: Essays in Postmodern Culture*, ed. Hal Foster (Seattle, WA: Bay Press, 1983), pp. 83–110; and Barthes, *A Lover's Discourse; Fragments* (1977), trans. Richard Howard (London: Vintage, 2002). Anastasia-Erasmia Peponi has suggested that, in its evolution out of the 1981 doctoral thesis, Carson's extended essay shows the influence of French *écriture*. See Anastasia-Erasmia Peponi, "*Écriture* and the Budding Classicist," in *Anne Carson/Antiquity*, ed. Jansen, pp. 51–61. Peponi proceeds to "single out Barthes . . . as a refreshing presence one can sense in the undercurrents of Carson's book" (p. 54), but does not discuss any of the striking formal and ideational similarities between Barthes's textual "simulation" of desire and Carson's. For a discussion of these similarities and of affinities and tensions with Derrida's iconic reading of the *Phaedrus*, see my Chapter 1.

43. Carson's description of Barthes appears in "The Sheer Velocity and Ephemerality of Cy Twombly."
44. Description from the conference brochure "Reinventing the Poet-Critic," Miami University Summer Institute for Literary History, June 2–4, 1994, https://sc.lib.miamioh.edu/handle/2374.MIA/6312?show=full.
45. Bernstein, "The Revenge of the Poet-Critic, or The Parts are Greater than the Sum of the Whole," in *My Way: Speeches and Poems*, p. 12.
46. DuPlessis, "f-Words," 17.
47. For example, Anne Carson, "Stillness," *Critical Inquiry* 48.1 (Autumn 2021), 1–22.
48. Cage's "Lecture on the Weather" was composed in 1975 and first performed in Toronto, on February 26, 1976. A database of Cage's work contains his complete technical specifications for the performance: https://johncage.org/pp/John-Cage-Work-Detail.cfm?work_ID=109.
49. Elaine Scarry, *Dreaming by the Book* (Princeton, NJ: Princeton University Press, 1999), p. 105. Carson, *The Beauty of the Husband*, p. 38, and Carson, "Epitaph: Evil," *Men in the Off Hours*, p. 29.
50. Anne Carson, "The Life of Towns," in her *Plainwater* (New York: Knopf, 1995; New York: Vintage Contemporaries, 2000), p. 93.
51. Barthes, "Cy Twombly," p. 167.
52. "Just for the Thrill" is the short title of an early scholarly essay by Carson, discussed in Chapter 8 of this book.
53. See Jim Fleming and Anne Carson, "Transcript for Poesis with Anne Carson," "To the Best of Our Knowledge," Wisconsin Public Radio, http://archive.ttbook.org/book/transcript/transcript-poesis-anne-carson.
54. Eric Hayot, "Then and Now," in *Critique and Postcritique*, ed. Elizabeth S. Anker and Rita Felski (Durham, NC, and London: Duke University Press, 2017), pp. 279–296 (p. 291).
55. D'Agata, "A __ with Anne Carson," 12.
56. Ibid., 17. It is interesting to read these remarks alongside Susan Howe's characterization of "the grace of scholarship," a grace that enables her to "know" her objects of study "just from reading" and that leaves her "indebted to everyone." See Susan Howe, *The Birth-mark: Unsettling the Wilderness in American Literary History* (Middletown, CT.: Wesleyan University Press, 1993), p. 39.
57. Howe, *The Birth-mark*, p. 38. Reflecting on her own creative, often mimetic, reading of Dickinson, Howe's comment reads: "Ask what form for the form. . . . Truth is water. Attraction makes it open," calling perhaps for a similar kind of formal transparency in response to the form of another work.
58. Oscar Wilde, *The Critic as Artist* (New York: David Zwirner Books, 2019), p. 84. Carson talks to Will Aitken about Wilde's influence during her teen years: "[Wilde] gave me an education in aesthetic sensibility, and also a kind of irony toward myself that was useful in later life." Aitken, "The Art of Poetry no. 88."
59. See scholar-poet Angela Leighton's discussion of "*forma efformans*" in her book, *On Form* (Oxford: Oxford University Press, 2007), p. 7.

60. Megan Berkobien, "An Interview with Anne Carson and Robert Currie," *Asymptote: A Journal of Translation*, https://www.asymptotejournal.com/interview/an-interview-with-anne-carson-and-robert-currie/.
61. Carson's vision of her work here bears strong affinities with Umberto Eco's famous ascription of a deliberate "openness" to chance and contingency in the arrangement and presentation of the work of art. See Umberto Eco, *The Open Work* (1962), trans. Anna Cancogni (Cambridge, MA: Harvard University Press, 1989). Kim Anno describes the "metaphorical" relation of text and image producing an "open reading" in remarks quoted by Berkobien, "An Interview with Anne Carson and Robert Currie" (n.p.), and reproduced on Anno's personal website: http://www.kimanno.com/books/ . *The Albertine Workout* was originally published in the New Directions "Poetry Pamphlet" series. The artist book edition is a boxed set of unbound sheets alternating Carson's text with Anno's illustrations (St. Joseph, MN: One Crow Press, The Literary Arts Institute of the College of St. Benedict, September 2014). Anno has also illustrated the original libretto of Carson's "Mirror of Simple Souls," a proto-version of the "Decreation" opera: Anne Carson and Kim Anno, *The Mirror of Simple Souls: An Opera Installation* (St. Joseph, MN: One Crow Press, The Literary Arts Institute of the College of St. Benedict, 2003). Images of Anno's illustrations to both the libretto and *The Albertine Workout* are available to view on Anno's website (as above).
62. The phrase is from Carson's justification of her "conversation" between Simonides and Celan as a means to sustain readers' attention. Carson, *Economy of the Unlost*, viii.
63. Friedrich Hölderlin, *Selected Poems and Fragments: Bilingual Edition,* trans. Michael Hamburger, ed. Jeremy Adler (London: Penguin, 1998), pp. 206–207. Quoted in Rüdiger Görner, "Hölderlin's Romantic Classicism," in *The Oxford Handbook of European Romanticism*, ed. Paul Hamilton (Oxford: Oxford University Press, 2016), pp. 274–292 (p. 279).
64. Brian Dillon, *Essayism* (London: Fitzcarraldo Editions, 2017), p. 16. Dillon cites Jean Starobinski's remarks on the etymological story of the French verb "essayer" in Jean Starobinski, "Can One Define the Essay?," first published in *La Revue des Belles-lettres* (1983), reproduced, in a translation by Lyndsey Scott, in Carl H. Klaus and Ned Stuckey French, eds., *Essayists on the Essay: Montaigne to Our Time* (Iowa City: University of Iowa Press, 2012), pp. 110–111.
65. Anne Carson, "The Glass Essay," in her *Glass, Irony and God* (New York: New Directions, 1995), pp. 1–38.
66. Ian Rae, "Verglas: Narrative Technique in Anne Carson's 'The Glass Essay,'" *ESC* 37.3–4 (September–December 2011), 163–186 (166).
67. Carson, *Economy of the Unlost*, vii; Carson, "The Glass Essay," p. 2.
68. Carson, "The Sheer Velocity and Ephemerality of Cy Twombly." See Barthes, "Cy Twombly," p. 166, on Twombly's marks uniting "by an inimitable stroke, both inscription and erasure."
69. Howe, *My Emily Dickinson* (1985; New York: New Directions, 2007), "Introduction" (unpaginated).
70. Carson, *Short Talks*, p. 23; and Carson, "Irony Is Not Enough: Essay on My Life as Catherine Deneuve (2nd Draft)," in *Men in the Off Hours*, pp. 119–126.

71. Roland Barthes, *Criticism and Truth* (1966), trans. Katrine Pilcher Keuneman (1987; London and New York: Continuum, 2004), p. 36.
72. For example, the essays collected in Hélène Cixous, *Reading with Clarice Lispector*, ed. and trans. Verena Andermatt Conley (Minneapolis: Minnesota University Press, 1990); Julia Kristeva, *Teresa My Love: An Imagined Life of the Saint of Avila*, trans. Lorna Scott Fox (2008; New York: Columbia University Press, 2015); Carol Mavor, *Reading Boyishly: Roland Barthes, J. M. Barrie, Jacques Henri Lartigue, Marcel Proust, and D. W. Winnicott* (Durham, NC, and London: Duke University Press, 2007).
73. Sarah Chihaya, "A Glass Essay: Reading Anne Carson Post-breakup," *The Yale Review*, June 1, 2022 https://yalereview.org/article/sarah-chihaya-anne-carson.

    A doctoral thesis by Paul Meyer (University of Toronto, 2016) is structured around a series of short "fractal" chapters whose titles mimic Carson; e.g., "little blues for (On Encyclopaedism in Anne Carson)." McNeilly's "Five Fairly Short Talks on Anne Carson" plays a similar riffing game. See Kevin McNeilly, "Five Fairly Short Talks on Anne Carson," *Canadian Literature* 176 (Spring 2003), 6–10.
74. D'Agata, "A__ with Anne Carson," 12.
75. Barthes, *Criticism and Truth*, p. 36; Roland Barthes, *Critique et Vérite* (Paris: Éditions du Seuil, 1966), p. 77.
76. Stephen Halliwell's account of mimesis suggests the history of Western literature is also a history of misreading or misapprehension of Plato's image of the mirror in Book X of *The Republic*. See Stephen Halliwell, *The Aesthetics of Mimesis: Ancient Texts and Modern Problems* (Princeton, NJ, and Oxford: Princeton University Press, 2002), especially pp. 118–150.
77. After Duchamp, Anish Kapoor and Gerhard Richter have both used mirrors to turn the viewer-object relation on its head.
78. From the poem "What Is the Language Using Us for?," W. S. Graham, *New Collected Poems* (London: Faber and Faber, 2004), p. 202. See David Nowell-Smith, *W. S. Graham: The Poem as Art Object* (Oxford: Oxford University Press, 2022), "to make / An object," pp. 1–42 (p. 4).
79. Howe, *My Emily Dickinson*, p. 134.
80. Joan Brossa et al., *Poesía Brossa: Imagen, texto y performatividad / Brossa Poetry: Image, Text and Performativity* (Mexico City: Museo Universitario de Arte Contemporáneo, 2021), p. 69. The Catalan poet's original Spanish reads: "Estos versos se han escrito / para que pasen desapercibidos como / un cristal" (p. 68).
81. See in particular Carson, *Eros the Bittersweet*, pp. 30–61 (p. 39). Carson's thesis in the book builds on the work of Denys Page and Bruno Snell (see my Chapter 1 for a fuller discussion of the book's central ideas).
82. Bruno Snell (1948), *The Discovery of the Mind in Greek Philosophy and Literature*, trans. T. G. Rosenmeyer (Oxford: Basil Blackwell, 1953), p. 53, quoted in Carson, *Eros the Bittersweet*, p. 38.
83. Carson, *Eros the Bittersweet*, p. 45.
84. Ibid., pp. 152–153.
85. Ibid., pp. 20–21.
86. McNeilly, "Gifts and Questions," 20.

87. *If Not, Winter: Fragments of Sappho*, trans. Anne Carson (2002; London: Virago Press, 2003), x.
88. Carson, *Economy of the Unlost*, vii.
89. Eleanor Wachtel and Anne Carson, "An Interview with Anne Carson," *Brick* 89 (Summer 2012), 29–47, https://brickmag.com/an-interview-with-anne-carson/.
90. The collective began under the name "EgoCircus: a Workshop in Collaboration."
91. Berkobien, "An Interview with Anne Carson and Robert Currie" (n.p.).
92. For example, the constrained vocabularies of Carson's sequential translations of Ibykos fragment 286 in "Variations on the Right to Remain Silent" and recent collaborations with Currie using random integer generators to produce aleatory lineation patterns, recall the techniques of Oulipo. For an illuminating study of Oulipo and its legacy after the mid-century, see Daniel Levin Becker, *Many Subtle Channels: In Praise of Potential Literature* (Cambridge, MA: Harvard University Press, 2012).
93. John Cage, *Silence: Lectures and Writings* (Middletown, CT: Wesleyan University Press, 1961), p. 69.
94. David Solway, "The Trouble with Annie: David Solway Unmakes Anne Carson," *Books in Canada* (July 2001), 26, 25, http://www.booksincanada.com/article_view.asp?id=3159. Ian Rae has written an elegant riposte to the Solway piece: Ian Rae, "Anne Carson and the Solway Hoaxes," *Canadian Literature* 176 (2003), 45–65. See Kenneth Goldsmith, *Uncreative Writing: Managing Language in the Digital Age* (New York: Columbia University Press, 2011); Marjorie Perloff, *Unoriginal Genius: Poetry by Other Means* (Chicago: University of Chicago Press, 2010), p. 20, and Kaya Marczewska, *This Is Not a Copy: Writing at the Iterative Turn* (London and New York: Bloomsbury, 2018).
95. From Robert Potts's well-known critique: see Robert Potts, "Neither Rhyme nor Reason," *The Guardian*, January 26, 2002, https://www.theguardian.com/books/2002/jan/26/poetry.tseliotprizeforpoetry.
96. Jacques Derrida, *La Dissémination* (Paris: Éditions du Seuil, 1972), p. 175 (*L'illusioniste, le technicien du trompe-l'oeil, le peintre, l'ecrivain, le pharmakeus*); Derrida, *Dissemination*, p. 140. See Plato, "Sophist," trans. F. M. Cornford, *The Collected Dialogues*, ed. Edith Hamilton and Huntington Cairns, Bollingen Series LXXI (Princeton, NJ: Princeton University Press, 1961), pp. 1016–1017 (268c).
97. Plato, "Sophist," *The Collected Dialogues*, p. 1016, and Derrida, *Dissemination*, p. 140. Stephen Halliwell makes a strong case for caution in translating Plato and Aristotle's *mimēsis* as imitation, given the word's negative associations of fraudulence and impersonation. He opts, instead, to preserve the word "mimesis" as is. Halliwell, *The Aesthetics of Mimesis*, pp. 13–14.
98. Adorno, "The Essay as Form," p. 21.
99. See Colin Burrow, *Imitating Authors: From Plato to Futurity* (Oxford: Oxford University Press, 2019); Halliwell, *The Aesthetics of Mimesis*; and Linda Hutcheon, *A Theory of Parody: The Teachings of Twentieth-Century Art Forms* (New York and London: Methuen, 1985). Daphne Merkin, "Last Tango," *New York Times*, September 30, 2001, p. 12, online edition: https://www.nytimes.com/2001/09/30/books/last-tango.html.

100. Burrow, *Imitating Authors*, pp. 2–3. In his "Posthuman Postscript," Burrow discusses the work of Canadian author Christian Bök, whose uncreative writing practice includes implanting a particularly resonant verse from Virgil's *Georgics* into the DNA of thale cress, thus allowing the poem to reproduce permutatively across time. See Christian Bök, *The Xenotext: Book I* (Toronto: Coach House Books, 2015).
101. See Reena Sastri, "'Wildly Constant': Anne Carson's Poetics of Encounter," *Contemporary Literature* 62.3 (Fall 2021), 307–337; Stanton, "'I am writing this to be as wrong as possible to you': Anne Carson's Errancy"; and Gillian Sze, "Erring and Whatever," in *Anne Carson/Antiquity*, ed. Jansen, pp. 63–74. My thanks to Reena Sastri for sharing her article with me in draft form.
102. In Harold Bloom's theory of creative influence, "strong misreading" (and its alternative term, "misprision") is how poets read other poets. See Harold Bloom, *Agon: Towards a Theory of Revisionism* (Oxford: Oxford University Press, 1982).
103. Burrow, *Imitating Authors*, p. 10.
104. Gérard Genette, *Palimpsests: Literature in the Second Degree*, trans. Channa Newman and Claude Doubinsky (Lincoln, NE: University of Nebraska Press, 1997), p. 83, cited in Burrow, *Imitating Authors*, p. 12.
105. See Carson's own definition of *eidōlon* in *Norma Jeane Baker of Troy*, p. 5. Liddell and Scott's definition is "shape, image, spectre, phantom": Henry George Liddell and Robert Scott, *Liddell and Scott's Greek-English Lexicon Abridged* (n.p.: Simon Wallenberg Press, 2007), p. 196. Burrow's reference is to Plato, *Theaetetus; Sophist*, trans. H. N. Fowler (London, 1921), lines 235d–e, cited in Burrow, *Imitating Authors*, p. 60.
106. Burrow, *Imitating Authors*, pp. 60–61.
107. See Bloom, *Agon*, and Bloom, "The Breaking of Form," in *The Lyric Theory Reader*, ed. Jackson and Prins, p. 278.
108. René Girard, *The Scapegoat*, trans. Yvonne Freccero (Baltimore, MD: Johns Hopkins University Press, 1986), p. 165.
109. Virginia Woolf, *How Should One Read a Book?*, Introduction and Afterword by Sheila Heti (1935; London: Lawrence King, 2020), p. 42.
110. T. W. Adorno, "The Actuality of Philosophy," *Telos* 31 (1977), 120–133 (131): "An exact fantasy; fantasy which abides strictly within the material which the sciences present to it, and reaches beyond them only in the smallest aspects of their arrangement: aspects, granted, which fantasy itself must generate."
111. Carson, "Stillness," 2.
112. Carson, *The Beauty of the Husband*, p. 38.
113. Carson's comments appear in Sara Elkamel, "Anne Carson and Robert Currie in Conversation with Sara Elkamel and NYU Undergrads—On Starting in the Middle," *Washington Square Review* (May 5, 2021), https://www.washingtonsquarereview.com/online-features/2021/5/4/anne-carson-amp-robert-currie-on-starting-in-the-middle-in-conversation-with-sara-elkamel-amp-nyu-undergrads.
114. McNeilly, "Gifts and Questions," 17 (italics mine).
115. Anne Carson, "Cassandra Float Can," in *Float* (unpaginated), and McNeilly, "Gifts and Questions," 22. My Postscript discusses this anti-descriptive element as it emerges in *Short Talks*.

116. See Johanna Drucker's fantastic essay on concrete "visual performativity": Johanna Drucker, "Visual Performance of the Poetic Text," in *Close Listening*, ed. Bernstein, pp. 131–161. Also see Susan Howe, "The End of Art," *Archives of American Art Journal* 14.4 (1974), 2–7.
117. Carson, "Variations on the Right to Remain Silent." The intermedia piece was first performed in Dún Laoghaire, Ireland, in 2012.
118. See Scarry, *Dreaming by the Book*.
119. Carson, "'Just For the Thrill,'" 148.
120. Ibid., 147 (Carson's line reference in the *Poetics* is 456a, 36–37).
121. Virginia Jackson and Yopie Prins, "Introduction," in *The Lyric Theory Reader*, ed. Jackson and Prins, p. 2. "The survey of twentieth- and twenty-first-century criticism offered here shows that this general definition of the lyric (whether valued or devalued) now seems to us a given only because twentieth-century literary criticism made it up."
122. Jonathan Culler, *Theory of the Lyric* (Cambridge, MA: Harvard University Press, 2017), p. 226.
123. See Stanton, "I am writing this to be as wrong as possible to you."
124. Carson, "'Just for the Thrill,'" 150 (Carson's line reference is *Poetics*, 1450b 17).
125. McNeilly, "Gifts and Questions," 22. She expresses similar sentiments in an interview with Peter Constantine: "[I] still seem to approach writing as a very complicated, rule-bound form of drawing." Peter Constantine and Anne Carson, "Ancient Words, Modern Words: A Conversation with Anne Carson," *World Literature Today* 88.1 (January–February 2014), 36–37 (37). For a sensitive and intelligent discussion of Carson's collaboration with Currie in the composition of "Wildly Constant," see Sastri, '"Wildly Constant".' For a reading of Carson's visual art alongside her poems, see Oran McKenzie, "'to see matter stumble out of its forms': Anne Carson's Poetry and Visual Art," *mémoire* submitted at the English Department of the University of Geneva, August 2015. Monique Tschofen has written powerfully on the work of artist Betty Goodwin, to which Carson responds in the ekphrastic poem "Seated Figure with Red Angle by Betty Goodwin (1988)," in *Decreation*, pp. 95–102. See Monique Tschofen, "Drawing out a New Image of Thought: Anne Carson's Radical Ekphrasis," *Word and Image* 2.2 (2013), 233–243, and my discussion of the poem in Chapter 5 of this book.
126. Northrop Frye, *Anatomy of Criticism: Four Essays*, foreword by Harold Bloom (Princeton, NJ, and Oxford: Princeton University Press, 1957; 2000), p. 280 ("the radical of opsis in the lyric is riddle, which is characteristically a fusion of sensation and reflection, the use of an object of sense to stimulate a mental activity in connection with it"). The title of Sam Anderson's profile for the *New York Times*, "The Inscrutable Brilliance of Anne Carson," is suggestive in this regard.
127. Carson, "Stillness," 1. The text was first presented as a "lecture," in which the word "lecture" substitutes "essay" here.
128. Jarvis, "An Undeleter for Criticism," 16.
129. DuPlessis, "f-Words," 28.

130. Raoul Eshelman, *Performatism or the End of Postmodernism* (Aurora, CO: Davies Group, 2008).
131. The term is Barthes's to describe the lyric texture of *A Lover's Discourse*. See Barthes, *A Lover's Discourse: Fragments*, p. 7.
132. Carson's interest in these questions can be traced back to *Glass, Irony and God*, in particular "The Truth About God" (pp. 39–54) and "Book of Isaiah" (pp. 107–118) sequences.
133. Anne Carson, "Mimnermos: The Brainsex Paintings," *Plainwater*, pp. 1–26. Her "Pinplay: A Version of Euripides' *Bacchae*" was commissioned by the artist Elliott Hundley as an accompaniment piece to his installation, *The Bacchae*, Wexner Center for the Arts, Ohio (2011). The piece was performed, Carson's performance notes state, by members of the Ohio State Department of Greek and Latin, and is published in *Float* (unpaginated). Carson's "Twelve-Minute Prometheus (After Aiskhylos)" appears in *London Review of Books* 30.20 (October 23, 2008), https://www.lrb.co.uk/v30/n20/anne-carson/twelve-minute-prometheus-after-aiskhylos. Her version of Euripides's *Herakles*, *H of H Playbook*, was published by New Directions in 2021. *Norma Jeane Baker of Troy* (subtitled "a version of Euripides' *Helen*") premiered at The Shed in New York, with fragments from the work performed at London's Southbank Centre later in 2019.
134. See Edith Hall's excellent essay on *Autobiography of Red*: Edith Hall, "Autobiography of the Western Subject: Carson's Geryon," in *Living Classics*, ed. S. J. Harrison (Oxford: Oxford University Press, 2009), pp. 218–237; also see Edith Hall, "Subjects, Selves and Survivors," *Helios* 34.2 (Fall 2007), 125–160. A recent study provides exhaustive commentary on the extant text of the *Geryoneis*, including the distinctive metrical organization of the poem as choral song, and the myth and cult of Geryon: Paul Curtis, *Stesichoros's Geryoneis*, Mnemosyne Supplements: Monographs on Greek and Latin Language and Literature, no. 333 (Leiden and Boston: Brill, 2011).
135. Jansen's edited collection, *Anne Carson/Antiquity*, includes chapters on Carson's adaptations, translations, "transcreations" (Haroldo de Campos's term), and Carson's early academic relationship to the Classical canon. Louis A. Ruprecht Jr.'s *Reach Without Grasping* approaches Carson's classicism in dialogue with her commitments to "embodied spirituality." Several articles and short essays in Joshua Marie Wilkinson's edited collection address individual Carson adaptations. See, for example, Harmony Holiday, "Masters of the Open Secret: Meditations on Anne Carson's *Autobiography of Red*" (pp. 69–73); Vanessa Place, "What's So Funny About *Antigonick*?," (pp. 165–171); and Bianca Stone, "Your Soul Is Blowing Apart: *Antigonick* and the Influence of Collaborative Process" (pp. 152–155), in ed. Wilkinson, *Anne Carson: Ecstatic Lyre*. Illuminating recent work has been done on the contemporary adaptation and translation of classical texts by authors including Carson, Seamus Heaney, and Derek Walcott. See ed. Harrison, *Living Classics*. Another collection analyses the specific case of contemporary adaptations of Greek tragedy: see eds. Vayos Liapis and Avra Sidiropoulou, *Adapting Greek Tragedy: Contemporary Contexts for Ancient Texts* (Cambridge: Cambridge

University Press, 2021). Classicist Daniel Mendelsohn has discussed the wider question of "updating" Classical texts in translation and adaptation: Daniel Mendelsohn and Alec Ash, "Daniel Mendelsohn on Updating the Classics (of Greek and Roman Literature," interview, *Five Books*: https://fivebooks.com/best-books/classics-daniel-mendelsohn/. For Mendelsohn's response to Carson's translation of Sappho, see my Chapter 8.
136. This translation of the *Antigone* was premiered at the Grand Théâtre de Luxembourg, in collaboration with The Barbican, London. The production was directed by Ivo van Hove and starred Juliette Binoche as Antigone. Sophokles, *Antigone*, trans. Anne Carson (London: Oberon Books, 2015), and Anne Carson, trans., *Antigonick: Sophokles* (Tarset: Bloodaxe Books, 2012).
137. Carson, *If Not, Winter*, x, xi.
138. See Carson's entry in Charles Simic et al., "Reading 9-11-01," *Artforum* (November 2001), 41–42.

Chapter 1

1. "Uncle Falling: A Pair of Lyric Lectures with Shared Chorus," in *Float* (unpaginated). Copyright © 2016 by Anne Carson. Used by permission of Alfred A. Knopf, an imprint of the Knopf Doubleday Publishing Group, a division of Penguin Random House LLC, and Jonathan Cape, a division of the Penguin Random House Group Limited. All rights reserved.
2. The "Performance Notes" included among the pamphlets of *Float* state that "Lecture I" was first performed at Housing Works Bookstore Café, New York, in 2008 by Carson, Robert Currie, and others, including the visual artist Tacita Dean and performance artist Laurie Anderson. "Lecture II" was added in 2010 for a performance at "The Poetry Project" at St. Mark's Church-in-the-Bowery, New York: https://www.poetryproject.org/david-shapiro-anne-carson-excerpts-10610/.
3. "Uncle Falling: A Pair of Lyric Lectures with Shared Chorus," in *Float* (unpaginated).
4. Streb's description of her work's main goal in the context of her studio, SLAM: Streb Lab for Action Mechanics, Brooklyn: https://streb.org/elizabeth-streb/. Streb understands the audience as "co-conspirators" in her work, and the mobilization of audience expectations is crucial to the effect of the controlled fall. Streb's own stunts, her webpage tells us, include diving through glass.
5. Carson, "Essay on What I Think About Most," *Men in the Off Hours*, p. 35. The "Essay," along with its redraft or companion piece "Essay on Error," was first published in *Raritan* 18.3 (Winter 1999). Carson's short disquisition on Aristotelian error and its performative or mimetic quality echoes her reading of the same passage from the *Poetics* and her discussion of the same Alkman fragment in the academic article, "'Just for the Thrill,'" 151–152. Her phrase "the true mistakes of poetry," also in the "Essay on What I Think About Most," appears in this article (151). Carson's line references in Aristotle are *Poetics* (1460b15–17), and, for "How true, yet I mistook!," *Rhetoric* (3.11.6).

6. Carson uses the term "accidents" to describe her unorthodox reading combinations. See Aitken, "The Art of Poetry no. 88."
7. "Scheduled mischief" is her term for the channeling of erotic instinct in the psychoanalytic transference; see Carson, *Eros the Bittersweet*, p. 64.
8. See Carson-Giacomelli, "Odi et Amo Ergo Sum."
9. Plato, "Phaedrus," trans. R. Hackforth, in *The Collected Dialogues*, ed. Hamilton and Cairns, p. 477 (228b1).
10. Catherine Bush, "A Short Talk with Anne Carson," unpublished email interview, 2000, http://catherinebush.com/articles/a-short-talk-with-anne-carson/
11. These arguments from Carson's thesis, which draw on the work of Classicists Bruno Snell and Denys Page, are reprised in *Eros the Bittersweet*, e.g., pp. 32–60. Carson's principal sources here include Bruno Snell's magnum opus, *The Discovery of the Mind in Greek Philosophy and Literature*.
12. Carson and D'Agata discuss this in his interview with the poet. D'Agata, "A__ with Anne Carson," 8.
13. Several academic articles engage with Carson's reading of desire. Jessica Fisher writes on what she calls Carson's "stereoscopic poetics," drawing on Carson's own description of "the difference between what is and what could be visible" as "a kind of stereoscopy" in *Eros the Bittersweet*. See Jessica Fisher, "Anne Carson's Stereoscopic Poetics," in *Anne Carson: Ecstatic Lyre*, ed. Wilkinson, pp. 17, 11.
14. D'Agata, "A__ with Anne Carson," 12, 13.
15. *Eros the Bittersweet* was published as an academic book in 1986 by Princeton University Press, and was re-released by the Dalkey Archive Press in 1998 as a trade paperback.
16. Guy Davenport, remarks reproduced in the front matter of *Eros the Bittersweet* (Dalkey Archive paperback edition). Davenport's full response to Carson's book is published in *Grand Street*: Guy Davenport, "Review [*Eros the Bittersweet*]," *Grand Street* 6, no. 3 (Spring 1987), 184–191.
17. Carson, *Men in the Off Hours*, p. 30. See Anne Carson, "Essay on What I Think About Most," *Raritan*, 18.3 (Winter 1999), https://raritanquarterly.rutgers.edu/issue-index/all-volumes-issues/volume-18/volume-18-number-3.
18. Carson, *Men in the Off Hours*, p. 30.
19. The italics here are Carson's.
20. The essay was first delivered as one of Carson's Clark Lectures, held at Trinity, College, Cambridge: "Stillness," March 12, 2018; "Corners," March 13, 2018; "The Chair (And a Dance)," March 15, 2018. Lectures in the series have since been presented at the City University of New York, the New York Public Library, and other venues.
21. Carson, "Stillness," 1.
22. Carson, *Eros the Bittersweet*, p. 17.
23. Cited in ibid., p. 7.
24. Carson, "'Just for the Thrill,'" 148. See the definition of *mimēsis* and the infinitive verb form *mi-me'omai* in Liddell and Scott, p. 447, and Halliwell's extensive discussion of the term in Halliwell, *The Aesthetics of Mimesis*.

25. Susan Howe's phrase in *The Birth-mark* ("Ask what form for the form," p. 38), quoted in the Introduction to this book.
26. See Liddell and Scott, *Liddell and Scott's Greek-English Lexicon Abridged*, (*metaphora*), p. 440.
27. From Guy Davenport's "Introduction," to Carson, *Glass, Irony and God*, p. viii.
28. Though Carson's image sequence is built out of a series of verbal figures and literary anecdotes, it recalls the collage form or *Bilderreihen* of Aby Warburg's *Mnemosyne Atlas* to the extent that the images fulfill the dual function of repository (content, source material) and rehearsal (argumentative structure). It is also the method famously employed by Walter Benjamin in the unfinished *Arcades Project* (*Das Passagenwerk*, 1982), structured around alphabetically organized "convolutes," including quotations with and without commentary. Walter Benjamin, *The Arcades Project*, trans. Howard Eiland and Kevin McLaughlin (Cambridge, MA, and London: Harvard University Press, 1999).
29. Carson provides the reference *Poetarum Lesbiorum Fragmenta*, ed. E. Lobel and D. Page (Oxford: Oxford University Press, 1955), fr. 31, for the original Greek text. The English translation is Carson's (*Eros the Bittersweet*, p. 13). A revised translation appears in Carson, trans., *If Not, Winter*, p. 63.
30. Girard, *The Scapegoat*, p. 165.
31. Joanne O'leary, "Pulling out the Screams: A Scattershot Collection of Unsettling Poems" [Review of *Float*], *Times Literary Supplement*, September 1, 2017, https://www.the-tls.co.uk/articles/pulling-out-the-screams/.
32. McNeilly, "Gifts and Questions," 17.
33. Ibid.
34. John D'Agata and Susan Steinberg, "John D'Agata Redefines the Essay," an interview with Susan Steinberg, *Electric Literature* (July 14, 2016).
35. Karen Solie, "On the Irreconcilable Temptations of Anne Carson," *Literary Hub*, October 1, 2019, https://lithub.com/on-the-irreconcilable-temptations-of-anne-carson/.
36. T. J. Sienkewicz, "Anne Carson: *Eros the Bittersweet*," *The Classical Bulletin*, 63.3 (Summer 1987), 89, 90.
37. Derrida, *Dissémination*, p. 70.
38. Ibid., xvi (in Barbara Johnson's Introduction).
39. Ulmer, "The Object of Post-Criticism," (p. 94).
40. Carson, *Eros the Bittersweet*, p. 87. Her reference is Montaigne, 1603, bk. 5, ch. 3.
41. Barthes, *A Lover's Discourse: Fragments*, pp. 3, 4, 7, 3.
42. Barthes, *A Lover's Discourse*, p. 9.
43. Ibid.
44. Peponi suggests that *Eros the Bittersweet* bears the influence of *écriture*: "a book written by a budding classicist, with antiquity at its thematic core, but creatively aligned with contemporary debates in Europe, and especially in France, regarding the very nature and function of writing. I use *écriture* here to evoke precisely that period in recent history rather than a specific definition of the term" (p. 54). She mentions Barthes as a "refreshing presence one can sense in the undercurrents of Carson's book" (p. 54),

but does not note the striking formal, stylistic, and citational similarities between *Eros the Bittersweet* and Barthes's more famous account of desire, or his significance more broadly in Carson, who praises explicitly his "golden persuasions." See Peponi, "Ècriture and the Budding Classicist," *Anne Carson/Antiquity*, pp. 51–62, and Carson, "The Sheer Velocity and Ephemerality of Cy Twombly."

45. D'Agata, "A __ with Anne Carson," 9.
46. Ibid., 11.
47. Plato, *Phaedrus*, trans. Walter Hamilton (London and New York: Penguin, 1973; 1995), p. 57. Plato, "Phaedrus," *The Collected Dialogues*, p. 509 (263b): "to say of it what you said just now, namely that it is harmful both to the beloved and the lover, and then to turn around and say that it is really the greatest of goods." Quotations in the text hereafter are from Walter Hamilton's lively, reader-friendly translation. I include translations from the Bollingen edition of *The Collected Dialogues* in these notes to provide readers with the standard paragraph reference.
48. Plato, *Phaedrus*, p. 57; Plato, "Phaedrus," p. 509 (263d): "thanks to my inspired condition I can't quite remember. Did I define love at the beginning of my speech?"
49. Longinus, "On Sublimity," in *Classical Literary Criticism*, ed. D. A. Russell and Michael Winterbottom (Oxford: Oxford University Press, 1972; 1998), p. 158 (13.2). For Carson's remarks on the treatise, see *Decreation*, p. 45. I discuss Carson's "Essay with Rhapsody" briefly in Chapter 5.
50. Barthes, *A Lover's Discourse*, p. 3.
51. D'Agata, "A __ with Anne Carson," 8.
52. Roland Barthes, "Interview for *Les Lettres Françaises*, February 9, 1972," in *The Grain of the Voice: Interviews 1962–1980*, trans. Linda Coverdale (New York: Hill and Wang, 1985), p. 161.
53. Sienkewicz, "Anne Carson: *Eros the Bittersweet*," 90. Carson opens *Eros the Bittersweet* with a series of brief remarks on Kafka's short story "The Top," about, she says, "a philosopher who spends his time around children so he can grab their [spinning] tops in spin" (xi) to confirm his belief, she quotes, "'that the understanding of any detail, that of a spinning top for instance, was sufficient for the understanding of all things.'"
54. D'Agata, "A __ with Anne Carson," 14.
55. See my discussion in Chapter 8.
56. Derrida, *Dissémination*, p. 71.
57. Transcribed from Carson's reading of "59 Paragraphs About Albertine" at the Mercantile Library Center for Fiction, New York, September 10, 2013, https://www.youtube.com/watch?v=ofR3Qd2E_A0.
58. Anne Carson, "The Albertine Workout," *London Review of Books* 36.11 (June 5, 2014), https://www.lrb.co.uk/the-paper/v36/n11/anne-carson/the-albertine-workout. The full version of *The Albertine Workout*, including appendices, was published in New Directions "Poetry Pamphlet" series on June 25, 2014. A limited edition of the *London Review of Books* version also appeared in artist book format, illustrated with photogravures by the artist Kim Anno: Anne Carson and Kim Anno, *The Albertine Workout* (St. Joseph, MN: One Crow Press, The Literary Arts Institute of the College of St. Benedict, 2014).

59. For example, the following image of Albertine and her girlfriends: "They form a frieze in [Marcel's] mind, pushing their bicycles across the beach with the blue waves breaking behind them" (entry 37) and "Albertine's eyes are blue and saucy. Her hair is like crinkly black violets" (entry 32). See Adam Watt's detailed account of the relationship between Carson's descriptions and Proust's: Adam Watt, "Poetry as Creative Critique: Notes on the Desert of After Proust (On Anne Carson's The Albertine Workout)," *Contemporary French and Francophone Studies*, 20.4–5 (2016), 648–656.
60. Carson's remark on the appendices to her doctoral thesis comes from her 1997 interview with John D'Agata. See D'Agata, "A___ with Anne Carson," 10.
61. Marcel Proust, *À la recherche du temps perdu*, III, édition publiée sous la direction de Jean-Yves Tadié avec, pour ce volume, la collaboration d'Antoine Compagnon et de Pierre-Edmond Robert (Paris: Gallimard, 1988). "La Prisonnière," p. 570.
62. Barthes expresses something similar when he says "there is no sincere boredom. . . . Boredom is not far from bliss: it is bliss seen from the shores of pleasure." Roland Barthes, *The Pleasure of the Text* (1973), trans. Richard Miller (New York: Hill and Wang, 1975), pp. 25–26.
63. See T. Clutch Fleischmann, "The Transposition Workout," *Brooklyn Rail*, September 2014, https://brooklynrail.org/2014/09/books/the-transposition-workout.
64. "Appendix 59 on a bad photograph" describes a photograph of Proust and Alfred Agostinelli seated side by side in a motorcar. Carson tells us that the photograph would have been one of those "that arouses merely a docile interest and is then forgotten—as Barthes says, a photograph with no fissure in its surface, no *punctum* to draw you in and disturb you (*Camera Lucida*, p. 41)—except for the posture of Alfred Agostinelli's head," which, she goes on to say, is tilted back at an angle that suggests motion at some velocity when the two are in fact sitting, "stock-still in the car" (p. 38). Carson alludes to Barthes's famous distinction between the *punctum* and *studium* of a photograph, where the studium of an image "arouses a merely docile interest," in Carson's words—or in Barthes's, that "derives from an average affect, almost from a certain training. . . . the studium is that very wide field of unconcerned desire." See Roland Barthes, *Camera Lucida* (1980), trans. Richard Howard (London and New York: Vintage, 2000), pp. 26–27). Barthes goes on to explain in *Camera Lucida*, in language that chimes with the Albertine question, that the studium "is a kind of education . . . which allows me to discover the Operator, to experience the intentions which establish and animate his practices, but to experience them "in reverse," according to my will as a *Spectator*" (p. 28).
65. Barthes, *The Pleasure of the Text*, p. 36.
66. Barthes, *Le Neutre: Notes de cours au Collége de France, 1977–1978* ed. Thomas Clerc (Paris: Seuil, 2002), p. 58 (*scintillations de la délicatesse . . . Non pas "traits," "éléments," "composants," mais ce qui brille par éclats [but what shines by bursts], en désordre, fugitivement, successivement, dans le discours "anecdotique"*).
67. See Barthes, *Le Neutre*, e.g., pp. 183–185. An excellent article on Barthes's unwritten novel discusses the "notational" form in relation to contemporary novels of process, including Sheila Heti's *How Should a Person Be?* (2012). See Rachel Sagner Buurma and Laura Heffernan, "Notation After "The Reality Effect": Remaking Reference with Roland Barthes and Sheila Heti," *Representations* 125.1 (Winter 2014), 80–102.

68. The artist Kim Anno has described the "metaphorical" relation of text and image in her and Carson's artist book edition of *The Albertine Workout* as inviting an "open reading," one that readers can arrive at "on their own." Quoted in Berkobien, "An Interview with Anne Carson and Robert Currie" (n.p.). Carson and Anno's artist book edition is a boxed set of unbound sheets alternating Carson's text with Anno's illustrations, published by One Crow Press and The Literary Arts Institute of the College of St. Benedict.
69. Philippe Lacoue-Labarthe and Jean-Luc Nancy, *The Literary Absolute* (1978), trans. Philip Barnard and Cheryl Lester (Albany: State University of New York Press, 1988), pp. 43, 47.
70. Watt, "Poetry as Creative Critique," 650.
71. See Justin O'Brien, "Albertine the Ambiguous: Notes on Proust's Transposition of Sexes," *PMLA* 64, no. 5 (December 1949), 933–952. O'Brien's article is where the overdeterministic transposition theory is first and most powerfully set out. Later studies set out to "unmask" Marcel's homosexuality and Proust's "lesbianism." His representation of lesbianism or "Gomorrah," as determined by a homosexual male gaze, has been discussed by authors including Colette, Djuna Barnes, and Monique Wittig. See Mark D. Guenette, "Le Loup et le Narrateur: The Masking and Unmasking of Homosexuality in Proust's *À la recherche du temps perdu*," *Romanic Review* 80.2 (March 1, 1989), and Elisabeth Ladenson, *Proust's Lesbianism* (Ithaca, NY, and London: Cornell University Press, 1999), in which Ladenson writes that "no account of lesbianism in literature could be complete without coming to terms with Proust" (p. 4).
72. Carson, *Nox*, entry 1.3. The idea can be traced to Heidegger (see my Chapter 7).
73. Sontag, "On Style," *Against Interpretation and Other Essays* (1961; London and New York: Penguin Classics, 2009), pp. 15–36 (p. 28); Lisa Ruddick, 'When Nothing Is Cool', *The Future of Scholarly Writing*, ed. A. Bammer and R.-E. Boetcher Joeres (New York: Palgrave Macmillan, 2015), p. 71.
74. See Samuel Beckett, *Proust/Three Dialogues* (London: J. Calder, 1965).
75. René Girard, *Deceit, Desire and the Novel: Self and Other in Literary Structure*, trans. Yvonne Freccero (Baltimore, MD: Johns Hopkins University Press, 1965), p. 35.
76. Ibid.
77. See Jacqueline Rose, *Albertine* (2001; London: Vintage, 2002), and Angela Carter, *The Infernal Desire Machines of Doctor Hoffman* (1972; London: Penguin Books, 1986).
78. See Jeanette Winterson, *Frankissstein* (London and New York: Jonathan Cape, 2019); Marina Warner, *Indigo or Mapping the Waters* (London: Chatto and Windus, 1992), and Jean Rhys, *Wide Sargasso Sea* (1966; London: Penguin Books, 2000).
79. See "Appendix 40 on sleep theory," *The Albertine Workout*, p. 36. There are allusions to Heraklitos in *La Prisonnière* that may be Carson's source for the fictional letter. See Jacob Sider Jost, "Bergotte's Other Patch of Yellow: A Fragment of Heraclitus in Proust's *La prisonnière*," *Modern Philology* 112.4 (May 2015), 713–720. The context of the letter throws it off balance in ways that recall Carson's own essay on sleep in *Decreation*. Before writing the letter, Proust wakes in the aftermath of a dream, "swept aside by something that had passed; he wakes, we are told, 'on the wrong shore,'"

echoing Carson's paraphrasing of Jacques Lacan in "Every Exit Is an Entrance (A Praise of Sleep)": "sleep is a space from which the sleeper can travel in two directions, both of them a kind of waking" (*Decreation*, p. 22; see Chapter 5 of this book). Carson speaks of waking on the wrong side of sleep, entering a scene from real life "from the sleep side" (*Decreation*, p. 20). The things that theory cannot prevent from existing, the apocryphal letter scene suggests, are themselves of dubious origin, unplumbable things anchored deep in the life of fantasy, sleep, and dreams.

80. See Brady, *Poetry and Bondage* on the relationships between formal constraint in poetry and the experiences it transacts of freedom and liberty. Brady also proposes that notions of constraint (the "fetters of verse") depend, in turn, on the experiences of people in actual bondage.

81. Traces of Barthes's thinking are all over *Eros the Bittersweet* and *The Albertine Workout*. Carson quotes from *A Lover's Discourse*, *The Pleasure of the Text*, and *Camera Lucida*, but we can also find echoes of Barthes's many fantasies of neutralizing discursive power. This from *Roland Barthes par Roland Barthes* is perhaps the most powerful of his reflections on hermeneutic as well as linguistic forms of capture: Barthes recalls a childhood game, "prisoner's base," where, he says, "what I liked best was to free the prisoners—the effect of which was to put both teams back into circulation. . . . In the great game of the powers of speech, we also play prisoner's base: one language has only temporary rights over another." *Roland Barthes by Roland Barthes* (1975), trans. Richard Howard (Berkeley and Los Angeles: University of California Press, 1977), p. 50.

82. "Uncle Falling: A Pair of Lyric Lectures with Shared Chorus" in *Float* (unpaginated; the italics are Carson's).

83. The sonnet sequence was first performed at Harvard University's English Institute in 2007, following a commission by the University.

84. The sequence of sonnets has since been performed at the 92nd Street Y in New York and at Princeton University: https://english.princeton.edu/events/possessive-used-drink-me-lecture-pronouns-form-15-sonnets. A number of the sonnets are available to view on the University of Michigan's "Play Gallery" site: https://archive.org/details/podcast_play-gallery-posessive-used_431518246.

85. "Merce Sonnet" in "Possessive Used as Drink (Me): A Lecture on Pronouns in the Form of 15 Sonnets," *Float* (unpaginated). See Carson's performance of the sonnet at the 92nd Street Y, New York: https://www.youtube.com/watch?v=pLdAkDi5u9E.

86. Roger Copeland, *Merce Cunningham: The Modernizing of Modern Dance* (New York and London: Routledge, 2004), pp. 97–98.

87. Copeland, *Merce Cunningham*, p. 114. See Harriet and Sidney Janis, "Marchel Duchamp: Anti-Artist," *View: The Modern Magazine [Duchamp Issue]*, Series V, no. 1 (March 1945), reprinted in Robert Motherwell, ed., *The Dada Painters and Poets: An Anthology* (1951; Cambridge, MA: Harvard University Press, 1981), pp. 306–316 (p. 307: the correct quotation reads, "I have forced myself to contradict myself in order to avoid conforming to my own taste"). "Sonnet Isolate" was published in *London Review of Books* 32.21 (November 4, 2010), http://www.lrb.co.uk/v32/n21/anne-carson/sonnet-isolate. For a recording of the performance at the 92nd Street Y: https://www.youtube.com/watch?v=j8y5SvhpbwU from minute 4:32.

88. See Linda Hutcheon, "Interdisciplinary Opera Studies," *PMLA* 121.3 (May 2006), 802–810, and Linda Hutcheon and Michael Hutcheon, "Interdisciplinary Opera," *Journal of the Royal Musical Association* 134.1 (2009), 149–159.
89. Carson, *Eros the Bittersweet*, p. 14.
90. Berkobien, "An Interview with Anne Carson and Robert Currie."
91. Carson touches on related ideas in the long poem "Pronoun Envy," included among the pamphlets of *Float*.
92. From Carson, "Reticent Sonnet" in "Possessive Used as Drink (Me)," *Float* (unpaginated).
93. Carson, "The Glass Essay," in *Glass, Irony and God*, p. 2; Carson, *The Beauty of the Husband*, p. 34 ("There is something pure-edged and burning about the first infidelity in a marriage.... I cannot live without her. / Her, this word that explodes").
94. Anne Carson, "Triple Sonnet of the Plush Pony," published in *London Review of Books* 29.16 (August 16, 2007), 16, reprinted in *Float* (unpaginated). For a recording of "Triple Sonnet of the Plush Pony" at the 92nd Street Y: https://www.youtube.com/watch?v=j8y5SvhpbwU.
95. Carson, "Triple Sonnet of the Plush Pony Part II," "Triple Sonnet of the Plush Pony Part III," *Float* (unpaginated). Copyright © 2016 by Anne Carson. Used by permission of Alfred A. Knopf, an imprint of the Knopf Doubleday Publishing Group, a division of Penguin Random House LLC, and Jonathan Cape, a division of the Penguin Random House Group Limited. All rights reserved.
96. Carson, "Cassandra Float Can" in *Float* (unpaginated).
97. See Jean-Luc Nancy, *Le Partage des voix* (Paris: Éditions Galilée, 1982) on a "rhapsodic" hermeneutics; also see Jean-Luc Nancy, *À L'écoute* (Paris: Éditions Galilée, 2002), on the "sound"—the tone and timbre—of "listening" (p. 17). The phrase "dialogical rhapsody" is from Max Statkiewicz, *Rhapsody of Philosophy: Dialogues with Plato in Contemporary Thought* (University Park: Penn State University Press, 2009), p. 193.
98. Pickstock, *After Writing*, p. 5. See Derrida, *Dissémination*, p. 128.
99. Derrida's "insistence on the transcendental writtenness of language is," Pickstock says, "... a rationalistic gesture which suppresses embodiment and temporality." Pickstock, *After Writing*, p. 4.
100. Jorie Graham, "The Art of Poetry No. 85," interview by Thomas Gardner, *The Paris Review* (Spring 2003), no. 165, http://www.theparisreview.org/interviews/263/the-art-of-poetry-no-85-jorie-graham.
101. Carson, "Variations on the Right to Remain Silent," *Float* (unpaginated).
102. See Adorno, *Prisms*, p. 27 on the "hubris" of criticism and his remarks on criticism's "self-satisfied contemplation" (p. 34). In the same interview, Jorie Graham speaks of her poetry's efforts to "rebuild the shattered community of the *we*" through crossing into the reading time of the reader, even asking for his help. Graham, "The Art of Poetry no. 85."

Chapter 2

* This essay has received funding from the European Union's Horizon 2020 research and innovation program under the Marie Skłodowska-Curie grant agreement no. 887344.
1. "Letter to Hans Bender" (1960) in Paul Celan, *Collected Prose*, translated and with an introduction by Rosemarie Waldrop (1986; New York: Routledge, 2003), p. 26. Copyright © Rosemarie Waldrop 1986, 1999, 2003. Used by permission of Taylor and Francis Group LLC (Books) US through PLSclear.
2. "The Meridian" in Celan, *Collected Prose*, p. 53.
3. In the words of Bruce Krajewski in his review of the book for *Bryn Mawr Classical Review*. See Bruce Krajewski, "*Economy of the Unlost: Reading Simonides of Keos with Paul Celan* [Review]," *Bryn Mawr Classical Review* 2.39 (2003), https://bmcr.brynmawr.edu/2003/2003.02.39/. As Krajewski points out later in the review, the reception of Carson's book shows just how polarizing a figure she is: Stanley Corngold's review in *Modernism/Modernity* is awash with praise for the ingenuity of her reading: see Stanley Corngold, "*Economy of the Unlost: Reading Simonides of Keos with Paul Celan*" (review), *Modernism/Modernity* 7.2 (2000), 322–324. Steven Willett is strongly critical of its philological weaknesses: see Steven Willett, "*Economy of the Unlost: Reading Simonides of Keos with Paul Celan*," *Bryn Mawr Classical Review* 2.28 (2000), https://bmcr.brynmawr.edu/2000/2000.02.28.
4. "Grandiose" is one of the adjectives thrown at Carson's book by Willett, for whom this "slim" book suggests "the academic subgenre, the 'lyrical' meditation that rests on a few scholarly posts and often shows a distinct lack of interest in truth or lucidity." Willett highlights what he calls Carson's "casual respect for care, accuracy, evidence and logical reasoning," and concludes this scathing review, which includes a raft of appendices listing Carson's errors, that "the errors are of such extent and magnitude that they could seriously mislead someone not familiar with the scholarship, especially when Leslie Kurke assures us in the book jacket puff that it is a work of 'meticulous scholarship'" (Willett, "*Economy of the Unlost*," n.p.).
5. Carson, "Now What?," 43–45. Ian Rae describes Carson's use of adjoining scholarly introductions as a kind of hypotaxis, understood as the arrangement of unequal constructs in a sentence. See Rae, "Verglas," 164, 182. On the function of *scholia* throughout the history of Ancient Greek scholarship, see eds. Franco Montanari and Lara Pagani, *From Scholars to Scholia: Chapters in the History of Ancient Greek Scholarship* (Berlin: De Gruyter, 2011).
6. In Hölderlin, *Selected Poems and Fragments*, pp. 206–207. Quoted in Görner, "Hölderlin's Romantic Classicism," in ed. Hamilton, *The Oxford Handbook of European Romanticism*, p. 279.
7. Willett, "*Economy of the Unlost*" (n.p.). Willett is particularly severe in his remarks on the "Note on Method." In his view, the final paragraph of the extract I quote here can be parsed as follows: "If we unpack this statement, it tells us that (1) only some facts will be retained, (2) there will be little method behind their retention, (3) they will be employed capriciously as they excite attention and (4) 'creative' exploitation will take

precedence over careful reasoning from evidence. That is a good summary of what EU. gives us."

8. Carson's reference is to Lukács, "Die Subjekt-Objekt Beziehung in der Ästhetik" (1917), *Logos* (1917–1918), 14–28 (19).

9. See the extended discussion of *Short Talks* in the Postscript to this book. The remark on *Short Talks* is from Rachel Wyatt, quoted on the dust jacket of the Brick Books edition.

10. Alongside Lukacs's proposed excision of the world beyond *Erlebbarkeit*, Carson's remarks also invoke Martin Heidegger's notion of *Lichtung* (translated as "Clearing" but rooted in *Licht*, so a space opened for light to pass). The word suggests not just excision—clearing away, clearing out—but an open, illuminated space into which less readily heeded forms of meaning can be perceived; a counterpoint to the "darkening landscape" of material fact.

11. Carson, *Short Talks*, p. 23.

12. Hans Georg Gadamer, *Gadamer on Celan: "Who Am I and Who Are You?" and Other Essays*, ed. and trans. Richard Heinemann and Bruce Krajewski (Albany: State University of New York Press, 1997), pp. 149–150. The similarity of this statement to Carson's was suggested to me by Amador Vega, who quotes Gadamer's confession in an illuminating comparative essay on Celan, Meister Eckhart, and the German priest, poet, and mystic Angelus Silesius: Amador Vega, *Tres poetas del exceso: La hermenéutica imposible en Eckhart, Silesius y Celan* (Barcelona: Fragmenta Editorial, 2011), pp. 90–91.

13. The listing of etymological and historical facts also appears in *Norma Jeane Baker of Troy*, Carson's adaptation of Euripides's *Helen*, as a means of calling attention to ambiguities and lacunae in the narratives of both the mythic Helen and the historical Marilyn Monroe. The use of associative "footnotes" can also be seen in Carson's experimental "Lecture on the History of Skywriting," performed at the Whitney Museum of American Art in collaboration with Robert Currie and Faisal bin Ali Jaber, an engineer from Yemen, on May 27, 2016: https://whitney.org/education/education-blog/skywriting-lecture.

14. The phrase appears in the second line of Catullus's "Poem 101" in Carson's translation. See *Nox*, 7.2 (facing the glossary entry for "prisco").

15. See Paul Celan, *The Meridian. Final Version. Drafts. Materials*, ed. Bernhardt Böschenstein and Heino Schmull, trans. Pierre Joris (Palo Alto, CA: Stanford University Press, 2011), p. 104 (from Celan's notes on "The Poem"). Celan's remarks on the poem as "encounter" (*Begegnung*) are discussed and referenced in note 40 below.

16. John Felstiner, *Paul Celan: Poet, Survivor, Jew* (New Haven, CT, and London: Yale University Press, 1995), p. xvi. Felstiner notes that the word *du* is "voiced some 1,300 times in over three decades of verse" (p. xvi). Felstiner discusses Celan's use of both "the intimate "you"" (*du*) and the "addressable thou" of "*Du / und Aber-Du*" in "Zurich, at the Stork" (p. 158).

17. Carson, ""Echo with No Door on Her Mouth," 255–256.

18. See D'Agata, "A___ with Anne Carson," 17. Carson also responds to the following question from Kevin McNeilly: "Do you see poems as gifts?"—"Ideally." McNeilly, "Gifts and Questions," 15.
19. Danielle Allen, "Review (*Economy of the Unlost*)," *Chicago Review*, 46.1 (2000), 162–164 (164).
20. George Steiner, *Real Presences* (Chicago: University of Chicago Press, 1989), p. 157. Steiner's utopian argument for interpretation as the performance (as in virtuoso "execution") of a source object, as in the live interpretation of a musical score, and his call, after Geoffrey Hartman, for a form of criticism "answerable" to its object, is an argument borne out, to a certain extent, by Carson's reading of Celan. (Steiner, incidentally, was an avowed admirer of both poets). See G. Douglas Atkins, *Geoffrey Hartman: Criticism as Answerable Style* (London and New York: Routledge, 1990).
21. According to records of the Charles Beebe Martin Classical Lectures held at Oberlin College, Carson's original lecture series was titled as follows: Anne Carson (McGill University), *Greed: A Fractal Approach to Simonides* (1992). April 27, "The Art of Negative Attention"; April 28, "Radical Defect Radical Eye: Greed for the Invisible"; April 30, "Writing on the World: Greed for Exactitude"; May 1, "Your Money or Your Life."
22. Carson's academic output in the years running up to the Lectures bears this out. Material and ideas revisited in the lectures and in *Economy of the Unlost* first appears in several earlier journal articles and prose pieces. See, e.g., Anne Carson, "Simonides Negative," *Arethusa* 21.2 (Fall 1988), 147–157; "'Just for the Thrill,'" 144–146; and "Economy, Its Fragrance," 14–16 ("If I were marketing the poetry/prose distinction as a perfume, I would call it *Economy*" . . . "Economic measures allow poetry to practice what I take to be its principal subversion. That is, insofar as it is economic, poetry relies on a gesture which it simultaneously dismantles," 14). It should be emphasized that Celan is not an afterthought to Carson's early work on economy. The reading of his "No More Sand Art" that appears in *Economy of the Unlost* makes an unexpected appearance in the final part of "Economy, Its Fragrance" (15). Indeed, the essay might be read as a compact early rehearsal of *Economy of the Unlost*.
23. Carson, *Economy of the Unlost*, p. 15. The phrase also makes a cameo appearance in the title of Elizabeth Lowry's review of *Economy of the Unlost* and *Autobiography of Red*: Elizabeth Lowry, "The Man Who Would Put to Sea on a Bathmat," *London Review of Books* 22.19 (October 5, 2000), https://www.lrb.co.uk/the-paper/v22/n19/elizabeth-lowry/the-man-who-would-put-to-sea-on-a-bathmat.
24. Carson's reference for her quotation from Bourdieu is J. G. Peristiany, *Honor and Shame: The Values of Mediterranean Society* (Chicago: University of Chicago Press, 1966), p. 210.
25. See J. Hillis Miller, "The Critic as Host," *Critical Inquiry* 3.3 (Spring 1977), 439–447.
26. Carson also discusses uses and forms of the *symbolon* in *Eros the Bittersweet*, pp. 70–76. For broader definitions of the Greek term, see Liddell and Scott, p. 663.
27. At the end of his highly critical review of *Economy of the Unlost*, Willett compiles a long list of philological and biographical "blunders" littering Carson's essay, and is particularly censorious of what he suggests is her naïveté or wishful thinking in her

treatment of the biographical myths grown up around Simonides of Keos. Curiously, given Carson's Classical training, most of the errors Willett attributes to her essay apply to her readings of Simonides, where unattributed sources and the scarcity of corroboratory material are the condition for a degree of poetic license that, Willett argues, would be impermissible in the case of Celan. Willett, "*Economy of the Unlost.*"

28. See Homer, *The Odyssey*, trans. Emily Wilson (London and New York: Norton, 2018). Odysseus's vivid recounting runs from Book 9 to Book 13, whereupon we hear his audience "praised his words ... since he had spoken well" (p. 318, Book 13, lines 48–49).

29. E.g., M. M. Austin and P. Vidal-Naquet, *Economic and Social History of Ancient Greece: An Introduction* (Berkeley: University of California Press, 1977); Ian Morris, "Gift and Commodity in Archaic Greece," *Man* 21.1 (March 1986), 1–17; in addition to Marcel Mauss's *The Gift: Forms and Functions of Exchange in Archaic Societies*, trans. I. Cunnison (1925; New York: Norton, 1967). Carson explores the versatility of *charis*, whose meaning moves between "return favour" and "free gift," in the essay "Echo with No Door on Her Mouth: A Notional Refraction through Sophokles, Plato, and Defoe."

30. Jacques Derrida, *Given Time: I. Counterfeit Money* (1991), trans. Peggy Kamuf (Chicago: University of Chicago Press, 1992), p. 30.

31. Roland Barthes, "The Death of the Author" (1967), in his *Image, Music, Text*, trans. Stephen Heath (London: Fontana Press, 1977), p. 142.

32. Barthes, *A Lover's Discourse*, p. 75.

33. In his attempted takedown of Carson, Solway reads Carson's chapter "No More Sand Art" and argues "the few interesting things Carson does have to say about Celan's poem are cribbed almost verbatim" from Felstiner's *Paul Celan: Poet, Survivor, Jew*. See Solway, "The Trouble with Annie," 24. Also see Rae's strong riposte to Solway in "Anne Carson and the Solway Hoaxes," where Rae acknowledges Carson "draws heavily from Felstiner" but notes that Felstiner is referenced frequently throughout the book, suggesting Carson makes no attempt to hide her debt to Celan's biographer and one of his finest readers. Rae, "Anne Carson and the Solway Hoaxes," 46.

34. Barthes, *Criticism and Truth*, p. 37.

35. Walter Benjamin, "The Task of the Translator" (1923), in *Selected Writings, Volume I: 1913–1926*, ed. Marcus Bullock and Michael W. Jennings (Cambridge, MA: Harvard University Press, 1996), pp. 253–263. Benjamin, citing Rudolf Pannwitz, argues in favor of the translator "allowing his language to be powerfully affected by the foreign tongue": in this case, then, of Carson allowing her English to be Germanized (p. 262).

36. The most famous instance of the demand placed by Celan on individual letters is in the final lines of the poem "No More Sand Art" ["Keine Sandkunst mehr"]: "Your song, what does it know? // Deepinsnow, / Eepinnow, / Ee-i-o." ["Dein Gesang, was weiß er? // Tiefimschnee, / Iefimnee, / I–i–e"]: Paul Celan, *Poems of Paul Celan*, trans. Michael Hamburger (1972; London: Anvil Press, 2007), pp. 268–269. John Felstiner notes that "translated into Hebrew, which has no vowel letters, this poem would verge on silence—a testimony to the literal truth that Celan sought" (Felstiner, *Paul Celan*, p. 220). Carson makes a similar observation in her essay: "For one cannot help but think, watching 'Deepinsnow' melt away, that if this poem were translated into

Hebrew, a language in which vowels are not usually printed, it would vanish even before its appointed end. As did many a Hebrew": Carson, *Economy of the Unlost*, p. 116.

37. A similar reading of "with" and the first lines of John 1 is presented in Forrest Gander's collection *Be With*, in the poem "First Ballad: A Wreath," a loose translation of the first ballad of St. John of the Cross: In the beginning the Word / was as being / In happiness / infinitely the Word possessed // The same Word being was / said to be beginning // Beginninglessly / it went on." See Forrest Gander, *Be With* (New York: New Directions, 2018), p. 32.

38. See André Furlani, "Reading Paul Celan with Anne Carson: What Kind of Withness Would That Be?," *Canadian Literature* 176 (Spring 2003), 84–104. The question in the title of Furlani's article is taken from Carson's poem, "God's Christ Theory" (Carson, *Glass, Irony and God*, p. 51).

39. See "L.A.," a selection of works composed for Laurie Anderson, in *Float* (unpaginated).

40. Celan speaks of the "encounter" (*Begegnung*) of poetry in the following terms: "The poem is lonely. It is lonely and *en route*. Its author stays with it. Does this very fact not place the poem already here, at its inception, in the encounter, *in the mystery of encounter?*" [*im Geheimnis der Begegnung*]. Celan, *Collected Prose*, p. 49. See Martin Heidegger, *Being and Time*, trans. John Macquarrie and Edward Robinson (Oxford: Blackwell, 1962, 2005), Part I: IV, pp. 149–162.

41. Willett, "*Economy of the Unlost*" (n.p.).

42. Ibid. (n.p.).

43. See Rita Felski's discussion of description and redescription as alternatives to "suspicious" critique: Rita Felski, *The Limits of Critique*, e.g., pp. 17, 30.

44. Carson's "slapdash" use of sources in her readings of Simonides, making the case for the distant closeness of his and Celan's poetics, is one of the points criticized most heavily by Steven Willett (Willet, "*Economy of the Unlost*," n.p.). He states: "She begins by comparing Celan's "Matière de Bretagne," which combines a wide range of other poetic traditions focused on a single dramatic moment when the false sail appears to Tristan, with two citations from Simonides: (1) a passage from Plutarch's *Life of Theseus* (17.4, fr. 550 PMG) in which Simonides says that the false sail which misled Theseus' father was red and (2) a scholiast who reports the words of the messenger sent to inform Aegeus of the true story (fr. 551 PMG). Celan's use of negatives and negative theology is well known, but C. now argues that the negative in the first and the counterfactual in the second passage show that 'Negation links the mentalities of Simonides and Celan' (9). They do no such thing. In the *Life of Theseus*, the statement that the sail was "not white" belongs to Plutarch's prose, the statement that it was a kind of red belongs to Simonides' poem. Whether Simonides used a negative here is unknown."

45. Paul Celan, *Gesammelte Werke*, 5 vols. (Frankfurt: Suhrkamp, 1983), vol. 1, p. 171, translated by Carson in *Economy of the Unlost*, p. 5.

46. *Poems of Paul Celan*, pp. 142–143.

47. Ibid., pp. 70–71.

48. Benjamin, "The Task of the Translator," p. 260.

49. Ibid.

50. On the reproduction of meter in her own practice of translation, Carson has said: "I wouldn't say there's metrical fidelity to the original meters, which isn't reproducible, but there's a new rhythmic design to take in the English sounds and the shifting content." See Berkobien, "An Interview with Anne Carson and Robert Currie" (n.p.).
51. See Hutcheon, *A Theory of Parody*, p. 38.
52. Ibid., p. 32.
53. Carson, *Decreation*, p. 175.
54. Willett, "*Economy of the Unlost*" (n.p.).
55. Ibid. (n.p.).
56. Ibid. (n.p.).
57. Carson cites this description of Mallarmé from Jean-Paul Sartre, marking out the lines of a poetic tradition joining Mallarmé to Celan (and perhaps Carson herself). Jean-Paul Sartre, *Mallarmé or the Poet of Nothingness*, trans. E. Sturm (University Park: Penn State University Press, 1988), cited in Carson, *Economy of the Unlost*, p. 6.
58. Culler, *Theory of the Lyric*, p. 226.
59. See Mutlu Konuk Blasing's powerful argument for the public, emotional resonances of language, the community invoked in the mother tongue, as what sustains the lyric "I." Mutlu Konuk Blasing, *Lyric Poetry: The Pain and the Pleasure of Words* (Princeton, NJ, and Oxford: Princeton University Press, 2007).

Chapter 3

* This essay has received funding from the European Union's Horizon 2020 research and innovation program under the Marie Skłodowska-Curie grant agreement no. 887344.
1. Carson, *Glass, Irony and God*, "Introduction" by Guy Davenport, ix.
2. John D'Agata and Deborah Tall, "New Terrain: the Lyric Essay," *Seneca Review* 27.2 (Fall 1997), 7. Ian Rae has discussed the influence of essayistic practices such as those of Michel de Montaigne in "The Glass Essay": see Rae, "Verglas," 164–165.
3. Mary Gannon, "Anne Carson: Beauty Prefers an Edge," *Poets and Writers* 29.2 (March–April 2001), 26–33 (33).
4. Carson, *Glass, Irony and God*, "Introduction" by Guy Davenport, ix.
5. The phrase summarizes a critical tradition long nourished on what Brontë scholar Lucasta Miller calls the "Brontë myth": a reading of her work that assumes its visionary, metaphysical inspiration. See Lucasta Miller, *The Brontë Myth* (London: Jonathan Cape, 2001).
6. Carson, *Economy of the Unlost*, p. viii.
7. See, e.g., Carson, "Ordinary Time: Virginia Woolf and Thucydides on War" and "Appendix on Ordinary Time," *Men in the Off Hours*, pp. 3–8 and pp. 165–166, as well as *The Beauty of the Husband* (discussed in Chapter 4 of this book) and *Nox* (discussed in Chapter 7).
8. Carson, "God's Christ Theory," in *Glass, Irony and God*, p. 51.

9. See the poem sequences "The Truth About God" and "Book of Isaiah" in *Glass, Irony and God*, pp. 39–54 and pp. 107–118. The poem "Teresa of God" appears halfway through the first of these sequences (pp. 44–45).
10. See D'Agata, "A __ with Anne Carson," 12.
11. As per my benchmarks for the lyric in this book: Vendler's "performance of the mind in solitary speech," often in Carson a performance of the mind in and after reading, and especially Culler's "iterative and iterable performance of an event in the lyric present." See Helen Vendler, "Introduction" to *The Art of Shakespeare's Sonnets*, reproduced in *A Lyric Theory Reader*, ed. Jackson and Prins, pp. 128–140 (p. 129), and Culler, *Theory of the Lyric*, p. 226.
12. Juliana Spahr, "Introduction" to *American Women Poets in the 21st Century: Where Lyric Meets Language* (2002), reprinted in ed. Jackson and Prins, *The Lyric Theory Reader*, p. 557.
13. Emily Brontë's original punctuation, prior to the intervention of her sister, can be seen in the first published edition of poems by Charlotte, Emily, and Anne Brontë: *Poems by Currer, Ellis and Acton Bell* (London: Aylott and Jones, 1846), access courtesy of the Munby Rare Books Room, Cambridge University Library. The edition of Brontë's poems to which I refer in this chapter, unless otherwise stated, is *The Poems of Emily Brontë*, ed. Barbara Lloyd-Evans (London: B. T Batsford, 1992, hereafter *Poems*). Emily Brontë's "erratic" spellings are listed in Appendix 2 of the *Poems*, beside an editorial rationale for their excision and regularization. See *Poems*, p. 185.
14. See John Milton, "When I Consider..." (Sonnet XIX), in *Complete Poems and Major Prose*, ed. Meritt Y. Hughes (1957; Cambridge and Indianapolis: Hackett, 2003), p. 168 (lines 2 and 4).
15. See Carson's remarks in Dean, "Anne Carson Punches a Hole Through Greek Myth."
16. See Rae, "Verglas," 168–171. See also Aitken, "The Art of Poetry No. 88," 206, where the poem's image of "a frozen ditch" is cited.
17. See Erica McAlpine's work on mistakes in poems and on the history of their reading. Erica McAlpine, *The Poet's Mistake* (Princeton, NJ: Princeton University Press, 2020).
18. The phrase appears in Charlotte Bronte's preface to *Wuthering Heights*, and is quoted at several points by Stevie Davies in her book, *Emily Brontë: Heretic* (London: The Women's Press, 1994). Carson makes much of Charlotte Brontë's interventions, setting them up as an analog to the role of the narrator's mother in the text. Ian Rae, for example, discusses several possibilities for the pronunciation of "whacher." Where the word has been read as belonging to a category of "portmanteaux" (a single word composed of two separate words), Rae suggests such words "might better be defined as nonce-words": "because the terms are personal, provisional, and often irregular in spelling" ("Verglas," 176).
19. Carson also reflects on the loneliness of Charlotte after Emily's death in "Short Talk on Charlotte," *Short Talks*, p. 58.
20. See Carson, "Appendix to Ordinary Time," *Men in the Off Hours*, pp. 165–166 (p. 166).
21. Howe, *The Birth-mark*, p. 1.
22. Ibid. pp. 15, 9. Howe also speaks in *My Emily Dickinson* of a misreading that begins with "canonical criticism [... that] persists in dropping [Dickinson and other's]

names and ignoring their work": Howe, *My Emily Dickinson*, p. 11. The poet Claudia Rankine proclaims her own romantic attachment to Dickinson, though she appeals to a very different set of circumstances—the history of disqualification of black lives—in her address to her reclusive predecessor: "sadness lives in the recognition that a life can not matter. Or, as there are billions of lives, my sadness is alive alongside the recognition that billions of lives never mattered. I write this without breaking my heart, without bursting into anything. Perhaps this is the real source of my sadness. Or, perhaps, Emily Dickinson, my love, hope was never a thing with feathers." Rankine's reference is to Dickinson's famous poem "'Hope' is the Thing with Feathers," for which hope "perches in the soul - / And sings the tune without the words —": in this prose section of Rankine's poem, and for the historical injustices she invokes without hope of redress, the words are to be sung without the tune. See Rankine, *Don't Let Me Be Lonely*, pp. 22–23.

23. Walter Benn Michaels writes illuminatingly on Howe's commitment to the material ontology of the Dickinson fascicles. See Walter Benn Michaels, *The Shape of the Signifier, 1967 to the End of History* (Princeton, NJ: Princeton University Press, 2006), Introduction: "The Blank Page" (especially pp. 3–5).

24. Susan Howe quotes a remarkably similar reading of Emily Dickinson by T. H. Johnson, editor of Dickinson's poems for Harvard University Press: "'her creative energies were at flood, and she was being overwhelmed by forces which she could not control' (PED xviii)." See Howe, *The Birth-mark*, p. 149. The origin of Brontë's *poiesis* has long been the object of scholarly mystification, linked for almost as long to her alleged Mystical experiences. Although there is evidence for Brontë's conversancy with elements of Kantian idealism—Thomas Carlyle's essay on Novalis in *Critical and Miscellaneous Essays* of 1839 is a likely candidate—Brontë scholar Lucasta Miller is at pains to stress the extent to which Brontë's writing process has been mythologized at the expense of her work's critical reading. See Miller, *The Brontë Myth*, in particular the chapter "The Mystic of the Moors" (pp. 251–288). Miller cites May Sinclair's idiosyncratic 1912 study, *The Three Brontës*, as instantiating a twentieth-century tradition of transcendental explanations for Emily Brontë's writing.

25. This again tallies with predominant readings of Emily Dickinson, whose relation to the figure she addresses as "Master" has been understood as decisive, Susan Howe shows, in transforming her from a maker of "verses" into a poet. See Howe, *The Birth-mark*, pp. 132–134 (133).

26. Margaret Homans, *Women Writers and Poetic Identity* (Princeton, NJ: Princeton University Press, 1980), p. 104.

27. Ibid., p. 108.

28. *Poems*, p. 50. In poem 26 in the earliest available manuscript of Brontë's poems, the "EJB MS," transcribed in February 1844, Brontë figures this expansive ambivalence to the muse: "Thee, ever present, phantom thing, / My slave, my comrade and my King!" See *Poems*, p. 56.

29. F. R. and Q. D. Leavis, *Lectures in America* (London: Chatto and Windus, 1969), pp. 83–152, my italics. Leavis's criticism is a strong example of the "Intentional

Fallacy" theorized by W. K. Wimsatt and M. C. Beardsley in *The Verbal Icon* (1954; London: Methuen, 1970).

30. In his essay "Experimentum Linguae," Giorgio Agamben writes of the "unwritten work" to which every text is prologue or afterword. See Giorgio Agamben, *Infancy and History* (1979), trans. Liz Heron (London: Verso, 1993), p. 3.
31. Frank Kermode, *The Classic: Literary Images of Permanence and Change* (Cambridge, MA: Harvard University Press, 1983), p. 133.
32. A list of Brontë's "erratic" spellings can be found in Appendix 2 of the *Poems*, alongside an editorial rationale for their excision and regularization. See *Poems*, p. 185.
33. Rae, "Verglas," 177. Rae proposes that the poem be understood as staging a dialogue between "I" and "Aw," the latter the Yorkshire dialect term for "I" as spoken by minor characters in *Wuthering Heights* (176–177).
34. Carson, "Stanzas, Sexes, Seductions," *Decreation*, pp. 72–73.
35. See *A Concordance to the Complete Poems of Emily Jane Brontë*, eds. S. Akiho and T. Fujita (Tokyo: Shohakusha, 1976). Carson quotes the line from Brontë's "At Castle Wood," in "The Glass Essay," *Glass, Irony and God*, p. 30.
36. In Brontë's "The Prisoner. A Fragment," sight and sounding are described as an affliction for the soul bound to the sensible body: "Oh, dreadful is the check—intense the agony—When the ear begins to hear, and the eye begins to see; When the pulse begins to throb, the brain to think again; The soul to feel the flesh, and the flesh to feel the chain."
37. See David James's powerful inquiry into the consolations of fiction and life-writing, and "the critical work contemporary literature itself can perform when evoking consolation's experiential and representational complexities": David James, *Discrepant Solace: Contemporary Literature and the Work of Consolation* (Oxford: Oxford University Press, 2019), p. 8.
38. Chihaya, "A Glass Essay: Reading Anne Carson Post-breakup."

Chapter 4

1. Wachtel, "An Interview with Anne Carson." Carson speaks in similar terms of her handling of classical sources: "to jump from what you know into empty space and see where you end up." See Rehak, "Things Fall Together."
2. See Stanton, "I am writing this to be as wrong as possible to you."
3. Carson, "Uncle Falling: A Pair of Lyric Lectures with Shared Chorus," *Float* (unpaginated).
4. Gannon, "Beauty Prefers an Edge," 33.
5. The remarks appear in DuPlessis's landmark essay "For the Etruscans," in *The Pink Guitar*, p. 5. In the freeform essay, DuPlessis inquires into "the production of formal, epistemological, and thematic strategies by members of the group Woman," which she considers in relation to the rhetorical limitations of "formal argument" (p. 6). Woolf's remarks, quoted by DuPlessis (p. 5), appear in Virginia Woolf, "Mrs. Thrale,"

in Woolf, *The Moment and Other Essays* (1949; New York: Harcourt Brace Jovanovich, 1974), p. 52.

6. Barthes, *A Lover's Discourse*, p. 7. Barthes's confession of his "piratical law"—"I follow a somewhat piratical law that doesn't always recognize original property. Not at all from a spirit of contestation, but from the immediacy of desire"—appears in Barthes, *The Grain of the Voice*, p. 277. Andrea Rexilius has remarked on the relevance of Barthes to Carson's representation of desire in *The Beauty of the Husband*, and is one of few readers to engage with the significance of the tango in the work. See Andrea Rexilius, "The Light of This Wound: Marriage, Longing, Desire in Anne Carson's *The Beauty of the Husband*," in ed. Wilkinson, *Anne Carson: Ecstatic Lyre*, pp. 107–113.
7. Barthes, *A Lover's Discourse*, p. 3 (italics mine).
8. Ibid.
9. Culler, *Theory of the Lyric*, p. 226.
10. B. K. Fischer remarks that "Carson's dominant mode in *The Beauty of the Husband* ... is not painterly but dancerly ... the poem's tempo and pacing mimic the dance's alternation of long steps with quick complicated ones, as well as its exaggerated posturing. Carson's frequent use of tercets with lines of shortening lengths evokes the tango's centrifugal arc." See B. K. Fischer, "Review: Carson, Fulton, Rankine," *Boston Review*, July 15, 2014, https://bostonreview.net/articles/bk-fischer-review-carson-fulton-rankine/.
11. Anne Carson, "The Keats Headaches," *Times Literary Supplement*, February 22, 2019, https://www.the-tls.co.uk/articles/the-keats-headaches/. See note 54 below on the Foucauldian affiliations of Carson's expression.
12. See Elizabeth S. Anker on the extreme metafiction of J. M. Coetzee, which poses comparable difficulties for suspicious reading models. See Elizabeth S. Anker, "Why We Love Coetzee; or, *The Childhood of Jesus* and the Funhouse of Critique," in *Critique and Postcritique*, ed. Anker and Felski, pp. 183–210.
13. Barthes, *A Lover's Discourse*, p. 75. Barthes, *Fragments d'un discours amoureux*, p. 89 (*le délire—ou le leurre dans lequel je suis pris*).
14. See Carson, "The Keats Headaches," which stages the narrator's blending and unblending with the biography of Keats as she wrestles with headaches "crashing on all coasts of me." The exchanges between these stories recalls the staged identifications with Emily Brontë in "The Glass Essay."
15. This is also a concern of Barthes's (see Chapter 1, note 81).
16. In Euripides's *Helen*, one of the principal literary transmissions of the Persephone myth, Demeter is referred to as "the Mother." Carson's text sets up a structural parallel with the *Hymn to Demeter*, casting the narrator's mother as a stalwart against seduction. Carson's 2018 version of the *Helen* is discussed in Chapter 6 of this book.
17. Cleanth Brooks, *The Well Wrought Urn: Studies in the Structure of Poetry* (1947; London: Methuen, 1949), p. 124.
18. John Keats, "Ode on a Grecian Urn," in *Keats: Poetical Works*, ed. H. W. Garrod (Oxford: Oxford University Press, 1956; 1990), pp. 209–210 (p. 210).
19. Ibid.
20. McNeilly, "Gifts and Questions," 20.

21. C. Namwali Serpell, "A Heap of Cliché," in Anker and Felski, eds., *Critique and Postcritique*, pp. 153–182 (p. 159). Serpell's remarks refer to literary cliché in general.
22. Paul Ricoeur, *The Rule of Metaphor* (1975), trans., Robert Czerny with Kathleen McLaughlin and John Costello, Routledge Classics (London and New York: Routledge, 2004), p. 6.
23. The characterization of metonymy as "devouring" is Roland Barthes's. See Barthes, *A Lover's Discourse*, p. 75.
24. Carson, "Stanzas, Sexes, Seductions," *Decreation*, p. 72.
25. The term is Robert Potts's, though Solway's sentiments toward Carson are similar. See Potts, "Neither Rhyme nor Reason."
26. See James Longenbach, *The Resistance to Poetry* (Chicago: University of Chicago Press, 2004), where Longenbach argues that the elements in poetry that push against or sabotage themselves are in fact "the wonder of poetry." Resistance is what distinguishes poetry from writing whose function is to transmit knowledge or information without obstructing it.
27. Carson, "Stillness," 12.
28. See Fredric Jameson, *Valences of the Dialectic* (New York: Verso, 2009), pp. 475–509 (p. 475).
29. *Keats: Poetical Works*, pp. 207–209.
30. See Culler's powerful, synthetic definition in Culler, *Theory of the Lyric*, p. 226.
31. Carson seems, too, to have Walter Benjamin's "one true language" in mind. See Walter Benjamin, "The Task of the Translator," *Selected Writings*, Volume 1, pp. 253–263 (p. 259).
32. Giorgio Agamben, *The Idea of Prose* (1985), trans. Michael Sullivan and Sam Whitsitt (Albany: State University of New York Press, 1995), pp. 47–48.
33. Ibid., p. 48.
34. See Carson's vignette in the "Decreation" essay in which she describes a childhood urge to eat the pages of *The Lives of the Saints* (*Decreation*, p. 175). Though Carson's "Notes" mention neither Dante nor Agamben, they refer to "Johann Sebastian Bach, Cantata, BWV, 56; Rev. 7.15–17." Bach's so-called cross cantata (from its title "Ich will den Kreuzstab" [I shall willingly carry the cross-staff]) departs from the text of Matthew 1–18 to reflect on the suffering of man's "pilgrimage" "to God, in the promised land" ("zu Gott in das gelobte Land"), a journey which is compared in the cantata to a sea voyage and arrival at the "port of my rest" ("Port der Ruhe"). Resonances with Dante's pilgrimage in *The Divine Comedy*, with the mother tongue as a "port of rest," are possible but oblique. See the entry for "Ich will den Kreuzstab gerne tragen," *Oxford Composer Companions: J. S. Bach*, ed. Malcolm Boyd (Oxford: Oxford University Press, 1999), p. 489.
35. Agamben, *The Idea of Prose*, p. 48.
36. Barthes, *A Lover's Discourse*, p. 9. A small but significant cache of material absorbed by Carson's narrative concerns the work of Marcel Duchamp, as discussed toward the end of this chapter.
37. Carson's reference is to "Plato, *Phaedrus*, 264." The idea of "cuts" expressed here returns in Carson's experimental lecture "Cassandra Float Can," in which she

describes "cuts" and "incisions" revealing the internal structures of, respectively, the Trojan language as uttered by Aeschylus's Cassandra, the thought and shorthand of Edmund Husserl, and the buildings into which "anarchitect" Gordon Matta-Clark made his interventions (*Float*, unpaginated). See my Chapters 7 and 8 for discussions of the lecture.

38. McNeilly, "Gifts and Questions," 20.
39. Both texts were published in the 1848 volume *Literary Remains*. See *Keats: Poetical Works*, pp. 247–306 and pp. 316–340.
40. It is perhaps easy to see why Carson chose these works, given their parallels with the jealous intrigues of her narrator. However, her own remarks on the spuriousness of the fragments (which she chose for their "shininess") suggest we would do best not to take these parallels too seriously. See McNeilly, "Gifts and Questions," 20.
41. Carson provides references for a number of her allusions to Keats at the end of the book, but the reference for this sighting is not among them. The vignette is taken from a letter sent in 1817 from the Isle of Wight, in which Keats reports local opinion that the island had been ruined by the presence of soldiers, an opinion he later finds expressed in the graffiti on glass: "In the room where I slept at Newport I found this on the window "O Isle spoilt by the Milatary." See John Keats, "Letter to J. H. Reynolds, 17–18 April 1817," in *The Letters of John Keats, 1814–1821*, ed. Hyder Edward Rollins, 2 vols. (Cambridge, MA: Harvard Univ. Press, 1958), volume I, pp. 131–132.
42. See Howe, *My Emily Dickinson*.
43. Howe, *The Birth-mark*, p. 9.
44. See Marcel Duchamp, *The Essential Writings of Marcel Duchamp*, ed. Michel Sanouillet and Elmer Peterson (London: Thames and Hudson, 1973), p. 26.
45. Duchamp famously expressed his preference for the work following the damage ("It's a lot better with the breaks, a hundred times better. It's the destiny of things."). See Pierre Cabanne, *Dialogues with Marcel Duchamp*, trans. Ron Padgett (London: Thames and Hudson, 1971), pp. 75–76.
46. Carson, "Variations on the Right to Remain Silent," *Float*, unpaginated.
47. Barthes, *The Responsibility of Forms*, p. 234.
48. *Keats: Poetical Works*, p. 209.
49. Brooks, *The Well Wrought Urn*, pp. 130, 129.
50. Ronald Alley, *Catalogue of the Tate Gallery's Collection of Modern Art other than Works by British Artists* (London: Tate Gallery and Sotheby Parke-Bernet, 1981), pp. 186–191 (p. 186).
51. Octavio Paz, *Apariencia desnuda: La obra de Marcel Duchamp* (Mexico City: El Colegio nacional/Ediciones Era, 2008), pp. 39, 15 (my translation).
52. See Eco, *The Open Work*.
53. Paz, *Apariencia desnuda*, pp. 46, 38.
54. Carson's reference in the "Notes" is to Jean Baudrillard, *Forget Foucault* [1977], trans. Nicole Dufresne (New York, 1987), 34, where Baudrillard speaks of "the agony of sexual reason" and summarizes Foucault's notion of "transparence" in *Discipline and Punish*. Unconvinced, Baudrillard explains how the "simulating device" ostensibly replicates the work of the "original" or "desiring machines" of "libidinal energy" (33–34). See also Jerrold Seigel, *The Private Worlds of Marcel Duchamp: Desire, Liberation*

and the Self in Modern Culture (Berkeley: University of California Press, 1997), p. 120, and Lawrence Steefel, "Marcel Duchamp and the Machine," in *Marcel Duchamp*, ed. Anne D'Harnoncourt and Kynaston McShine (New York: Museum of Modern Art, 1973), pp. 69–80.

55. Examples include Duchamp's *Rotary Demiphere (Precision Optics)*, 1924. See the wonderful essay by Rosalind Krauss, "The Story of the Eye," *New Literary History* 21.2 (Winter 1990), 283–298, which provides a fascinating account of the theoretical foundations of "Op' Art."

56. It should be emphasized that Duchamp was strongly against this notion: "One has to be on guard because, despite oneself, one can become invaded by things of the past. Without wanting to, one puts in some detail. There [in *The Bride Stripped Bare by Her Bachelors, Even*] it was a constant battle to make an exact and complete break." See Cabanne, *Dialogues with Marcel Duchamp*, p. 38.

57. J. M. Bernstein, *Against Voluptuous Bodies: Late Modernism and the Meaning of Painting* (Stanford, CA: Stanford University Press, 2006), p. 247.

58. Brooks, *The Well Wrought Urn*, pp. 124, 134.

59. See Jacques Herzog and Pierre De Meuron, *Treacherous Transparencies: Thoughts and Observations Triggered by a Visit to the Farnsworth House* (Barcelona: Actar/IITAC Press, 2016); Leighton, *On Form*, p. 3.

60. Brooks discusses the readings suggested by "enigmatic parable" of the "Ode," including the suggestion, if we emphasize the second variant, "*truth* [is] beauty" of "a propaganda art." Brooks, *The Well Wrought Urn*, p. 125.

61. Paz describes the Readymade as a form of "active critique," suggesting its critical function is performative, not expository. Paz, *Apariencia desnuda*, p. 31.

62. See Rachel Blau Duplessis, "Sub Rrosa: Marcel Duchamp and the Female Spectator," in DuPlessis, *The Pink Guitar*, pp. 68–82 (p. 80).

Chapter 5

1. Carson's "Foam (Essay with Rhapsody): On the Sublime in Longinus and Antonioni" was first published in *Conjunctions* 37 (Twentieth Anniversary Issue, 2001), 96–104.

2. Oran McKenzie has written on what Carson describes here as "the sense of banditry" and its resonances with the wider spilling-over of moments and quotations in Carson. McKenzie's complex argument offers that new notions of poetic value are required to account for Carson's forms of "derivation" (the "spillage" of sources) in the age of "financial derivatives." See Oran McKenzie, "Spillage and Banditry: Anne Carson's Derivatives," *Economies of English. SPELL: Swiss Papers in English Language and Literature* 33 (2016), 225–243 (232–235 on "Foam").

3. Carson's reference is Seymour Chatwin, *Antonioni, or, the Surface of the World* (Berkeley: University of California Press, 1985), p. 57.

4. Dan Disney, "Sublime Disembodiment? Self-as-Other in Anne Carson's Decreation," *Orbis Litterarum* 67.1 (2012), 25–38. See also McKenzie, "Spillage and Banditry," which takes its central metaphors from Carson's essay.

5. Carson, "Longing: A Documentary," in *Decreation*, p. 244. The work introduces terms (Emily Dickinson's "overtakelessness"/Heidegger's *das Unumgängliche*) and ideas that are later developed and reused in *Nox* (see my Chapter 7).
6. Carson uses the word "stereoscopic" in *Eros the Bittersweet* to describe "the difference between what is and what could be visible": Carson, *Eros the Bittersweet*, p. 17. See Jessica Fisher, "Anne Carson's Stereoscopic Poetics," in *Anne Carson: Ecstatic Lyre*, ed. Wilkinson, pp. 10–16.
7. John Berryman, *77 Dream Songs* (New York: Farrar, Straus and Giroux, 1964).
8. Carson, *Decreation*, p. 152 and epigraph. Carson's reading of the "incongruous ideas" in the literature of eclipse echoes what she describes as "sustained incongruence" in *Eros the Bittersweet* (which Fisher discusses in relation to Carson's idea of stereoscopy in the book). The epigraph is taken from John Florio's 1603 translation of the *Essais* of Michel de Montaigne's ("Essay on Some Verses of Virgil"). See Michel de Montaigne, "Essay on Some Verses of Virgil," in *The Essays of Michel de Montaigne: Done into English by John Florio* (London: David Nutt, 1892), Third Book. Carson also takes the title of the chapter of *Eros the Bittersweet*, "My Page Makes Love," from Montaigne's essay.
9. Fisher, "Anne Carson's Stereoscopic Poetics," 10. See also Disney, "Sublime Disembodiment."
10. Fisher, "Anne Carson's Stereoscopic Poetics," 10. While Fisher's essay is strong and largely convincing, I disagree with her reading of decreation as a philosophy proposing to "literalise the deprivation of the self in choosing death" (10). Weil does not imagine decreation as choosing "death" but as the renunciation of an "apparent" existence grown up in the absence of God: "God created me as a non-being which has the appearance of existing, in order that through love I should renounce this apparent existence and be annihilated by the plenitude of being. . . . The 'I' belongs to non-being." Simone Weil, *First and Last Notebooks*, trans. Richard Rees (Oxford: Oxford University Press, 1978), pp. 96–97. For an in-depth discussion of Weil's "decreation" and how Carson reads it, see Elizabeth Coles, "The Sacred Object: Anne Carson and Simone Weil," *Acta Poetica* 34.1 (2013), 127–154.
11. Carson, *Eros the Bittersweet*, p. 21.
12. Simone Weil, *Gravity and Grace* (1948), trans. A Wills (Lincoln: University of Nebraska Press, 1997), pp. 89, p. 88. I cite here from the text used by Carson (*Decreation*, pp. 169, 168).
13. Few readers have sought to engage with Carson's reading of mysticism and decreation theology, tending instead to approach *Decreation* as an example of Carson's "intergenericity" and "multimodality" (Van Praet) or the characteristic "spillage" of sources in her work (McKenzie). Helena Van Praet makes the case for *Decreation* as a "project of re-engagement that is underpinned by synthetic disjunctions of competing viewpoints" and as a model of literary "iteration." Carson's conceptual reading in *Decreation*, Van Praet argues with recourse to "literary semiology," is "better conceptualized as a *network* of relations." See Helena Van Praet, "Writer's Writer Revisits Authorship: Iteration in Anne Carson's *Decreation*," *Canadian Literature* 241 (2020), 18–35 (18 and abstract).

14. Aitken, "The Art of Poetry no. 88" (italics mine).
15. Several instances in *Decreation* suggest Carson's engagement with the ideas of phenomenology, in particular the writings of Husserl and Martin Heidegger, whose concept of "overtakelessness" (*das Unumgängliche*) appears in the book's final text, "Longing, A Documentary," p. 245, as well as in *Nox* (see my Chapter 7). See Edmund Husserl, *Analyses Concerning Passive and Active Synthesis: Lectures on Transcendental Logic*, trans. Anthony J. Steinbock (Dordrecht, Boston, and London: Kluwer Academic, 2001).
16. Wachtel, "An Interview with Anne Carson."
17. See Kurt Flasch, *Meister Eckhart: Philosopher of Christianity* (2011; New Haven, CT: Yale University Press, 2015), p. 205 ("God's exit is his entrance"). Carson does not cite Eckhart in *Decreation*, but she does refer to his distinctive syntactic inversions in her recent essay on "Stillness."
18. This bold translation of Adorno's remark is cited in Benson and Connors, *Creative Criticism*, p. 82. A more tepid translation appears in Adorno, "The Essay as Form," p. 4.
19. Plato, *The Republic*, pp. 283–285 (Book X); Plato, "Republic," *The Collected Dialogues*, pp. 820–821 (596b–597). See de Man on "material vision" in Paul de Man, "Phenomenality and Materiality in Kant," in de Man, *Aesthetic Ideology* (Minneapolis: University of Minnesota Press, 1996), p. 88. Several thinkers in the phenomenological tradition are evoked here. See Martin Heidegger, "The Origin of the Work of Art," in *Basic Writings*, ed. and trans. David Farrell Krell (London: Routledge, 1993), whose thesis on the non-instrumental life of objects is picked up by Carson on "the emptiness of things before we make use of them" (*Decreation*, p. 24), and Edmund Husserl (see notes 36 and 38 below), whose theories of attention are suggested in several texts in *Decreation*, and whose writing is discussed explicitly in "Cassandra Float Can," *Float* (unpaginated). A more recent philosophical affinity is with the "object-oriented ontology" of speculative realism, which seeks a non-relational, disinterested philosophy of objects in the world. E.g., Graham Harman, *Object-Oriented Ontology: A New Theory of Everything* (London: Penguin, 2018) and Harman's essay on "Art Without Relations," *Art Review* 66 (November 4, 2014), 144–147, https://artreview.com/features/september_2014_graham_harman_relations/.
20. Sigmund Freud, *The Interpretation of Dreams: The Complete and Definitive Text*, ed. and trans. James Strachey (1955; New York: Basic Books, 2010), p. 101.
21. Carson, "Uncle Falling: A Pair of Lyric Lectures with Shared Chorus," *Float* (unpaginated).
22. Carson, "Every Exit is an Entrance," in *Decreation*, pp. 17–40 (p. 22).
23. Spoken by Lecturer II in Carson, "Uncle Falling: A Pair of Lyric Lectures with Shared Chorus," *Float* (unpaginated).
24. Carson, "Sleepchains," *Decreation*, p. 3.
25. See Carson, "God's Christ Theory," *Glass, Irony and God*, p. 51, and "Note on Method," *Economy of the Unlost*, viii.
26. Gillian Rose, "Angry Angels: Simone Weil and Emmanuel Levinas," *Judaism and Modernity* (Oxford: Blackwell, 1993), p. 221.

27. Simone Weil, *Gravity and Grace* (1947), eds. Emma Crawford and M. von du Ruhr (1953; London: Routledge, 2002), p. 22. See Weil's original French in Simone Weil, *La Pesanteur et la grâce* (Paris: Plon, 1947), p. 25.
28. Weil, *Gravity and Grace* (2002), p. 13; *La Pesanteur et la grâce*, p. 61.
29. I am grateful to Gaétan Charbonneau, for the estate of Betty Goodwin, for permission to reproduce the image.
30. Betty Goodwin (1923–2008) was a Canadian painter and printmaker. The themes of her work include, according to a review of a 2009 exhibition in *Frieze*, "fragility, empathy, self, absence." See James D. Campbell, "Review: Betty Goodwin: Musée d'art contemporain, Montreal, Canada" *Frieze* (October 1, 2009), https://frieze.com/article/betty-goodwin. See Monique Tschofen's compelling article on Carson's poem and its relationship to the themes of Goodwin's work. Tschofen, "Drawing out a New Image of Thought."
31. Carson, "*Seated Figure with Red Angle* by Betty Goodwin (1988)," *Decreation*, pp. 99–101. An earlier version of the poem was published under the title "Betty Goodwin 'Seated Figure with Red Angle (1988),'" *Art Forum* 38.1 (September 1999), 156–157. A recording of Carson reading "*Seated Figure*" can be found on YouTube.com: http://www.youtube.com/watch?v=HmJJpR_bP74.
32. See Tschofen, "Drawing out a New Image of Thought," 235–240.
33. Sigmund Freud's recommendation was that analysts listen with an "evenly suspended attention" (*gleichschwebende Aufmerksamkeit*) to the discourse of the patient. See also Simone Weil's aim "to empty desire, finality of all content, to desire in the void, to desire without any wishes. To detach our desire from all good things and to wait" in *Gravity and Grace*, p. 13 ("Détacher notre désir de tous les biens et attendre," *La Pesanteur et la grâce*, p. 61). Compare Carson's "to keep attention strong means to keep it from settling," "Note on Method," *Economy of the Unlost*, viii. Also see Weil's remarks in *Waiting on God* (*Attente de Dieu*, 1950): "[a]bove all, our thought should be empty, waiting, not seeing anything, but ready to receive in its naked truth the object that is to penetrate it." Simone Weil, *Waiting on God* (1950), trans. Emma Crawford (London: Routledge, 1951), p. 111–112.
34. Carson-Giacomelli, "Odi et Amo Ergo Sum," and Carson, *Eros the Bittersweet*, p. 20.
35. See Tschofen, "Drawing out a New Image of Thought," note 26, and Husserl, *Analyses Concerning Passive and Active Synthesis*, p. 196, lines 11–13.
36. Husserl, *Analyses Concerning Passive and Active Synthesis*, p. 196, lines 26, 28 (italics mine).
37. Ibid., p. 196, line 15.
38. Husserl uses the term "transcendental association" in his *Analyses* to refer to the characteristic mode of thought under passive synthesis, as opposed to active connections.
39. See McNeilly, "Gifts and Questions," 14 ("I like the space between languages because it's a place of error or mistakenness.... And that's useful I think for writing because it's always good to put yourself off balance, to be dislodged from the complacency in which you normally go at perceiving the world and saying what you've perceived."—"[a] kind of tension that's disruptive," McNeilly summarizes). See Chapter 8 for a discussion of error and mimesis in Carson's early writing.

40. See the following discussion of Carson's lecture and writer's workshop hosted by *Critical Inquiry*: Reema Saleh, "Stillness Complicated by Corners: A Reflection on Anne Carson's Lecture Series," *The Official University of Chicago Arts Blog*, December 2019, https://www.uchicagoartsblog.art/archive/2019/12/19/stillness-complicated-by-corners-a-reflection-on-anne-carsons-lecture-series.
41. Mark C. Taylor has written extensively on ideas of figuration and disfiguration in twentieth-century art and religious thought: Mark C. Taylor, *Disfiguring: Art, Architecture, Religion* (Chicago: University of Chicago Press, 1992).
42. Weil reads *The Iliad* with an extraordinary sensitivity, arguing that the poem models the transformation of the object of violence from person into thing. See Simone Weil, "The Iliad, or the Poem of Force" [trans. Mary McCarthy], *Chicago Review* 18.2 (1965), 5–30. The essay is a remarkable exception to the coolness of Weil's aphoristic writing.
43. While numerous recordings of performances and readings can be consulted online, this recent recording of a "Lecture on the History of Skywriting" provides a classic example: https://www.youtube.com/watch?v=9F9xUhaimTY.
44. Quoted in Carson, *Decreation*, p. 169. Emma Crawford and Mario von du Ruhr's translation reads: "To see a landscape as it is when I am not there. . . . When I am in any place, I disturb the silence of heaven and earth by my breathing and the beating of my heart." Weil, *Gravity and Grace*, p. 42. Weil refers to herself as the "unwelcome third" in the presence of two lovers; as Weil sees it, she "ought to go away so that they can really be together": *Gravity and Grace*, p. 41.
45. Carson, "Stanzas, Sexes, Seductions," *Decreation*, pp. 72–73.
46. In Aitken, "The Art of Poetry no. 88," Carson remarks: "Well, I think there are different gradations of personhood in different poems. Some of them seem far away from me and some up close, and the up-close ones generally don't say what I want them to say. And that's true of the persona in the poem, but it's also true of me as me."
47. While she seeks the annihilation of lover into lover, what the poet gets instead is tied up in the avid life of words. "There are things unbearable. / Scorn, princes, this little size / of dying": the line looks like a list of "things unbearable." It is also a near appropriation of a line by the poet, Lucy Hutchinson: "Scorn, princes, your embroidered canopies. And painted roofs: the poor whom you despise." While Hutchinson's meaning makes the line more an imperative address to "princes" ("Scorn, [you] princes"]) than a list, Carson's might equally allude to the borrowing of the line, the "little size" of typeface, the smallness and bathos of all that has been written, all of it drunk, an immense human production on the problem of mortality. Human remains are, after all, also these things: the accumulated history, the "little size," of writing. See Lucy Hutchinson, *Order and Disorder* (Oxford: Blackwell, 2001). With thanks to Peter Howarth for drawing my attention to the similarity.
48. In "The Glass Essay," Carson has ex-lover "Law" diagnose their relationship as "not enough spin on it." Carson, "The Glass Essay," *Glass, Irony and God*, p. 11.
49. See Andrew Marvell, "The Garden," in Marvell, *Selected Poems*, ed. Bill Hutchings (New York: Routledge, 2002), p. 60.

50. Barthes, *Image Music Text*, p. 142. For Barthes's French, see Roland Barthes, "La Mort de l'auteur," in Barthes, *Le Bruissement de la langue: Essais critiques IV* (Paris: Seuil, 1984), p. 61.
51. See Barthes, *Le Neutre* ("Non pas 'traits,' 'éléments,' 'composants,' mais ce qui brille par éclats, en désordre, fugitivement, successivement, dans le discours 'anecdotique,'" p. 59).
52. Barthes's *S/Z* deals in a similar defiance of sexual difference in his reading of Balzac's *Sarrasine*. Barthes discusses the case of the castrato, La Zambinella, a "female impersonator" whom Sarrasine mistakes for a woman. See Roland Barthes, *S/Z* (1970), trans. Richard Miller (New York: Hill and Wang, 1975).
53. See Wachtel, "An Interview with Anne Carson," and McNeilly, "Gifts and Questions," 20.
54. See Carson, "By Chance the Cycladic People" and the Ibykos translation exercise in "Variations on the Right to Remain Silent," both in *Float* (unpaginated), and Carson, *Red Doc>*. Reena Sastri situates the Ibykos translations in relation to Carson's wider "wild constancy" to her sources. See Sastri, "'Wildly Constant.'"
55. See Levin Becker, *Many Subtle Channels*, on "literature in the conditional mood" post-Oulipo.
56. See Goldsmith, *Uncreative Writing*.
57. Perloff, *Unoriginal Genius*.
58. Burrow, *Imitating Authors*, "Posthuman Postscript: Poems more Durable than Brass," pp. 407–425.
59. Burrow's example of the genetic generation of verse is Canadian experimental poet Christian Bök, who embedded a particularly resonant line from Virgil's *Georgics* in the DNA of the bacterium *Deinococcus radiodurans*: "Nec vero terrae ferre omnes Omnia possunt" ("Nor can all of the earth bring forth all fruit alike"). See Burrow, pp. 422–423, and Bök, *The Xenotext*.
60. See Harold Bloom's essay on the writings of second-century gnostic, Valentinus, "Lying Against Time: Gnosis, Poetry, Criticism," in *The Rediscovery of Gnosticism: Proceedings of the International Conference on Gnosticism at Yale, New Haven, Connecticut, March 28-31, 1978*, ed. Bentley Layton, 2 vols. (Leiden: Brill, 1981), vol. 1, pp. 57–72, and Eric Voegelin's discussion of the gnostic dialectic of knowledge and captivity, by which gnosis is both the knowledge of captivity and the means of escape: Eric Voegelin, *Science, Politics and Gnosticism* (Washington, DC: Regnery, 1968), pp. 10–11.
61. Readers of Susan Howe will note an echo in the title of her 2010 work, *That This*. Susan Howe, *That This* (New York: New Directions, 2010).
62. In the words of "Gnosticism VI": "The language knew" (p. 93).
63. Carson, "Stillness," 9.
64. Carson, "Stillness," 13 (the Woolf diary entry cited by Carson is dated January 26, 1920, and referenced *The Diary of Virginia Woolf*, vol. 2, p. 14. She provides no page references for quotations from *Between the Acts* (1941).
65. Carson, "Stillness," 13.
66. See Liddell and Scott, p. 51 (*analogia*) and p. 46 (preposition *ana-*).

67. Gillian Rose, *Mourning Becomes the Law: Philosophy and Representation* (Cambridge: Cambridge University Press, 1996), p. 10.

Chapter 6

* This essay has received funding from the European Union's Horizon 2020 research and innovation program under the Marie Skłodowska-Curie grant agreement no. 887344.
1. The essay was first published under the same title in the journal *Common Knowledge* 8.1 (Winter 2002), 188–203.
2. See Carson, *Decreation*, p. 180. Carson's source in her remarks on the term is an article by Paul Verdeyen, "Le process d'inquisition contre Marguerite Porete," *Revue d'histoire ecclesiastique* 81 (1986), 47–94. Following her questioning by the king's confessor, William of Paris, excerpts of Porete's book were presented before a panel of twenty-one theologians tasked with judging its content for heresy. The expression *pseudo-mulier* was used by the Continuer of William of Nangis, in his account of Porete's trial and execution. See Sean Fields, *The Beguine, the Angel, and the Inquisitor* (Notre Dame, IN: University of Notre Dame Press, 2012), for a full discussion of the trial proceedings. An illuminating discussion of the possible meanings of *pseudo-mulier* (a gloss for her controversy, writing with the help of no known scribe or confessor, or even a reference to "Porete" as a false surname, derived from *poret* or "leek" in Middle French) is published on the website of the Leverhulme-funded international research network "Women's Literary Culture and the Medieval Canon," based at the University of Surrey (December 2015): https://blogs.surrey.ac.uk/medievalwomen/2015/12/07/a-burnable-book-and-a-pseudo-woman-the-case-of-marguerite-called-porete/.
3. Victoria Blut writes in "A Burnable Book and a Pseudo-Woman: The Case of Marguerite, called Porete" that in Porete, Virginia Woolf's observation that "Anon . . . was often a woman" finds something of an "early test-case" (see "Women's Literary Culture and the Medieval Canon," University of Surrey). Laura Moncion's blog for the "Dangerous Women Project"(May 2016) at the Institute for Advanced Studies in the Humanities (IASH), University of Edinburgh, features an entry on Porete, noting she "refused to submit to the Church's idea of what proper female piety should be": https://dangerouswomenproject.org/2016/05/28/marguerite-porete/#_ftn3.
4. The expression "wiles of woman" is from Euripides's *Helen*. See Colin Burrow on the feminizing power of imitation in *Imitating Authors*, pp. 46–50, and the influence the ideas of mimesis dramatized in the *Helen* (and Aristophanes's *imitatio* of its author) had on Plato (pp. 50–62).
5. See Simone Pétrement, *Simone Weil: A Life*, trans. Raymond Rosenthal (New York: Pantheon Books, 1976), p. 45. Writing on Weil, Toril Moi observes that Weil "never defined herself as a woman, any more than as a Jew." See Toril Moi, "I

Came with a Sword: Simone Weil's Way," *London Review of Books* 43.13 (July 1, 2021), https://www.lrb.co.uk/the-paper/v43/n13/toril-moi/i-came-with-a-sword. Sophie Bourgault observes, "Many biographers have commented at length on Weil's discomfort with bodily contact, food, and sexuality (the disturbing subtext here is that it is particularly strange for a woman to eschew romantic love, children, or sex)." S. Bourgault, "Beyond the Saint and the Red Virgin: Simone Weil as Feminist Theorist of Care," *Frontiers: A Journal of Women's Studies* 35.2 (2014), 1–27 (1).

6. Weil, *La Pesanteur et la grâce*, p. 11. Emma Crawford translates the phrase "I also am other than what I imagine myself to be. To know this is forgiveness": Weil, *Gravity and Grace*, p. 9.

7. Carson, "Cassandra Float Can," *Float* (unpaginated).

8. Weil's mystical-theological concept of "decreation" has several antecedents in the "annihilating detachment" of fourteenth-century mysticism (Eckhart, Porete). See Bernard McGinn, *The Harvest of Mysticism in Medieval Germany (1300–1500), The Presence of God: A History of Western Mysticism*, vol. IV (New York: Herder and Herder, 2005), p. 170. Unless otherwise indicated, quotations from Porete are my translations from the Middle French text established by Romana Guarnieri (*Le Mirouer des simples ames*), reproduced in the following edition with extensive annotations and with a modern Italian translation en face: Margharita Porete, *Lo Specchio delle anime semplici*, trans. Giovanna Fozzer, with a preface by Romana Guarnieri and commentary by Marco Vannini (Milano: Edizioni San Paolo, 1994), p. 422, line 30. References hereafter are to *Le Mirouer/Lo Specchio*.

9. Carson is not the first to link "decreation" to practices of writing and particularly to a lyric poetics. In *My Emily Dickinson*, Susan Howe seeks to emphasize "the implications of a nineteenth century American penchant for linguistic decreation ushered in by their [Sandra M. Gilbert and Susan Gubar's] representative poet Emily Dickinson" (p. 13). Decreation of syntax and grammatical law, but so as to move the "I" out of its center (or in Howe's words, "breaking the law just short of breaking off communication with a reader" (p. 11). Carson discusses Dickinson's poem "I heard a Fly buzz / when I died" in terms that echo her concerns in the "Decreation" essay. See Carson, "Stillness," 9–10.

10. See Bernstein, *Shadowtime*, p. 13. The libretto is the result of a collaboration between Bernstein and Brian Ferneyhough, who composed the music and is credited with the concept for the opera. Marjorie Perloff discusses *Shadowtime* (premiered in 2004) in terms of its citational poetics: the libretto, according to Bernstein, uses appropriated text as a means of "writing-through" Benjamin. See Perloff, *Unoriginal Genius*, p. 17.

11. Burrow, *Imitating Authors*, p. 3.

12. See my comments in the Introduction on Plato's late variation on the theory of *mimēsis* in *The Sophist*.

13. Michel de Certeau, *La fable mystique: XVIe—XVIIe siècle* (Paris: Gallimard, 1982), p. 257. My references are to the French edition and translations are my own.

14. The term "Appellstruktur" is employed by Wolfgang Iser in *Die Appellstruktur der Texte* (1970) but is taken up by Haas to describe the invocational structure of Eckhart's sermons. See Alois M. Haas, *Sermo mysticus: Studien zu Theologie und Sprache der*

deutschen Mystik (Freiburg, Schweiz: Universitätsverlag, 1979), p. 15. Haas's term is cited by Niklaus Largier in "Recent Work on Meister Eckhart: Positions, Problems, New Perspectives," *Recherches de Théologie et Philosophie Médiévales* 65.1 (1998), 147–167 (p. 158).

15. The tradition runs from the biblical Song of Songs through the commentary of Bernard of Clairvaux (*Sermones super Cantica canticorum*), the *Cántico espiritual* of St. John of the Cross, Marguerite Porete's *Le Mirouer*, Teresa of Ávila's *Libro de la vida*, to list some well-known examples.
16. See Barbara Newman on Porete's *Mirror* in the context of what she calls "la mystique courtoise" or a mysticism modeled on the structural conceits of courtly love. See Barbara Newman, *From Virile Woman to WomanChrist: Studies in Medieval Religion and Literature* (Philadelphia: University of Pennsylvania Press, 1995), pp. 137–139. Also see Amy Hollywood, *Sensible Ecstasy: Mysticism, Sexual Difference and the Demands of History* (Chicago: University of Chicago Press, 2001).
17. Solway, "The Trouble with Annie," 25.
18. See Goldsmith, *Uncreative Writing*; Marczewska, *This Is Not a Copy*; and Perloff, *Unoriginal Genius*.
19. Scholarly readings of *Decreation* customarily focus on the same textual features that attracted the negative attention of Solway, namely Carson's formal technique, usually praised as iterative or post-structuralist in character. See e.g., Van Praet, "Writer's Writer Revisits Authorship" and Jennifer Thorp, "Prowling the Meanings: Anne Carson's Doubtful Forms," PhD thesis, University of Manchester, 2015.
20. Rae, "Anne Carson and the Solway Hoaxes," 49.
21. Derrida, *Dissemination*, p. 107.
22. D'Agata, "A _ with Anne Carson," 5.
23. Carson's essay first appears in D. Halperin and F. Zeitlin, eds., *Before Sexuality*. See also Burrow, *Imitating Authors*, and Halliwell, *The Aesthetics of Mimesis*, on the history of anxieties surrounding mimesis.
24. Carson, *Men in the Off Hours*, p. 133 (Carson's note 7).
25. Carson. *Eros the Bittersweet*, pp. 13–14.
26. Ibid., pp. 15, 16.
27. Carson, *Eros the Bittersweet*, p. 16; Carson, *Decreation*, p. 161. Carson's reading of Sappho's ecstasy/decreation echoes another early reading in a journal article from 1990. Fragment 55, Carson argues, stages the "invisibility" of an unnamed woman in such a way that draws us into her place: "the second person singular verbs of the poem locate us within some woman by calling her 'you.' You transact your own invisibility by living in the present as if you were already dead—which, by the time you realize it, you are." Carson, " 'Just for the Thrill,' " 147. Her reading of fragment 31 appears on pages 148–151.
28. Italics in original. The translation is as appears in *If Not, Winter*.
29. The work's full title in the Middle French is *Le Miroir des âmes simples anéanties et qui seulement demeurent en vouloir et désir d'amour*. A good English translation, which Carson adapts in her own translations, is Marguerite Porete, *The Mirror of Simple Souls*, trans. Ellen Babinsky (Mahwah, NJ: Paulist Press, 1993).

30. Guarnieri's unaccented Middle French text is reproduced in facing page in the edition from which I cite, and includes an illuminating preface discussing her attribution of the work to Porete.
31. Corinthians I, 13: 12; "in a mirror dimly" in the English Standard Version; "an indistinct image in a mirror" in the International Standard Version. For discussions of the genre of miroir-livres, see Fabienne Pomel, ed., *Miroirs et jeux de miroirs dans la littérature médiévale* (Rennes: Presses universitaires de Rennes, 2016) and in particular Einar Mar Jonsson, *Miroir, Naissance d'un genre littéraire* (Paris: Les Belles Lettres, 1995), p. 12.
32. Carson, *Decreation*, p. 181. Porete, *Le Mirouer/Lo Specchio*, p. 434.
33. See Manuela Ceballos, "Life and Death by the Book: A Dramatic Reading of Marguerite Porete's *Mirror of Simple Souls*," *English Language Notes* 56.1 (April 2018), 183–196 (183).
34. Or, in St. John of the Cross, "Adonde te escondiste / amado y me dexaste con gemido?" ("Where have you hidden, / beloved, and left me moaning?"). Werner G. Jeanrond writes that "[t]he mystical discourse of love thus shows that the erotic and the sacred need not be understood in terms of radical opposition." Werner G. Jeanrond, *A Theology of Love* (New York: T & T Clark, 2010), p. 18.
35. Certeau, *Le fable mystique*, pp. 258, 26; 258, 27.
36. Carson speaks of the "thrill—at the inside edge where [Sappho's] words go missing" in the introductory notes to *If Not, Winter* (xiii). She also uses the word emphatically in a reading of Sappho fragments 31 and 55 in "'Just for the Thrill,'" describing the effect of mimetic forms on emotional reasoning (*dianoia*). See Chapter 8 of this book for further discussion. The phrase "Just for the Thrill" also appears in the title of a text in "The Anthropology of Water," "Just for the Thrill: An Essay on the Difference Between Women and Men," *Plainwater*, pp. 192–244.
37. Carson, *Decreation*, p. 165; Porete, *Le Mirouer/Lo Specchio*, pp. 476–478.
38. Carson, *Decreation*, p. 164; Porete, *Le Mirouer/Lo Specchio*, p. 308 ("l'] apareil du divin estre, don't j'ay estre, qui es estre").
39. Carson, *Decreation*, p. 165; Porete, *Le Mirouer/Lo Specchio*, p. 479 ("Et tant estoie aise, et me amoye 'avec' luy, que je ne povoye pour rien me contenir, ne avoir en muy maniere: j'estoye tenue en destroit, par quoy je n'aloye pas l'ambleure").
40. Hutcheon quotes this fortuitous description of parody from Bakhtin: "The genre itself, the style, the language are all put in cheerfully irreverent quotation marks (1981, 55)." Hutcheon, *A Theory of Parody*, p. 41.
41. Niklaus Largier, "Recent Work on Meister Eckhart: Positions, Problems, New Perspectives," 158. On the relationship between Porete's and Eckhart's writings, see Maria Lichtmann, "Marguerite Porete and Meister Eckhart: The Mirror of Simple Souls Mirrored," in *Meister Eckhart and the Béguine Mystics: Hadewijch of Brabant, Mechthild of Magdeburg, and Marguerite Porete*, ed. Bernard McGinn (New York: Continuum Press, 1994), pp. 65–86.
42. Carson and Anno, *The Mirror of Simple Souls: An Opera Installation*.
43. Porete, *Le Mirouer/Lo Specchio*, p. 282. *Loingprès* has a clear antecedent in the Neoplatonism of St. Augustine, for whom God is paradoxical in location and nature,

both everywhere and nowhere. My thanks to Amador Vega, whose conversations on Augustine, Eckhart, Porete, and Weil made this chapter possible.

44. Giovanna Fozzer discusses the presentation of *Le Mirouer* in her introduction to the bilingual text. Commentary below the Middle French text by Marco Vannini states that this remark, the first reference to *auditeurs* in the text, shows that the author read her book aloud in public or before a small group of listeners. See Porete, *Le Mirouer/Lo Specchio*, p. 282.

45. See Carson, "Blended Text," *Decreation*, p. 79, and Porete, *Le Mirouer/Lo Specchio*, p. 439.

46. Giorgio Agamben, *Profanations*, trans. Jeff Fort (New York: Zone Books, 2007), p. 41. Quoted in Carson, "Stillness," 22.

47. Burrow, *Imitating Authors*, p. 12.

48. Cole Swensen has written on the machinic elements of Carson's opera libretto, which he links back to the *deus ex machina* of Greek tragedy, the *mekhane* or crane-like structure by which gods were lowered onto the stage. Cole Swensen, "Opera Povera: Decreation, an Opera in Three Parts," in ed. Wilkinson, *Anne Carson: Ecstatic Lyre*, p. 127.

49. In Homer, Hephaistos's trap succeeds but, likewise, the capture of his beloved brings him no relief: "I am horrified to see it," he says; "Her eyes stare at me like a dog." Homer, *The Odyssey*, p. 230.

50. Susan Sontag, *Notes on Camp*, Penguin Modern Series (Harmondsworth, UK: Penguin, 2018), p. 1. See Carson, *Decreation*, pp. 192, 197.

51. Sontag, *Notes on Camp*, p. 2.

52. Ibid.

53. Hutcheon, *A Theory of Parody*, p. 36. Hutcheon notes that "if the decoder [the reader] does not notice quotation he will just naturalize it," eliminating the point and meaning of the work (p. 34).

54. Porete, *Le Mirouer/Lo Specchio*, pp. 178–180 (*Prenez ce Sacrement, mectez le en ung mortier avec aultres choses, et breez ce Sacrement tant que vous n'y puissez point veoir ne point sentir de la Personne que vous y avez mis*). The *Sacrement* refers to the consecrated host, the "bread" and body of the Eucharist.

55. Carson, *Decreation*, p. 170 ("Such a Soul ... swims in a sea of joy"); Porete, *Le Mirouer/Lo Specchio*, p. 212. "FarNear" (*Loingprès*) was customarily translated as "far night" before the work's attribution to Porete. For references to nothingness (e.g., "*comment elle est venue cognoissance de son nient*" and "*Hee Amour, dit ceste Ame, le sens de ce qui est dit m'a fait nulle, et le nient de ce seul m'a mis en abysme dessoubs moins que nient sans mesure*") see Porete, *Le Mirouer/Lo Specchio*, pp. 256, 264.

56. The textual source for the duet is quoted in the "Decreation" essay: Carson, *Decreation* p. 165 (Porete, *Le Mirouer/Lo Specchio*, p. 478).

57. Manuela Ceballos has asked how the various transformations and "un-making" undergone by Porete's characters in *The Mirror* might be realized in performance. I suggest Carson's mise-en-scène offers a compelling example of how contemporary audio-visual technologies make it possible to represent psychic phenomena such as ecstatic self-separation. See Ceballos, "Life and Death by the Book."

58. Burrow, *Imitating Authors*, p. 13.
59. Carson-Giacomelli, "Odi et Amo Ergo Sum," p. 299 (elision mine). The reference Carson gives is *The Simone Weil Reader*, ed. G. A. Panichas (New York: David McKay, 1977), p. 212. The full quotation can be found in Weil, *Gravity and Grace*, p. 65, and runs on a parallel with Carson's arguments regarding *aidos* in the thesis: "To soil is to modify, it is to touch. The beautiful is that which we cannot wish to change. To assume power over is to soil, to possess is to soil. To love purely is to consent to distance, to adore the distance between ourselves and that which we love."
60. Carson gives the reference "1977, 364" (*The Simone Weil Reader*, p. 364). Quoted in Carson, *Eros the Bittersweet*, p. 10.
61. See Pétrement, *Simone Weil*. On "desire without an object," see, e.g., Weil, *Gravity and Grace*, p. 65.
62. See Susan Sontag, "Simone Weil" [Review of Simone Weil, *Selected Essays*], *New York Review*, February 1, 1963, https://www.nybooks.com/articles/1963/02/01/simone-weil/. In a less vehement example, Claire Wolfteich finds Weil's gnostic "distaste for the material" "reinforce[d]" by the details of Weil's biography: "[Weil's] conception of Creation, and her emphasis on annihilation of the self and the Crucifixion, similarly may indicate a rejection of mater and an unhealthy focus on death. In addition, Weil's own dangerous eating habits and body denial reinforces such an interpretation." Claire Wolfteich, "Attention or Destruction: Simone Weil and the Paradox of the Eucharist," *The Journal of Religion* 81.3 (2001), 359–376 (360).
63. Sontag, "Simone Weil."
64. See Sharon Cameron, "The Practice of Attention: Simone Weil's Performance of Impersonality," *Critical Inquiry* 29.2 (Winter 2003), 216–252, where Cameron speaks of the "minimalist economy" governing Weil's prose (218).
65. Simone Weil, *Lectures on Philosophy*, trans. Hugh Price (Cambridge: Cambridge University Press, 1978), p. 193.
66. Quoted in Carson, *Decreation*, p. 171. Carson cites from Weil, *Gravity and Grace*, trans. A. Wills, p. 148.
67. Weil, *Gravity and Grace*, p. 64.
68. See Joan Dargan, *Simone Weil: Thinking Poetically* (Albany: State University of New York Press, 1999), p. 5, for Dargan's remarks on Weil's "clear rejection of autobiography in favour of abstraction," and Carson, *Decreation*, p. 174 (Carson's description of Gustave Thibon's strategy in handling Weil's notebooks: Thibon, she says, "extracted punchy passages"). Citing Pétrement's biography of Weil, Toril Moi notes Weil's perfectionism as signaled by the absence of cross-outs or corrections of any kind in her manuscript for *The Need for Roots*. See Moi, "I Came with a Sword."
69. Sharon Cameron describes the "I" in Weil's writing as an "I" that "has been deprived of its particularity; it is positional rather than substantive, an abstraction, an 'I' that *is* a figure." Cameron, "The Practice of Attention," 220.
70. Rose, *Judaism and Modernity*, p. 221.
71. Weil, "The Iliad, or the Poem of Force," 9.
72. Ibid., 6.
73. Simone Weil, *L'Enracinement* (Paris: Gallimard, 1949), p. 283.

74. Carson, *Decreation*, p. 174; Carson cites *Gravity and Grace*, trans. A. Wills, p. 11.
75. Simone Weil, *The Notebooks of Simone Weil*, trans. A. Wills, 2 vols. (New York: Routledge & Kegan Paul, 1956), vol. 2, p. 411. Cited in Cameron, "The Practice of Attention," 233.
76. Though parodic in tone, this imitation of a Weil letter is close in tone and content to actual letters sent by Weil. See note 78 below for several examples.
77. Carson, *Decreation*, pp. 230–233..
78. Letters sent from London to Weil's parents include references to light summer clothing (not usually needed in London, she reassures them, first in a letter dated June 15, then again in a letter dated June 25, 1943, pp. 191, p193); and a request for her parents to post an article on the Romans to her "as quickly as possible" (March 1, 1943, p. 182). A letter sent by Weil to Jean Posternak in 1938 discusses tensions and brutal attacks against the organizations and parties of the Left (p. 95), in Simone Weil, *Seventy Letters: Personal and Intellectual Windows on a Thinker*, trans. Richard Rees (Eugene, OR: Wipf and Stock, 1965).
79. See Levin Becker, *Many Subtle Channels*, for a compelling account of the formal variants in Oulipo and "potential literature." Carson's translations of Ibykos fragment 286 employ a different form of remix, retaining the fragment's constative structure while substituting vocabularies, where in the remixed Weil letter, a single vocabulary is reorganized internally.
80. Moi, "I Came with a Sword."
81. See Gillian Rose on the complexities of mediated self-relation: "my relation to myself is mediated by what I recognise or refuse to recognise in your relation to yourself; while your self-relation depends on what you recognise of my relation to myself," Rose, *Mourning Becomes the Law*, p. 74.
82. See Weil, *Gravity and Grace*, p. 10 ("Grace fills empty spaces but it can only enter where there is a void to receive it"), and *La Pesanteur et la grâce*, p. 12 ("... comble, mais elle ne peut entrer que là où il y a un vide pour la recevoir").
83. Rose, *Judaism and Modernity*, p. 221.
84. Ibid., pp. 221–222 (221).
85. Weil, *Gravity and Grace*, p. 40.
86. Ibid., p. 41.
87. Hutcheon, *A Theory of Parody*, p. 41.
88. See Carson's remarks in "Stillness" on the "third voice" or "another voice" to which Woolf refers in *Between the Acts*. Carson, "Stillness," 13.
89. Hutcheon, *A Theory of Parody*, pp. 36, 35.
90. Judith Butler, "Merely Cultural," *Social Text*, 52/53, Queer Transexions of Race, Nation, and Gender (Autumn–Winter 1997), 265–277 (277).
91. Ibid., 266.
92. Weil, *Gravity and Grace*, p. 13.
93. Ibid., p. 22.
94. A letter sent from Weil to her parents on June 15, 1943, mentions the fruit currently in season: "what one sees now is cherries, strawberries, ripe peaches." See Weil, *Seventy Letters*, p. 190.

95. Perloff, *Unoriginal Genius*, p. 17; Carson, *Economy of the Unlost*, p. 34.
96. Carson, *Decreation*, p. 175.
97. Jean Tortel quoted in Moi, "I Came with a Sword." "Performance of impersonality" is Sharon Cameron's expression; see Cameron, "The Practice of Attention."
98. Gillian Rose quotes Thibon in Rose, *Judaism and Modernity*, p. 222. Rose calls this failure to pass unnoticed Weil's "spiritual . . . *supernatural*, failing."
99. Cameron has suggested that the "resistance between [the] positions [Weil represents in her writing] is what makes Weil's writing interesting"; Cameron, "The Practice of Attention," 218.
100. Carson, *Grief Lessons*, p. 309.
101. Ibid., p. 309.
102. Ibid., p. 310.
103. Carson, "Cassandra Float Can," *Float* (unpaginated).
104. Ibid.
105. See Carson, "Teresa of God," *Glass, Irony and God*, pp. 44–45.
106. On St. Teresa's performance of naming, see Certeau, *La fable mystique*, pp. 257–279.
107. Kristeva, *Teresa My Love*, p. 105. Kristeva's French reads "l'extase de Thérèse ne serait ni plus ni moins qu'un effet d'écriture!": Julia Kristeva, *Thérèse mon amour* (Paris: Fayard, 2008), p. 129.
108. Carson, *Autobiography of Red*, p. 5.
109. "Fragment 192 poetae melici graeci," "Appendix B," in Carson, *Autobiography of Red*, p. 17.
110. Euripides, *Euripides in Four Volumes, I: Iphigeneia at Aulis, Rhesus Hecuba, The Daughters of Troy, Hecuba*, trans. Arthur S. Way (London: William Heinemann, 1916), pp. 468, 469 (line 34).
111. "Does the presence of this *mimēma* make the heroic tradition into a kind of ghostly charade?" asks Burrow in *Imitating Authors*, p. 47.
112. See Jacqueline Rose, *Women in Dark Times* (London: Bloomsbury, 2014), p. 101.
113. In Arthur S. Way's translation of the *Helen*, Theoclymenus, betrothed to Helen but finds himself deceived when she and Menelaus escape, bemoans having been "by wiles of woman cozened, caught as in the net." See *Euripides: In Four Volumes*, p. 603 (lines 1621–1622). See also Weil's words in *Gravity and Grace*: "what is more terrible than discovery that through a bodily appearance we have been loving an imaginary being?," (p. 65).
114. In Rose's reading of Monroe, the actress is made to pay for thwarted fantasies bound up in the American Dream: Rose, *Women in Dark Times*, pp. 100–138.
115. "(Norma Jeane speaking as Fritz Lang): 'we can't jeopardize the cloud scam'": Carson, *Norma Jeane Baker of Troy*, p. 15.
116. Quoted in Rose, *Women in Dark Times*, p. 126.
117. Andrew David King, "Unwriting the Books of the Dead: Anne Carson and Robert Currie on Translation, Collaboration, and History," *Kenyon Review*, October 6, 2012, https://kenyonreview.org/2012/10/anne-carson-robert-currie-interview/.

Chapter 7

1. Carson, *Grief Lessons*, p. 7.
2. See the transcript of "Freaks and Greeks. Antigone: A Roundtable Between Anne Carson, Simon Critchley, and Trajal Harrell," hosted by Lauren O'Neill-Butler, *ArtForum*, September 22, 2015: https://www.artforum.com/slant/antigone-a-rou ndtable-with-anne-carson-simon-critchley-and-trajal-harrell-55046.   Stephen Halliwell argues that the expressions of culture on which Plato based his critique of *mimēsis* not only required their audiences to emote, but were conditional on a total, emotionally saturating performance—the ecstatic "intense assimilation, the self-likening identification" of the actor or poet with his role or object—whose function was exemplary: its "self-likening" position could be occupied by audiences and readers. See Halliwell, *The Aesthetics of Mimesis*, p. 80 (see also pp. 76–80 and p. 52).
3. In *The Republic*, Plato describes how reason constrains the spectator in his identification with the spectacle and in the pity and fear he feels. Aristotle, in book VI of the *Poetics*, refers to the telos or endgame of tragedy as the purgation of emotion through the pity and fear aroused during the spectacle. See Halliwell, *The Aesthetics of Mimesis*, p. 77, and Plato, "Republic," p. 831, line 606b1 ("the woes of others"). Also see Edith Hall, "Aristotle's Theory of Katharsis in Its Historical and Social Contexts," in *Transformative Aesthetics*, ed. Erika Fischer-Lichte and Benjamin Wihstutz (London: Routledge, 2017), pp. 26–47.
4. Carson, *Grief Lessons*, p. 7.
5. Sigmund Freud, "Thoughts for the Time on War and Death" ["Zeitgemäßes über Krieg und Tod," 1915], *The Standard Edition of the Complete Psychological Works of Sigmund Freud*, trans. James Strachey, vol. XIV (1914–1916), "On the History of the Psychoanalytic Movement, Papers on Metapsychology and Other Works" (London: Hogarth Press and the Institute of Psycho-analysis, 1957), p. 291.
6. Carson, "Variations on the Right to Remain Silent," *Nay Rather*, p. 32.
7. Ibid., italics mine.
8. McNeilly, "Gifts and Questions," 14, 21.
9. Carson, *Economy of the Unlost*, p. vii.
10. See my discussion of the fragments of Sappho in Chapter 8.
11. Numerous studies account for this textual history. Examples discussed in this book include Burrow, *Imitating Authors* (pp. 37–138), and a fascinating recent study on the appropriation and "citation" of Old Comedy and comic tropes in Greek tragedy: Craig Jendza, *Paracomedy: Appropriations of Comedy in Greek Tragedy* (Oxford: Oxford University Press, 2020).
12. See Jansen's introduction to *Anne Carson/Antiquity*, ed. Jansen, p. 2. Though Carson's originality lies in probing the "afterlife" of classical antiquity "somewhere off-centre from its mainstream traditions," the essays in Jansen's collection, she notes, largely suggest that "[Carson's] classicism responds in philosophical terms more consistently to certain European and Anglophone schools of thought" (p. 1).

13. See Stephanie Burt, "Professor or Pinhead," *London Review of Books* 33.14 (July 14, 2011), https://www.lrb.co.uk/the-paper/v33/n14/stephanie-burt/professor-or-pinhead; and *If Not, Winter*, xiii.
14. Nancy and Lacoue-Labarthe, *The Literary Absolute*, p. 47.
15. Jansen reminds us in her introduction to *Anne Carson/Antiquity* that Carson is not alone in her "turn on the Classics," citing the poems of Alejandra Pizarnik, the poetry and performance art of classicist Phoebe Giannisi, and the translations and poems of classicist Josephine Balmer (p. 1). Several other recent examples might be cited, including Alice Oswald's long poem, *Nobody: A Hymn to the Sea* (New York: Norton, 2020), whose meditation on the sea "lives between the murkiness between [two] stories" in the *Odyssey*; the off-kilter versions of Catullus in Isobel Williams's *Shibari Carmina* (Manchester: Carcanet, 2021); and the poems of Fiona Benson in *Vertigo & Ghost* (London: Jonathan Cape, 2019), which includes a stunning sequence on the rapes of Zeus.
16. Sienkewicz, "Anne Carson: *Eros the Bittersweet*," 90.
17. Carson, *Eros the Bittersweet*, xi.
18. See Marjorie Perloff's discussion of "transcreation," as coined by Haroldo de Campos: Perloff, *Unoriginal Genius*, pp. 16–17.
19. See King, "Unwriting the Books of the Dead," for a discussion with Carson and Currie on the thinking behind both works, as well as the relationships they invite between text and image.
20. Sophokles, *Antigone*, trans. Carson, hereafter "*Antigone*." The play was premiered in Luxembourg in 2015. See the account of the work's preparation and staging by Will Aitken, who accompanied Carson and the actors for the premiere: Will Aitken, *Antigone Undone: Juliette Binoche, Anne Carson, Ivo van Hove and the Art of Resistance* (Regina: University of Regina Press, 2018).
21. Bianca Stone, "Your Soul Is Blowing Apart: *Antigonick* and the Influence of Collaborative Process," in ed. Wilkinson, *Anne Carson: Ecstatic Lyre*, p. 152.
22. Judith Butler, *Antigone's Claim: Kinship Between Life and Death* (New York: Columbia University Press, 2002), p. 2.
23. Carson, *Grief Lessons*, p. 73.
24. See Celan, "Epitaph for François," in *Poems of Paul Celan*, pp. 84–85. Carson reproduces the poem on pages 86 and 87 of *Economy of the Unlost*.
25. Carson, *Economy of the Unlost*, p. 87.
26. Ibid., pp. 84–85.
27. Carson refers to it interchangeably as "epitaph" and "elegy," and explains this in interview with Andrew David King: " 'Elegy' was a polyvalent genre in ancient Greek poetry, used in the archaic period for exhorting troops to battle, outlining political views, pithy military wisdom, mild erotic description, consolation after shipwreck, and meditation on drunkenness. It was not until the time of Simonides of Keos that epitaphs for the dead began to be written in elegiac couplets and so to become almost synonymous with that genre functionally. That's why I used epitaph as well as elegy when referring to *Nox*. I did not use couplets but I did have in mind a range of function and tone." King, "Unwriting the Books of the Dead," n.p.

28. Ibid.
29. The term "multimodal" is increasingly used to describe works like *Nox* and Susan Howe's *The Midnight* (2003). Readings adopting the approaches of cultural material studies increasingly emphasize the material experiences of reading enabled by new technologies, and on "the book's materiality as a medium of sociality" (Plate). See, for example, Liedeke Plate, "How to Do Things with Literature in the Digital Age: Anne Carson's *Nox*, Multimodality, and the Ethics of Bookishness," *Contemporary Women's Writing* 9.1 (March 2015), 93–111. Howe's materialist reading of the Emily Dickinson fascicles, we saw in Chapter 3, offers an interesting framework to approach the materially driven textuality of *The Midnight*. For a polemical account of Howe's reading of Dickinson, see Benn Michaels, *The Shape of the Signifier*, pp. 3–18.
30. Carson, *Economy of the Unlost*, p. 89.
31. Ibid.
32. *Nox* is unpaginated, so I refer to Carson's glossary entries by word, when citing from them, or else to the book's numbered prose instalments.
33. See Charles M. Stang, "'Nox,' or the Muteness of Things," *Harvard Divinity Bulletin*, Poetry and Faith, Winter/Spring 2012, https://bulletin.hds.harvard.edu/nox-or-the-muteness-of-things/. Stang remarks on a striking parallel between the little Carson knew of her brother and the little that is known historically about Catullus's brother.
34. Leighton, *On Form*, p. 222.
35. Ibid., p. 220.
36. Parul Sehgal, "Evoking the Starry Lad Her Brother Was," *Irish Times*, March 19, 2011, https://www.irishtimes.com/culture/books/evoking-the-starry-lad-her-brother-was-1.577255.
37. See James, *Discrepant Solace*, on what James calls "consolatory form" (pp. 20–27) and his chapter "Elegy Unrestored" (pp. 88–113).
38. Carson, *Economy of the Unlost*, p. 73.
39. Wachtel, "An Interview with Anne Carson."
40. Sehgal, "Evoking the Starry Lad Her Brother Was."
41. E.g., Meghan O'Rourke, "The Unfolding," *New Yorker*, July 5, 2010, https://www.newyorker.com/magazine/2010/07/12/the-unfolding.
42. The glossary entries have been called "exhaustive definitions," though as I understand it their tendentiousness and *non*-exhaustiveness is Carson's point here. See Eleni Sikelianos, "Sentences on *Nox*," in ed. Wilkinson, *Anne Carson: Ecstatic Lyre*, p. 148.
43. Horace, *The Art of Poetry*, line 337 (my adapted translation), and *Epistles*, Book 1, Epistle XIX, line 44 (*fidis enim manare poetica mella*), in Horace, *Satires, Epistles, Ars Poetica*, trans. H. Rushton Fairclough, Loeb Classical Library 194 (Cambridge, MA: Harvard University Press, 1991), online edition, https://www.loebclassics.com/view/horace-ars_poetica/1926/pb_LCL194.479.xml.
44. Carson has said that she derived the idea for the structure of her book from facing-page translations of classical texts. She remarks that "you get used to thinking in that little channel in between the two languages where the perfect language exists." See Wachtel, "An Interview with Anne Carson."
45. Carson, *Economy of the Unlost*, p. 132.

46. Emily Dickinson, "1691 [Part Five: The Single Hound']," in *The Complete Poems* (1890; London: Faber & Faber, 2016), p. 690. The word also appears in Carson's "Longing: A Documentary," *Decreation*, pp. 245. See Martin Heidegger, "Science and Reflection," in *The Question Concerning Technology and Other Essays*, trans. William Lovitt (New York and London: Harper Colophon, 1977), pp. 155–182 (177–179). In William Lovitt's translation, *das Unumgängliche* is rendered "that which is not to be gotten around [*Unumgängliche*], intractable and inaccessible" (p. 177). With thanks to Amador Vega for explaining the word's significance in Heidegger.
47. See Hugh Macnaghten, *The Poems of Catullus: Done into English Verse* (Cambridge: Cambridge University Press, 1925), p. 148. The unattributed citation is also noted in a review of *Nox* for *Open Letters Monthly*, in which Abigail Deutsch links the borrowing to a wider "literary gamesmanship" in the work. See Abigail Deutsch, "Tribute and Farewell," *Open Letters Monthly*, December 1, 2012, https://www.openlettersmonthlyarchive.com/olm/nox-carson.
48. *Men in the Off Hours*, p. 166. See also Priscilla Uppal, *We Are What We Mourn: The Contemporary English-Canadian Elegy* (Montreal: McGill-Queen's University Press, 2009) on the contemporary elegy form and its shifting affective requirements. Uppal discusses Carson's "Appendix to Ordinary Time" as an "elegy" for her mother, and offers a sensitive reading of Woolf's cross-outs in Carson's text: "A writer's cross-outs are preserved evidences of revision, of changes to expression. If the cross-out can be understood as the textual equivalent of a death, then death merely revises life instead of permanently erasing it." See Uppal, *We Are What We Mourn*, pp. 96–100 (p. 98).
49. Gannon, "Beauty Prefers an Edge," 33.
50. See Wachtel, "An Interview with Anne Carson."
51. See Carson, *Men in the Off Hours*, p. 42, "Odi et Amo (I Hate and I Love Perhaps You Ask Why)," which includes the epigraph "Catullus is in conflict." The poem is an adaptation of Catullus's poem "85," also known by the title Carson provides.
52. See Carson, "The Life of Towns," *Plainwater*, p. 94.
53. See Sehgal, "Evoking the Starry Lad Her Brother Was."
54. Benjamin, "The Task of the Translator," pp. 258–259.
55. Ibid., p. 261.
56. E.g., Plate, "How to Do Things with Literature in the Digital Age," and Tatiana G. Rapatzikou, "Anne Carson's *Nox*: Materiality and Memory," *Book 2.0*, 7.1 (2017), 57–65.

    The majority of articles published on the work approach it from the perspective of cultural material studies. An interesting exception is an article by Gillian Sze, whose approach to the work in terms of a "melancholic archive" reads it against Freud's "Mourning and Melancholia" (and implicitly, against Carson's protestations that the work is "not about grief"). See Gillian Sze, "The Consolatory Fold: Anne Carson's *Nox* and the Melancholic Archive," *Studies in Canadian Literature* 44.1 (2019), 66–80.
57. See Carson and Currie's discussion in King, "Unwriting the Books of the Dead." A Master's thesis is dedicated to the photographic images in Carson's book: Rebecca Anne Macmillan, "The Languages of *Nox*: Photographs, Materiality, and Translation in Anne Carson's Epitaph," University of Texas at Austin, May 2013;

as well as several academic articles, including Sophie Mayer, "Picture Theory: On Photographic Intimacy in Nicole Brossard and Anne Carson," in *Studies in Canadian Literature* 33.1 (2008), 97–117, and Kiene Brillenburg Wurth, "Re-Vision as Remediation: Hypermediacy and Translation in Anne Carson's *Nox*," *Image (&) Narrative* 14.4 (2013), 20–33.

58. Barthes, *Camera Lucida*, p. 6 (italics mine). ("Quoi qu'elle donne à voir et quelle que soit sa manière, une photographie est toujours invisible. Ce n'est pas elle qu'on voit": Roland Barthes, *La Chambre Claire: Note sur la photographie* (Paris: Gallimard, 1980), p. 18). Barthes, citing Sontag's famous description, describes the photograph of his mother as touching him "like the delayed rays of a star" (*Camera Lucida*, p. 81).

59. Judith Butler "Speaking of Rage and Grief," filmed in The Great Hall, The Cooper Union, April 28, 2014, at the 2014 PEN World Voices Festival: https://www.youtube.com/watch?v=ZxyabzopQi8. Butler also quotes Carson's lines in her review of *Antigonick*: Judith Butler, "Can't Stop Screaming (Review)," *Public Books*, May 9, 2012, https://www.publicbooks.org/cant-stop-screaming/.

60. Carson, trans., *Antigone*, p. 28, p. 30. For a charismatic account of the production and performance of Carson's translation under van Hove's direction, see Aitken, *Antigone Undone*.

61. See Philippe Lacoue-Labarthe, "On Ethics: A Propos of Antigone," *European Journal of Psychoanalysis* 5.1 (2018) https://www.journal-psychoanalysis.eu/articles/on-ethics-a-propos-of-antigone-2/. George Steiner writes extensively on the embedding of the Antigone in the history of Western philosophy, see George Steiner, *Antigones: How the Antigone Legend Has Endured in Western Literature, Art, and Thought* (1984; New Haven, CT: Yale University Press, 1996), pp. 6–8 especially.

62. Lacoue-Labarthe, "On Ethics," n.p.

63. Ibid. The quotation from Lacan appears in his famous reading of the Antigone. See Jacques Lacan, *The Seminar of Jacques Lacan, Book VII*, "The Ethics of Psychoanalysis 1959–1960," ed. Jacques-Alain Miller, trans. Dennis Porter (London and New York: Norton, 1997), pp. 241–284, in particular p. 278–280.

64. See Lacoue-Labarthe, "On Ethics," and Butler, *Antigone's Claim*.

65. *Antigone*, trans. Carson, p. 5 ("A Note from the Translator"). Antigone's line appears on page 42 of this translation, line 1034 in line-numbered translations such as Robert Fagles's, which renders the line: "all for reverence, my reverence for the gods." See Sophocles, *The Three Theban Plays*, trans. Robert Fagles (Harmondsworth, UK: Penguin, 1982), p. 107 (hereafter *Three Theban Plays*).

66. Euripides, *The Trojan Women: A Comic*, by Rosanna Bruno, text by Anne Carson (Hexham: Bloodaxe Books, 2021).

67. See Carson, *Economy of the Unlost*, p. 82. Carson describes the chromatic structure of epitaphic text, with alternating red and black lines producing an "economical" double epitaph—the red letters forming one sentence, the black another.

68. See Charlotte Salomon, *Charlotte Salomon: Life? or Theatre?* (1942), trans. Leila Vennewitz, ed. Judith C. E. Belinfante et al. (Zwolle: Waanders, 1998), p. 43.

69. See Stone's essay in *Anne Carson: Ecstatic Lyre*, ed. Wilkinson, p. 152, where she describes her drawings as "an element of form."

70. Ibid., p. 153.
71. Steiner, *Antigones*, Preface. A review of the recent, handwritten and illustrated *H of H Playbook* (2021) in *The New Yorker* describes the work as "A cross between a dramaturge's dream journal and a madman's diary, it features Carson's transformed version of the Euripides play, rendered in handwritten lines and blocky paragraphs of pasted word-processor text, alongside original illustrations." See Casey Cep, "Anne Carson's Obsession with Herakles," *New Yorker*, November 1, 2021, https://www.newyorker.com/magazine/books/11/08/anne-carsons-obsession-with-herakles.
72. *Antigonick* is unpaginated. For orientation, I provide line numbers and page references for the equivalent passages in Fagles's translation. The lines I quote here are Carson's rendering of lines 1310–1312 of the *Antigone*, in *Three Theban Plays*, p. 121. In Sophokles's play, Eurydice does not exit but remains onstage until after messenger's speech, when she "turns and reenters the palace," *Three Theban Plays*, p. 123 (between lines 1373–1374).
73. Lacan, "The Ethics of Psychoanalysis," p. 275.
74. The performance was held on June 26, 2014, curated by Ben Hjorth and held in collaboration between the University of Paris-Sorbonne, the University of Paris-Diderot, Paris-Ouest, the University of Avignon, the Laboratory of the Arts and Philosophies of the Stage (Labo LAPS), and the international Performance Philosophy network. The performance can be viewed online: https://www.youtube.com/watch?v=6ygeQDu-4EU.
75. *Antigonick*; *Three Theban Plays*, p. 108 (lines 1035–1040).
76. Fagles's translation of the same lines reads: "Danaë, Danaë— / even she endured a fate like yours, / in all her lovely strength she traded / the light of day for the bolted brazen vault, / buried within her tomb, her bridal chamber, wed to the yoke and broken."
77. *Antigone*, trans. Carson, p. 42.
78. *Antigonick*. Carson's 2015 translation is similar in tone, minus the metadramatic interpolation "I delete this line." The equivalent lines in Fagles's translation read: "Far be it from me—I haven't the skill, / and certainly no desire, to tell you when, / if ever, you make a slip in speech . . . though / someone else might have a good suggestion." *Three Theban Plays*, p. 95 (lines 766–769). Fagles alludes to an unsayable portion of Haemon's discourse, insinuating the deleted line Carson's Haimon confesses in real time.
79. Lacan, "The Ethics of Psychoanalysis," p. 243.
80. Butler, *Antigone's Claim*, pp. 2–3.
81. "'The Antigone [is] one of the most sublime and in every respect most excellent works of art of all time'—G. W. F. Hegel, *Aesthetics*," reads the back cover of *Antigonick* in the 2012 Bloodaxe Books edition.
82. The equivalent lines in *Three Theban Plays* read: "But think of Niobe—well I know her story—think what a living death she died," p. 102 (lines 915–916). Antigone recognizes her story through the story of Niobe—just as we, Carson suggests, see our lives reflected on the stage. See Andrew Benjamin on Hegel's critique of Antigone and invocation of Niobe in pursuing the problem of justice: Andrew Benjamin, *Towards a Relational Ontology* (Albany: State University of New York Press, 2015), p. 33.

83. The equivalent of lines 1–12 in *Three Theban Plays*, p. 59, and in *Antigone*, trans. Carson, p. 13. Other comparable examples in *Antigonick* spoken by Antigone include: "Hegel says people want to see their / lives on stage look at me people I go my last / road I see my last light look, death who / gathers / all of us into his old bent arms in the end is / gathering me but I am still alive," and "let's say my / unconscious while remaining unconscious could / also know the laws of consciousness."
84. Andrew David King admits his unsuccessful attempts to trace the line in Hegel, coming up with Estragon in Godot as the closest parallel: "We are all born mad. Some remain so." When asked about the rationale behind the play's opening controversy, Carson responded: "sheer sensationalism." See King, "Unwriting the Books of the Dead."
85. Carson heavily abridges Sophokles's dialogue, covering lines 102–116 in the Fagles translation: *Three Theban Plays*, p. 64 ("you're wrong from the start . . ." appears at line 107).
86. *Three Theban Plays*, p. 59 (lines 5–8). Carson's 2015 translation of the *Antigone* reads: "what bitterness pain disgust disgrace or moral shock / have we been spared" (p. 13).
87. Simone Weil, *Seventy Letters*, p. 161 (a letter to her parents dated December 16, 1942). Weil had published an important essay on *Antigone* several years earlier: see the opening chapter of Simone Weil, *Intimations of Christianity Among the Ancient Greeks* (London: Routledge 1957).
88. Lacan, "The Ethics of Psychoanalysis," pp. 270–283.
89. Ibid., p. 281. There is no equivalent line in the *Antigone*. Carson seems to have inserted the declaration between Antigone's remarks on her piety—"my reverence only brands me for irreverence" in Fagles's translation (1016); "they call my piety impiety" in *Antigonick*—and her invocation of suffering as the measure of justice: "once I suffer I will know that I was wrong. / But if these men are wrong, let them suffer . . ." (1017–1020), *Three Theban Plays*, p. 106. Carson's equivalent line in *Antigonick* is "Who suffers more I wonder."
90. An interpolation by Carson, replacing the Chorus Leader's "still the same rough winds, the wild passion / raging through the girl" in *Three Theban Plays*, p. 106 (lines 1022–1023).
91. See Stone, "Your Soul Is Blowing Apart," in *Anne Carson: Ecstatic Lyre*, ed. Wilkinson, pp. 152–155.
92. King, "Unwriting the Books of the Dead."
93. Virginia Woolf, *To the Lighthouse*, Vintage Classics Woolf Series (1927; London: Vintage, 2016), p. 143. See, for example, the essay on "Stillness" and "Every Exit is an Entrance."
94. In his introductory notes, Bernard Knox includes an interesting discussion of Brecht's interpretation, a "radical revision of Hölderlin's translation." Brecht famously cast Antigone as a symbol of the resistance to fascism in Germany. *Three Theban Plays*, p. 36–37.

95. The Chorus's reference to Brecht is an interpolation following lines 943–946, and is followed by an abridged and transformed rendering of lines 947–958 spoken by Antigone, who, in Sophokles's play, recounts the "coiling horrors" of her mother's marriage bed and the griefs borne as a result. *Three Theban Plays*, p. 103.
96. The equivalent lines in Fagles's translation read: "O dear brother, doomed / in your marriage—your marriage murders mine, / your dying drags me down to death alive!" *Three Theban Plays*, p. 103 (lines 956–958).
97. See Hutcheon, *A Theory of Parody*, p. 31, where Hutcheon argues parody can be used to point to the artifices of a text, not just to signal forms of derivation and/or mockery. Her theory of parody, here, is conceived as a modification to Gérard Genette's notion of "hypertextuality," which, Hutcheon argues here, is "not just about formal borrowing" (p. 30). Joshua Marie Wilkinson's edited collection contains a revelatory essay on *Antigonick* and comedy, covering the play's in-jokes, lawyer jokes, potential for self-mockery, etc. See Vanessa Place, "What's So Funny about *Antigonick*?," in ed. Wilkinson, *Anne Carson: Ecstatic Lyre*, pp. 165–171. Also see Rodolphe Gasché, "Self-Dissolving Seriousness: On the Comic in the Hegelian Conception of Tragedy, in *Philosophy and Tragedy*, ed. Miguel de Beistegui and Simon Sparks, Warwick Studies in European Philosophy Series (London and New York: Routledge, 2000), pp. 37–56.
98. Butler, *Antigone's Claim*, p. 68. See also Butler, "Merely Cultural," on parody's capacity as an expression of dissent. On the *Antigone*, parody, and political action, see Honig, "Antigone's Two Laws," 4–8.
99. See Bonnie Honig, "Antigone's Two Laws: Greek Tragedy and the Politics of Humanism, *New Literary History* 41.1 (Winter 2010), 1–33 (4) and Bonnie Honig, "Antigone's Laments, Creon's Grief: Mourning, Membership, and the Politics of Exception, *Political Theory* 37.1 (February 2009), 5–43.
100. George Steiner, "Anne Carson 'Translates' *Antigone*," *The Times Literary Supplement* 5705 (August 3, 2012), 8–9.
101. For example, A. E. Housman's mock "Fragment of a Greek Tragedy," which sends up tragic diction and sensibility. Contemporary to Greek tragic drama, Aristophanean comedy also sends up key elements of tragedy: a well-known example is Aristophanes's featuring of Euripides himself (and referencing his *Helen*) in the play *Thesmophoriazusae* or *Women at the Thesmophoria*. See Burrow, *Imitating Authors* (pp. 46–50), and Jendza, *Paracomedy*, which also shows how tragedy appropriated aspects of comedy to the emotive enrichment of tragedy and tragic irony.
102. See Jendza, *Paracomedy*, Introduction (esp. pp. 5–9). Jendza discusses a key case of sexual innuendo spoken by Clytemnestra in the *Agamemnon* (p. 8).
103. Comments made by Jendza: https://today.ku.edu/2020/05/22/paracomedy-examines-appropriation-humor-greek-tragedy).
104. See Place, "What's So Funny about *Antigonick*?," in ed. Wilkinson, *Ecstatic Lyre*.
105. King, "Unwriting the Books of the Dead."
106. Carson, "Variations on the Right to Remain Silent," *Nay Rather*, p. 18; reprinted in *Float* (unpaginated).

107. These objections are described in Carson, "Variations on the Right to Remain Silent," *Nay Rather*, p. 20.
108. Ibid., pp. 24, p. 22. "Vocabulary of excess" is an expression from David Constantine, whom Carson cites in the piece (pp. 20–22).
109. Carson, "Cassandra Float Can," unpaginated. For discussions of Cassandra's cry, see Nicole Loraux, *The Mourning Voice: An Essay on Greek Tragedy*, trans. Elizabeth Trapnell Rawlings (Ithaca, NY: Cornell University Press, 2002), pp. 74–75, and Honig, "Antigone's Two Laws," 5–7, on the capacity of "non-discursive sound" to generate identifications, promoting a humanism that overcomes political divisions. Cassandra's cry "OTOTOTOI POPOI DA," Honig clarifies, is not the *aiai* cry of bereavement that Loraux identifies with the "anti-politics" of mourning (Honig, "Antigone's Two Laws," 7).
110. The equivalent lines in Carson's 2006 translation of the *Agamemnon* are as follows: "No longer now out from veils like some / firstblush bride / shall my oracle glance / but as brightness blows the rising sun open / it will rush my oceans forward onto light-- / a wave of woes far worse than these." Carson, *An Oresteia*, p. 54.
111. *Nox*, 7.1. "all those little kidnaps in the dark" cites without citing Aristotle on the "kidnapping of the soul" (*psychagōgikon*) that occurs in the abrupt immediacy of seeing or spectacle. See my discussion of Aristotle's term in Chapter 8. Carson, trans., *If Not, Winter*, x.
112. A review piece in the *Harvard Review* seems to pick up on the play's prophetic function: "Out of Sophokles' timeless work, she has crafted a taut, weirdly prescient reinvention." Dawn Tripp, "Revisiting Anne Carson's Antigonick," *Harvard Review Online*, November 21, 2019, https://www.harvardreview.org/content/revisiting-anne-carsons-antigonick// Also see Zawacki, "Standing / in the Nick of Time," in *Anne Carson: Ecstatic Lyre*, ed. Wilkinson, on a "temporal rift" in *Antigonick* (p. 156).
113. Carson, "Cassandra Float Can," *Float* (unpaginated).
114. Sarah Kane, "Phaedra's Love," *Complete Plays*, introduced by David Grieg (London: Methuen, 2001), pp. 63–104. Dean, "Anne Carson Punches a Hole Through Greek Myth."
115. Carson, "Variations on the Right to Remain Silent, *Nay Rather*, p. 22.
116. "Cassandra Float Can," an iteration of the same "Essay on Translation" she claims to have spent her life rehearsing, goes on to perform these actions—"cuts" is the descriptor she settles on—on the matter of its own text. See the final section of my Chapter 8.
117. Carson, *Economy of the Unlost*, p. vii. See my Chapter 2 for a discussion of the epigraph.
118. The equivalent lines in *Three Theban Plays* read: "My countrymen, / all of you—I caught the sound of your words / as I was leaving to do my part, / to appeal to queen Athena with my prayers. / I was just loosing the bolts when a voice filled with sorrow, family sorrow, / struck my ears, and I fell back, terrified, / into the women's arms–everything went black. / Tell me the news, again, whatever it is . . . / sorrow and I are hardly strangers. / I can bear the worst" (p. 121, lines 1301–1312).

119. Andrew Zawacki suggests the inverse becomes true: that the "nick of time" does not carry a sense of "speed and reprieve" but a sense of arriving "too late." Zawacki, "Standing in / the Nick of Time," in *Anne Carson: Ecstatic Lyre*, ed. Wilkinson, p. 156.
120. Carson, "Twelve Minute Prometheus (After Aiskhylos)."
121. Tacita Dean, *Complete Works and Filmography* (London: Royal Academy of Arts, 2018), pp. 293–300.
122. Anne Carson, "TV Men: Antigone (Scripts 1 and 2)" in *Men in the Off Hours*, pp. 100–101. Though Carson reads from "TV Men: Antigone (Scripts 1 and 2) during the work, Dean's extracts from *Antigone* come from Fagles's translation (Dean, p. 295). My quotations are from Tacita Dean, *Selected Writing 1992–2018* (London: Royal Academy of Arts, 2018), p. 107.
123. Dean, *Selected Writing*, pp. 109–110.
124. Ibid., p. 110.
125. Carson cites the work in her early essay, "Simonides Negative," 157.
126. Ulrich von Wiliamowitz-Moellendorff, *Greek Historical Writing and Apollo*, trans. Gilbert Murray (Oxford: Clarendon Press, 1908), p. 25. Quoted in Simon Critchley, *Tragedy, the Greeks and Us* (London: Profile Books, 2019), p. 7 (italics mine). With thanks to Simon Critchley for a conversation on the untimeliness of prophecy and philosophy at Barcelona's Escola Europea d'Humanitats in 2019.
127. Carson, *Grief Lessons*, pp. 8–9.

Chapter 8

1. At the time of writing, a trilingual edition exists in Greek, English, and Spanish: Anne Carson, *Si no, el invierno: Fragmentos de Safo*, trans. Aurora Luque (Madrid and Mexico City: Vaso Roto, 2019).
2. In her introductory notes, Carson clarifies that her text excludes some of Voigt's single-word fragments. See Eva-Maria Voigt, *Sappho et Alcaeus. Fragmenta* (Amsterdam: Polak & van Gennep, 1971).
3. Emma Heath, "Theatre Reimagined in H of H Playbook," *Chicago Review of Books*, October 27, 2021, https://chireviewofbooks.com/2021/10/27/h-of-h-playbook/
4. See Emily Wilson, "Tongue Breaks," *London Review of Books* 26.1 (January 8, 2004), 27–28, https://www.lrb.co.uk/v26/n01/emily-wilson/tongue-breaks.
5. Greenwood, "Review [untitled]," 159. Bruce Whiteman, whose prodigious article compares versions including Sappho imitations by H. D., Ezra Pound, and translations by Mary Barnard and Guy Davenport, says Carson's versions "sound more like trots than fully achieved English poems. She prints every scrap that has survived, including single words, and her translations hew very closely to the Greek. . . . This is useful for the reader lacking Greek, but the English demonstrably needs more, well, poetry." See Bruce Whiteman, "Sappho; or, On Loss," *The Hudson Review* 66.4 (2014), 673–688.
6. See Meryl Altman, "Looking for Sappho [Review article]," *The Women's Review of Books* 21.4 (January 2004), 8–10 (10).

7. Monique Wittig and Sande Zweig, *Lesbian Peoples: Materials for a Dictionary* (New York: Avon Books, 1976), "Sappho" entry.
8. The grammarian Tzetzes notes that "the passage of time has destroyed Sappho and her works, her lyre and her songs." Quoted in Margaret Williamson, *Sappho's Immortal Daughters* (Cambridge, MA: Harvard University Press, 1998), p. 43.
9. Margaret Reynolds discusses Winterson's fiction, as well as a short story, "The Poetics of Sex" (1993), on the same theme: Margaret Reynolds, *The Sappho Companion* (New York: Palgrave Macmillan, 2000), pp. 375–376.
10. Ibid., p. 376.
11. Catullus and John Donne have both impersonated the lyric voice of fragment 31. See Ellen Greene, "Refiguring the Feminine: Catullus Translating Sappho," *Arethusa* 32.1 (Winter 1999), 1–18; and Page DuBois, *Sappho* (London: Bloosmbury, 2015), pp. 105, 118, on Donne's cross-dressing identification with Sappho's lyric speaker. DuBois also discusses translations by Aphra Behn, Monique Wittig, and imitations of Sappho's aesthetics by H. D., etc. See also Joan de Jean, *Fictions of Sappho* (Chicago: Chicago University Press, 1989).
12. Carson's examples are given on pages xii and xiii of the introductory notes to *If Not, Winter*.
13. I allude here to the title of Joan de Jean's *Fictions of Sappho*.
14. Carson, "Simonides Negative," 155.
15. Carson's reference is to Lu Chi's "Exposition on Literature" [also translated "Essay on Literature" or "The Art of Writing"], reproduced in J. J. Y. Liu, *Chinese Theories of Literature* (Chicago: University of Chicago Press, 1975).
16. The poem also echoes sentiments of short "Simonidean" poem in Carson, *Men in the Off Hours*, "Epitaph: Evil" (p. 29), which I quote later in the chapter.
17. Thinking of Carson's "Essay on What I Think About Most" and "Essay on Error" (*Men in the Off Hours*, pp. 30–36, 37), "Possessive Used as Drink (Me): A Lecture on Pronouns in the Form of 15 Sonnets," in *Float*, and, at a push, *The Beauty of the Husband*.
18. In addition to the poems from *Men in the Off Hours* cited above, the reading appears in Carson's essays, "'Just for the Thrill,'" and "Stillness."
19. Carson, "Simonides Negative," 155. The title of a recent Carson lecture bears same message: "Zero Is a Number and Nothing Is Something," the Turnbull Poetry Lecture, Johns Hopkins University, November 10, 2021. Carson's comment also echoes sentiments expressed by Carson's mother in *Nox* when, sensing that her son is no longer alive, she says, "When I pray for him nothing comes back" (*Nox*, 4.2).
20. Carson refers to Dickinson's poem in "Stillness," 9.
21. See Altman, "Looking for Sappho," 8, and Sehgal, "Evoking the Starry Lad Her Brother Was."
22. Constantine and Carson, "Ancient Words, Modern Words," 37. See Andrea Brady's *Poetry and Bondage* for an original exploration of the human conditions of possibility for the idea of verse as constraint, bondage, chains, etc. In Brady's argument, these conditions of possibility are writers and non-writers who have suffered actual bondage.

23. Nancy and Lacoue-Labarthe, *The Literary Absolute*, p. 47.
24. Sappho, "87D [youth]" in Carson, *If Not, Winter*, pp. 170–171. Copyright © 2002 by Anne Carson. Reproduced with permission of Little Brown Book Group Limited through PLSclear and used by permission of Alfred A. Knopf, an imprint of the Knopf Doubleday Publishing Group, a division of Penguin Random House LLC. All rights reserved.
25. Sienkewicz, "Anne Carson: *Eros the Bittersweet*," 90. Carson opens *Eros the Bittersweet* with remarks on Kafka's short story "The Top," a story about, she says, "a philosopher who spends his time around children so he can grab their [spinning] tops in spin" (xi), in order to confirm his belief, she quotes, "that the understanding of any detail, that of a spinning top for instance, was sufficient for the understanding of all things."
26. See Daniel Mendelsohn, "In Search of Sappho," *New York Review of Books*, August 14, 2003, https://www.nybooks.com/articles/2003/08/14/in-search-of-sappho/. See Williamson, *Sappho's Immortal Daughters*, p. 5, where Williamson asks whose image has most often been inscribed on the blank page—"[Sappho's] or her readers'?"
27. Carson, *Eros the Bittersweet*, p. 27.
28. Carson, trans., *If Not, Winter*, p. xiii.
29. Carson, *Economy of the Unlost*, p. 10.
30. Culler, *Theory of the Lyric*, p. 226.
31. Carson, *Eros the Bittersweet*, p. 32.
32. Snell, *The Discovery of the Mind*, p. 53, quoted in Carson, *Eros the Bittersweet*, p. 38. The ellipsis and second parenthetical insertion are Carson's.
33. "Fondation Hardt 1963, 119," is Carson's reference, cited in *Eros the Bittersweet*, p. 43.
34. John D'Agata makes a similar observation regarding *Eros the Bittersweet* in his interview with Carson: "you say it's because there's perhaps no true lover suggested?—no guy or gal that's literally intended in the poems?—but instead that the real lover and recipient of this desire is language itself. At least I think that's what you say." Carson seems to assent to his reading ("Isn't that profound?"). D'Agata, "A __ with Anne Carson," 8.
35. Fragment 31 is one of precious few near-complete poems in the Sappho oeuvre (several more were added following the discoveries in 2004 and 2014 of several lots of fragments, including the "Brothers Poem" and "Kypris Poem," along with a host of smaller fragments. The fragments, and the two longer poems, were confirmed to be Sappho's by Dirk Obbink, a papyrologist at the University of Oxford. For a detailed philological profile of the discoveries, see Anton Bierl and André Lardinois, eds., *The Newest Sappho: P. Sapph. Obbink and P. GC inv. 105, Frs. 1–4: Studies in Archaic and Classical Greek Song*, vol. 2 (Leiden: Brill, 2016).
36. Carson, *Decreation*, p. 179.
37. Carson, "'Just for the Thrill,'" 148.
38. Ibid., 146.
39. Ibid., 147.
40. Ibid., 150.
41. Ibid.

42. Ibid.
43. The same fragment appears in Carson, "Essay on What I Think About Most," *Men in the Off Hours*, p. 32. I discuss the poem's argument about error briefly in Chapter 1.
44. Carson, "'Just for the Thrill,'" 153. See her later iteration of these ideas (and the Chinese proverb) in Carson, "Essay on What I Think About Most," *Men in the Off Hours*, p. 30.
45. Carson, *Economy of the Unlost*, p. 52.
46. See Carson, *Nox* (7.1).
47. Aitken, "The Art of Poetry no. 88," 203. Also see Anderson's interview with Carson for *The New York Times*, in which Carson says: "I'm really trying to make people's minds move, you know, which is not something they're naturally inclined to do ... it's really important to get somehow into the mind and make it move somewhere it has never moved before. That happens partly because the material is mysterious or unknown but mostly because of the way you push the material around from word to word in a sentence. And it's that that I'm more interested in doing, generally, than mystifying by having unexpected content or bizarre forms.... [To just] throw in a bit of Hegel. Who knows what that means? But to actually take a piece of Hegel and move it around in a way that shows you something about Hegel is a satisfying challenge." Anderson, "The Inscrutable Brilliance of Anne Carson."
48. Culler, *Theory of the Lyric*, p. 226.
49. See Vendler, "Introduction" to *The Art of Shakespeare's Sonnets* in *A Lyric Theory Reader*, eds. Jackson and Prins, p. 130.
50. Sappho, "22," in Carson, *If Not, Winter*, pp. 40–41. Copyright © 2002 by Anne Carson. Reproduced with permission of Little Brown Book Group Limited through PLSclear and used by permission of Alfred A. Knopf, an imprint of the Knopf Doubleday Publishing Group, a division of Penguin Random House LLC. All rights reserved.
51. Dimitrios Yatromanolakis, "Fragments, Brackets, and Poetics: On Anne Carson's *If Not, Winter*," *International Journal of the Classical Tradition* 11.2 (Fall 2004), 266–272.
52. Ibid., 267.
53. Ibid.
54. Ibid.
55. Margaret Williamson, "Sappho and the Other Woman," in *Reading Sappho: Contemporary Approaches*, ed. Ellen Greene (Berkeley: University of California Press, 1996), pp. 248–264. See my discussion of fragment 31 in Chapter 1.
56. Williamson, "Sappho and the Other Woman," p. 255.
57. Greenwood, "Review," p. 159. Greenwood calls *Eros the Bittersweet* the "logical companion" to *If Not, Winter*.
58. Carson, *Economy of the Unlost*, p. 95.
59. On the deictic elements in Sappho's verse, see André Lardinois, "Sappho's Brothers Song and the Fictionality of Early Greek Lyric Poetry," in eds. Bierl and Lardinois, *The Newest Sappho*, 167–187. See the epigraph and opening paragraph in Chapter 2 on Celan's idea.
60. McNeilly, "Gifts and Questions," 17 (italics mine).

61. Mendelsohn, "In Search of Sappho." On the prerogatives of the composer (*troubadour*) and the performer (*jongleur*), not a "strict dichotomy" between the "creative" and the "recreative," see Gregory Nagy, *Poetry as Performance: Homer and Beyond* (Cambridge: Cambridge University Press, 2016), p. 20.
62. Scarry, *Dreaming by the Book*, p. 105.
63. Burt, "Professor or Pinhead."
64. Eleanor Wachtel, "Anne Carson on Writing from the Margins of Her Mind," *CBC Radio*, Writers and Company series, May 6, 2016, https://www.cbc.ca/radio/writersandcompany/anne-carson-on-writing-from-the-margins-of-her-mind-1.3568450.
65. See Page DuBois, *Sappho Is Burning* (Chicago: University of Chicago Press, 1995), p. 31. On the "many bodies of Sappho [that] express her contradictions," see Reynolds, *The Sappho Companion*, p. 7, and Wilson, "Tongue Breaks." Wilson's comments refer to Margaret Reynolds's *The Sappho History* (London: Palgrave Macmillan, 2003), and to the "body/text" metaphor that is, Wilson says, "all too common in writing about Sappho."
66. Burt, "Professor or Pinhead."
67. Carson, trans., *If Not, Winter*, pp. 349, 241.
68. See Carson, "The Glass Essay," *Glass, Irony and God*, p. 8.
69. Ezra Pound's poem "Papyrus," from *Lustra* (London: Elkin Matthews, 1916) reads: "Spring .... Too long .... Gongula," turning the historically contingent state of the fragment into a formal poetics. In the same volume, "Ιμερρω" ends with the line "Thou restless, ungathered." In their understated aesthetics, these poems could have come from *If Not, Winter*.
70. Whiteman, "Sappho; or, On Loss." See Rebecca Varley-Winter, *Reading Fragments and Fragmentation in Modernist Literature* (Brighton: Sussex Academic Press, 2019). A research project on precisely the question of "Fragmentary Modernisms" is led by researchers at Durham University: "Fragmentary Modernisms: The Classical Fragment in Literary and Visual Cultures 1896–1950": https://gtr.ukri.org/projects?ref=AH%2FS01201X%2F1. See also Paul Hamilton, *Metaromanticism: Aesthetics, Literature, Theory* (Chicago: University of Chicago Press, 2003), on the complex backstory to the twentieth-century literary fascination with the fragment.
71. D'Agata, "A __ with Anne Carson," 14.
72. Ibid.
73. Ibid.
74. Carson, "Cassandra Float Can," *Float* (unpaginated), and McNeilly, "Gifts and Questions," 22. The Postscript of this book reflects on the origins and futures of this anti-descriptive element in Carson.
75. See my discussion of the poem in Chapter 5.
76. Carson, "Apostle Town," *Plainwater*, p. 95.
77. Carson, *Plainwater*, pp. 93–94.
78. Quoted in Carson, "Essay on What I Think About Most," *Men in the Off Hours*, p. 31.
79. See Ernest Fenollosa and Ezra Pound, *The Chinese Written Character as a Medium for Poetry*, ed. Haun Saussy, Jonathan Stalling, and Lucas Klein (New York: Fordham University Press, 2008).

80. See Haun Saussy, "Outside the Parenthesis (Those People Were a Kind of Solution)," *Comparative Literature* 15.5 (December 2000), 849–891, a fascinating, roaring critique of post-structuralism's "resort to Asia" and the fantasies of an Asian culture "beyond" writing and therefore transcendent, "underdetermined" antitype to determinism of alphabetic culture (851).
81. *If Not, Winter*, p. 185; Voigt, *Sappho et Alcaeus. Fragmenta*, pp. 102–103.
82. With thanks to Antonio Rigo for clarifications on the Greek text. See note 59 for further reading on the deictic elements of Sappho's poetry.
83. Carson, "Epitaph: Evil," in *Men in the Off Hours*, p. 29.
84. Carson, "Stillness," 7.
85. Constantine and Carson, "Ancient Words, Modern Words," 37.
86. See the description of Holzer's intervention on the Ekeberg Park website: https://ekebergparken.com/en/kunst/cliff-sappho). My quotations are taken from Constantine and Carson, "Ancient Words, Modern Words," 37.
87. Carson, "Cassandra Float Can," *Float* (unpaginated).
88. Quoted in Carson, "Cassandra Float Can" (unpaginated) and, in an alternative translation, in *An Oresteia*: "a wave of woes far worse than these" (p. 54).
89. Carson, "Cassandra Float Can: Final Cut," *Float* (unpaginated). Copyright © 2016 by Anne Carson. Used by permission of Alfred A. Knopf, an imprint of the Knopf Doubleday Publishing Group, a division of Penguin Random House LLC, and and Jonathan Cape, a division of the Penguin Random House Group Limited. All rights reserved.
90. DuPlessis, "f-Words," 19.
91. Michael Fried, "Art and Objecthood," *Minimal Art: A Critical Anthology*, ed. Gregory Battcock, introduction by Anne M. Wagner (Berkeley: University of California Press, 1995), pp. 116–147 (pp. 125, 135).
92. Vendler, "Introduction" to *The Art of Shakespeare's Sonnets* in *A Lyric Theory Reader*, eds. Jackson and Prins, pp. 130, 132.
93. Ibid., p. 132.

Postscript

1. The keynote lecture was delivered at the interdisciplinary "Visualizing Theory Conference" on Thursday, May 10, 2018: https://visualizingtheoryconference.wordpress.com/keynote-lecture/. A full recording of the lecture is available to view: https://www.youtube.com/watch?v=CYiMmCLRIQ0. The lecture was originally delivered as one of Carson's Clark Lectures—a series of three lectures including "Stillness," "Corners," and "Chairs"—at Trinity College, Cambridge.
2. For example, the "Short Talk on the Witness of the Body," a "short talk" in three parts, which appears in "L.A.," a collection of pieces composed for performance artist Laurie Anderson, printed in *Float*. The "Talk" was produced for the catalog of Anderson's multimedia show, *Forty-Nine Days in the Bardo* (2012).

3. Carson, "Short Talk on Aeroplane Takeoff," *Short Talks*, p. 66. © 1992 by Anne Carson. Used with permission of Brick Books.
4. I was in the audience at Carson's performance of the talk along with excerpts from *Norma Jeane Baker of Troy*, at London's Southbank Centre on October 30, 2019. I refer here to my own experience of participating in Carson's "interactive lecture."
5. Carson performs the same "Short Talk" in her message of gratitude on receipt of the Princesa de Asturias award in 2020, referring to the piece as an "interactive poem."
6. See Nancy, *Le Partage des voix*, cited in Chapter 1.
7. Carson, *Economy of the Unlost*, viii.
8. Carson, "Essay on What I Think About Most," in *Men in the Off Hours*, p. 31.
9. In the tradition of Allan Kaprow, Claes Oldenburg, Oscar Masotta, etc.
10. Carson's "Lecture on the History of Skywriting" was performed at the Whitney Museum of American Art in collaboration with Robert Currie and Faisal bin Ali Jaber, an engineer from Yemen, on May 27, 2016. "Possessive Used as Drink (Me): A Lecture on Pronouns in the Form of 15 Sonnets" was first presented at Harvard's English Institute in 2007 in collaboration with dancers from the Merce Cunningham Dance Company, whose original choreography was presented in a recording by Sadie Wilcox, with an audio composition by sound artist Stephanie Rowden. "Cassandra Float Can," described as "a lecture in three parts," was first performed at the Brooklyn Academy of Music in 2008 accompanied by an intervention by Robert Currie based on images of the work of Gordon Matta-Clark in slide and poster format. Lecture I of "Uncle Falling" was first presented at Housing Works Bookstore Café in New York in 2008, with Lecture II added for a collaborative performance at the Poetry Project, St. Mark's Church in-the-Bowery, New York, in 2010, as listed in the Performance Notes of *Float*.
11. Carson, "Stillness," 1 (the original lecture spoke of a "lecture" instead of an "essay").
12. Ibid., 22.
13. Anne Carson and Maria Negroni, "Entrevista a Anne Carson por Maria Negroni," a Zoom interview forming the final installment of a course on "Poetry: The Art of Impertinence" at the Museo Malba (Museo Latinoamericano de Buenos Aires, Argentina): https://www.youtube.com/watch?v=haJbVh8arOM. A reviewer of *Men in the Off Hours* describes the work: "as though someone standing in a room cluttered with papers and books suddenly opened a door on a windstorm"; Hilbert, "On and Off Parnassus."
14. Anne Carson, "Corners," a lecture given at the New York Public Library, December 7, 2018: https://www.youtube.com/watch?v=iE7R9n8aOxg.
15. Hayot, "Then and Now," in *Critique and Postcritique*, ed. Anker and Felski, p. 291.
16. Graham Galt Harpham, *Scholarship and Freedom* (Cambridge, MA: Harvard University Press, 2020), p. 66; citing Max Weber, "Science as a Vocation," in *The Vocation Lectures*, trans. Rodney Livingston, ed. David Owen and Tracy B. Strong (Indianapolis: Hackett, 2004).
17. See Fleming, "Transcript for Poesis with Anne Carson."
18. Davenport, "Review [Untitled]," 185.

19. Carson, "Stillness," 12, 8. Carson's reference is John Cage, "An Autobiographical Statement," www.johncage.org/beta/autobiographical_statement.html, a statement she presumes to have been made in Kyoto, 1989, on receiving the Kyoto Prize, though she notes the statement is "variously attested."
20. Taken from the testimony of "EgoCircus" participant Matthew Whittinger, following the workshop at Poets House, New York: http://matthewwhittinger.com/2011/02/26/egocircus/.
21. See the article "Lecture on the Weather: John Cage in Buffalo," Burchfield Penney Art Center at Buffalo State College, January 23, 2010–February 14, 2010: https://burchfieldpenney.org/exhibitions/exhibition:01-23-2010-02-14-2010-lecture-on-the-weather-john-cage-in-buffalo/.
22. John Cage, "Thoreau Said the Same," "Composition in Retrospect," in *X: Writings '79-'82* (Middletown, CT: Wesleyan University Press, 1983), p. 133. © 1983 by John Cage. Used by permission.
23. See Jann Pasler, "Inventing a Tradition: Cage's 'Composition in Retrospect,'" in *John Cage: Composed in America*, ed. Marjorie Perloff and Charles Junkerman (Chicago and London: University of Chicago Press, 1994), p. 134.
24. See Carson, "Thirst: Introduction to Kinds of Water" and "Kinds of Water: An Essay on the Road to Compostela" in *Plainwater*, pp. 119–123 and pp. 124–187.
25. See Octavio Paz, "Water Writes Always in Plural," *Diacritics* 8.4 (Winter 1978), 41–54; Paz, *Apariencia desnuda*, pp. 105–187, in the original Spanish. Paz traces the phrase to Duchamp's *The* (1915), the artist's first text in English, in which the word "the" was systematically replaced with asterisks (p. 105). See Howe, *The Birth-mark*, p. 38.
26. See Susan Howe, "Hinge Picture" (1974), in *Frame Structures: Early Poems 1974–1979* (New York: New Directions, 1996), pp. 31–56.
27. Carson, "Short Talk on Sylvia Plath," *Short Talks*, p. 53. © 1992 by Anne Carson. Used with permission of Brick Books.
28. Carson, "Short Talk on the End," *Short Talks*, p. 52. © 1992 by Anne Carson. Used with permission of Brick Books.
29. Rembrandt van Rijn, *The Three Crosses* (1653), dry point and burin on vellum, Metropolitan Museum of Art: https://www.metmuseum.org/art/collection/search/354631. The Museum's description of the work goes some way to accounting for Carson's "darker. / Darker": "When Rembrandt created this [later] impression, he deliberately left ink on the printing plate . . . a thicker layer almost completely covers the bushes along the right edge. By creatively inking the copperplate, Rembrandt in a certain sense painted each impression." Examples from several of the four stages of printing are also held at the Bibliothèque Nationale de France and the National Gallery of Art, Washington, DC.
30. Images of *The Three Crosses* corresponding to each of the four stages of printing can be consulted on the website of the Bibliothèque Nationale de France: http://expositions.bnf.fr/rembrandt/grand/048_4.htm.
31. See the opening paragraph of Chapter 3. Davenport quotes Laughlin's observation in the introduction to Carson, *Glass, Irony and God* (ix).

32. See "Merce Sonnet" in "Possessive Used as Drink (Me): A Lecture on Pronouns in the Form of 15 Sonnets," *Float* (unpaginated).
33. Woolf, *To the Lighthouse*, p. 218.
34. Theodor W. Adorno, "Late Style in Beethoven" (1937), in *Essays on Music*, selected with an introduction, commentary, and notes by Richard Leppert, trans. Susan H. Gillespie et al. (Berkeley, Los Angeles, and London: University of California Press, 2002), pp. 564–568 (p. 564).
35. Galt Harpham, *Scholarship and Freedom*, pp. 7, 4.
36. Ibid., pp. 7, 9.
37. D'Agata, "A_ with Anne Carson," 1.
38. Ibid., 13.
39. Carson, *Economy of the Unlost*, p. viii.

Bibliography

Adorno, Theodor W. "The Actuality of Philosophy." *Telos* 31 (1977), 120–133.

Adorno, Theodor W. *Essays on Music*, selected with an introduction, commentary, and notes by Richard Leppert, trans. Susan H. Gillespie et al. (Berkeley, Los Angeles, and London: University of California Press, 2002).

Adorno, Theodor W. *Notes to Literature*, Volume I, ed. Rolf Tiedemann, trans. Shierry Weber Nicholsen (New York: Columbia University Press, 1991).

Adorno, Theodor W. *Prisms* (1955), trans. S. Weber and S. Weber (Cambridge, MA: MIT Press, 1983).

Agamben, Giorgio. *Homo Sacer: Sovereign Power and Bare Life* (1995), trans. Daniel Heller Roazen, Meridian: Crossing Aesthetics Series (Stanford, CA: Stanford University Press, 1998).

Agamben, Giorgio. *The Idea of Prose* (1985), trans. Michael Sullivan and Sam Whitsitt (Albany: State University of New York Press, 1995).

Agamben, Giorgio. "Image and Silence." *Diacritics* 40.2 (2012), 94–98.

Agamben, Giorgio. *Infancy and History* (1979), trans. Liz Heron (London: Verso, 1993).

Agamben, Giorgio. *Profanations* (2005), trans. Jeff Fort (New York: Zone Books, 2007).

Aitken, Will. "Anne Carson, the Art of Poetry No. 88." *The Paris Review* 171 (Fall 2004), 190–226, https://www.theparisreview.org/interviews/5420/anne-carson-the-art-of-poetry-no-88-anne-carson.

Aitken, Will. *Antigone Undone: Juliette Binoche, Anne Carson, Ivo van Hove and the Art of Resistance* (Regina: University of Regina Press, 2018).

Akiho, S., and T. Fujita, eds. *A Concordance to the Complete Poems of Emily Jane Brontë* (Tokyo: Shohakusha, 1976).

Allen, Danielle. "Review (*Economy of the Unlost*)." *Chicago Review* 46.1 (2000), 162–164.

Alley, Ronald. *Catalogue of the Tate Gallery's Collection of Modern Art Other than Works by British Artists* (London: Tate Gallery and Sotheby Parke-Bernet, 1981).

Altman, Meryl. "Looking for Sappho [Review article]." *The Women's Review of Books* 21.4 (January 2004), 8–10.

Anderson, Sam. "The Inscrutable Brilliance of Anne Carson." *New York Times Magazine*, March 14, 2013, https://www.nytimes.com/2013/03/17/magazine/the-inscrutable-brilliance-of-anne-carson.html.

Anker, Elizabeth S. "Why We Love Coetzee; or, *The Childhood of Jesus* and the Funhouse of Critique." In *Critique and Postcritique*, ed. Anker and Felski (Durham, NC: Duke University Press, 2017), pp. 183–210.

Anker, Elizabeth S., and Rita Felski, eds. *Critique and Postcritique* (Durham, NC: Duke University Press, 2017).

Aristotle. *Poetics*, trans. Malcolm Heath (London: Penguin Books, 1996).

Atkins, G. Douglas. *Geoffrey Hartman: Criticism as Answerable Style* (London and New York: Routledge, 1990).

Attridge, Derek. *The Work of Literature* (Oxford: Oxford University Press, 2015).

Auerbach, Erich. *Mimesis: The Representation of Reality in Western Literature* (1946), trans. Willard R. Trask (Princeton, NJ: Princeton University Press, 2013).

Austin, M. M., and P. Vidal-Naquet. *Economic and Social History of Ancient Greece: An Introduction* (Berkeley: University of California Press, 1977).

Barthes, Roland. *Le Bruissement de la langue: Essais critiques IV* (Paris: Seuil, 1984).

Barthes, Roland. *Camera Lucida* (1980), trans. Richard Howard (London: Vintage, 2000).

Barthes, Roland. *La Chambre Claire: Note sur la photographie* (Paris: Gallimard, 1980).

Barthes, Roland. *Criticism and Truth* (1966), trans. Katrine Pilcher Keuneman (1987; London and New York: Continuum, 2004).

Barthes, Roland. *Critique et Vérite* (Paris: Éditions du Seuil, 1966).

Barthes, Roland. *The Grain of the Voice: Interviews 1962–1980*, trans. Linda Coverdale (New York: Hill and Wang, 1985).

Barthes, Roland. *Image, Music, Text*, trans. Stephen Heath (London: Fontana Press, 1977).

Barthes, Roland. *A Lover's Discourse; Fragments* (1977), trans. Richard Howard (London: Vintage, 2002).

Barthes, Roland. *Le Neutre: Notes de cours au Collège de France (1977–1978)* (Paris: Seuil, 2002).

Barthes, Roland. *The Pleasure of the Text* (1973), trans. Richard Miller (New York: Hill and Wang, 1975).

Barthes, Roland. *The Responsibility of Forms: Critical Essays on Music, Art, and Representation*, trans. Richard Howard (Oxford: Blackwell, 1986).

Barthes, Roland. *Roland Barthes by Roland Barthes* (1975), trans. Richard Howard (Berkeley and Los Angeles: University of California Press, 1977).

Baudrillard, Jean. *Forget Foucault* (1977), trans. Nicole Dufresne (New York: Semiotext(e), 1987).

Becker, Daniel Levin. *Many Subtle Channels: In Praise of Potential Literature* (Cambridge, MA: Harvard University Press, 2012).

Beckett, Samuel. *Proust/Three Dialogues* (London: J. Calder, 1965).

Bell, Currer, Ellis Bell, and Acton Bell. *Poems by Currer, Ellis and Acton Bell* (London: Aylott and Jones, 1846).

Benjamin, Andrew. *Towards a Relational Ontology* (Albany: State University of New York Press, 2015).

Benjamin, Walter. *The Arcades Project* (1983), trans. Howard Eiland and Kevin McLaughlin (Cambridge, MA, and London: Harvard University Press, 1999).

Benjamin, Walter. "The Task of the Translator" (1923). In *Selected Writings*, Volume I: *1913–1926*, ed. Marcus Bullock and Michael W. Jennings (Cambridge, MA: Harvard University Press, 1996), pp. 253–263.

Benson, Fiona. *Vertigo & Ghost* (London: Jonathan Cape, 2019).

Benson, Stephen, and Clare Connors. *Creative Criticism: An Anthology and Guide* (Edinburgh: Edinburgh University Press, 2014).

Berk, Hannah. "Review: *Antigonick* and the *Fragments of Sappho* from Taffety Punk." *DC Theatre Scene*, May 28, 2019, https://dctheatrescene.com/2019/05/28/review-antigonick-and-the-fragments-of-sappho-from-taffety-punk/.

Berkobien, Megan. "An Interview with Anne Carson and Robert Currie." *Asymptote: A Journal of Translation*, October 2013, https://www.asymptotejournal.com/interview/an-interview-with-anne-carson-and-robert-currie/.

Bernadac, Marie-Laure, and Cy Twombly. *The Ceiling: Un Plafond pour le Louvre*, ed. Marie-Laure Bernadac (Paris: Éditions du Regard, Musée du Louvre, 2010).

Bernstein, Charles, ed. *Close Listening: Poetry and the Performed Word* (New York and Oxford: Oxford University Press, 1998).
Bernstein, Charles. *My Way: Speeches and Poems* (Chicago: University of Chicago Press, 1999).
Bernstein, Charles. *A Poetics* (Cambridge, MA: Harvard University Press, 1992).
Bernstein, Charles. *Shadowtime* (Los Angeles: Green Integer Editions, 2014).
Bernstein, J. M. *Against Voluptuous Bodies: Late Modernism and the Meaning of Painting* (Stanford, CA: Stanford University Press, 2006).
Berryman, John. *77 Dream Songs* (New York: Farrar, Straus and Giroux, 1964).
Bierl, Anton, and André Lardinois, eds. *The Newest Sappho: P. Sapph. Obbink and P. GC inv. 105, Frs. 1–4*: Studies in Archaic and Classical Greek Song, vol. 2 (Leiden: Brill, 2016).
Blasing, Mutlu Konuk. *Lyric Poetry: The Pain and the Pleasure of Words* (Princeton, NJ, and Oxford: Princeton University Press, 2007).
Bloom, Harold. *Agon: Towards a Theory of Revisionism* (Oxford: Oxford University Press, 1982).
Bloom, Harold. "The Breaking of Form." In *The Lyric Theory Reader: A Critical Anthology*, ed. Virginia Jackson and Yopie Prins, (Baltimore, MD: Johns Hopkins University Press, 2014), pp. 275–286.
Bloom, Harold. "Lying Against Time: Gnosis, Poetry, Criticism." In *The Rediscovery of Gnosticism: Proceedings of the International Conference on Gnosticism at Yale, New Haven, Connecticut, March 28–31, 1978*, ed. Bentley Layton, 2 vols. (Leiden: Brill, 1981), vol. 1, pp. 57–72.
Blut, Victoria. "Women's Literary Culture and the Medieval Canon." University of Surrey Blogs, December 2015, https://blogs.surrey.ac.uk/medievalwomen/2015/12/07/a-burnable-book-and-a-pseudo-woman-the-case-of-marguerite-called-porete/.
Bök, Christian. *The Xenotext: Book I* (Toronto: Coach House Books, 2015).
Bourgault, S. "Beyond the Saint and the Red Virgin: Simone Weil as Feminist Theorist of Care." *Frontiers: A Journal of Women's Studies* 35.2 (2014), 1–27.
Boyd, Malcolm, ed. *Oxford Composer Companions: J. S. Bach* (Oxford: Oxford University Press, 1999).
Brady, Andrea. *Poetry and Bondage: A History and Theory of Lyric Constraint* (Cambridge: Cambridge University Press, 2021).
Brontë, Emily. *The Poems of Emily Brontë*, ed. Barbara Lloyd-Evans (London: B. T Batsford, 1992).
Brontë, Emily. *Wuthering Heights* (London: Everyman's Library, 1991).
Brooks, Cleanth. *The Well Wrought Urn: Studies in the Structure of Poetry* (1947; London: Methuen, 1949).
Bruno, Rosanna, and Anne Carson. *Euripides: The Trojan Women: A Comic* (Manchester: Bloodaxe Books, 2021).
Brossa, Joan. *Poesía Brossa: Imagen, texto y performatividad / Brossa Poetry: Image, Text and Performativity* (Mexico City: Museo Universitario de Arte Contemporáneo, 2021).
Burrow, Colin. *Imitating Authors: From Plato to Futurity* (Oxford: Oxford University Press, 2019).
Burt, Stephanie. "Professor or Pinhead," *London Review of Books* 33.4 (July 14, 2011), https://www.lrb.co.uk/the-paper/v33/n14/stephanie-burt/professor-or-pinhead.
Bush, Catherine. "A Short Talk with Anne Carson," unpublished email interview, 2000, http://catherinebush.com/articles/a-short-talk-with-anne-carson/.

Butler, Judith. *Antigone's Claim: Kinship Between Life and Death* (New York: Columbia University Press, 2002).

Butler, Judith. "Can't Stop Screaming (Review)." *Public Books*, May 9, 2012, https://www.publicbooks.org/cant-stop-screaming/.

Butler, Judith. "Merely Cultural." *Social Text* 52–53, Queer Transexions of Race, Nation, and Gender (Autumn–Winter 1997), 265–277.

Butler, Judith. "Speaking of Rage and Grief." Filmed at The Cooper Union, April 28, 2014, PEN World Voices Festival, 2014, https://www.youtube.com/watch?v=ZxyabzopQi8.

Cabanne, Pierre. *Dialogues with Marcel Duchamp*, trans. Ron Padgett (London: Thames and Hudson, 1971).

Cage, John. "Composition in Retrospect." In Cage, *X, Writings '79–'82* (Middletown, CT: Wesleyan University Press, 1983), pp. 123–152.

Cage, John. *Silence: Lectures and Writings* (Middletown, CT: Wesleyan University Press, 1961).

Cairns, Douglas. *Aidos: The Psychology and Ethics of Honour and Shame in Ancient Greek Literature* (Oxford: Oxford University Press, 1993).

Cameron, Sharon. "The Practice of Attention: Simone Weil's Performance of Impersonality." *Critical Inquiry* 29.2 (Winter 2003), 216–252.

Campbell, James D. "Review: Betty Goodwin: Musée d'art contemporain, Montreal, Canada" *Frieze* (October 1, 2009), https://frieze.com/article/betty-goodwin.

Carson, Anne. "The Albertine Workout." *London Review of Books* 36.11 (June 5, 2014), https://www.lrb.co.uk/the-paper/v36/n11/anne-carson/the-albertine-workout.

Carson, Anne. *The Albertine Workout*. "Poetry Pamphlet" Series (New York: New Directions, 2014).

Carson, Anne, trans. *Antigonick: Sophokles*, illustrated by Bianca Stone, design by Robert Currie (Tarset: Bloodaxe Books, 2012).

Carson, Anne. *Autobiography of Red: A Novel in Verse* (New York: Knopf, 1998).

Carson, Anne. *The Beauty of the Husband: A Fictional Essay in 29 Tangos* (London: Vintage, 2001).

Carson, Anne. "Betty Goodwin 'Seated Figure with Red Angle (1988).'" *ArtForum* 38.1 (September 1999), 156–157.

Carson, Anne. *Decreation: Poetry, Essays Opera* (2005; London: Jonathan Cape, 2006).

Carson, Anne. "'Echo with No Door on Her Mouth': A Notional Refraction through Sophokles, Plato, and Defoe." *Stanford Literature Review* 3.2 (Fall 1986), 247–261.

Carson, Anne. "Economy, Its Fragrance." *The Threepenny Review* 69 (Spring 1997), 14–16.

Carson, Anne. *Economy of the Unlost: (Reading Simonides of Keos with Paul Celan)* (Princeton, NJ: Princeton University Press, 1999).

Carson, Anne. *Eros the Bittersweet: An Essay* (1986; Champaign, IL: Dalkey Archive Press, 1998).

Carson, Anne. "Essay on What I Think About Most." *Raritan*, 18.3 (Winter 1999), https://raritanquarterly.rutgers.edu/issue-index/all-.

Carson, Anne. *Float* (New York: Knopf, 2016).

Carson, Anne. "Foam (Essay with Rhapsody): On the Sublime in Longinus and Antonioni." *Conjunctions* 37 (Twentieth Anniversary Issue, 2001), 96–104.

Carson, Anne. *Glass, Irony and God* (New York: New Directions, 1995).

Carson, Anne. *Grief Lessons: Four Plays by Euripides* (New York: New York Review of Books, 2006).

Carson, Anne. *H of H Playbook* (New York: New Directions, 2021).

Carson, Anne, trans. *If Not, Winter: Fragments of Sappho* (2002; London: Virago Press, 2003).
Carson, Anne. "'Just for the Thrill': Sycophantizing Aristotle's *Poetics*." *Arion: A Journal of Humanities and the Classics* (Winter 1990), 142–154.
Carson, Anne. "The Keats Headaches." *Times Literary Supplement*, February 22, 2019, https://www.the-tls.co.uk/articles/the-keats-headaches/.
Carson, Anne. *Men in the Off Hours* (New York: Vintage, 2000).
Carson, Anne. *Nay Rather*. The Cahiers Series (no. 21). Centre for Writers and Translators, the American University of Paris (Paris: Sylph Editions, 2013).
Carson, Anne. *Norma Jeane Baker of Troy: A Version of Euripides' Helen* (London: Oberon Books, 2019).
Carson, Anne. "Now What?" *Grand Street Journal* 9.3 (Spring 1990), 43–45.
Carson, Anne. *Nox* (New York: New Directions, 2010).
Carson, Anne, trans. *An Oresteia: Agamemnon by Aiskhylos, Elektra by Sophokles, Orestes by Euripides* (New York: Faber and Faber, 2009).
Carson, Anne. *Plainwater* (New York: Knopf, 1995; New York: Vintage Contemporaries, 2000).
Carson, Anne. "Putting Her in Her Place: Woman, Dirt and Desire." In *Before Sexuality*, ed. D. Halperin and F. Zeitlin (Princeton, NJ: Princeton University Press, 1990), pp. 135–170.
Carson, Anne. *Red Doc>* (London: Jonathan Cape, 2013).
Carson, Anne. "The Sheer Velocity and Ephemerality of Cy Twombly." *LitHub*, October 22, 2020, https://lithub.com/anne-carson-the-sheer-velocity-and-ephemerality-of-cy-twombly/.
Carson, Anne. *Short Talks* (Kingston, ON: Brick Books, 1992).
Carson, Anne. "Simonides Negative." *Arethusa* 21.2 (Fall 1988), 147–157.
Carson, Anne. *Si no, el invierno: Fragmentos de Safo*, trans. Aurora Luque (Madrid and Mexico City: Vaso Roto, 2019).
Carson, Anne. "Sonnet Isolate." *London Review of Books* 32.21 (November 4, 2010), https://www.lrb.co.uk/the-paper/v32/n21/anne-carson/sonnet-isolate.
Carson, Anne. "Stillness." *Critical Inquiry* 48.1 (Autumn 2021), 1–22.
Carson, Anne. "Triple Sonnet of the Plush Pony." *London Review of Books* 29.16 (August 16, 2007), 16.
Carson, Anne. "Twelve Minute Prometheus (After Aiskhylos)." *London Review of Books* 30.20 (October 23, 2008), https://www.lrb.co.uk/v30/n20/anne-carson/twelve-minute-prometheus-after-aiskhylos.
Carson, Anne, et al. "Freaks and Greeks. Antigone: A Roundtable Between Anne Carson, Simon Critchley, and Trajal Harrell." Hosted by Lauren O"Neill-Butler. *ArtForum*, September 22, 2015, https://www.artforum.com/slant/antigone-a-roundtable-with-anne-carson-simon-critchley-and-trajal-harrell-55046.
Carson, Anne, and Kim Anno. *The Albertine Workout* (St. Joseph, MN: One Crow Press, The Literary Arts Institute of the College of St. Benedict, September 2014).
Carson, Anne, and Kim Anno. *The Mirror of Simple Souls: An Opera Installation* (St. Joseph, MN: One Crow Press, The Literary Arts Institute of the College of St. Benedict, 2003).
Carson-Giacomelli, Anne. "Odi et Amo Ergo Sum" (University of Toronto, 1981).
Carter, Angela. *The Infernal Desire Machines of Doctor Hoffman* (1972; London: Penguin Books, 1986).

Ceballos, Manuela. "Life and Death by the Book: A Dramatic Reading of Marguerite Porete's *Mirror of Simple Souls*." *English Language Notes* 56.1 (April 2018), 183–196.

Celan, Paul. *Collected Prose*, trans. Rosmarie Waldrop (1986; New York: Routledge, 2003).

Celan, Paul. *Gesammelte Werke*. 5 vols. (Frankfurt: Suhrkamp, 1983), vol. 1.

Celan, Paul. *The Meridian. Final Version. Drafts. Materials*, ed. Bernhardt Böschenstein and Heino Schmull, trans. Pierre Joris (Palo Alto, CA: Stanford University Press, 2011).

Celan, Paul. *Poems of Paul Celan*, trans. Michael Hamburger (1972; London: Anvil Press, 2007).

Cep, Casey. "Anne Carson's Obsession with Herakles." *New Yorker*, November 1, 2021, https://www.newyorker.com/magazine/books/11/08/anne-carsons-obsession-with-herakles.

Certeau, Michel de. *La fable mystique: XVIe–XVIIe siècle* (Paris: Gallimard, 1982).

Chatwin, Seymour. *Antonioni, or, the Surface of the World* (Berkeley: University of California Press, 1985).

Chihaya, Sarah. "A Glass Essay: Reading Anne Carson Post-breakup." *The Yale Review* 110.2 (June 1, 2022), https://yalereview.org/article/sarah-chihaya-anne-carson.

Chihaya, Sarah, Merve Emre, Katherine Hill, and Jill Richards. *The Ferrante Letters: An Experiment in Collective Criticism* (New York: Columbia University Press, 2020).

Cixous, Hélène. *Reading with Clarice Lispector*, ed. and trans. Verena Andermatt Conley (Minneapolis: University of Minnesota Press, 1990).

Clutch Fleischmann, T. "The Transposition Workout." *Brooklyn Rail*, September 2014, https://brooklynrail.org/2014/09/books/the-transposition-workout.

Coles, Elizabeth. "The Sacred Object: Anne Carson and Simone Weil." *Acta Poetica* 34.1 (2013), 127–154.

Coles, Elizabeth. "Thérèse mon amour: Julia Kristeva's St. Teresa of Avila." *Feminist Theology* 24.2 (2016), 156–170.

Constantine, Peter, and Anne Carson. "Ancient Words, Modern Words: A Conversation with Anne Carson." *World Literature Today* 88.1 (January–February 2014), 36–37.

Copeland, Roger. *Merce Cunningham: The Modernizing of Modern Dance* (New York and London: Routledge, 2004).

Corngold, Stanley. "*Economy of the Unlost: Reading Simonides of Keos with Paul Celan*." (review). *Modernism/Modernity* 7.2 (2000), 322–324.

Critchley, Simon. *Tragedy, the Greeks and Us* (London: Profile Books, 2019).

Culler, Jonathan. *Theory of the Lyric* (Cambridge, MA: Harvard University Press, 2017).

Curtis, Paul. *Stesichoros's Geryoneis*. Mnemosyne Supplements: Monographs on Greek and Latin Language and Literature, no. 333 (Leiden and Boston: Brill, 2011).

D'Agata, John. "A__ with Anne Carson." *The Iowa Review* 27.2 (1997), 1–22.

D'Agata, John. "A Talk with Anne Carson (Interview)." *Brick* 57 (Fall 1997), 14–22.

D'Agata, John. "Review: Men in the Off Hours." *Boston Review*, June 1, 2000, http://bostonreview.net/poetry/john-dagata-review-men-hours.

D'Agata, John. "We Might as Well Call it the Lyric Essay." *Seneca Review* 44 (2014), 6–10, https://www.hws.edu/senecareview/dagata_le.pdf.

D'Agata, John, and Susan Steinberg. "John D'Agata Redefines the Essay," an interview with Susan Steinberg. *Electric Literature* (July 14, 2016), https://electricliterature.com/john-dagata-redefines-the-essay/.

D'Agata, John, and Deborah Tall. "New Terrain: The Lyric Essay." *Seneca Review* 27.2 (Fall 1997), 7–8, https://www.hws.edu/senecareview/lyricessay.aspx.

Danto, Arthur C. *The Philosophical Disenfranchisement of Art*, foreword by Jonathan Gilmore (New York: Columbia University Press, 1986, 2005).

Davenport, Guy. "Introduction" to Anne Carson, *Glass, Irony and God* (New York: New Directions, 1995).

Davenport, Guy. "Review [*Eros the Bittersweet*]." *Grand Street* 6.3 (Spring 1987), 184–191.

Davies, Stevie. *Emily Brontë: Heretic* (London: The Women's Press, 1994).

Dean, Tacita. "Anne Carson Punches a Hole Through Greek Myth." *Interview Magazine*, December 16, 2021, https://www.interviewmagazine.com/culture/anne-carson-punches-a-hole-through-greek-myth.

Dean, Tacita. *Complete Works and Filmography* (London: Royal Academy of Arts, 2018).

Dean, Tacita. *Selected Writing 1992–2018* (London: Royal Academy of Arts, 2018).

De Man, Paul. "Phenomenality and Materiality in Kant." In *Aesthetic Ideology*, ed. Andrej Warminski (Minneapolis and London: University of Minnesota Press, 1996), pp. 70–90.

Deresiewicz, William. "In Defense of Facts." *The Atlantic*, January–February 2017, https://www.theatlantic.com/magazine/archive/2017/01/in-defense-of-facts/508748/.

Derrida, Jacques. *La Dissémination* (Paris: Seuil, 1972).

Derrida, Jacques. *Dissemination* (1972), translated and with an introduction by Barbara Johnson (London: The Athlone Press, 1981).

Derrida, Jacques. *Given Time: I. Counterfeit Money* (1991), trans. Peggy Kamuf (Chicago: University of Chicago Press, 1992).

Derrida, Jacques. *Glas*, trans. John P. Leavey and Richard Rand (Lincoln: University of Nebraska Press, 1990).

Dess, G. D. "The Perils and Pitfalls of the Lyric Essay." *Los Angeles Review of Books*, May 22, 2019, https://lareviewofbooks.org/article/the-perils-and-pitfalls-of-the-lyric-essay/.

Deutsch, Abigail. "Tribute and Farewell." *Open Letters Monthly*, December 1, 2012, https://www.openlettersmonthlyarchive.com/olm/nox-carson.

Dickinson, Emily. *The Complete Poems* (1890; London: Faber & Faber, 2016).

Dillon, Brian. *Essayism* (London: Fitzcarraldo Editions, 2017).

Disney, Dan. "Sublime Disembodiment? Self-as-Other in Anne Carson's Decreation." *Orbis Litterarum* 67.1 (2012), 25–38.

Drucker, Johanna. "Visual Performance of the Poetic Text." In *Close Listening: Poetry and the Performed Word*, ed. Charles Bernstein (New York and Oxford: Oxford University Press, 1998), pp. 131–161.

DuBois, Page. *Sappho* (London: Bloosmbury, 2015).

DuBois, Page. *Sappho Is Burning* (Chicago: University of Chicago Press, 1995).

Duchamp, Marcel. *The Essential Writings of Marcel Duchamp*, ed. Michel Sanouillet and Elmer Peterson (London: Thames and Hudson, 1973).

Du Plessis, Rachel Blau. "f-Words: An Essay on the Essay." *American Literature* 68.1, Write Now: American Literature in the 1980s and 1990s (March 1996), 15–45.

DuPlessis, Rachel Blau. *The Pink Guitar: Writing as Feminist Practice* (Tuscaloosa: University of Alabama Press, 2006).

Eco, Umberto. *The Open Work* (1962), trans. Anna Cancogni (Cambridge, MA: Harvard University Press, 1989).

Elkamel, Sara. "Anne Carson and Robert Currie in Conversation with Sara Elkamel and NYU Undergrads: On Starting in the Middle." *Washington Square Review* (May 5, 2021), https://www.washingtonsquarereview.com/blog/2021/5/4/anne-car

son-amp-robert-currie-on-starting-in-the-middle-in-conversation-with-sara-elkamel-amp-nyu-undergrads.

Erickson, Steve, and Angela Stubbs. "An Interview with Steve Erickson." *Bookslut* (December 2007), http://www.bookslut.com/features/2007_12_012067.php.

Euripides. *Euripides in Four Volumes, I: Iphigeneia at Aulis, Rhesus Hecuba, The Daughters of Troy, Hecuba*, trans. Arthur S. Way (London: William Heinemann, 1916).

Eve, Martin Paul. *Literature Against Criticism: University English and Contemporary Fiction in Conflict* (Cambridge: Open Book, 2016).

Felski, Rita. *The Limits of Critique* (Chicago: University of Chicago Press, 2015).

Felstiner, John. *Paul Celan: Poet, Survivor, Jew* (New Haven, CT, and London: Yale University Press, 1995).

Fenollosa, Ernest, and Ezra Pound. *The Chinese Written Character as a Medium for Poetry*, ed. Haun Saussy, Jonathan Stalling, and Lucas Klein (New York: Fordham University Press, 2008).

Fields, Sean. *The Beguine, the Angel, and the Inquisitor* (Notre Dame, IN: University of Notre Dame Press, 2012).

Fischer, B. K. "Review: Carson, Fulton, Rankine." *Boston Review*, July 15, 2014, https://bostonreview.net/articles/bk-fischer-review-carson-fulton-rankine/.

Fisher, Jessica. "Anne Carson's Stereoscopic Poetics." In *Anne Carson: Ecstatic Lyre*, ed. Joshua Marie Wilkinson (Ann Arbor: University of Michigan Press, 2015), pp. 10–16.

Flasch, Kurt. *Meister Eckhart: Philosopher of Christianity* (2011; New Haven, CT: Yale University Press, 2015).

Fleming, Jim, and Anne Carson. "Transcript for Poesis with Anne Carson." "To the Best of Our Knowledge." Wisconsin Public Radio, http://archive.ttbook.org/book/transcript/transcript-poesis-anne-carson.

Freud, Sigmund. *The Interpretation of Dreams: The Complete and Definitive Text*, ed. and trans. James Strachey (1955; New York: Basic Books, 2010).

Freud, Sigmund. "Thoughts for the Time on War and Death." In *The Standard Edition of the Complete Psychological Works of Sigmund Freud*, trans. James Strachey, vol. XIV (1914–1916), "On the History of the Psychoanalytic Movement, Papers on Metapsychology and Other Works" (London: The Hogarth Press and the Institute of Psycho-analysis, 1957), pp. 275–300.

Fried, Michael. "Art and Objecthood." In *Minimal Art: A Critical Anthology*, ed. Gregory Battcock, introduction by Anne M. Wagner (Berkeley: University of California Press, 1995), pp. 116–147.

Frus, Phyllis, and Christy Williams, eds. *Beyond Adaptation: Essays on Radical Transformations of Original Works* (Jefferson, NC: McFarland, 2010).

Furlani, André. "Reading Paul Celan with Anne Carson: What Kind of Withness Would That Be?" *Canadian Literature* 176 (Spring 2003), 84–104.

Gadamer, Hans Georg. *Gadamer on Celan: "Who Am I and Who Are You?" and Other Essays*, ed. and trans. Richard Heinemann and Bruce Krajewski (Albany: State University of New York Press, 1997).

Gander, Forrest. *Be With* (New York: New Directions, 2018).

Gannon, Mary. "Anne Carson: Beauty Prefers an Edge." *Poets and Writers* 29.2 (March–April 2001), 26–33.

Gasché, Rodolphe. "Self-Dissolving Seriousness: On the Comic in the Hegelian Conception of Tragedy." In *Philosophy and Tragedy*, ed. Miguel de Beistegui and

Simon Sparks. Warwick Studies in European Philosophy Series (London and New York: Routledge, 2000), pp. 37–56.

Genette, Gerard. *Palimpsests: Literature in the Second Degree*, trans. Channa Newman and Claude Doubinksy (Lincoln, NE: University of Nebraska Press, 1997).

Girard, René. *Deceit, Desire and the Novel: Self and Other in Literary Structure* (1961), trans. Yvonne Freccero (Baltimore, MD: Johns Hopkins University Press, 1965).

Girard, René. *The Scapegoat* (1982), trans. Yvonne Freccero (Baltimore, MD: Johns Hopkins University Press, 1986).

Glück, Louise. *Poems 1962–2012* (New York: Farrar, Strauss and Giroux, 2012).

Goldsmith, Kenneth. *Uncreative Writing: Managing Language in the Digital Age* (New York: Columbia University Press, 2011).

Görner, Rüdiger. "Hölderlin's Romantic Classicism." In *The Oxford Handbook of European Romanticism*, ed. Paul Hamilton (Oxford: Oxford University Press, 2016), pp. 274–292.

Graham, Jorie. "The Art of Poetry No. 85." interview by Thomas Gardner. *The Paris Review* 165 (Spring 2003), 165, http://www.theparisreview.org/interviews/263/the-art-of-poetry-no-85-jorie-graham).

Graham, Jorie. *The Errancy* (Manchester: Carcanet Press, 1997).

Graham, W. S. *New Collected Poems* (London: Faber and Faber, 2004).

Greene, Ellen. "Refiguring the Feminine: Catullus Translating Sappho." *Arethusa* 32.1 (Winter 1999), 1–18.

Greenwood, Emily. "Review [untitled]." *The Journal of Hellenic Studies* 125 (2005), 158–159.

Guenette, Mark D. "Le Loup et le Narrateur: The Masking and Unmasking of Homosexuality in Proust's *À la recherche du temps perdu.*" *Romanic Review* 80.2 (March 1, 1989), 229–247.

Haas, Alois M. *Sermo mysticus: Studien zu Theologie und Sprache der deutschen Mystik* (Freiburg, Schweiz: Universitätsverlag, 1979).

Hall, Edith. "Aristotle's Theory of Katharsis in Its Historical and Social Contexts." In *Transformative Aesthetics*, ed. Erika Fischer-Lichte and Benjamin Wihstutz (London: Routledge, 2017), pp. 26–47.

Hall, Edith. "Autobiography of the Western Subject: Carson's Geryon." In *Living Classics*, ed. S. J. Harrison (Oxford: Oxford University Press, 2009), pp. 218–237.

Hall, Edith. "Subjects, Selves and Survivors." *Helios* 34.2 (Fall 2007), 125–160.

Halliwell, Stephen. *The Aesthetics of Mimesis: Ancient Texts and Modern Problems* (Princeton, NJ, and Oxford: Princeton University Press, 2002).

Hamburger, Michael. *Art as Second Nature: Occasional Pieces* (Manchester: Carcanet New Press, 1975).

Hamilton, Paul. *Metaromanticism: Aesthetics, Literature, Theory* (Chicago: University of Chicago Press, 2003).

Harman, Graham. "Art Without Relations." *ArtReview* 66 (November 4, 2014), 144–147, https://artreview.com/features/september_2014_graham_harman_relations/.

Harman, Graham. *Object-Oriented Ontology: A New Theory of Everything* (London: Penguin, 2018).

Harpham, Graham Galt. *Scholarship and Freedom* (Cambridge, MA: Harvard University Press, 2020).

Hartman, Geoffrey. "Crossing Over: Literary Commentary as Literature." *Comparative Literature* 28 (1976), 257–276.

Hayot, Eric. "Then and Now." In *Critique and Postcritique*, ed. Elizabeth S. Anker and Rita Felski (Durham, NC, and London: Duke University Press, 2017), pp. 279–296.

Heaney, Seamus. *The Burial at Thebes: Sophokles' Antigone* (London: Faber and Faber, 2004).

Heath, Emma. "Theatre Reimagined in *H of H Playbook*." *Chicago Review of Books*, October 27, 2021, https://chireviewofbooks.com/2021/10/27/h-of-h-playbook/.

Heidegger, Martin. *Being and Time*, trans. John Macquarrie and Edward Robinson (Oxford: Blackwell, 1962, 2005).

Heidegger, Martin. *Basic Writings*, ed. and trans. David Farrell Krell (London: Routledge, 1993).

Heidegger, Martin. "Science and Reflection." In Heidegger, *The Question Concerning Technology and Other Essays*, trans. William Lovitt (New York and London: Harper Colophon, 1977), pp. 155–182.

Hertz, Neil. "Lurid Figures." In *Reading De Man Reading*, ed. Lindsay Waters and Wlad Godzich (Minneapolis: Minnesota University Press, 1989), pp. 82–104.

Herzog, Jacques, and Pierre De Meuron. *Treacherous Transparencies: Thoughts and Observations Triggered by a Visit to the Farnsworth House* (Barcelona: Actar/IITAC Press, 2016).

Hilbert, Ernest. "On and Off Parnassus [Review article]." *Contemporary Poetry Review*, July 8, 2005, https://www.cprw.com/on-and-off-of-parnassus.

Hillis Miller, J. "The Critic as Host." *Critical Inquiry* 3.3 (Spring 1977), 439–447.

Hölderlin, Friedrich. *Selected Poems and Fragments: Bilingual Edition*, trans. Michael Hamburger, ed. Jeremy Adler (London: Penguin, 1998).

Hollywood, Amy. *Sensible Ecstasy: Mysticism, Sexual Difference and the Demands of History* (Chicago: University of Chicago Press, 2001).

Homans, Margaret. *Women Writers and Poetic Identity* (Princeton, NJ: Princeton University Press, 1980).

Homer. *The Odyssey*, trans. Emily Wilson (London and New York: Norton, 2018).

Honig, Bonnie. "Antigone's Laments, Creon's Grief: Mourning, Membership, and the Politics of Exception." *Political Theory* 37.1 (February 2009), 5–43.

Honig, Bonnie. "Antigone's Two Laws: Greek Tragedy and the Politics of Humanism." *New Literary History* 41.1 (Winter 2010), 1–33.

Horace. *Satires, Epistles, Ars Poetica*, trans. H. Rushton Fairclough, Loeb Classical Library 194 (Cambridge, MA: Harvard University Press, 1991), https://www.loebclassics.com/view/horace-ars_poetica/1926/pb_LCL194.479.xml.

Howe, Susan. *The Birth-mark: Unsettling the Wilderness in American Literary History* (Middletown, CT: Wesleyan University Press, 1993).

Howe, Susan. "The End of Art." *Archives of American Art Journal* 14.4 (1974), 2–7.

Howe, Susan. *Frame Structures: Early Poems 1974–1979* (1974; New York: New Directions, 1996).

Howe, Susan. *The Midnight* (New York: New Directions, 2003).

Howe, Susan. *My Emily Dickinson* (1985; New York: New Directions, 2007).

Howe, Susan. *Sorting Facts, or Nineteen Ways of Looking at Marker* (1996; New York: New Directions, 2013).

Howe, Susan. *That This* (New York: New Directions, 2010).

Husserl, Edmund. *Analyses Concerning Passive and Active Synthesis: Lectures on Transcendental Logic*, trans. Anthony J. Steinbock (Dordrecht, Boston, and London: Kluwer Academic, 2001).

Hutcheon, Linda. "Interdisciplinary Opera Studies." *PMLA* 121.3 (May 2006), 802–810.

Hutcheon, Linda. *A Theory of Parody: The Teachings of Twentieth-Century Art Forms* (New York and London: Methuen, 1985).

Hutcheon, Linda, and Michael Hutcheon. "Interdisciplinary Opera." *Journal of the Royal Musical Association* 134.1 (2009), 149–159.

Hutchinson, Lucy. *Order and Disorder* (Oxford: Blackwell, 2001).

Jackson, Virginia, and Yopie Prins, eds. *The Lyric Theory Reader: A Critical Anthology* (Baltimore, MD: Johns Hopkins University Press, 2014).

James, David. *Discrepant Solace: Contemporary Literature and the Work of Consolation* (Oxford: Oxford University Press, 2019).

Jameson, Fredric. *Valences of the Dialectic* (New York: Verso, 2009).

Janis, Harriet, and Sidney Janis. "Marchel Duchamp: Anti-Artist." *View: The Modern Magazine [Duchamp Issue]*, Series V, no. 1 (March 1945), reprinted in *The Dada Painters and Poets: An Anthology*, ed. Robert Motherwell (1951; Cambridge, MA: Harvard University Press, 1981), pp. 306–316.

Jansen, Laura, ed. *Anne Carson/Antiquity*. Bloomsbury Studies in Classical Reception (London: Bloomsbury, 2022).

Jarvis, Simon. "An Undeleter for Criticism." *Diacritics* 32.1, Rethinking Beauty (Spring 2002), 3–18.

Jean, Joan de. *Fictions of Sappho* (Chicago: Chicago University Press, 1989).

Jeanrond, Werner G. *A Theology of Love* (New York: T & T Clark, 2010).

Jendza, Craig. *Paracomedy: Appropriations of Comedy in Greek Tragedy* (Oxford: Oxford University Press, 2020).

Jonsson, Einar Mar. *Miroir, Naissance d'un genre littéraire* (Paris: Les Belles Lettres, 1995).

Kane, Sarah. *Complete Plays*, introduced by David Grieg (London: Methuen, 2001).

Keats, John. *Keats: Poetical Works*, ed. H. W. Garrod (Oxford: Oxford University Press, 1956, 1990).

Keats, John. *The Letters of John Keats, 1814–1821*, ed. Hyder Edward Rollins, 2 vols. (Cambridge, MA: Harvard University Press, 1958), volume I.

Kellaway, Kate, and Anne Carson. "I Do Not Believe in Art as Therapy." *The Guardian*, October 30, 2016, https://www.theguardian.com/books/2016/oct/30/anne-carson-do-not-believe-art-therapy-interview-float.

Kermode, Frank. *The Classic: Literary Images of Permanence and Change* (Cambridge, MA: Harvard University Press, 1983).

King, Andrew David. "Unwriting the Books of the Dead: Anne Carson and Robert Currie on Translation, Collaboration, and History." *Kenyon Review*, October 6, 2012, https://kenyonreview.org/2012/10/anne-carson-robert-currie-interview/.

Klaus, Carl H., and Ned Stuckey French, eds. *Essayists on the Essay: Montaigne to Our Time* (Iowa City: University of Iowa Press, 2012).

Kondoleon, Christine, et al. *Cy Twombly: Making Past Present* (Boston: MFA Publications, 2020).

Krajewski, Bruce. "Economy of the Unlost: Reading Simonides of Keos with Paul Celan [Review]." *Bryn Mawr Classical Review* 2.39 (2003), https://bmcr.brynmawr.edu/2003/2003.02.39/).

Krauss, Rosalind. "Cy's Up." *Artforum International*, September 1994, https://www.artforum.com/print/199407/cy-s-up-33352.

Krauss, Rosalind. "The Story of the Eye." *New Literary History* 21.2 (Winter 1990), 283–298.

Kristeva, Julia. *Teresa My Love: An Imagined Life of the Saint of Avila* (2008), trans. Lorna Scott Fox (New York: Columbia University Press, 2015).
Kristeva, Julia. *Thérèse mon amour* (Paris: Fayard, 2008).
Lacan, Jacques. *The Seminar of Jacques Lacan, Book VII, The Ethics of Psychoanalysis 1959–1960*, ed. Jacques-Alain Miller, trans. Dennis Porter (London and New York: Norton, 1997).
Lacoue-Labarthe, Philippe. "On Ethics: A Propos of Antigone." *European Journal of Psychoanalysis* 5.1 (2018), https://www.journal-psychoanalysis.eu/articles/on-ethics-a-propos-of-antigone-2/.
Lacoue-Labarthe, Philippe, and Jean-Luc Nancy. *The Literary Absolute* (1978), trans. Philip Barnard and Cheryl Lester (New York: State University of New York Press, 1988).
Ladenson, Elisabeth. *Proust's Lesbianism* (Ithaca, NY, and London: Cornell University Press, 1999).
Landes, Michael. "Anne Carson: Icon of Intellect." *Washington Square News*, February 6, 2017, https://nyunews.com/2017/02/06/anne-carson-icon-of-intellect/.
Largier, Niklaus. "Recent Work on Meister Eckhart: Positions, Problems, New Perspectives." *Recherches de Théologie et Philosophie Médiévales* 65.1 (1998), 147–167.
La Rocco, Claudia. "Amid a Sculptural Physicality, a Poet Walks and Talks Onstage" (Review of Carson's performance pieces "Stacks" and "Bracko"), *New York Times*, December 7, 2008, https://www.nytimes.com/2008/12/08/arts/dance/08stac.html.
Lauterbach, Ann. "As (It) Is: Toward a Poetics of the Whole Fragment." In *American Women Poets in the 21st Century: Where Lyric Meets Language*, ed. Claudia Rankine and Juliana Spahr (Middletown, CT: Wesleyan University Press, 2002), pp. 363–366.
Leavis, F. R., and Q. D. Leavis. *Lectures in America* (London: Chatto and Windus, 1969).
Leighton, Angela. *On Form: Poetry, Aestheticism, and the Legacy of a Word* (Oxford: Oxford University Press, 2007).
Liapis, Vayos, and Avra Sidiropoulou. *Adapting Greek Tragedy: Contemporary Contexts for Ancient Texts* (Cambridge: Cambridge University Press, 2021).
Lichtmann, Maria. "Marguerite Porete and Meister Eckhart: The Mirror of Simple Souls Mirrored." In *Meister Eckhart and the Béguine Mystics: Hadewijch of Brabant, Mechthild of Magdeburg, and Marguerite Porete*, ed. Bernard McGinn (New York: Continuum Press, 1994), pp. 65–86.
Liddell, Henry George, and Robert Scott. *Liddell and Scott's Greek-English Lexicon Abridged* (n.p.: Simon Wallenberg Press, 2007).
Lista, Michael. "Is Anne Carson the Only Poet with More Fans than Readers?" *The Walrus*, October 2016, https://thewalrus.ca/audens-opposite/.
Liu, J. J. Y. *Chinese Theories of Literature* (Chicago: University of Chicago Press, 1975).
Lobel, E., and D. Page, eds. *Poetarum Lesbiorum Fragmenta* (Oxford: Oxford University Press, 1955).
Loman, Andrew. "Anne Carson, Antigone, and the State of Exception." *Independent*, March 5, 2016, https://theindependent.ca/uncategorized/anne-carson-antigone-and-the-state-of-exception/
Longenbach, James. *The Resistance to Poetry* (Chicago: University of Chicago Press, 2004).
Longinus. "On Sublimity." In *Classical Literary Criticism*, ed. D. A. Russell and Michael Winterbottom (Oxford: Oxford University Press, 1972, 1998), pp. 143–187.
Loraux, Nicole. *The Mourning Voice: An Essay on Greek Tragedy*, trans. Elizabeth Trapnell Rawlings (Ithaca, NY: Cornell University Press, 2002).

Love, Heather. "Close Reading and Thin Description." *Public Culture* 25.3 (Fall 2013), 401–434.

Lowry, Elizabeth. "The Man Who Would Put to Sea on a Bathmat." *London Review of Books* 22.19 (October 5, 2000), https://www.lrb.co.uk/the-paper/v22/n19/elizabeth-lowry/the-man-who-would-put-to-sea-on-a-bathmat.

Lukács, Georg. *Writer and Critic, and Other Essays*, ed. and trans. Arthur Kahn (London: Merlin, 1970).

Macmillan, Rebecca Anne. "The Languages of *Nox*: Photographs, Materiality, and Translation in Anne Carson's Epitaph." MA thesis, University of Texas at Austin (2013).

Macnaghten, Hugh. *The Poems of Catullus: Done into English Verse* (Cambridge: Cambridge University Press, 1925).

Marczewska, Kaja. *This Is Not a Copy: Writing at the Iterative Turn* (London and New York: Bloomsbury, 2018).

Marvell, Andrew. *Selected Poems*, ed. Bill Hutchings (New York: Routledge, 2002).

Mauss, Marcel. *The Gift: Forms and Functions of Exchange in Archaic Societies* (1925), trans. I. Cunnison (1925; New York: Norton, 1967).

Mayer, Sophie. "Picture Theory: On Photographic Intimacy in Nicole Brossard and Anne Carson." *Studies in Canadian Literature* 33.1 (2008), 97–117.

McAlpine, Erica. *The Poet's Mistake* (Princeton, NJ: Princeton University Press, 2020).

McGinn, Bernard. *The Harvest of Mysticism in Medieval Germany (1300–1500)*, *The Presence of God: A History of Western Mysticism*, vol. IV (New York: Herder and Herder, 2005).

McGurl, Mark. *The Program Era: Postwar Fiction and the Rise of Creative Writing* (Cambridge, MA: Harvard University Press, 2009).

McKenzie, Oran. "Spillage and Banditry: Anne Carson's Derivatives." *Economies of English*, SPELL: Swiss Papers in English Language and Literature 33 (2016), 225–243.

McKenzie, Oran. "'To see matter stumble out of its forms': Anne Carson's Poetry and Visual Art." *Mémoire* submitted to the English Department, University of Geneva (August 2015).

McNeilly, Kevin. "Five Fairly Short Talks on Anne Carson." *Canadian Literature* 176 (Spring 2003), 6–10.

McNeilly, Kevin. "Gifts and Questions: An Interview with Anne Carson." *Canadian Literature* 176 (Spring, 2003), 12–25.

Mendelsohn, Daniel, and Alec Ash. "Daniel Mendelsohn on Updating the Classics of Greek and Roman Literature [Interview]." *Five Books*, April 4, 2012, https://fivebooks.com/best-books/classics-daniel-mendelsohn/.

Mendelsohn, Daniel. "In Search of Sappho." *New York Review of Books*, August 14, 2003, https://www.nybooks.com/articles/2003/08/14/in-search-of-sappho/.

Merkin, Daphne. "Last Tango." *New York Times*, September 30, 2001, p. 12, https://www.nytimes.com/2001/09/30/books/last-tango.html.

Meyer, Paul. "She] ⟨Ha?⟩ She." PhD thesis, University of Toronto (2016).

Michaels, Walter Benn. *The Shape of the Signifier: 1967 to the End of History* (Princeton, NJ: Princeton University Press, 2006).

Miller, Lucasta. *The Brontë Myth* (London: Jonathan Cape, 2001).

Milton, John. *Complete Poems and Major Prose*, ed. Meritt Y. Hughes (1957; Cambridge and Indianapolis: Hackett, 2003).

Moi, Toril. "I Came with a Sword: Simone Weil's Way." *London Review of Books* 43.13 (July 1, 2021), https://www.lrb.co.uk/the-paper/v43/n13/toril-moi/i-came-with-a-sword.

Moncion, Laura. "The Dangerous Women Project (Marguerite Porete)." Institute for Advanced Studies in the Humanities (IASH), University of Edinburgh, May 2016, https://dangerouswomenproject.org/2016/05/28/marguerite-porete/#_ftn3.

Montaigne, Michel de. *The Essays of Michel de Montaigne: Done into English by John Florio* (London: David Nutt, 1892).

Montanari, Franco, and Lara Pagani. *From Scholars to Scholia: Chapters in the History of Ancient Greek Scholarship* (Berlin: De Gruyter, 2011).

Morris, Ian. "Gift and Commodity in Archaic Greece." *Man* 21.1 (March 1986), 1–17.

Nagy, Gregory. *Poetry as Performance: Homer and Beyond* (Cambridge: Cambridge University Press, 2016).

Nancy, Jean-Luc. *Le Partage des voix* (Paris: Éditions Galilée, 1982).

Newman, Barbara. *From Virile Woman to WomanChrist: Studies in Medieval Religion and Literature* (Philadelphia: University of Pennsylvania Press, 1995).

Ngai, Sianne. *Our Aesthetic Categories: Zany, Cute, Interesting* (Cambridge, MA: Harvard University Press, 2012).

Nowell-Smith, David. *W. S. Graham: The Poem as Art Object* (Oxford: Oxford University Press, 2022).

O'Brien, Justin. "Albertine the Ambiguous: Notes on Proust's Transposition of Sexes." *PMLA* 64.5 (December 1949), 933–952.

O'leary, Joanne. "Pulling out the Screams: A Scattershot Collection of Unsettling Poems [Review of *Float*]." *Times Literary Supplement*, September 1, 2017, https://www.the-tls.co.uk/articles/pulling-out-the-screams/.

O'Rourke, Megan. "The Unfolding." *New Yorker*, July 5, 2010, https://www.newyorker.com/magazine/2010/07/12/the-unfolding.

Oswald, Alice. *Nobody: A Hymn to the Sea* (New York: Norton, 2019).

Pasler, Jann. "Inventing a Tradition: Cage's 'Composition in Retrospect.'" In *John Cage: Composed in America*, ed. Marjorie Perloff and Charles Junkerman (Chicago and London: University of Chicago Press, 1994), pp. 125–143.

Paz, Octavio. *Apariencia desnuda: La obra de Marcel Duchamp* (Mexico City: El Colegio nacional/Ediciones Era, 2008).

Paz, Octavio. "Water Writes Always in Plural." *Diacritics* 8.4 (Winter 1978), 41–54.

Peponi, Anastasia-Erasmia. "*Ècriture* and the Budding Classicist." In *Anne Carson/Antiquity*, ed. Laura Jansen (London: Bloomsbury, 2022), pp. 51–62.

Perloff, Marjorie. *Unoriginal Genius: Poetry by Other Means* (Chicago: University of Chicago Press, 2010).

Pétrement, Simone. *Simone Weil: A Life*, trans. Raymond Rosenthal (New York: Pantheon Books, 1976).

Pickstock, Catherine. *After Writing: On the Liturgical Consummation of Philosophy* (Oxford: Blackwell, 1998).

Place, Vanessa. "What's So Funny about *Antigonick*?" In *Anne Carson: Ecstatic Lyre*, ed. Joshua Marie Wilkinson (Ann Arbor: University of Michigan Press, 2015), pp. 165–171.

Plate, Liedeke. "How to Do Things with Literature in the Digital Age: Anne Carson's *Nox*, Multimodality, and the Ethics of Bookishness." *Contemporary Women's Writing* 9.1 (March 2015), 93–111.

Plato. *The Collected Dialogues*, ed. Edith Hamilton and Huntington Cairns. Bollingen Series LXXI (Princeton, NJ: Princeton University Press, 1961).

Plato. *Phaedrus*, trans. Walter Hamilton (London and New York: Penguin, 1973; 1995).

Plato. *The Republic*, trans. A. D. Lindsay (London: Everyman's Library, 1992).
Plato. *Theaetetus; Sophist*, trans. H. N. Fowler (1921; Cambridge, MA: Harvard University Press, 1966).
Pomel, Fabienne Pomel. *Miroirs et jeux de miroirs dans la littérature médiévale* (Rennes: Presses universitaires de Rennes, 2016).
Porete, Margharita. *Lo Specchio delle anime semplici*, bilingual edition, trans. Giovanna Fozzer, with a preface by Romana Guarnieri and commentary by Marco Vannini (Milano: Edizioni San Paolo, 1994).
Porete, Marguerite. *The Mirror of Simple Souls*, trans. Ellen Babinsky (Mahwah, NJ: Paulist Press, 1993).
Potts, Robert. "Neither Rhyme nor Reason." *The Guardian*, January 26, 2002, https://www.theguardian.com/books/2002/jan/26/poetry.tseliotprizeforpoetry.
Pound, Ezra. *Lustra* (London: Elkin Matthews, 1916).
Proust, Marcel. *À la recherche du temps perdu*, III, édition publiée sous la direction de Jean-Yves Tadié avec, pour ce volume, la collaboration d'Antoine Compagnon et de Pierre-Edmond Robert (Paris: Gallimard, 1988).
Proust, Marcel. *In Search of Lost Time*, Volume V: *The Captive and The Fugitive*, trans. C. K. Scott Moncrieff and Terence Kilmartin. Modern Library Classics (New York: Random House, 1993).
Rae, Ian. "Anne Carson and the Solway Hoaxes." *Canadian Literature* 176 (2003), 45–65.
Rae, Ian. "'Dazzling Hybrids': The Poetry of Anne Carson." *Canadian Literature* 166 (Autumn 2000), 17–41.
Rae, Ian. "Verglas: Narrative Technique in Anne Carson's 'The Glass Essay.'" *ESC* 37.3–4 (September–December 2011), 163–186.
Rapatzikou, Tatiana G. "Anne Carson's *Nox*: Materiality and Memory." *Book 2.0*, 7.1 (2017), 57–65.
Rankine, Claudia and Juliana Spahr, eds. *American Women Poets in the 21st Century: Where Lyric Meets Language* (Middletown CT: Wesleyan University Press, 2002).
Rankine, Claudia. *Don't Let Me Be Lonely: An American Lyric* (Minneapolis: Graywolf Press, 2004).
Rankine, Claudia. *The End of the Alphabet* (New York: Grove Press, 1998).
Rehak, Melanie. "Things Fall Together." *New York Times*, March 26, 2000, https://www.nytimes.com/2000/03/26/magazine/things-fall-together.html.
Rexilius, Andrea. "The Light of This Wound: Marriage, Longing, Desire in Anne Carson's *The Beauty of the Husband*." In *Anne Carson: Ecstatic Lyre*, ed. Joshua Marie Wilkinson (Ann Arbor: University of Michigan Press, 2015), pp. 107–113.
Reynolds, Margaret. *The Sappho Companion* (New York: Palgrave Macmillan, 2000).
Reynolds, Margaret. *The Sappho History* (London: Palgrave Macmillan, 2003).
Rhys, Jean. *Wide Sargasso Sea* (1966; London: Penguin Books, 2000).
Ricks, Christopher. *Essays in Appreciation* (Oxford: Oxford University Press, 1996).
Ricoeur, Paul. *The Rule of Metaphor* (1975), trans. Robert Czerny with Kathleen McLaughlin and John Costello. Routledge Classics (London and New York: Routledge, 2004).
Riding, Laura. *Anarchism Is Not Enough*, ed. Lisa Samuels (Berkeley: University of California Press, 2001).
Rooney, Ellen. "Live Free or Describe: The Reading Effect and the Persistence of Form." *Differences* 21.3 (2010), 112–139.
Rose, Gillian. *Judaism and Modernity* (Oxford: Blackwell, 1993).

Rose, Gillian. *The Melancholy Science: An Introduction to the Thought of T. W. Adorno.* Verso Radical Thinkers (1978; London and New York: Verso, 2014).

Rose, Gillian. *Mourning Becomes the Law: Philosophy and Representation* (Cambridge: Cambridge University Press, 1996).

Rose, Jacqueline. *Albertine* (2001; London: Vintage, 2002).

Rose, Jacqueline. *Women in Dark Times* (London: Bloomsbury, 2014).

Ruddick, Lisa. "When Nothing Is Cool." In *The Future of Scholarly Writing*, ed. A. Bammer and R.-E. Boetcher Joeres (New York: Palgrave Macmillan, 2015), pp. 71–86.

Ruprecht, Louis A., Jr. *Reach Without Grasping: Anne Carson's Classical Desires* (Lanham, MD: Lexington Books, 2021).

Russell, D. A., and Michael Winterbottom, eds. *Classical Literary Criticism* (Oxford: Oxford University Press, 1972, 1989).

Sagner Buurma, Rachel, and Laura Heffernan. "Notation after 'The Reality Effect': Remaking Reference with Roland Barthes and Sheila Heti." *Representations* 125.1 (Winter 2014), 80–102.

Saleh, Reema. "Stillness Complicated by Corners: A Reflection on Anne Carson's Lecture Series." *The Official University of Chicago Arts Blog*, December 2019, https://www.uchicagoartsblog.art/archive/2019/12/19/stillness-complicated-by-corners-a-reflection-on-anne-carsons-lecture-series.

Salomon, Charlotte. *Charlotte Salomon: Life? or Theatre?* (1942), trans. Leila Vennewitz, ed. Judith C. E. Belinfante et al. (Zwolle: Waanders, 1998).

Sartre, Jean-Paul. *Mallarmé or the Poet of Nothingness*, trans. E. Sturm (University Park: Penn State University Press, 1988).

Sastri, Reena. "'Wildly Constant': Anne Carson's Poetics of Encounter." *Contemporary Literature* 62.3 (Fall 2021), 307–337.

Saussy, Haun. "Outside the Parenthesis (Those People Were a Kind of Solution)." *Comparative Literature* 15.5 (December 2000), 849–891.

Scarry, Elaine. *Dreaming by the Book* (Princeton, NJ: Princeton University Press, 1999).

Sedgwick, Eve Kosofsky. *Touching Feeling: Affect, Pedagogy, Performativity* (Durham, NC: Duke University Press, 2003).

Sehgal, Parul. "Evoking the Starry Lad Her Brother Was." *Irish Times*, March 19, 2011, https://www.irishtimes.com/culture/books/evoking-the-starry-lad-her-brother-was-1.577255.

Serpell, C. Namwali. *Seven Modes of Uncertainty* (Cambridge, MA: Harvard University Press, 2014).

Serpell, C. Namwali. "A Heap of Cliché." In *Critique and Postcritique*, ed. Elizabeth S. Anker and Rita Felski (Durham, NC, and London: Duke University Press, 2017), pp. 153–182.

Shakespeare, William. *The Oxford Shakespeare: The Complete Works*, ed. Stanley Wells and Gary Taylor (Oxford: Clarendon Press, 1986, 2005).

Siegel, Jerrold. *The Private Worlds of Marcel Duchamp: Desire, Liberation and the Self in Modern Culture* (Berkeley: University of California Press, 1997).

Sienkewicz, T. J. "Anne Carson: *Eros the Bittersweet*." *The Classical Bulletin* 63.3 (Summer 1987), 89–90.

Simic, Charles. "The Spirit of Play." *New York Review of Books*, November 3, 2005, https://www.nybooks.com/articles/2005/11/03/the-spirit-of-play/.

Simic, Charles, et al. "Reading 9-11-01." *Artforum* 40.3 (November 2001), 41–42, https://www.artforum.com/print/200109/reading-9-11-01-1866.

Snell, Bruno. *The Discovery of the Mind in Greek Philosophy and Literature* (1948), trans. T. G. Rosenmeyer (1948; Oxford: Basil Blackwell, 1953).
Solie, Karen. "On the Irreconcilable Temptations of Anne Carson." *Literary Hub*, October 1, 2019, https://lithub.com/on-the-irreconcilable-temptations-of-anne-carson/.
Soloski, Alexis. "Greek Tragedies Lost in Anne Carson's Translation." *The Guardian* (Theatre blog), April 27, 2009, https://www.theguardian.com/stage/theatreblog/2009/apr/27/greek-tragedies-anne-carson-translation.
Solway, David. "The Trouble with Annie: David Solway Unmakes Anne Carson." *Books in Canada*, July 2001, http://www.booksincanada.com/article_view.asp?id=3159.
Sontag, Susan. *Against Interpretation and Other Essays* (1961; London and New York: Penguin Classics, 2009).
Sontag, Susan. *Notes on Camp*, Penguin Modern Series (Harmondsworth, UK: Penguin, 2018).
Sontag, Susan. "Simone Weil [Review of Simone Weil, *Selected Essays*]." *New York Review*, February 1, 1963, https://www.nybooks.com/articles/1963/02/01/simone-weil/.
Sophocles. *The Three Theban Plays*, trans. Robert Fagles (Harmondsworth, UK: Penguin Books, 1982).
Sophokles. *Antigone*, trans. Anne Carson (London: Oberon Books, 2015).
Sophokles. *Antigonick*, trans. Anne Carson, illustrated by Bianca Stone (Tarset: Bloodaxe Books, 2012).
Spahr, Juliana. *Everybody's Autonomy: Connective Reading and Collective Identity* (Tuscaloosa: University of Alabama Press, 2001).
Spahr, Juliana. "Introduction." In *American Women Poets in the 21st Century: Where Lyric Meets Language*, ed. Claudia Rankine and Juliana Spahr (Middletown, CT: Wesleyan University Press, 2002), pp. 1–17.
Stang, Charles M. "'Nox,' or the Muteness of Things." *Harvard Divinity Bulletin*, Poetry and Faith, (Winter/Spring 2012), https://bulletin.hds.harvard.edu/nox-or-the-muteness-of-things/.
Stanton, Robert. "'I am writing this to be as wrong as possible to you': Anne Carson's Errancy." *Canadian Literature* 176 (Spring 2003), 28–43.
Starobinski, Jean. "Can One Define the Essay?" (1983), trans. Lyndsey Scott. In *Essayists on the Essay: Montaigne to Our Time*, ed. Carl H. Klaus and Ned Stuckey French (Iowa City: University of Iowa Press, 2012), pp. 110–111.
Statkiewicz, Max. *Rhapsody of Philosophy: Dialogues with Plato in Contemporary Thought* (University Park: Penn State University Press, 2009).
Steefel, Lawrence. "Marcel Duchamp and the Machine." In *Marcel Duchamp*, ed. Anne D'Harnoncourt and Kynaston McShine (New York: Museum of Modern Art, 1973), pp. 69–80.
Steiner, George. "Anne Carson 'Translates' Antigone." *Times Literary Supplement* 5705 (August 3, 2012), 8–9.
Steiner, George. *Antigones: How the Antigone Legend Has Endured in Western Literature, Art, and Thought* (1984; New Haven, CT: Yale University Press, 1996).
Steiner, George. *Real Presences* (Chicago: University of Chicago Press, 1989).
Stone, Bianca. "Your Soul Is Blowing Apart: *Antigonick* and the Influence of Collaborative Process." In *Anne Carson: Ecstatic Lyre*, ed. Joshua Marie Wilkinson (Ann Arbor: University of Michigan Press, 2015), pp. 152–155.

Swensen, Cole. "Opera Povera: Decreation, an Opera in Three Parts." In *Anne Carson: Ecstatic Lyre*, ed. Joshua Marie Wilkinson (Ann Arbor: University of Michigan Press, 2015), pp. 127–131.

Sze, Gillian. "The Consolatory Fold: Anne Carson's *Nox* and the Melancholic Archive." *Studies in Canadian Literature* 44.1 (2019), 66–80.

Sze, Gillian. "Erring and *Whatever*." In *Anne Carson/Antiquity*, ed. Laura Jansen (London: Bloomsbury, 2022), pp. 63–74.

Taylor, Mark C. *Disfiguring: Art, Architecture, Religion* (Chicago: University of Chicago Press, 1992).

Thorp, Jennifer. "Oases and Mirages in the Desert of 'After Proust.'" *Oxonian Review* 25.5 (June 30, 2014), http://www.oxonianreview.org/wp/oases-and-mirages-in-the-desert-of-after-proust/.

Thorp, Jennifer. "Prowling the Meanings: Anne Carson's Doubtful Forms." PhD thesis, University of Manchester (2015).

Timpane, John. "Nox Is a Moving Story—and an Art Object." *Philadelphia Inquirer*, October 3, 2010, https://www.inquirer.com/philly/entertainment/20101003__quot_Nox_quot__is_a_moving_book_-_and_an_art_object.html.

Trilling, Lionel. *The Liberal Imagination* (New York: Scribner's Sons, 1976).

Tripp, Dawn. "Revisiting Anne Carson's *Antigonick*." *Harvard Review Online*, November 21, 2019, https://www.harvardreview.org/content/revisiting-anne-carsons-antigonick/.

Tschofen, Monique. "Drawing out a New Image of Thought: Anne Carson's Radical Ekphrasis." *Word and Image* 29.2 (2013), 233–243.

Ulmer, Gregory L. "The Object of Post-Criticism." *The Anti-Aesthetic: Essays in Postmodern Culture*, ed. Hal Foster (Seattle, WA: Bay Press, 1983), pp. 83–110.

Uppal, Priscilla. *We Are What We Mourn: The Contemporary English-Canadian Elegy* (Montreal: McGill-Queen's University Press, 2009).

Van Praet, Helena. "Writer's Writer Revisits Authorship: Iteration in Anne Carson's *Decreation*." *Canadian Literature* 241 (2020), 18–35.

Varley-Winter, Rebecca. *Reading Fragments and Fragmentation in Modernist Literature* (Brighton, UK: Sussex Academic Press, 2019).

Vega, Amador. *Tres poetas del exceso: La hermenéutica imposible en Eckhart, Silesius y Celan* (Barcelona: Fragmenta Editorial, 2011).

Vendler, Helen. *The Art of Shakespeare's Sonnets* (Cambridge, MA: Harvard University Press, 1997).

Voegelin, Eric. *Science, Politics and Gnosticism* (Washington, DC: Regnery, 1968).

Voigt, Eva-Maria. *Sappho et Alcaeus: Fragmenta* (Amsterdam: Polak & van Gennep, 1971).

Wachtel, Eleanor. "Anne Carson on Writing from the Margins of Her Mind." *CBC Radio*, Writers and Company series, May 6, 2016, https://www.cbc.ca/radio/writersandcompany/anne-carson-on-writing-from-the-margins-of-her-mind-1.3568450.

Wachtel, Eleanor, and Anne Carson, "An Interview with Anne Carson." *Brick* 89 (Summer 2012), 29–47, https://brickmag.com/an-interview-with-anne-carson/.

Warner, Marina. *Indigo or Mapping the Waters* (London: Chatto and Windus, 1992).

Watt, Adam. "Poetry as Creative Critique: Notes on the Desert of After Proust (On Anne Carson's 'The Albertine Workout')." *Contemporary French and Francophone Studies* 20.4–5 (2016), 648–656.

Weber, Max. "Science as a Vocation." In Weber, *The Vocation Lectures*, trans. Rodney Livingston, ed. David Owen and Tracy B. Strong (Indianapolis: Hackett, 2004), pp. 1–31.
Weil, Simone. *L'Enracinement* (Paris: Gallimard, 1949).
Weil, Simone. *Gravity and Grace* (1947), trans. A Wills (Lincoln: University of Nebraska Press, 1997).
Weil, Simone. *Gravity and Grace* (1947), eds. Emma Crawford and M. von du Ruhr (1953; London: Routledge, 2002).
Weil, Simone. "The Iliad, or the Poem of Force [trans. Mary McCarthy]." *Chicago Review* 18.2 (1965), 5–30.
Weil, Simone. *Intimations of Christianity Among the Ancient Greeks* (London: Routledge 1957).
Weil, Simone. *Lectures on Philosophy*, trans. Hugh Price (Cambridge: Cambridge University Press, 1978).
Weil, Simone. *The Notebooks of Simone Weil*, trans. A. Wills, 2 vols. (New York: Routledge & Kegan Paul, 1956), vol. 2.
Weil, Simone. *La Pesanteur et la grâce* (Paris: Plon, 1947).
Weil, Simone. *Seventy Letters: Personal and Intellectual Windows on a Thinker*, trans. Richard Rees (Eugene, OR: Wipf and Stock, 1965).
Weil, Simone. *Waiting on God* (1950), trans. Emma Crawford (London: Routledge, 1951).
Whiteman, Bruce. "Sappho; or, On Loss." *The Hudson Review* 66.4 (2014), 673–688.
Wilde, Oscar. *The Critic as Artist* (New York: David Zwirner Books, 2019).
Wiliamowitz-Moellendorff, Ulrich von. *Greek Historical Writing and Apollo*, trans. Gilbert Murray (Oxford: Clarendon Press, 1908).
Wilkinson, Joshua Marie, ed. *Anne Carson: Ecstatic Lyre* (Ann Arbor: University of Michigan Press, 2015).
Willett, Steven. "Economy of the Unlost: Reading Simonides of Keos with Paul Celan." *Bryn Mawr Classical Review* 2.28 (2000), https://bmcr.brynmawr.edu/2000/2000.02.28.
Williams, Isobel. *Catullus: Shibari Carmina* (Manchester, UK: Carcanet, 2021).
Williamson, Margaret. "Sappho and the Other Woman." In *Reading Sappho: Contemporary Approaches*, ed. Ellen Greene (Berkeley: University of California Press, 1996), pp. 248–264.
Williamson, Margaret. *Sappho's Immortal Daughters* (Cambridge, MA: Harvard University Press, 1998).
Wilson, Emily. "Tongue Breaks." *London Review of Books* 26.1 (January 8, 2004), 27–28, https://www.lrb.co.uk/v26/n01/emily-wilson/tongue-breaks.
Wimsatt, W. K., and M. C. Beardsley. *The Verbal Icon* (1954; London: Methuen, 1970).
Winterson, Jeanette. *Frankissstein* (London and New York: Jonathan Cape, 2019).
Wittig, Monique, and Sande Zweig. *Lesbian Peoples: Materials for a Dictionary* (New York: Avon Books, 1976).
Wolfteich, Claire. "Attention or Destruction: Simone Weil and the Paradox of the Eucharist." *The Journal of Religion* 81.3 (2001), 359–376.
Woolf, Virginia. *How Should One Read a Book?* Introduction and afterword by Sheila Heti (1935; London: Lawrence King, 2020).
Woolf, Virginia. *The Moment and Other Essays* (1949; New York: Harcourt Brace Jovanovich, 1974).
Woolf, Virginia. *To the Lighthouse*. Vintage Classics Woolf Series (1927; London: Vintage, 2016).

Wurth, Kiene Brillenburg. "Re-Vision as Remediation: Hypermediacy and Translation in Anne Carson's *Nox*." *Image (&) Narrative* 14.4 (2013), 20–33.
Yatromanolakis, Dimitrios. "Fragments, Brackets, and Poetics: On Anne Carson's *If Not, Winter*." *International Journal of the Classical Tradition* 11.2 (Fall 2004), 266–272.
Zawacki, Andrew. "Standing in / the Nick of Time: *Antigonick* in Seven Short Takes." In *Anne Carson: Ecstatic Lyre*, ed. Joshua Marie Wilkinson (Ann Arbor: University of Michigan Press, 2015), pp. 156–164.
Zwicky, Jan. *Lyric Philosophy* (1992; Edmonton and Calgary: Brush Education, 2014).
Zwicky, Jan. *Wittgenstein Elegies* (Kingston, ON: Brick Books, 1986).

Index

For the benefit of digital users, indexed terms that span two pages (e.g., 52–53) may, on occasion, appear on only one of those pages.

Abanthis (Sappho), 213, 214
Adorno, Theodor, 17–19, 129, 233–34
Agamben, Giorgio, 112–13, 154–55, 194, 226–27
Agamemnon (Aiskhylos), 148, 168, 197, 221
Agostinelli, Alfred, 46–47, 48, 251n.64
aidōs, 15–16, 17–18, 33, 106, 137, 278n.59
Aiskhylos (Aeschylus), 148, 168, 197
  See also specific works
Aitken, Will, 232–33
Akhmatova, Anna, 150
À la recherche du temps perdu (Proust), 34–35, 43, 44–51
Albertine (Rose), 49–50
Albertine Simonet (Proust), 44–45, 46–47, 48–50, 51, 59–60
The Albertine Workout (Carson)
  aesthetics of notation and, 46
  À la recherche du temps perdu as a source for, 34–35, 43, 44–51
  appendices of, 44–46, 50–51, 121
  artist book edition of, 46
  Barthes and, 45–46, 50–51
  hermeneutics and, 45, 49–50, 65, 187
  Mallarmé and, 47–48
  nonsequitur connections in, 52
  Proust's letter to Heraklitos in, 49–50
  transposition theory and, 46–47
Alkestis (*Alcestis*, Euripides), 176
Alkman, 14–15, 211
Allen, Danielle, 66–67
Altman, Meryl, 202, 205–6
Anakreon (Anacreon), 14–15, 36–37
Andrews, Bruce, 8
Anne Carson/Antiquity (Jansen), 26–27
Anno, Kim, 11–12, 46, 252n.68
Antigone (Dean film), 200
Antigone (Sophokles)
  burial rites and, 189–90
  Carson's 2015 translation of, 2–3, 189–90, 195–96

Chorus's appeal to precedent in, 192
Hegel's critique of, 192–95
Hölderlin's translation of, 196–97, 198–99
killing of Polyneikes in, 178–79, 189–90
sisters' dispute in, 193–94
as source for *Antigonick*, 27, 178–79
Antigonick (Carson)
  Antigone as a source for, 27, 178–79
  Barthes and, 39–40
  Beckett and, 194
  Brecht and, 195
  Chorus of, 192–95
  Eurydike's monologue in, 199
  as found text, 191–92
  illustrations in, 178–79, 190–91
  imitation and pastiche in, 158
  as immanent commentary, 15–16
  "nick" in, 198–200
  Sorbonne performance (2014) of, 192–93
  transparency and, 27, 191–92
  Woolf and, 190–91, 194
Antonioni, Michelangelo, 125–26, 130–31, 136, 144–45
Aphrodite, 153, 156–57
"Apostle Town" (Carson), 218
Appellstruktur (Haas), 149, 153–54
"Appendix to Ordinary Time" (Carson), 90–91, 185
Archilochos, 14–15, 126
Ares, 156–57
Aristotle
  dianoia and, 209–10
  on error, 204–5
  on metaphor, 35–36
  mimesis and, 211, 218–19, 227–28, 230
  on the poet as imitator of reality, 31–32
  on visual spectacle (*opsis*), 22, 210–11
Ars Poetica (Horace), 183–84
Art and Lies (Winterson), 203
Auden, W. H., 109–10, 141
Augustine, 1–2, 276–77n.43

Austin, M. M., 69–70
Autobiography of Red (Carson)
    commercial success of, 3
    Geryoneis as a source for, 19–20, 26–27, 149–50, 202–3
    as immanent commentary, 15–16
    paratexts of, 169, 203, 233–34
    Red Doc> and, 26–27
    verse-novel form of, 2–3

Bacon, Francis, 21, 59–60
Baker, Norma Jeane. *See* Monroe, Marilyn
Bakhtin, Mihkail, 153–54
Barnard, Mary, 217
Barthes, Roland. *See also specific works*
    on criticism as lifting and variation of signs, 13
    on the critic's language, 41–42, 70–71
    on dedication, 105–6, 111–12
    on "destruction of every voice," 69–70, 142–43
    eros and, 39–40, 41–42, 43
    on form as "what is between the thing and its name," 117
    on fusion of first-person voice with source text, 13
    horizontal discourse and, 103, 115
    on language without adjectives, 50–51
    the neuter and, 143
    on the photograph's invisibility, 188–89
    Proust and, 45–46
    on the *punctum*, 251n.64
    "simulation" and, 8, 39–40, 103, 249n.42
    on time's visibility in Twombly, 1
    on writing as a neutral space, 143
Bataille, Georges, 7–8
Baudrillard, Jean, 120
The Beauty of the Husband: A Fictional Essay in 29 Tangos (Carson)
    autofictional response to Keats in, 3–4, 19–20, 24–25, 72, 102, 106–7, 108–9, 110–11, 116, 119
    dedication of, 104–9
    eros and, 34
    fatalism of, 109, 121–22
    form of, 102–3
    The Large Glass and, 13–14, 103–4, 116–17, 119–20
    lyric essay and, 103
    marriage in, 101–2
    metaphor in, 101, 103–4, 107, 121–22
    Persephone in, 106–7
    Phaedrus and, 111–12, 113, 118–19
    on poetic imitation, 108–9
    pronouns and, 51, 54–55
    "too much self" in, 121
    transparency and self-exposure in, 24–25, 102–4, 110–11, 116, 120, 191–92, 202–3
    visibility of time and, 12–13, 110–11
Beckett, Samuel, 44, 48, 101–2, 179, 193–94
Benjamin, Walter, 7–8, 13, 70–71, 74–75, 148, 187–88, 189, 215
Benson, Fiona, 282n.15
Bernstein, Charles, 2–3, 7–8, 13, 148
Bernstein, Jay, 120
Between the Acts (Woolf), 144–45
Binoche, Juliette, 189–90
Bishop, Elizabeth, 126
Bloom, Harold, 1–2, 5, 19, 144
"Book of Isaiah" (Carson), 86–87
Bourdieu, Pierre, 68–70
Brecht, Bertolt, 1, 20–21, 194–97, 199
Brontë, Charlotte, 90–92
Brontë, Emily. *See also specific works*
    Ellis Bell pseudonym of, 93
    "The Glass Essay" as reading of, 12–13, 24–25, 62, 72, 78, 85–88, 99, 185
    liberty in the writing of, 86–87, 92–93
    "Nudes" (Carson) and, 89–90, 96–99
    "thou" as muse of, 86–88, 92–93, 95–96, 97–99
    "whaching" by, 88–92, 94
Brooks, Cleanth, 107, 118, 121
Brossa, Joan, 13–14
Bruno, Rosanna, 190–91
Burrow, Colin, 18–19, 144, 148–49, 155, 158
Burt, Stephanie, 176–77, 216, 220
Butler, Judith, 164–65, 179, 189–93, 194, 195
"By Chance the Cycladic People" (Carson), 143–44

Cage, John, 17, 36, 143–44, 159–60, 228–29
    Cunningham and, 17, 228
    on silence, 228
    struggle "to get every Me out of the way" of, 143–44, 159–60, 228–29
Cameron, Sharon, 159, 166–67
The Cap and Bells; Or, The Jealousies (Keats), 114
Carson, Anne. *See also specific works*
    on "being an amateur," 10, 227
    classical education of, 2–3, 176–78
    direct address to readers in the works of, 3–4, 5–6, 66, 77, 101–2, 110, 116, 187
    on the essay as gift, 10, 66
    on form arising "out of the thing itself," 10, 35
    on imitation, 20

on lecturing, 28
on mimesis and "painting notion" of writing 4–5, 217–18
on poetry and the academy, 3
on reading Proust, 43–44, 51
teaching posts held by, 6–7
Carson, Michael, 3–4, 180–83, 184–86
Carter, Angela, 7–8, 49–50
Cassandra
"fake women" and, 150–51, 168
prophecy on house of Atreus by, 197–98
Trojan emotion and, 168
Twombly and, 1
"Cassandra Float Can" (Carson), 52, 197–98, 199, 220–22, 225–26
Catullus
Catullus 85 and, 14–15
Catullus 101 and, 3–4, 15–16, 27, 178–79, 180–81, 183–85, 188, 212
Nox and, 3–4, 15–16, 27, 65, 72, 178–79, 180–81, 183–85, 188, 212
Twombly and, 1, 12–13
Ceballos, Manuela, 152
Celan, Paul. *See also specific works*
Carson on Simonides in "conversation" with, 62–63, 65–66, 67–68, 69–70, 72, 80–81, 205
Carson's identification in *Economy of the Unlost* with, 24, 77–78, 79–80
on "encounter" *(Begegnung)* of poetry, 65–66
Gadamer's readings of, 64–65
mimesis and, 218–19
on the poem as gift, 58, 61, 179–80
Tristan and Isolt legend in "Matière de Bretagne" by, 73–77
"unlost *(unverloren)*" and, 64–65, 78–79
Certeau, Michel de, 149, 153
"Chairs" (Carson), 138–39
Chihaya, Sarah, 13, 99
Chorus
in "Decreation: An Opera in Three Parts," 156–58, 162, 165–66
improvised, 224–25
in Greek tragedy, 224–25
lecture with, 130–31, 225–26
Cixous, Hélène, 13
Clark Lectures (Carson), 6–7, 225–26, 234
Cliff Sappho (Carson and Holzer), 220
Coleridge, Samuel Taylor, 10–11
"Composition in Retrospect" (Cage), 228
Constantine, Peter, 206
Copeland, Roger, 53
Corinthians, Paul's First Letter to, 152
"Corners" (Carson), 224, 225, 226–27, 233–34

Cratylus (Plato), 204
Creative Criticism: An Anthology and Guide (Benson and Connors), 7–8
Critchley, Simon, 281n.2, 290n.126
"The Critic as Artist" (Wilde), 10–11
Culler, Jonathan, 21–22, 79, 103, 212
Cunningham, Merce, 3, 17, 52–54, 228
Currie, Robert
Antigonick and, 179, 190–91
Carson's collaborations with, 22
EgoCircus Collective and, 17, 228
on "Merce Sonnet" in performance, 54
Nox and, 187

D'Agata, John
Carson's interviews with, 4–5, 10, 40–41
on Carson's "creative" work, 234
on Carson's "very formal" oeuvre, 23–24
on *Eros of the Bittersweet*, 41–42
on the essay's lyric action, 39
on "The Glass Essay," 13, 87–88
on lyric essay's "overt desire to engage with facts," 85–86
Dante Alighieri, 112–13
Davenport, Guy, 18–19, 35–36, 37, 85–86, 227–28, 229–30
Dean, Tacita, 1, 15–16, 19, 198, 200
decreation
contradictions of, 26, 127–28, 140, 146, 160–61
dementia and, 130–31
displacement of the conceptual center and, 127–28
ecstasy and, 127, 138–39
everyday emotion and, 132
Marvell and, 142
performance and, 151–55
as "self-undoing," 25–26, 126, 146, 159–60
uncreativity and, 143–44
Weil's articulation of the concept of, 109–10, 125–26, 127–28, 160–61
the will and, 138–39
writing and, 127–28, 142–43
"Decreation: An Opera in Three Parts" (Carson)
camp aesthetics and, 19, 156–57, 166–67
"fake women" and, 155, 157, 167
imitation and citational poetics in, 155, 157–58, 164, 167
love triangle of Aphrodite and, 156–57
"The Mirror of Simple Souls" opera (Carson) and, 154–55
Porete in, 157–58
Sappho's fragment 31 and, 156

"Decreation: An Opera in Three Parts" (Carson) (*cont.*)
   as "thought opera," 148
   tripartite structure of, 151, 155
   Weil in, 157, 161–66
"Decreation: How Sappho, Marguerite Porete and Simone Weil Tell God" (Carson)
   Carson's reading of Weil in, 25–26, 78
   Carson's rehearsal of "conversations" in, 65–66
   "fake women" and, 26, 146–48, 167
   imitation and, 148–49
   mysticism and, 25–26, 130, 136
   on Porete's "FarNear," 152–53, 154–55
   prepositions in, 72
   problem of self in, 16–17, 51
   Sappho's fragment 31 and, 37, 151
   solemnity of, 156–57
Decreation: Poetry, Essays, Opera (Carson). *See also specific essays and poems*
   blended text in, 154–55
   conceptual jumps in, 127, 128–29, 145
   eros and, 34
   fatalism in, 121–22
   mysticism and, 127, 138–39
   paratactic organization in, 127–28
   on phenomenology and mystical thinking, 130
   problem of self in, 25–26, 86–87, 125–26, 127, 144–45
   the Sublime in, 126, 127
   transparency in, 24–25, 121–22
   "withness" in, 72
Defoe, Daniel, 65–66
deixis, 8–9, 215, 219–20, 293n.59, 295n.82
   apostrophe and, 154, 215
de Kooning, Willem, 226–27
Deneuve, Catherine, 13
Derrida, Jacques. *See also specific works*
   on gifts, 69–70, 80–81
   logos and, 42–43, 59
   mimetic reading of Plato by, 8, 17–18, 39
   "paraliterature" and, 39
   on philosophy and writing, 39, 150
Dickinson, Emily
   Howe's readings of, 12–13, 91–92, 114, 274n.9
   "I heard a Fly buzz" by, 144–45, 205
   "overtakelessness" and, 184–85
   Rankine on black lives and, 261–62n.22
Dillon, Brian, 11–12
"Dirt and Desire: Essay on the Phenomenology of Female Pollution in Antiquity" (Carson), 8–9, 150

Donne, John, 20–21
"Drop't Sonnet" (Carson), 55
Drucker, Johanna, 21
DuBois, Page, 216
Duchamp, Marcel
   Cunningham and, 53
   hinge principle of, 230
   The Large Glass and, 13–14, 103–4, 116–17, 118–21
   machine célibataire of, 120
   "readymades" of, 116–17, 119
   on water writing in plural, 228–29
DuPlessis, Rachel Blau, 8, 23, 103, 121–22, 222–23

Eckhart, Meister, 36, 129, 154, 226–27, 276–77n.43
Eco, Umberto, 119
Economy of the Unlost (Carson)
   distinction between academic and aesthetic work in, 63–65, 79–80
   Carson's comparison of herself and Celan in, 24, 77–78, 79–80
   on Celan's retelling of Tristan and Isolt legend in "Matière de Bretagne," 73–76
   on classical training and sticking to "verbal facts," 176
   "conversation" between Celan and Simonides in, 62–63, 65–66, 67–68, 69–70, 72, 80–81, 205
   copying of names and noting activity in, 63–65, 70–71
   on despair and poetry, 80
   on epitaphs, 179–80, 182, 198–99
   on the essay as gift, 66
   gift exchange (*xenia*) and, 24, 67–69, 78–79, 80
   Hölderin's "The Rhine" and, 63
   Martin Classical Lectures as a source for, 16–17, 24, 67–68
   Marxist analysis of commodity economics in, 67–68, 69–71
   mimesis and, 212
   "Note on Method" section in, 11–12, 16–17, 62–67, 70–73, 76–77, 78–79
   poetic economy and, 61–62, 66–67, 71, 80
   on poetry's surplus, 71
   on praise poems, 80–81
   reader address in, 66, 77
   reciprocity in, 62, 68
   reviews of, 61–62, 66–67, 72–73, 78–79
   on *symbola*, 69
   on "too much self" in writing, 63, 78–79

on "vibration," 63–65, 73, 74–75, 78–79, 219–20
on wasting and saving of words, 61–62, 72–73
"windowless room" (Lukács) in, 63, 99, 185
"withness" in, 71–72
"The EgoCircus Collective" (Carson and Currie), 17, 228
eidōlon/eidōla, 18–19, 169–70
"Epitaph: Evil" (Carson), 219–20
"Epitaph for François" (Celan), 65–66, 179–80, 188, 207
eros (erōs). See also Eros the Bittersweet (Carson)
  aidōs and, 15, 17–18, 33
  À la recherche du temps perdu and, 34–35, 43, 44–51
  "crisis of contact" and, 14–15, 32
  "discovery of the mind" and, 14–15
  lyric poetry and, 34, 37
  mimetic desire and, 37–38
  paradoxes and contradictions of, 32–34, 41
  personal sovereignty and, 15
  as a verb, 20–21, 36–37, 39, 43, 51
Eros the Bittersweet (Carson)
  alphabetization and, 208–9
  Barthes and, 39–40, 41–42
  Carson on the process of writing, 34, 40–41
  dance and, 53–54
  form of chapters in, 38
  Kafka's "The Top" and, 41–42, 177–78, 227–28
  "logic at the edge" and, 208–9
  on the lover's confrontation with time, 32
  love triangles and, 38, 54–55, 156
  metaphor in, 35–37
  on "the moment Eros enters you," 15
  "Odi et Amo Ergo Sum" as a source for, 15, 32–33, 34
  on oral poetics, 59
  Phaedrus and, 33–34, 40, 107, 111–12, 156
  pointillist structure of, 50
  Princeton University Press's publishing of, 35–36, 79
  privacy of reading in, 28
  reviews of, 35–36, 39, 41–42
  on rhetorical possession, 42–43
  Sappho's fragment 31 and, 37–38, 151
  scholarly and poetic "impulses" in, 40–41, 43
  Weil and, 158–59
Eshelman, Raoul, 23
"Essay on Error" (Carson), 8–9, 21–22, 138
"Essay on What I Think About Most" (Carson), 21–22, 31–32, 35–37, 108, 138

Euripides
  Alkestis and, 176
  Grief Lessons (Carson) and, 149–50, 175–76, 179–80
  Hekabe and, 176
  Herakles and, 3–4, 26–27, 176, 179–80
  Norma Jeane Baker of Troy (Carson) and, 15–16, 18–19, 26–27, 39–40, 158, 169–70, 195–96
  The Trojan Women and, 190–91
Eurydike (Eurydice, Sophokles), 191–93, 194–95, 199
Eve, Martin Paul, 49–50
"Every Exit Is an Entrance: A Praise of Sleep" (Carson), 7–8, 129, 142

"fake women"
  critiques of Carson's writing and, 149–50
  "Decreation: An Opera in Three Parts" and, 26, 146–48, 167
  "Decreation: How Sappho, Marguerite Porete and Simone Weil Tell God" and, 26, 146–48, 167
  mimesis and, 147–48
  Porete's inquisitorial trial and, 26, 146–47, 149–50, 157
  "position" and epistemology of, 147, 148–49, 150–51
Felski, Rita, 7
Felstiner, John, 65–66, 70–71
Fenollosa, Ernest, 218–19
Ferrante, Elena, 7–8
Fisher, Jessica, 127
Float (Carson). See also specific poems and performance works
  aleatory presentation of, 187
  eros and, 24, 34
  mimesis and, 220
  "reading is freefall" and, 52, 143–44
  reviews of, 1–2
"Foam (Essay with Rhapsody): On the Sublime in Longinus and Antonioni" (Carson), 9, 41, 125–26
Fränkel, Herman, 59
Frankissstein (Winterson), 49–50
Freud, Sigmund, 130, 133, 136–37, 175–76
Fried, Michael, 222–23
Frye, Northrop, 22
Furlani, André, 72

Gadamer, Hans Georg, 64–65
Genette, Gérard, 18–19
Geryon (Stesichoros), 246n.134

Geryoneis (Stesichoros), 19–20, 26–27, 202–3
The Gift (Mauss), 69–70
Girard, René, 19, 38, 49–50
glass
    as figure, 13–14, 19–20, 101, 103–4, 105–6, 116–18, 120, 121, 126, 147, 152, 202–3
    as medium, 13–14, 19–20, 87, 90, 96, 101, 114, 116–17, 119–20, 121, 126, 228–29. See also Duchamp, *The Large Glass*
Glass, Irony and God (Carson), 37, 85–87. See also specific essays and poems
"The Glass Essay" (Carson)
    Charlotte Brontë as critical interlocutor in, 92
    Chihaya's mimetic variation on, 13, 99
    idiosyncratic spelling in the poetry of Emily Brontë and, 94
    "I'll Come When Thou Art Saddest" quoted in, 95
    loneliness of Emily Brontë in, 88, 93–94, 95, 96–97
    lyric essay and, 85–86
    "Nudes" in, 89–90, 96–99
    poem and commentary speaking in "one consistent voice" in, 87–88
    pronouns in, 54–55
    reading of Emily Brontë in, 12–13, 24–25, 62, 72, 78, 85–88, 99, 185
    real time in, 86–87
    structure of, 85–86
    "thou" as muse in Emily Brontë's work and, 86–88, 92–93, 95–96, 97–99
    "too much self" in, 121
    transparency in, 24–25, 90, 191–92, 202–3
    visibility of time and, 12–13
    "whaching" by Emily Brontë in, 88–92, 94
"Gnosticisms" (Carson), 130, 132, 144
"God's Christ Theory" (Carson), 72, 86–87, 132
Goldsmith, Kenneth, 143–44
Gongyla (Sappho), 213, 214
Goodwin, Betty, 132–38, 134*f*, 139, 218
Graham, Jorie, 59–60
Graham, W. S., 13–14
Gravity and Grace (*La Pesanteur et la grâce*, Weil), 140, 147–48, 270n.33, 271n.44, 274n.6, 278n.59
"Greed: A Fractal Approach to Simonides" (Carson), 67–68
The Green Box (Duchamp), 116–17
Greenwood, Emily, 202, 215
Grenfell, Bernard Pyne, 213–14
Grief Lessons: Four Plays by Euripides (Carson), 149–50, 175–76, 179–80

Guarnieri, Romana, 151–52

Haas, Alois M., 149
Haimon (Haemon, Sophokles), 192–93, 196–97
Hamburger, Michael, 74
Harpham, Graham Galt, 227, 234
Hayot, Eric, 10, 227
H. D. (Hilda Doolittle), 7–8, 217
Hegel, G.W.F., 1, 162, 179, 192–95, 287n.83
Heidegger, Martin, 72, 184–85, 269n.15
Hekabe (Euripides), 176
Helen (Euripides). See *Norma Jeane Baker of Troy* (Carson)
Helen of Troy, 150, 169
Hephaistos, 156–57, 166
Herakles (Euripides), 3–4, 26–27, 176, 179–80
Hertz, Neil, 3–4
"Hinge Picture" (Howe), 230
Hippolytos (Hippolytus, Euripides), 167, 176
H of H Playbook (Carson)
    Herakles and, 3–4, 26–27
    as immanent commentary, 15–16
    reviews of, 202, 286n.71
    scrapbook styling of, 233–34
    "too much self" in, 121
Hölderlin, Friedrich, 11–12, 63, 196–97, 198–99
Holzer, Jenny, 220, 226–27
Homans, Margaret, 93
Homeric Hymn to Demeter (anon.), 106–7
Homo Sacer (Agamben), 194
Honig, Bonnie, 195
"Hopper: *Confessions*" (Carson), 1–2, 19–20
Hopper, Edward, 1–2
Horace, 183–84, 186–87
Horn, Roni, 22
Howe, Susan
    anarcho-scholasticism and, 7–8
    Dickinson and, 12–13, 91–92, 114, 274n.9
    on editorial practices and official textuality, 91–92
    materialist arts of sound of, 8
    poetry compared to "sun against glass" by, 13–14
    on truth as water, 228–29
Hunt, Arthur Surridge, 213–14
Husserl, Edmund, 127–28, 138, 221
Hutcheon, Linda, 53–54, 76–77, 153–54, 157, 164, 195

If Not, Winter: Fragments of Sappho (Carson)
    appendix of, 202
    brackets in, 205–6, 208, 216
    Carson's restraint as translator in, 15–16

fragments' accidental perfection and, 41–42
layout and mise-en-page of, 205–6, 208, 216
mimesis and, 203–4, 213
performativity and, 27
reviews of, 202
transparency and, 74–75, 202–3
"I heard a Fly buzz" (Dickinson), 144–45, 205
"The Iliad, or The Poem of Force" (Weil), 139–40, 160–61
"I'll Come When Thou Art Saddest" (Emily Brontë), 95
Imitating Authors (Burrow), 18
imitation. *See also* mimesis
  critical responses to Carson's engagement in, 17–18, 26–27
  "deep analogies" (Burrow) and, 155
  derivative form and, 18–19
  doubles and, 148–49
  elasticity of, 18
  formal (Burrow), 18–19
  Helen (Euripides), *Norma Jeane Baker of Troy* (Carson) and, 169–70
  imitatio and, 17–18, 32, 148–49, 154–55, 156–57, 158, 164, 167, 228–29
  interpretation as a prerequisite for, 18
  parody and, 18, 32, 76–77, 148–49, 154–55, 157, 158, 164, 165, 166–67
  performativity and, 20–22, 39
  proportion and, 18–20
  as "strong reading" (Bloom), 19
impersonation, 13, 114, 141, 143, 149–50, 155, –68
Indigo (Warner), 49–50
The Infernal Desire Machines of Doctor Hoffman (Carter), 49–50
"Irony Is Not Enough: Essay on My Life as Catherine Deneuve" (Carson), 8–9, 13
Ismene (Sophokles), 189–90, 192–94, 195–96

James, David, 263n.37
Jameson, Fredric, 110–11
Jansen, Laura, 26–27, 176–77
Jarvis, Simon, 23
Jendza, Craig, 195–96
Johnson, Barbara, 17–18, 39
John the Evangelist, 71–72
"'Just for the Thrill': Sycophantizing Aristotle's Poetics" (Carson), 9–10, 21–22, 36–37, 204–5, 209–10, 218–19

Kafka, Franz, 41–42, 177–78, 227–28
Kane, Sarah, 198
Kant, Immanuel, 1–2, 19, 126

Keats, John. *See also specific works*
  "Beauty is truth" proclamation, 19–20, 25, 102–4, 106, 107–8, 113–14, 115–16, 119, 121–22
  Carson's autofiction in *The Beauty of the Husband* and, 3–4, 19–20, 24–25, 72, 102, 106–7, 108–9, 110–11, 116, 119
  Paradise Lost annotations of, 114–15
  water epitaph of, 228–29
"The Keats Headaches" (Carson), 104, 105–6
Kermode, Frank, 93–94
Kierkegaard, Søren, 39–40
Kreon (Creon, Sophokles), 189–90, 192–93
Kristeva, Julia, 13, 169

Lacan, Jacques, 189–94, 195–96
Lacoue-Labarthe, Philippe, 46, 177–78, 190, 194–95, 206
La Dissémination (*Dissemination*, Derrida), 39
La Prisonnière (*The Captive*, Proust), 44–45, 48–50
The Large Glass (*Le Grand verre*, Duchamp), 13–14, 103–4, 116–17, 118–21
Largier, Niklaus, 154
Laughlin, James, 85, 232–33
Lauterbach, Ann, 7
Leavis, Q. D., 93–94
lebendigkeit (Hölderlin), 196–97, 198
"Lecture on Pronouns." *See* "Possessive Used as Drink (Me): A Lecture on Pronouns in the Form of 15 Sonnets" (Carson)
"Lecture on the History of Skywriting" (Carson, Currie, Ali Jaber), 28, 228
"Lecture on the Weather" (Cage), 8–9, 228
Leda, 1
Leighton, Angela, 121, 181–82
Le Neutre (*The Neuter*, Barthes), 45–46, 143
Lewis, Wyndham, 7–8
"The Life of Towns" (Carson), 9–10, 62–63, 139–40, 187, 218
Life? or Theatre (Salomon), 190–91
Lispector, Clarice, 13
Lobel, Edgar, 213–14
"Longing: A Documentary" (Carson), 126, 127–28
Longinus, 41, 125–26
A Lover's Discourse (Barthes), 8, 39–40, 41–43, 103, 264n.6
Lu Chi, 204–6, 218–20
Lukács, György, 63
lyric
  accident and, 207–8
  eros and, 34, 37
  lyric essay and, 85–86

lyric (cont.)
    "lyric mimesis" and, 21–22, 37, 55, 203–4, 210–12
    lyric philosophy and, 7–8
    lyric transparency and, 25, 103–4, 116
    performative dimension of, 14–15, 21–22, 36–37
    private reading and, 14–15, 34
    song and, 21–22, 58–59, 111, 203, 216
    transcription and, 14–15

Mallarmé, Stéphane, 47–48, 63
Man Ray, 120
Marcel (Proust), 44–47, 48–51
Martin Classical Lectures (Carson), 16–17, 24, 67–68, 176
Marvell, Andrew, 142
"Matière de Bretagne" (Celan), 72–77
Matta-Clark, Gordon, 221, 226–27
Mauss, Marcel, 69–70
Mavor, Carol, 13
Mendelsohn, Daniel, 207, 215–16
Men in the Off Hours (Carson), 1–2, 7–8, 186–87, 204–5. *See also specific essays and poems*
"Merce Sonnet" (Carson), 53–54
"The Meridian" (Celan), 61, 65–66
Merkin, Daphne, 18
Miller, J. Hillis, 68–69
Milton, John, 89–90
mimēma, 157
mimesis (*mimēsis*). *See also* imitation
    Aristotle and, 210–11, 218–19, 227–28, 230
    capture of mind and, 4–5, 212
    Derrida and, 8, 17–18, 39
    "fake women" and, 147–48
    glass and, 13–14, 117–18, 119–4, 121
    "lyric mimesis" and, 21–22, 37, 55, 203–4, 210–12
    mimetic desire and, 19, 38, 170–71
    performativity and, 20, 32
    Plato and, 15, 17–19, 210–11
    sophistry and, 17–19, 25, 39, 59
"Mimnermos: The Brainsex Paintings" (Carson), 26–27
The Mirror of Simple Souls (Porete), 146–47, 149, 151–55
"The Mirror of Simple Souls: An Opera Installation" (Carson), 154–55, 158–59
Moi, Toril, 163, 273–74n.5
Monroe, Marilyn (Norma Jeane Baker), 18–19, 150–51, 169, 171, 195–96
Montaigne, Michel de, 39, 126

Moore, Marianne, 109–10
Mourning Diary (Journal de deuil, Barthes), 188–89
Munnerlyn, Marcie, 54
Munro, Alice, 202–3
My Emily Dickinson (Howe), 12–13, 91–92, 114

Nagy, Gregory, 215
Nancy, Jean-Luc, 46, 58–59, 177–78, 206
Nay Rather (Carson), 20–21
The Neuter (Barthes). *See Le Neutre*
Norma Jeane Baker of Troy (Carson), 15–16, 18–19, 26–27, 39–40, 158, 169–70, 195–96
"Notes on Camp" (Sontag), 156–57
"Now What?" (Carson), 62–63
Nox (Carson)
    as "anti-book," 176–77
    Catulllus 101 and, 3–4, 15–16, 27, 65, 72, 178–79, 180–81, 183–85, 188, 212
    doubt of the translator in, 23
    as epitaph, 178–79, 180–83, 184–86, 188
    glossary format in, 182–84, 185–86
    grief and, 181–83
    mimesis and, 222–23
    on muteness in, 184–85
    open-endedness of, 187
    photographs in, 188–89
    residues and, 181–82, 183–84, 185, 186–87, 189
    scrapbook original of, 178–79, 180–81, 182–83, 233–34
    "too much self" in, 121
    transparency in composition of, 24–25, 27

"Ode on a Grecian Urn" (Keats), 102–4, 106–8, 113, 117–21
"Ode to a Nightingale" (Keats), 111
"Ode to Indolence" (Keats), 114
"Ode to Sleep" (Carson), 126
"Odi et Amo Ergo Sum" (Carson), 8, 14–15, 32–33, 34, 158–59
The Odyssey (Homer), 69, 156, 226–27
Oedipus at Colonus (Sophokles), 189–90
Oedipus the King (Sophokles), 189–90, 193–94
O'Hara, Frank, 223
"Oh What a Night (Alkibiades)" (Carson), 15–16
Olson, Charles, 7–8
On the Sublime (Longinus), 41, 125
opera. *See also* "Decreation: An Opera in Three Parts"
    interdisciplinary opera, 53–54
    "thought opera" and, 7–8, 148

opsis, 22, 41, 121–22, 210–11, 227–28, 229–30
"Ordinary Time: Virginia Woolf and Thucydides on War" (Carson), 90–91, 185
Oresteia (Carson's translation), 2–3
Oswald, Alice, 282n.15
Otho the Great (Keats), 114
Oulipo, 104, 243n.92, 279n.79

Page, Denys, 34, 208–9, 214
paranoid reading (Sedgwick), 7, 46–47, 48, 49–50, 104, 110, 115–16, 238n.27
Pasler, Jann, 228–29
Paz, Octavio, 119
Peace (Aristophanes), 68
Peponi, Anastasia-Erasmia, 39–40, 249–50n.44
performance
    aesthetics of, 28, 53, 57–58, 149, 154–55, 158, 187, 210–11, 215, 216, 219, 222–23, 224–25, 230, 232–33
    Carson on, 10–11, 20–21, 31, 75–76
    Currie on, 54
    decreation as, 151–55
    deixis and, 215, 219–20
    of impersonality (Cameron), 159
    improvisation and, 52, 224–25
    interactivity and, 23–24, 192–93, 222–23, 224, 225, 231, 237n.24
    Performance Philosophy and, 192–93, 234, 286n.74
Performatism (Eshelman), 23
Performative form, 5, 25–26, 27, 35, 46–47, 50, 126, 135, 138, 203–4, 221, 225
Perloff, Marjorie, 143–44
Pétrement, Simone, 159
Phaedrus (Plato)
    The Beauty of the Husband and, 111–12, 113, 118–19
    contradictions of eros in, 32–34, 41, 43, 166
    Derrida's mimetic reading of, 8, 39
    Eros the Bittersweet and, 33–34, 40, 107, 111–12, 156
    logos and, 59
    the lover in, 33, 130–31
    Lysias and, 33, 113, 118–19
    the nonlover in, 33, 40, 59, 113, 118–19, 130–31
    the spoken word in, 59
Phaidra, 150–51, 167, 170–71
Pickstock, Catherine, 59
"Pinplay: A Version of Euripides's *Bacchae*" (Carson), 26–27
Plath, Sylvia, 22, 230–31

Plato. *See also specific works*
    beds and, 130
    Carson's reading of Defoe and, 65–66
    on *eidōla* and likeness, 18–19
    mimesis and, 15, 17–19
    the spoken word and, 51, 59
Porete, Marguerite
    analogies of, 128–29
    "fake woman" charge leveled against, 26, 146–47, 149–50, 157
    "FarNear" (*Loingprès*) neologism of, 152–53, 154–55
    Inquisitorial trial of, 26, 146–47, 149–50, 152
    "undoing the creature" and, 148
"Possessive Used as Drink (Me): A Lecture on Pronouns in the Form of 15 Sonnets" (Carson)
    eros and, 24, 34–35
    grammar as inebriant and, 52
    grammar of difference and exchange in, 54–55
    Harvard University premiere (2006) of, 52
    onstage dance collaboration for, 3, 52, 53–54, 59–60
    pronouns as open form of address in, 54
    search for missing pronoun in, 55
    sonnet form and, 51, 52–53, 58–59
    "stands" as verb in, 58
    toy pony in, 56–57
post-critical, 23–24, 104, 109–10, 249n.39
Pound, Ezra, 7–8, 217–19
The Preparation of the Novel (Barthes), 45–46, 251n.67
"The Prisoner. A Fragment" (Emily Brontë), 98–99
"Prologue: False Sail" (Carson), 62–63
Prometheia (Aiskhylos), 199–200
Proust, Marcel. *See À la recherche du temps perdu* (Proust)
psychagōgikon, 22, 210–11, 227–28

Rae, Ian, 12, 90, 95, 150
Rankine, Claudia, 261–62n.22
Rauschenberg, Robert, 226–27
Reading Boyishly (Mavor), 13
Red Doc> (Carson), 26–27, 145
"Reinventing the Poet-Critic" Conference (1994), 8
Rembrandt van Rijn, 22, 232–33, 297n.29
The Republic (Plato), 17–19, 108–9, 130
Reynolds, Margaret, 203, 216
"The Rhine" (Hölderlin), 11–12, 63
Rhys, Jean, 49–50

Ricks, Christopher, 5–7
Ricoeur, Paul, 108
Riding, Laura, 7–8
Ronell, Avitall, 192
Rose, Gillian, 132, 145, 160–61, 163–64, 166–67
Rose, Jacqueline, 49–50, 169–70
Rowden, Stephanie, 52
Ruddick, Lisa, 48

Salomon, Charlotte, 190–91
Samuels, Lisa, 7–8
Sappho
    on "bittersweet desire" (*glukupikron*), 32–33, 36–37
    Carson's restraint in translating, 15–16
    erotics of the present tense in, 215
    "fake woman" charge and, 146
    fragment 22 and, 213–14, 216–17
    fragment 31 and, 37–38, 41, 151, 156, 170–71, 209–11
    fragment 55 and, 209–10
    fragment 87D, 206, 208
    fragment 94 and, 218–20
    fragment 105a and, 41–42, 207
    fragment 118 and, 216
    fragment 176 and, 216
    kletic hymns of, 149, 153
    mimesis and, 4–5
    postmodern aesthetics and reading of, 216
    preservation of poems through quotation, 176–77
    transcription of lyric song and, 14–15
Sartre, Jean-Paul, 39–40
Sastri, Reena, 18–19
Scarry, Elaine, 8–9, 215
"*Seated Figure with Red Angle* by Betty Goodwin (1988)" (Carson)
    allure and, 137–38
    the body in, 133–35
    contradiction and, 140
    Goodwin's artwork reproduced alongside, 133, 134f, 137
    open-ended inquiries and conditional syntax in, 133–35, 136, 138, 139, 143–44, 218
    opening of, 135
    violence in, 136–37
Sedgwick, Eve Kosofsky, 5–6, 7–8, 48, 104
Serpell, Namwali, 108
Shadowtime (Bernstein), 148
Short Talks (Carson)
    Carson on her motivations for writing, 7
    Carson's "interactive" lectures based on, 4–5, 224–25
    copying of names and activity in, 64–65
    drawings as origin of, 229–30
    mimesis and, 12–13, 225
    "Short Talk on Chromo-luminarism" and, 230, 231–32
    "Short Talk on Hölderlin's World Night Wound" and, 230
    "Short Talk on Sylvia Plath" and, 22, 230–31
    "Short Talk on the End" and, 231–32
    "Short Talk on the Sensation of Aeroplane Takeoff" and, 224–25, 230
Sienkewicz, T. J., 41–43, 177–78
"Simonides Negative" (Carson), 204
Simonides of Keos
    Carson on putting Celan in "conversation" with, 62–63, 65–66, 67–68, 69–70, 72, 80–81, 205
    Carson on the absence of despair in, 80
    invention of Greek letters and, 204, 205–6
    mimesis and, 4–5, 218–19
    poetic economy and sale of poems by, 61–62, 67–68, 78
    surplus in poetry of, 71
"Sleepchains" (Carson), 127–28, 131–32
Snell, Bruno, 14–15, 34, 208–9
Solway, David, 125–26, 149–50, 258n.33
"Sonnet Isolate" (Carson), 53
The Song of Songs, 153, 275n.15
Sontag, Susan, 5–6, 8, 48, 156–57, 159–60, 202–3
The Sophist (Plato), 17–20
Sophokles (Sophocles). *See specific works*
Stanton, Robert, 18–19
"Stanzas, Sexes, Seductions" (Carson), 97–98, 108–10, 132, 140–43
Steiner, George, 66–67, 191–92, 195–96
Stesichoros (Stesichorus), 5–6, 19–20, 26–27, 149–50, 169, 202–3
"Stillness" (Carson), 36, 53–54, 144–45, 219–20, 226–27, 228, 233–34
Stobaios, 207–8
Stone, Bianca, 22, 179, 190–91, 194
"Stops" (Carson), 129
St. Paul, 152, 160
Streb, Elizabeth, 31–32, 38, 100, 130–31
Symposium (Plato), 15–16, 202–3
Sze, Gillian, 18–19

Teresa of Avila, 13, 86–87, 150–51, 168
"Teresa of God" (Carson), 86–87, 168–69
Thoreau, Henry David, 228–29
The Three Crosses (Rembrandt), 22, 232, 297n.29
"The Top" (Kafka), 41–42, 177–78, 227–28

Tortel, Jean, 163, 166–67
To The Lighthouse (Woolf), 190–91, 194, 233–34
"Triple Sonnet of the Plush Pony" (Carson), 56–59
The Trojan Women (Euripides; Carson translation), 190–91
"The Truth About God" (Carson), 86–87, 168
Trilling, Lionel, 238n.34
Tschofen, Monique, 136–37, 138
"TV Men" (Carson), 19–20, 200, 203
  "TV Men: Antigone (Scripts 1 and 2)" and, 200
  "TV Men: Sappho" and, 203
"Twelve-Minute Prometheus (After Aiskhylos)" (Carson), 15–16, 26–27, 199–200
Twombly, Cy, 1, 8, 9–10, 12–13, 110–11
"The Tyger" (Blake), 141
Tzetzes, Joannes, 203

Ulmer, Gregory, 39
"Uncle Falling: A Pair of Lyric Lectures with Shared Chorus" (Carson), 8–9, 31–32, 52, 130–31, 225–26
das Unumgängliche (Heidegger), 46–47, 184–85, 268n.5, 269n.15, 284n.46

van Hove, Ivo, 189–90
"Variations on the Right to Remain Silent" (Carson), 8–9, 52, 117, 176, 196–98, 221, 230
Vega, Amador, 256n.12
Vendler, Helen, 212, 223
Vidal-Naquet, Pierre, 69–70
Virgil, 1, 268n.8, 272n.59
Vitti, Monica, 1–2, 19, 126
Voigt, Eva-Maria, 202, 213–14, 220

Waiting for Godot (Beckett), 194
Waiting on God (*Attente de Dieu*, Weil), 132–33, 270n.33
Warner, Marina, 49–50
Weber, Max, 227
Weil, Simone. *See also specific works*
  analogy in the works of, 127
  Antigone and, 193–94
  Being and personality as separate for, 147–48
  Carson's ventriloquizing of, 19, 25–26, 78, 164
  contradiction for, 160–61, 166–67
  decreation theology and, 109–10, 125–26, 127–28
  on desire, 132–33, 137
  desire to disappear of, 121, 159–60, 161, 166–67, 170–71
  dilemma of no contact for, 127
  "dream of distance" (Carson) and, 130
  "fake women" and, 146
  on impossible union with creation, 140
  on interpretation and attention, 136–37
  notebooks of, 151–52, 160–61, 268n.10, 278n.68
  paradox of self for, 160
  parents of, 147–48, 161–64, 165–66
  Sontag on the "fanatical asceticism" of, 159–60
  the Sublime and, 132
  "undoing the creature" and, 148
Whiteman, Bruce, 217
"Why I Wrote Two Plays About Phaidra" (Carson), 168
Wide Sargasso Sea (Rhys), 49–50
Wilcox, Sadie, 52
Wilde, Oscar, 10–11
Wiliamowitz-Moellendorff, Ulrich von, 200–1, 213–14
Willett, Steven, 63, 72–73, 78–79, 255n.4, 255n.7, 257–58n.27
Williams, Isobel, 282n.15
Williamson, Margaret, 214
Wilson, Emily, 202, 216
Winterson, Jeanette, 36, 203
Wittgenstein, Ludwig, 7–8, 13
Wittig, Monique, 203
"Woman's Constancy" (Donne), 20–21
Woolf, Virginia
  Between the Acts and, 144–45
  Carson writing "with," 86
  cross-outs in diary of, 90–91, 185, 205
  involuntary "shadow shape" of read texts posited by, 19
  To the Lighthouse and, 190–91, 194, 233–34
  techniques of reticence and, 144–45
  on writing as one speaks, 103
Wuthering Heights (Emily Brontë), 90–94

xenia, 24, 67–71, 80

Yatromanolakis, Dimitrios, 213–14

Zeus, 199–200, 282n.15
"Zurich, at the Stork" (Celan), 65–66
Zweig, Sande, 203
Zwicky, Jan, 7–8, 13